Window on Westminster

Window on Westminster

A Canon's Diary, 1976–1987

Trevor Beeson

SCM PRESS LTD

0 334 02745 4

First published 1998 by
SCM Press Ltd
9–17 St Albans Place London N1 0NX

Typeset by Regent Typesetting, London
Printed in Great Britain by
Biddles Ltd, Guildford and King's Lynn

Contents

To the memory of

Edward Carpenter

A godly and erudite Canon and
Dean of Westminster

1951–85

With gratitude and affection

Preface

London is sometimes described as a network of villages and two cities – of which Westminster is one. Within that city are institutions of major national and international significance, and during the years 1976–87 it was my privilege and delight to minister in two of these – Westminster Abbey, including St Margaret's Church, and the House of Commons. This brought me to that particular intersection of church and state which is peculiar to England and at once fascinating and demanding.

Westminster Abbey's status as a Royal Peculiar has a long and colourful history. Built originally by Edward the Confessor, the last but one of the Saxon kings, in the eleventh century, Westminster Abbey has been the place where all but two of England's monarchs have been crowned. Although for almost 500 years it was the home of a community of Benedictine monks, during that time it retained a close relationship with succeeding royal dynasties and, in common with some other major European abbeys, was exempted from local episcopal control.

This independence, granted by the Pope, was continued by King Henry VIII after the dissolution of the monastery in 1540 and is still symbolized by the reading of a 'Protest' whenever a new Archbishop of Canterbury makes his first official visit to the Abbey. So, although this great church is served by Church of England clergymen and administered in accordance with the beliefs and practices of the Established Church, it is independent of any external jurisdiction other than that of the Sovereign, its Visitor.

More than nine centuries of special relationship with the Crown has, paradoxically, secured for the Abbey not only a privileged place among the 'high and mighty' but also a place in the affections of the 'lowly and meek' in every part of the English-speaking world. And this is by no means confined to those who share the faith it exists to proclaim and express. Hence some special opportunities and challenges.

No one devising for the first time an appropriate relationship between the church and the state in the twentieth century would dream of creating the present English Establishment, which is full of anomalies and compromises that are not easy either to explain or to justify. But we are not required to devise a church-state relationship *ab initio*. Nor can we, for behind us are many centuries of history that have formed our culture and national identity. There is no escaping this influence, and the challenge is to use and develop our inheritance in ways that are creative rather than destructive.

The Coronation ceremony is a declaration that temporal power is derived ultimately from God and that those who exercise this power live always under the judgment of God. It is the duty of the Church of England to declare this truth in season and out of season, and of course to express it in its own life. Westminster Abbey stands as a living symbol of the supremacy of God over our national life, and what takes place within its walls is devised to demonstrate this in contemporary terms.

The worship of God is therefore the Abbey's primary function, for worship springs from a recognition of how we stand in relation to God and what is due to God. Day in, day out, worship has been offered in this national shrine since its consecration on Holy Innocents Day 1065. During the monastic years there were as many as seven daily services; today the number is reduced to four, sometimes five. At least one of these is led by a choir representing the best in the English choral tradition, and although it is rare for services to be attended only by members of the Abbey community, the worship is offered to God for his glory and is in no way dependent on public support. Many of the services in fact attract very large numbers.

Hourly acts of prayer between 10 a.m. and 4 p.m. every day, sermons, lectures and other educational activities, together with performances of great music, are also designed to remind those who come within reach that God stands first in human life and that a properly ordered individual and community life requires obedience to his will as this was revealed in Jesus Christ.

The Abbey's primary task cannot, however, be separated from its duty to welcome all who wish to experience something of its life. They come in their millions from all parts of the world and for many different reasons. The building's unique history has its own special attraction. The Coronation Chair (now sadly bereft of the Stone of Scone it was designed to house) and the Royal Tombs are a vivid reminder of key moments in English history. The confusing array of monuments and the stark simplicity of the grave of the Unknown Warrior speak of lives dedicated in different ways to the service of God and humanity.

And many come to pray. It is the special vocation of this royal church to embrace men and women of faith, and those in quest of faith, on their own terms, recognizing that God's love is always inclusive and that on the pilgrimage of faith, to which all are called, individuals and communities have reached differing stages. Westminster Abbey belongs to everyone.

This openness to all makes the Abbey a markedly secular church. It is a place for important ceremonies which have no direct religious significance, as for example the laying of wreaths on the grave of the Unknown Warrior by the visiting Heads of Foreign and Commonwealth countries. A large number of visitors belong to the post-Christian element in the Western world, and some are surprised to discover that the building is still used for religious purposes. It is necessary therefore to maintain a delicate balance between the sacred and the secular; thus intense forms of sacerdotalism are always likely to be out of place. The Abbey is more of a frontier post than it is a religious enclave.

My own entry into its full-time service was by way of an unusual route. The Dean and Canons of Westminster are appointed by the Crown. During the seventeenth and eighteenth centuries their number included many royal favourites, and during the nineteenth century, by which time the Sovereign was required to accept Prime Ministerial advice, the political views of candidates were rarely overlooked. The twentieth century has seen the development of a tradition in which scholars and elder ecclesiastical statesmen are nominated to serve both the Abbey and the wider church. The degree of church influence over these nominations has varied, but is greater now than at any other time during the last 400 years.

When, from a non-public-school, non-Oxbridge background, I was ordained in Durham Cathedral in 1951, it was in the happy expectation that my ministry would be spent in working-class parishes in the North of England. So it turned out – at least for the first fourteen years, when I served as a curate in a coal-mining parish in North West Durham, then as the pioneering vicar of a new housing-area parish on Tees-side.

I was then drawn into the realms of journalism and broadcasting related to the 1960s reform movements in church and society. When in the 1970s it proved impossible to combine this heavy commitment with responsibility for a lively parish in Hertfordshire, I was appointed to a Canonry of Westminster in the hope that this would provide sufficient freedom for me to continue and develop my work as a communicator.

Something of great significance had, however, been overlooked, or at least not yet been recognized. The oil crisis of 1974 led to rampant inflation in the Western world, which eventually destabilized the finances of many hitherto secure institutions – including Westminster Abbey. Escalating costs and uncertain income required active management by the

ix

Dean and Chapter, thus reducing seriously the amount of time available for extra-mural activity. What is more, the arrival of an ever-increasing number of visitors, conveyed in the new wide-bodied aircraft, raised questions about the character of the Abbey's ministry to them. How is the priority of God and his inclusive love for all to be affirmed among pressing crowds and in an ambience pervaded by the chink of money?

This proved to be no environment for leisurely reflection or for sustained writing, and although I achieved a fair amount of writing and broadcasting during my early years at the Abbey, the opportunity for this disappeared completely when I decided, with the agreement of my colleagues, to devote myself entirely to the on-the-spot opportunities offered by the Speaker's Chaplaincy in the House of Commons linked to the Rectory of St Margaret's Church.

These offices are another expression of the special relationship between church and state in England. Since 1661 the House of Commons has been served by a Chaplain, whose primary role is to conduct prayers before the opening of each day's business. This act is another reminder to those who exercise authority in the nation that they are themselves subject to an even higher authority than the High Court of Parliament.

With the encouragement and strong support of Speakers George Thomas and Bernard Weatherill, I sought to extend this particular witness through a pastoral ministry among MPs and staff, and by contributing to the thinking of that large community by means of talks, addresses and personal conversations. There was, it need hardly be said, no possibility of waging a private political campaign in the House of Commons. Like the Speaker, the Chaplain must be politically neutral, and in any case political decision-making is the task of the informed layman. My contribution was to try to lay bare some of the theological and moral issues that such decision-making inevitably raises and to support pastorally those who were rarely able to make black-and-white, right-or-wrong decisions, and nearly always had to settle for compromise.

Compromise is not, however, confined to politicians, and my appointment to Westminster in 1976 and my subsequent ministry there caused more than a few of my friends to wonder what degree of compromise was involved when a priest who had been among the foremost radical reformers of the 1960s moved to a position at the heart of the Establishment. I often wondered about this myself.

A number of my 1960s fellow-reformers decided, for entirely valid reasons, that the pace of change in the church was likely to be so slow that they would better serve the Kingdom of God by moving from ministry in the institutional church to ministry in such secular spheres as social services, politics and education. Those of us who remained with the institution were therefore confronted with the possibliity either of undertaking pioneering work in spheres where the constraints of tradition were greatly reduced or of seeking to be a reforming influence in spheres where tradition was most deeply entrenched. In practice, few had much choice in the matter, since appointments, then rarely advertised, were always in the hands of others.

On my arrival at Westminster Abbey I found as much freedom as any priest could find anywhere to express my views on any subject under the sun. A number of my broadcasts brought protests from politicians in Britain and abroad. I had regular columns in *The Guardian* and the Chicago-based *Christian Century*. I wrote for the British Council of Churches a book *Britain Today and Tomorrow* which was described by one reviewer as 'Jugoslavia without the sun', and this was followed by co-authorship of another book, *A Vision of Hope*, which was concerned with the role of the churches in rapidly-changing Latin America. A television series *The Controversialists* caused some viewers to enquire why such a series was being presented by a Canon of Westminster.

There was, however, no corresponding freedom to effect radical change in the life of the Abbey, had I ever believed this to be necessary, and this for two main reasons, the first being that ancient institutions cannot be changed quickly without seriously damaging their life. Like huge ocean-going liners, they can turn only slowly, and they have survived the storms of history largely because they have steered a straight and steady course. Constitution and culture combine to resist all but minor changes, though sometimes these can be significant, and over the course of the years an accumulation of modest modifications makes a difference. I had a part in the initiation and implementation of some such changes, but there were occasions when, through lack of agreement on the Chapter, it was necessary to accept that change was not yet possible.

The second buttress against change is that the Abbey's peculiar mission springs from its place in English history and the traditions it has accumulated along the way. From the moment of my arrival I was driven to take history much more seriously, since there was no possibility of understanding and participating in the Abbey's life without reference to its historical context. A programme of thorough modernization would always be self-defeating, for it would – if successful – remove that which enables the Abbey to engage most powerfully with the contemporary world. Effective communication runs deeper than prosaic understanding.

These extracts from my diary will, I hope, provide some glimpse of what was involved in my three-fold Westminster ministry. As I pointed out in *A Dean's Diary*, drawn from my Winchester years, limitation of space and consequent emphasis on the unusual runs the risk of distorting the overall picture – the main subject of which is the regular round of worship, reflection on the biblical revelation and proclamation of its implications, and pastoral care of individuals.

Some of my diary entries indicate that a Royal Peculiar is not exempt from human problems, foibles and eccentricities. Indeed, such is the style and atmosphere of this unique church that the quirky is frequently magnified. But under the leadership of a great Dean, to whose memory I dedicate this volume, our deeds and misdeeds were nearly always constrained by God's unconditional love and by the belief that the Abbey, in common with every other Christian community, is called to live as well as proclaim this love.

Once again I am deeply indebted to Esmé Parker for typing a difficult manuscript quickly and skilfully, and for being generous and encouraging enough to say that she enjoyed the experience.

TB

1976

Thursday 22 April 1976

The move into the Little Cloister was completed late yesterday and we now have the furnishings of three main rooms in place. The removal firm from Ware found it a much bigger job than they had bargained for, since their van could get no nearer than the Poets' Corner entrance to the Abbey, and every item of furniture had to be carried fifty yards through narrow gateways and across our small garden to the back door of the house.

The Little Cloister is a delightful haven of great beauty more or less hidden in the heart of London. From my bath this morning I could see Big Ben, and we had heard it strike most of the hours of the night. The first-floor drawing room and study overlook a small square of symmetrical arcades filled with wrought-iron railings which protect the cloister garth and a splendid fountain – all somewhat reminiscent of Spain.

Apparently this is the site of the monastic infirmary to which the Benedictine monks were despatched when they were ill, or simply in need of a rest. Parts of the original buildings were incorporated into the Cloister when it was rebuilt at the end of the seventeenth century, but all but two of the eight houses were either destroyed or severely damaged during an air raid in 1941.

Ours, No. 2, retained its ancient ground-floor walls, but the first and second floor were entirely rebuilt – copying, it would seem, the seventeenth-century design. The post-war architect, Lord Mottistone, evidently believed that Canons of Westminster should have fine staircases, and in our case servants' stairs – surely the last to be created in a London house. Bells in most of the rooms still connect to an indicator board in the kitchen, to Jo's wry amusement.

The long corridors give the place a somewhat institutional feel, but it has the makings of a comfortable, useful home, and it is of course an extraordinary privilege to be living here.

I

I was duly Installed as a Canon of Westminster at Evensong this afternoon. It was thought that May Day would be a specially appropriate day for me to begin my ministry at the Abbey, though it demanded considerable sacrifice of the Dean, Edward Carpenter, who is a football fanatic and was deprived of the opportunity to watch the Cup Final at Wembley.

The service contained no hint of revolution. After the first lesson at Evensong the Dean and Chapter's Legal Secretary read the Grant and Mandemus – formidable documents bearing the royal seal – declaring the Queen's appointment of me to the vacant Canonry for the period of my natural life and requiring the Dean to place me in an appropriate stall. I responded by stumbling through a lengthy Latin declaration, in which I promised to protect the Abbey's property, privileges and secrets, and the Dean then led me by the hand to a stall. This time the Latin was rather more edifying, for it exhorted me to occupy the Canonry to the glory of God and the edification of the church in the power of the Holy Spirit.

Evensong was then resumed, I read the second lesson, the prayers included some reference to me, a short hymn was sung, and immediately after the blessing I was escorted to the Jerusalem Chamber and, with more Latin, placed in a seat at the table where the formal meetings of the Dean and Chapter take place.

I was supported by a multitude of friends and Ware parishioners, and it was, I think, a specially moving, and in some ways a bewildering, experience for my parents, who are now in their mid-eighties and never dreamt that they would one day see their son installed as a Canon in Westminster Abbey. The music was a little disappointing as the Choristers are still on Easter holiday, and the ranks of the choirmen (Lay Vicars) included a number of elderly gentlemen, one of whom seemed to be asthmatic. The Organist and Master of the Choristers, Douglas Guest, was away at his country home because, I am told, he does not regard himself as being under any contractual obligation to direct the Choir when the Choristers are absent.

Monday 10 May 1976

This morning I attended my first Chapter meeting – a strange experience. The Jerusalem Chamber in which we met is replete with history. Built in the late fourteenth century by the then abbott, Nicholas

Litlyngton, as his withdrawing room, it is an elegant room, hung with splendid tapestries, and must, I suppose, accommodate seventy to eighty people seated.

It was here that Henry IV died in 1413, and that the translation of the Authorized Version of the Bible was master-minded from 1607–1611. The carved cedar-wood overmantel of the fireplace was erected by Dean Williams in 1624 to mark the betrothal of the Prince of Wales (soon to become Charles I) to Princess Henrietta Maria. Winston Churchill made a broadcast appeal from the Chamber for £1 million for the restoration of the Abbey in 1952 and surprised some people by the modesty of his own contribution – £1.

We, i.e. the Dean and four Canons, plus the Receiver General, occupied six chairs placed either side of the central section of a table extending over almost the entire length of the Chamber. We were in our scarlet cassocks, with bands and academic gowns. I had of course nothing to say for most of this first meeting, apart from acknowledging the warm welcome extended to me by the Dean, and I noted the formal style of the discussion. Each member of the Chapter speaks in turn, according to seniority of appointment, and titles, rather than names, are always used – Mr Dean, Mr Sub-Dean, Mr Treasurer, Mr Archdeacon. All of which must reduce the risk of heated debate.

Much of the time this morning was taken up by financial matters. I gather that prior to the oil crisis in 1974 the Abbey's finances were fairly stable (virtually every year producing a modest surplus), but the galloping inflation of the last two years has created considerable problems and the need for new sources of income has become urgent. Included in these is the possibility of setting up a brass-rubbing centre in the North Cloister and also in St Margaret's Church which, since 1972, has been fully integrated into the Abbey's administration. The introduction of such commercialism into the life of these two churches raises all sorts of problems, but we agreed in principle to do it.

The rest of the meeting was taken up with new proposals for dealing with tourists, appointments to parishes of which the Dean and Chapter are the patrons, and the visit of the President of France to the Unknown Warrior's grave on 22 June. Special services to mark the Independence of the Seychelles and the tenth anniversary of the Independence of Barbados were also briefly discussed. The financial problems did not preclude the doubling of the Dean and Chapter's contribution to private medical insurance – something in which I have declined to participate.

I absented myself this morning from the Chilean Navy Day ceremony – an occasion of increasing disquiet among those concerned with human rights in Latin America. At first sight the ceremony seems innocent enough: Admiral Thomas Cochrane, having been unfairly dismissed from the Royal Navy in 1814, later accepted command of the Chilean navy and secured the independence of Chile and Peru from the Spanish. He is apparently one of Chile's national heroes, though he subsequently returned to Britain, where he was reinstated in the Royal Navy and the Order of the Bath, and on his death in 1860 given burial in the Nave of the Abbey.

Every year on the anniversary of Cochrane's death the Chilean Ambassador and a detachment from his country's navy come to lay a wreath on his grave, in the context of a short address and prayers given by the Dean or the Canon-in-Residence. Shortly before I arrived, Michael Ramsey, the former Archbishop of Canterbury, wrote to the Dean expressing the disquiet of the Chile Committee for Human Rights, of which he is a sponsor, and suggesting that another ceremony should be held in the Abbey later in the day in remembrance of the victims of the present oppressive regime in Chile.

It was not an unreasonable suggestion, for the Pinochet government is a military dictatorship, and besides many thousands who have been murdered or simply 'disappeared' since it took power three years ago, a huge number have been forced to leave. This puts the Abbey in a very difficult position. As a royal church it is supposed to minister to everyone and not take sides in political matters. Furthermore, it cannot easily get out of step with the Government's foreign policy decisions. Individual members of the Chapter are of course entirely free to express their views on these matters but, as an institution, the Abbey is constrained.

In the event the problem was, apparently, thoroughly discussed in Chapter, and although Michael Ramsey's request was declined, the Dean – who is the decision-maker in these matters – readily undertook to include in his prayers some for those deprived of human rights. John Baker, who was present at the ceremony this morning, told me that Edward did exceedingly well both in his address and in the prayers; but the remark of the head of the Chilean Navy Mission that he had been touched and moved by every word the Dean had spoken makes me wonder just how much was understood.

The three elderly Lay Vicars whose presence in the Choir I noted at my Installation are clearly a considerable problem to the choral foundation and thus to the Dean and Chapter. All are over pensionable age, but each has a freehold office and none can be made to retire. Apparently the Elizabethan statutes provided for the appointment of Lay Vicars at the modest stipend of £10 per annum, plus accommodation, and security for life – unlikely to extend much beyond forty years in the sixteenth century.

The voices of the three men are now some way beyond the required standard, and one of them, Kenneth Tudor, has severe attacks of asthma which sometimes disrupt the Choir's performances. Discussion of this problem with Mr Tudor has led him to accuse us of trying to get rid of him, and he has had recourse to a solicitor, who has advised seeking the opinion of Counsel about his legal rights.

We are requesting that he should submit to examination by the Abbey's consultant physician, so that we have had evidence of his medical condition and future prospects. It should then be possible for us to make a firm proposal for his retirement, but all the signs suggest that the way forward is going to be hazardous. Already some of Ken Tudor's senior colleagues in the Choir are rushing to support him, and representations on his behalf from Equity and the Musicians' Union are expected any day now.

The professional aspect of the music in places like Westminster Abbey has been quite a revelation to me – and not a particularly edifying one. Money looms large on the agendas of the men who occupy the choir stalls to lead the daily worship of Almighty God. Suggestions of change involving a little extra time on duty are, I am told, invariably greeted with the question, How much are we to be paid for this?

The reasons for such a response are understandable enough. Most of the members of the Abbey Choir are not in the top flight of singers; those that are eventually leave to pursue national or international careers. The rest are very competent professionals who have a basic salary of just under £2,000 per annum for their regular work in the choir, pick up a bit more, perhaps £1,000, from special services, then have to earn what they can from solo work in local choral events or by teaching.

This does not constitute a very fat living, and sadly the insecurity seems to have created a tradition of preoccupation with money and an unwillingness to do anything without financial reward. So entrenched is this tradition that it seems unlikely that it would be modified by higher basic pay, were the necessary money ever to become available.

Monday 31 May 1976

Last evening I preached in the Abbey for the first time since I became a Canon. The preaching arrangements here are much the same as those observed in the major cathedrals: the Canons take it in turn to be on duty, usually for a month at a time, and during their period 'In Residence', as it is called, they must be present daily at Mattins and Evensong and also ensure that sermons are preached at these services on Sundays. They are themselves required to preach one sermon, but may invite someone else to preach the second. Curiously, the Dean can only preach at Mattins and Evensong on Christmas Day, Easter Day and Whitsunday unless invited by one of the Canons to preach on another Sunday.

Since I am not due to be in Residence until September I have, officially, no preaching duties until then, but we have a Sunday evening congregational service which is not controlled by the Statutes, at which the Dean or anyone invited by him may preach. In practice, the Dean and the Canons do most of the preaching at this service and, since there was a vacant slot yesterday, this was allocated to me to get me started.

It proved to be quite hard work. In the absence of a choir or set liturgy, the preacher is required to occupy almost one hour with a combination of addresses, prayers and hymns, led by himself and the organ. Since it was the Sunday after Ascension Day, I took the Ascension of Jesus as my theme – devoting one address to the biblical material, another to the theological implications of this material, and the third to some practical implications – mainly that the Ascended Christ is the Secular Christ and that those values and insights which Jesus shared with his friends in Palestine – love and reconciliation, self-sacrifice and service, truth and justice – are now to be expressed and worked out in every part of the earth and at every moment in time.

There were, I suppose, about 200 people present – mainly visitors from all parts of the world – and this service offers an opportunity in a quite informal context to do some fairly sustained preaching and teaching. I shall be responsible for four consecutive Sundays in November.

I have now been here for a month, though it seems much longer, and I am very conscious that I have joined an unusually gifted Chapter. Edward Carpenter, who came as a Canon in 1951 – just in time for the Queen's Coronation – and became Dean just a couple of years ago, is, I suppose, the most erudite leader of this community since the time of Armitage Robinson. He is one of the last of the liberal modernist churchmen who flourished for a time in the 1930s. His knowledge and love of the Abbey is unrivalled and he combines the eccentricity of a scholar with a warm humanity.

David Edwards, who is Rector of St Margaret's and also Sub-Dean, is the only Fellow of All Souls to have been ordained in the present century. He came here from Cambridge, where he was Dean of King's, and before that he was Editor of SCM Press during the *Honest to God* 1960s. We have been friends since those exciting and, I believe, creative days.

John Austin Baker, the Treasurer, came to the Abbey from Oxford, where he was a Fellow of Corpus Christi College. He is essentially an Old Testament scholar, but his chief claim to fame is his authorship of *The Foolishness of God* – a fine book of general theology which seeks to combine new insights with the traditional understanding of the Christian faith.

Edward Knapp-Fisher, the Archdeacon, arrived only last year from South Africa, where he was Bishop of Pretoria for fifteen years. Before that he was Principal of Cuddesdon Theological College, which was, by all accounts, an austere, semi-monastic training ground for the post-war generation of clergy. He is an uncompromising high churchman, but a severe exterior masks a warm pastoral heart, and he is the pastor of our community as well as responsible for the oversight of the parishes of which the Dean and Chapter are the patrons.

Reg Pullen, the Chapter Clerk and Receiver General, is not a member of the Chapter but attends all its meetings in a position akin to that of a Permanent Secretary or a Town Clerk. He came in 1947 and, as the chief lay administrator, has accumulated enormous power. Fortunately his commitment to the Abbey is total, and his contribution to virtually every facet of our corporate life is indispensable, but already I sense that little if anything can take place without his approval. This could create problems, particularly if significant change is ever mooted.

My own role here is not yet clear. I am not due to be Canon-in-Residence until September, and about that time I shall also become

Steward. Meanwhile, I have a regular weekly broadcast for the BBC and quite a lot of other broadcasting and writing commitments, so I shall not be idle. And I am greatly enjoying the daily worship in the Abbey, standing in for the Canon-in-Residence when he needs to be elsewhere, getting to know the building, and generally absorbing the atmosphere of this unique church.

Friday 4 June 1976

My daily encounter with the Abbey, through sharing and sometimes leading the worship, and wandering about the building, talking to visitors and exploring its recesses, is a constant source of amazement. Before I became a Canon I had been here on a number of occasions, mainly for services, but I didn't really know the place and had almost everything to learn. And after a mere couple of months living in its community I am still a beginner.

The building itself is extraordinary, and the combination of narrowness and great height – the nave roof is 102 feet above the floor – makes it the most French church in England. It bears a remarkable resemblance to Rheims Cathedral and there are those who believe it was designed by the same architect, but the experts say this is unlikely and that the similarity is due to the common factors in thirteenth-century Gothic architecture across Europe.

Where it differs from Rheims, of course, is in its vast collection of memorial stones and monuments which make it a kind of national Valhalla, though by no means all of those who are buried here were illustrious. In order to appreciate the great beauty of the building it is necessary to look upwards at angles of 45° and more. This takes one beyond the monuments, dating mainly from the seventeenth to nineteenth centuries, and into the realm of the pure Gothic – infinity made visible.

But most of the memorials and monuments offer fascinating reflections of the constituent parts of English history, not all of it edifying, and this helps to keep one's feet on the ground. There is that mixture of glory and shame which characterizes human nature everywhere and which this church, like every other, exists to redeem in Christ.

Not all our visitors – 1.5 to 2 million every year – see Westminster Abbey in these terms. I gather that after the mediaeval period, when hordes of pilgrims came to the shrine of St Edward the Confessor, visiting on a large scale began only after the burial of the Unknown Warrior in 1922.

The visitors, whose numbers have been greatly inflated by the ease of modern travel, come for a great variety of reasons – religious, historical, cultural, artistic, national – and sometimes out of sheer curiosity. Our responsibility, it seems to me, is to make them feel welcome and help them to discover a little more of the Abbey's prime purpose, which is the worship of God and the propagation of the truths and values of the Christian religion.

This cannot be forced on them – few of the visitors are in the building long enough for that, anyway – and we must largely rely on the building speaking for itself. At this point the monuments are quite a problem. Most of the chapels are so cluttered with them as to be unusable for liturgical purposes or even as places of prayer. During the seventeenth and eighteenth centuries the Dean and Chapter encouraged the erection of large monuments since fees were payable on the basis of square footage. What might therefore have been signs of devotion are now signs of death.

We ought, I believe, to encourage more visitors to share in the worship, especially the daily Evensong, so gloriously sung, and also to offer more information by means of leaflets and booklets. There is plenty of stuff about the history of the Abbey, but next to nothing about its spiritual purposes. The importance of the hourly prayers cannot be overestimated.

Saturday 5 June 1976

The financial position of this place is a long way from healthy, and the Abbey is nothing like as prosperous as it appears from the outside. I picked up something of this at my first Chapter meeting last month, and now that I've seen the accounts, the seriousness of the position is only too plain.

The year ended last September sustained a loss of more than £42,000 on the general income and expenditure account. This was an improvement on the previous year when the loss was about £61,000, but it means that reserves have been depleted by over £100,000 in two years.

Last year's improvement was achieved mainly by extending the area for which visitors must pay an admission fee and, since the new arrangement was introduced only half-way through the year, there is obviously some potential here. Certainly there doesn't seem much scope for cost-cutting unless the Abbey's ministry is to be seriously curtailed.

The annual running costs total about £520,000, of which £325,000 goes on the salaries, wages and pensions of the 170 people employed here. It is a very labour-intensive operation, and necessarily so, since it is an expression of the life of the church and therefore essentially a community. The music costs about £100,000 a year and the upkeep of our historic houses another £60,000. On the income side, we are heavily dependent upon visitors – last year they provided £261,000, excluding the profit of £47,000 from the Bookshop.

The Treasurer, John Baker, has produced a useful paper, 'Operation Solvency', in which he suggests a number of new money-raising projects and some modest economies, but, as he points out, increases of over 26% in the retail price index in the course of a single year cannot be met by a few adjustments here and there. The best hope lies in the Government's new pay policy, which should help to bring inflation under control, and a greater influx of overseas visitors encouraged by the weak pound.

Some improvement in our accounting procedures also looks urgent as budgets are not produced and the flow of financial information is inadequate for any kind of monitoring or control. The accounts office presents a scene of extraordinary chaos.

Tuesday 8 June 1976

The Choristers have been invited to take part in a television programme with Bing Crosby when he comes to London in July, but Douglas Guest is not keen on this and argues that there is insufficient time during the summer term for the necessary rehearsals.

The proposal, from an American company, is that the boys will sing in a television 'spectacular' to be presented world-wide at Christmas. The music will obviously be of the popular sort and likely to attract audiences numbering hundreds of millions. This cannot do the Abbey any harm; indeed it might well help to compensate for the fact that very few special services are now broadcast from the Abbey because the high Equity fees demanded for the Lay Vicars frighten away the television authorities. Our fund-raising efforts in America need this kind of exposure.

No doubt keeping company with Bing Crosby is not to Douglas Guest's taste and, although he doesn't say so, I imagine that he believes the proposed programme to be well beneath the dignity of the choir of Westminster Abbey. There are also signs that, as his career in church music nears its ending, he doesn't wish to be caught up in new enterprises involving additional work. The Chapter has asked the Dean to urge him to take the proposition seriously, and to investigate just how much additional rehearsal time is required, but I shall be surprised if the matter is resolved in time for the Choristers to become involved.

Wednesday 9 June 1976

At yesterday's Chapter meeting the Dean produced a small bronze bell, bearing the figures of an eagle, a lamb, a pelican and a lion, together with a Latin inscription. This had been left at the Deanery by a woman from Ontario acting for the parents of a Canadian soldier who was killed during the 1939–45 war. It seems that the soldier stole the bell from a church, believed to be Westminster Abbey, when he was passing through London on his way to France. Following his death, it was returned with his effects to his parents and they understood, presumably from something he had written, that he was full of remorse for having stolen the bell.

But Westminster Abbey, being middle-of-the-road Church of England, has never been a place where bells are left lying around. So we decided to send it along to Roman Catholic Westminster Cathedral, a much more likely scene of the crime.

Curious things come to us from Canada: we learned the other day that a Canadian benefactor had bequeathed to us twenty-seven acres of 'wild land' in British Columbia – more useful to us than a small bell, one might suppose, though its precise value has still be to ascertained.

Friday 11 June 1976

The Queen came to the annual Commonwealth Day Observance this afternoon and I was presented to her – the first time for me. On these grand occasions the Canons stand in line just inside the Great West Door. The Dean greets the visiting dignitary in the doorway and immediately brings him or her across to us to shake hands. Having been told that I had only recently arrived at the Abbey, the Queen expressed the hope that I would be happy here and quickly moved on to shake the hands of numerous Commonwealth officials.

This occasion has had a curious history. It was held just once in St Martin-in-the-Fields when I was on that church's part-time staff about ten years ago. But such an outcry was raised in the Church Assembly and elsewhere about its inter-faith character that it was immediately transferred to the secular setting of the Guildhall in the City of London.

The Queen soon became dissatisfied with this and asked Eric Abbott, the then Dean, to have it in the Abbey. This was an astute move because the Abbey, being a Royal Peculiar, is outside any sort of ecclesiastical jurisdiction and therefore beyond discussion in the Church Assembly. Equally, if the Archbishop of Canterbury or any other leading church-man is criticized for permitting inter-faith worship in a Christian church he can, with complete integrity, claim that anything taking place in Westminster Abbey is beyond his control. The Abbey is of course the ideal place for Commonwealth events, and it is somewhat surprising that this one did not come here in the first place.

As an event – great care is taken to describe it as an observance, rather than as a service – I found it impressive, indeed moving. The gathering together of so many people from so many different races, cultures and religions to affirm their belief in God and their solidarity within the Commonwealth can only be a good thing and must contribute something to the furthering of the unity of the human race.

As an act of worship it didn't seem to work. The different languages used and the very different understandings of God expressed in the readings and prayers militated against any corporate spiritual atmo-sphere, so it never 'took off'. But it is well worth doing and the Queen is obviously very committed to it.

Tuesday 29 June 1976

Today being St Peter's Day, and the Abbey's Patronal Festival, Jo and I attended the annual Collegiate Dinner held in the Jerusalem Chamber. This was a formal occasion, inasmuch as the Dean and Chapter and the other officers of the foundation wore their scarlet cassocks and academic gowns, with the ladies in their evening dresses, but because of the financial crisis neither caterers nor waiters were employed. The ladies of the Cloisters provided all the food, except the salmon, and it was organized as a serve-yourself buffet.

The salmon was brought to the event by the Prime Warden and Clerk of the Fishmongers Company and presented at the entrance to the Chamber to the accompaniment of a short ceremony which began 'Behold a man with a fish'. There indeed was a huge salmon, and at the end of the ceremony more were brought in to feed the assembled com-pany – about sixty of us, I suppose.

This tradition, while purporting to date from the Middle Ages, is – like many other of the Abbey's traditions – a fairly recent invention. It is derived from a monkish story which alleges that at the time of the dedi-cation of the first Abbey in the tenth century a fisherman in the Thames had a vision of St Peter, who instructed him to donate to the recently arrived Benedictine monks a tithe of his annual catch. On the strength of this story the Abbey claimed throughout the Middle Ages a tithe of all the salmon caught between Westminster and the Tower of London – a considerable amount, apparently.

The reflection of this at our St Peter's Day dinner is of course just a bit of fun, but the Fishmongers Company – one of the wealthiest in the City of London – seems happy to collaborate, and good relations with its Freemen have resulted. The less formal buffet meal is said to have been an improvement on the normal arrangement, though there is some uncertainty as to whether the ladies will be ready to provide most of the food every year.

Tuesday 13 July 1976

The Treasurer informed us today that a device has been invented that is capable of nullifying the Abbey's burglar alarm system. Chubb, the contractors responsible for our system, have offered to update it to counteract the possibility of interference, at a cost of £8,158.

The main purpose of the alarm is to protect the Coronation Stone, which is thought to be particularly vulnerable to theft by Scottish nationalists, but we simply do not have the money to pay for any updating of our system. So we readily agreed with the Treasurer's view that we cannot go ahead unless a substantial part of the cost is met either by the Government or by our insurers. In the present economic climate, however, it seems unwise to apply to them for grants towards an expenditure of this sort.

The Home Secretary is to be advised of the situation and of our inability to allocate such a large sum to the security of a national treasure. It will be interesting to see how he responds. I can't really see the Treasury being ready to cough up, even though the amount involved is minuscule for them.

Friday 16 July 1976

The drought which started soon after I arrived here in May continues, and it has become one of the hottest summers in living memory. The fountain in the Little Cloister has been turned off to save water and the grass in College Garden is scorched.

This morning I chanced to meet Chris Hildyard, who was a Minor Canon for forty-five years and still lives in No. 2 The Cloisters – a most beautiful house that was once the abode of the Benedictine guestmaster.

13

I asked Chris if he recalled an equally hot summer and he replied, 'Yes, in 1911 when I was a page boy at the Coronation of George V, and I remember guardsmen in their bearskins fainting in the heat.'

Chris is a delightful period piece. Now aged seventy-five, he became a Coronation page boy because his father had been a Minor Canon of St George's Chapel, Windsor since 1901 and was known to the Royal Family. Chris came to the Abbey in 1928 and joined the redoubtable Jocelyn Perkins, who had been Sacrist since 1899 and already done much to repair the liturgical neglect of the eighteenth and nineteenth centuries.

The two made a perfect combination, for although Chris knew very little about liturgy and even less about theology, he had a fine eye for colour, impeccable taste and an acute theatrical sense. The dignified, colourful ceremonial for which the Abbey is now famed owes everything to them, because both outstayed any Dean or Canon and eventually got their own ways.

A typical example of Hildyard flair is to be seen in the magnificent cope often worn by the Dean. While holidaying on the Greek island of Hydra, Chris noticed a soldier's uniform in a second-hand shop. It was badly worn but had splendid golden ornamentation, so he bought it for next to nothing, brought it back to London, and had the ornamentation remounted on blue velvet – with spectacular success.

A less happy story relates to the Coronation of the present Queen. Chris, who is a talented artist, decided to paint a picture of the Coronation ceremony, but when he reached the Canons in their seats near the High Altar he found himself unable to include Charles Smyth, the then Rector of St Margaret's, with whom he had frequently quarrelled and whom he greatly despised.

Tuesday 20 July 1976

The Choir School is in crisis. It has only thirty-six pupils, aged between eight and thirteen, twenty-four of whom are Choristers in the Abbey Choir and the remaining twelve Probationers who will in due course be admitted to the Choir. There is a teaching staff of eight, including the Headmaster, and a number of other peripatetic music teachers. It is more of a tutorial establishment than a school and over the years has served the Abbey and its Choristers exceedingly well – at enormous financial cost. There could be no possibility of producing music at the standard required here without such a school.

Now it has emerged that two of the masters, one of whom claims to be an Oxford MA and a PhD of Hanoi University, have developed an inappropriate relationship with some of the boys. A committee of enquiry has reported that, among other things, the boys have been encouraged to turn human biology books into obscene publications. Furthermore, at the annual Guy Fawkes night party held in the grounds of Lambeth Palace last November, one of these masters was observed lying with a boy beneath some bushes. The report also indicated, unsurprisingly, that the Headmaster lacks any real grip on the running of the school.

Never in my wildest dreams, or nightmares, did I suppose that within three months of arriving at Westminster I should be handling a matter of this sort. We had a very long discussion of the situation at today's Chapter Meeting in the course of which David Edwards suggested that we were responsible for managing what Evelyn Waugh would have described as a 'sink school'. The Headmaster is, in fact, a very agreeable, dedicated man, but quite obviously he will have to go and a new Head be recruited to make a fresh start and to restore confidence. Already, some parents are talking of withdrawing their boys from the school.

So we decided to terminate the appointment of one of the masters and not to renew the contract of the other which is about to expire. The former will be offered a term's pay in lieu of notice and the Dean will see the Headmaster personally next week to discuss his future.

Whatever happens, none of this must be allowed to get out, otherwise we shall be in even bigger trouble.

Sunday 1 August 1976

Our elder daughter, Jean, was married in the Abbey's Henry VII Chapel yesterday afternoon. This magnificent, early sixteenth-century, building with its fan-vaulted ceiling and canopied stalls, over which hang the banners of the senior knights of the Order of the Bath, makes a most memorable setting for any wedding and today's was a very happy occasion.

Originally, the wedding was to have taken place in the parish church at Ware, where we lived until just over three months ago, and it was something of a shock to Jean, who has a shy personality, and even more so to her non-churchgoing fiancé, Graham, to learn that it would have to be transferred to Westminster Abbey. The guests loved it, of course.

The service was conducted by her godfather, and my old friend from student days, Lawrence Jackson, who is now the Provost of Blackburn

Cathedral and came attired in ecclesiastical breeches and gaiters – much to the amusement of Jean, who had never before seen such a garb. The Abbey Choir being on holiday, the Ware choir took its place and did well. I gave Jean away and the Dean gave the blessing so, apart from one of the bridesmaids fainting briefly, everything went according to plan.

During the morning it seemed that the hot, dry summer was finally ended, for there was some rain, but it had recovered by the afternoon and we had the wedding reception in the delightful ruins of St Catherine's Chapel just outside our kitchen door. During its days as the Infirmary Chapel it was the place where, in 1176, the Archbishops of Canterbury and York quarrelled over precedence, the Papal Legate settling this in favour of Canterbury, and where Henry III, surrounded by the bishops, swore on the Gospels to maintain Magna Carta.

Set against these events, the failure of the bridegroom and bride to insert a knife in the wedding cake, because the icing had the constitution of concrete, could be seen only as a minor hiccup, and we danced the evening away on a boat plying between Westminster Bridge and Greenwich. The memory of Lawrence Jackson occupying a position in the bow, while still in his full ecclesiastical fig, will not quickly fade.

Tuesday 28 September 1976

I have been officially elected to the office of Steward – the position normally occupied by the most recent recruit to the Chapter and not a very demanding assignment. Historically, the Steward is the successor of the Guestmaster of the Benedictine Abbey, so he is responsible for present-day hospitality – dinners, receptions, and the like – and in recent times has been asked to ensure that the Abbey's two acres of grounds are properly maintained.

I suggested to the Chapter, however, and it was readily agreed, that the brief of the Steward should be enlarged. Hospitality should be seen not simply, or even primarily, in terms of official functions but rather in terms of the welcoming of the two million people who visit the Abbey every year from all parts of the world.

This represents a major challenge which so far has hardly been faced, and this for two main reasons. The numbers are often quite overwhelming and on most mornings of this summer the building has been crowded beyond its capacity. As Eric Abbott, the former Dean, once remarked, 'It isn't really a spiritual experience for the visitor if he is nearly trampled to death and then finds that his pocket has been picked.'

It is also the case that priests are not appointed to the Chapter of Westminster Abbey to deal with this kind of challenge. We are here because it is thought that we have a contribution to make to the life of the wider church as writers, scholars or teachers. So if the Abbey is ever to be seen as a dynamic centre of contemporary mission, different people will be needed.

Nonetheless, something has to be done about the visitors, and in the time remaining from my writing and broadcasting commitments I am prepared to have a go. I cannot believe, however, that it is going to be easy, since our sole welcoming resources are the twelve Vergers – an odd bunch who are interested mainly in candles and vestments and regard the visitors as a great nuisance. I have noticed that as soon as the building becomes crowded they disappear behind pillars or retreat to their supposed duties in the vestries. Last Saturday morning I found myself to be the only 'official' trying to marshal some thousands of people struggling to make their way from the nave to the restricted space of St Edward's Shrine and the Henry VII Chapel. This cannot continue.

Wednesday 29 September 1976

The size of the problem we are facing over the great influx of visitors to the Abbey was clearly demonstrated this afternoon when the Chapter was driven to consider the possibility of moving the Coronation Chair from its present site near the shrine of St Edward the Confessor to a more accessible place in Henry VII's Chapel.

The layout of the Abbey could hardly be worse for the movement of crowds. East of the nave, and in that part of the building which houses the shrine and the royal tombs, is a series of narrow bottle-necks, culminating in the shrine itself, which will accommodate no more than a dozen people. Congestion is inevitable and frequently there is absolute chaos.

The suggestion was that the Chair and the Stone of Scone which it accommodates should be placed on the steps of Henry VII's Chapel, where it would be more easily seen without holding up the flow of visitors, and that St Edward's Chapel should become a place of pilgrimage and prayer and be closed to conducted parties of tourists.

We had a long discussion about this and saw a drawing prepared by Peter Foster, the Surveyor of the Fabric, indicating how it might be done. Nicholas MacMichael, Keeper of the Muniments, also provided some historical statements about the positioning of the Chair. But in the

17

end we decided against change. It would be a fairly costly business and we thought it important that visitors should see the Chair and the Stone in their traditional places. We were, however, specially conscious of the fact that the removal would cause a great public outcry and, in any case, be unlikely to win the approval of the Queen.

So we must try other ways of controlling the crowds and sometimes, when things are getting out of hand, it may be necessary to close St Edward's Chapel for a time.

Thursday 30 September 1976

The brief act of prayer conducted every hour from the Nave pulpit is, I am sure, a valuable way of reminding the visitors what the Abbey is for and also of involving them in its chief activity. But it is not always easy to claim the attention of the multitudes – partly, I suspect, because many of them are in a hurry to move through the Abbey and on to Buckingham Palace, partly because many do not understand English and have no idea what we are talking about. It may also be the case that the growth of secularization is making the idea of prayer seem alien to the British and some other Europeans. Two minutes is about the bearable limit.

Hence the problem arising from Bishop Victor Pike's offer to give more of his time to the Abbey when he retires from the Bishopric of Sherborne next year. He is a dear man who before becoming a bishop was a greatly loved Chaplain General to the Forces. He belongs to a remarkable family of eleven children born in a rectory in County Tipperary – one died in infancy and of the remaining ten, three became bishops, two senior colonial administrators, one a headmaster, and the four girls all became doctors.

Victor is brimming over with Irish blarney and whenever he comes to us for a week to lead the hourly prayers he often occupies the pulpit for as long as ten minutes. This causes a fair amount of chaos because most of the visitors begin to get on the move well before he has attempted to bestow his final blessing upon them. More of this won't be at all helpful, which is a pity, because during the time between the prayers he makes himself available to the visitors and has a marvellous pastoral touch. We need to find some way of using him as a friend and pastor, but without the benefit of his prayers. This isn't going to be easy.

The Judges' service this morning, held every Michaelmas to mark the beginning of the legal year, was a remarkable new experience for me. I went into the Abbey at about 11.15 not knowing quite what to expect and was astonished to find the nave, from which all the chairs had been removed, absolutely packed with robed lawyers – High Court judges in their scarlet and ermine, Circuit judges in purple, QCs in full-bottom wigs and silver-buckled shoes and many others whom I took to be barristers.

It was the atmosphere of a market place with everyone milling around, greeting friends, discussing holidays and, for all I know, interesting recent cases. The hubbub was unbelievable, but shortly before 11.30 the arrival of the Lord Chancellor at the Great West Door brought a signal for silence and the beginning of a long procession, in which everyone had an appointed place, from the nave to the Choir.

As is customary in England, the most junior led the way, with the Lords of Appeal, the Law Lords, the Lord Chief Justice and the Lord Chancellor bringing up the rear. The procession in fact took longer than the short service which followed its completion. The contrast between the High Court judges, who looked like row upon row of Father Christmases, and the Law Lords, in their ordinary suits and mackintoshes, was striking. The Lord Chancellor, Lord Hailsham, read the lesson in Churchillian tones, and the ever-liberal Dean prayed that criminals should be corrected, rather than punished.

At the end of the service the Dean and Chapter were conducted to the Poets' Corner door, through which the entire assembly was to pass on its way to the House of Lords for the Lord Chancellor's reception. This time the senior people went first and, in accordance with custom, bowed to the Dean and Chapter as they passed. Thus in the space of about fifteen minutes I bowed many hundreds of times in response, trying always to look pleasant and to avoid a fixed grin.

The reception, to which we are apparently always invited, was a scrum and it was virtually impossible to move. Once upon a time, I was told, champagne was served, but the expansion of the legal profession has caused this to be reduced to white wine. I was buttonholed by a very tall QC who depressed me with the information that the Lawyers' Christian Fellowship, an evangelical group to which he belongs, has a membership in excess of 700.

After many meetings, much legal advice, some nasty financial negotiations and a good deal of mix-up, the worst of the Choir School crisis seems to be over, though there could still be some unpleasant repercussions. The master whose contract was about to expire milked us for £3,000 on some technical industrial-relations point, and the other one is claiming about £7,000.

The meeting between the Dean and the Headmaster had to be aborted because the Treasurer inadvertently advised him of the Dean and Chapter's decision that he should go. The legal ramifications of this were considerable and, although the majority of us thought that he should go this coming Christmas, it has now been agreed that he will stay until the end of the next Summer term and be given a year's salary as a lump sum when he goes.

Meanwhile three strong new teaching appointments (two of them women) have been made and we are in process of forming a Choir School Council on which such eminent people as David Willcocks and Dame Diana Reader-Harris have agreed to serve. Representatives of the parents are also to be brought in. Sadly, an attempt to link the Choir School with Westminster Under School failed simply because the Under School felt unable to accept responsibility for the education of boys who from time to time are required to leave the classroom in order to sing at special services in the Abbey. We discussed this problem at some length and there seems no acceptable solution. If the Queen were to be attending an Abbey service, it would be quite impossible to explain: 'Sorry, the Choristers are not here this morning, Ma'am: they could not be released from an English lesson.'

We are to advertise for a new Headmaster and need a strong character with good experience.

Sunday 24 October 1976

At a pleasant little ceremony last evening a memorial to Dame Sybil Thorndike was unveiled. This was quick work, since she died only a few months ago and often, as with the canonization of saints, some years have to elapse in order to test the candidate's staying power. In this instance the friendship and near-adoration of the Dean helped, but there is no doubting the great actress's outstanding gifts and her commitment to social reform and to good works far beyond the stage. A large company of stage people came to the ceremony together with representatives of the many causes she supported. J. B. Priestley composed the epitaph:

> Saint Joan or Hecuba, great actress of your age,
> All womenhood your part, the world your stage.
> To each good cause you lent your vigorous tongue,
> Swept through the years the champion of the young.
> And now the scripts lie fading on the shelf,
> We celebrate your finest role – yourself.
> The calls, the lights, grow dim but not this part,
> The Christian spirit, the great generous heart.

The stone also mentions that she was the wife of Lewis Casson, which is a nice touch, because theirs was a real partnership.

Wednesday 27 October 1976

Although Westminster Abbey was built primarily as a place of worship and prayer, it is now exceedingly difficult to experience between 10.00 a.m. and 5.00 p.m. the kind of peace and tranquillity that most people need if they are to engage in private prayer.

The beautiful and atmospheric St Faith's Chapel at the South end of the South Transept is set aside for prayer, but it is none too easy for occasional visitors to find and is used by relatively few people. In the rest of the building there is a continuous hubbub from the seething mass of visitors.

Edward Knapp-Fisher is, rightly, very troubled about this and has suggested that St George's Chapel, just inside the Great West Door, should also be set aside for private prayer and its purpose prominently advertised. It isn't one of my favourite chapels, having been created from a former consistory court and remodelled in 1932 in memory of the millions of men and women who died in the 1914–18 war. Although very small, it houses numerous military memorials as well as indifferent busts of F. D. Maurice, Charles Kingsley and William Booth, the founder of the Salvation Army.

Still, it is better than nothing, though it cannot be a quiet place, since it is exposed to the rest of the building. Edward Knapp-Fisher hopes that one day thick glass may be inserted in the screens to provide some protection from the noise, but Peter Foster, the Surveyor of the Fabric, says this would cost £15,000 – money we simply do not have at the moment.

There is also a question as to whether people will wish to pray in what may look like a large museum case, but in the present situation experiment is certainly called for if this church is to be truly a house of God and a place of prayer.

Tuesday 9 November 1976

I have lost my little battle to bring some influence to bear on Westminster City Council over its proposed cuts in welfare services and imposition of charges for various services to the elderly, the handicapped and the homeless. These proposals are, it is said, made necessary by cuts in national and overall Government spending, and when they were announced earlier this year in the national press the Bishop of Winchester, John Taylor, wrote to the Dean and Chapter expressing the hope that we might try to persuade the City Council to change its mind.

My own attempts to get something done about this have focussed on the fact that the City Council voted last year to donate £250,000 to the current appeal for the Abbey's restoration – this to be paid in annual instalments of £50,000. I suggested to the Chapter that we should not accept this money if it was to be at the expense of the underprivileged members of our exceedingly wealthy city.

This divided the Chapter. The Sub-Dean strongly supported me, but the Treasurer felt that we should show loyalty to the Trust, which under the active Presidency of the Duke of Edinburgh is working hard to raise the £10 million needed, while the Archdeacon thought that we might make our point simply by refraining from asking the City Council for the first instalment of its donation next year. The Receiver General, himself a former City Councillor and with many friends on its well-filled Conservative benches, strongly advised against any conflict with the local Establishment. The Dean, basically on my side, tried to find some middle way, such as having an informal discussion between himself and the Lord Mayor, but this did not seem to promise much likelihood of a change in policy. In the end my proposal lacked the support necessary for decisive action.

The problem is real enough. Although individual members of the Chapter – Charles Kingsley, Samuel Barnett, William Temple, Lewis Donaldson – have in times past campaigned on behalf of the poor, there is no precedent for Westminster Abbey as an institution challenging the political decision-makers at any level of government. We are deemed to be a part of the Establishment that hangs together for mutual support, therefore we must not agitate on behalf of groups which have grievances against their rulers. Support of the victims of apartheid in South Africa or of political repression in the Soviet Union is acceptable, but issues on our own doorstep must not be touched. I don't like this.

Quite a lot is now being said and written about the validity of the Establishment of the Church of England. My own problem is not with the existence of the church-state link, but with the little constructive use we are making of it.

Friday 12 November 1976

The ringing of cash tills and the chink of money is not a very edifying accompaniment to Mattins. Westminster Abbey and St Paul's Cathedral are the only remaining choral establishments that sing Mattins on weekdays – in our case on Tuesday and Friday. The attendance of worshippers at 9.20 a.m. is small, and although I go fairly often, the clergy are normally represented only by the Precentor and the Canon-in-Residence.

Soon after 9.30 a.m., however, the visitors begin to pour in, and after a brief inspection of the Nave make their way to the East end via the ticket desk at the entrance to the Nave Choir aisle. In theory, this is fine, and there is always the hope that some of the visitors may feel drawn to share in the worship. A few do. But most are simply intent on reaching the royal tombs and the Coronation Chair, and quite a number are being led by London Tourist Board guides who are anxious to display their knowledge of the building.

We have, more or less, managed to forbid lecturing while Mattins is in progress, but the sound of the tills and the chink of money is, at the moment, beyond control. During the summer months when tourism was at its peak Mattins was sung in St Margaret's, and this solved the problem of intrusive noise. Now the service is back in the Abbey and we don't quite know what to do. The Lay Vicars, who travel to the Abbey from all parts of Greater London and beyond, cannot get here any earlier, and the VAT inspector and the auditor require us to issue tickets in return for the entrance fees to the Royal Chapels. Refusal of admission until the service is ended at 10 o'clock would dislocate the pattern of tourism, which has to take in Buckingham Palace, St Paul's and the Tower of London before mid-afternoon.

One possible solution is to remain in St Margaret's all the year round, but this would represent a reduction in the public worship offered in the Abbey and a subordination to money of the very activity that the Abbey exists to promote. This won't do, and we have asked the cashiers not to issue tickets through their automatic machines while Mattins is going on, and to be ultra-careful over the handling of coins. A Verger is to be posted in the North Choir Aisle to enjoin silence and to enforce the ban on lecturing before ten o'clock.

Friday 19 November 1976

The Dean has discussed with me another batch of letters he has received about some of the Vergers who are unhelpful to people trying either to attend services or simply to sit in the Abbey for a short time when services are about to begin or are in progress. The daily choral services are held in the Choir, and there is no reason why people should not be carefully ushered in to join us at appropriate points in the worship or encouraged to sit in the Nave if they cannot stay for long.

This is a long-standing problem, going back for as far as the Dean can remember, and of course as the number of visitors and potential worshippers increases, the volume of frustration and complaint is also bound to increase. On any reckoning the attitude of the Vergers is crazy. The primary function of Westminster Abbey is to be a place of worship, and in our increasingly secularized age it is absolutely vital that this function should be maintained. Yet over the course of a year many hundreds, perhaps thousands, of people are actively discouraged from joining in the worship because their time-tables are not precisely synchronized with ours.

There seem to be two explanations – or excuses. The Vergers, possibly inheriting a former tradition, regard our worship chiefly as the activity of the Abbey community and something that needs to be protected from 'intruders'. It is true that people who arrive a little late or leave early sometimes create a disturbance, but this is exceedingly rare and can easily be coped with.

The other factor is that Vergers, in common with some others who deal with our public, like to throw their weight about and are, apparently, never happier than when exercising their authority negatively. Signs of this are to be found in most of the major cathedrals.

Responsibility for the Vergers here actually lies with the Dean, and only he has authority to deal with them, but he shared the problem with me this morning because I am now actively engaged in what we are beginning to call our 'ministry of welcome' to visitors and worshippers. The next step must be to convene a meeting of the Vergers, doorkeepers, stewards and anyone else dealing with the public in order to lay down the law about the required attitude towards anyone who enters the

Abbey for whatever purpose. But I gather that similar meetings have been held previously and made not a scrap of difference.

Thursday 25 November 1976

A great service at noon to mark the bicentenary of the American Constitution was virtually ruined by the sermon. It was intended to be, and mostly was, a marvellously festive occasion. The demand for tickets from the American community in London exceeded the supply weeks ago and the Abbey was packed with families intent on celebrating their identity and something important in their national life.

Being Americans, they were far less formal than their British counterparts would have been, and although we had the usual array of ambassadors and other dignitaries, including Princess Alexandra, the atmosphere was akin to a party. But then came the sermon delivered by this year's Moderator of the General Assembly of the Church of Scotland, Professor T.F.Torrance, and this soon put a damper on things.

The choice of preacher was not an unreasonable one – at least not to anyone unaware of his outlook and style. Tom Torrance is a very distinguished theologian and churchman who taught for some years in the United States and is in great demand there for special lectures. His position in the Church of Scotland also brought a necessary ecumenical dimension to the service. But the organizers had not bargained on a sermon of inordinate length, couched in academic terms, and devoted mainly to the question of whether or not there was room for a Bill of Rights in Britain.

I don't think I have ever experienced a more serious misjudgment of the requirement of a particular public occasion, and the effect was to reduce the emotional, and I would say the spiritual, temperature dramatically. The Dean was furious about it, as we all were, and the lunch with the Moderator in the Deanery afterwards was a long way from easy. We felt unable as much as to mention the sermon, to which he had obviously given much time and thought, though Edward, in his great charity, made a few rambling remarks about the connection between freedom and justice.

What one doesn't know, however, is how adequately Tom Torrance was briefed when he was invited to preach. He may have been quite unaware of the planned composition of the congregation he was required to address; in which case he must have been horrified, too. But there were no signs of this, and I am not sure that I would trust his judgment on matters of popular piety.

The first day of my second spell as Canon-in-Residence has been marked by the theft of a rather fine oriental carpet from St George's Chapel. Apparently two men, dressed as removal contractors' staff, arrived this morning, walked into the Chapel, rolled up the carpet, and without arousing the slightest suspicion carried it off to a van waiting outside the Great West Door. Nothing could have been more simple. It is now being suggested that a Verger should always be on duty at this main entrance to the Abbey, but while this would be a good thing any-way, I doubt if it would have saved the carpet. Internal communication is so weak that a duty Verger might well have believed the thieves to be on official business. There is a nice story of a nineteenth-century Canon losing a good deal of silver as a result of a burglary at his house in the Little Cloister during the night. Questioned by the police the following morning, one of his daughters reported that she had been disturbed, but when she saw from her bedside clock that it was only 4.00 a.m. she assumed that the noise was caused 'by the maids blacking the grates'.

Sunday 12 December 1976

Bishop John Robinson came to preach for me at Mattins this morning and was in his usual lucid and stimulating form. It being the Third Sunday in Advent, when the appointed Bible readings focus on the church's ordained ministry, he spoke about the distinctive roles of the priesthood and the laity and, while noting with approval the long overdue revival in our understanding of the crucial importance of the ministry of the latter, emphasized the significance of the representative character of the former.

He pointed out something which I am sure is true, namely that because the priesthood is a representative ministry, the level of ministry in the church will seldom in practice rise much above that of the ordained ministry. 'The longer I go on in this job,' he added, 'the more convinced I become that bad priests are worse than no priests. The ordained ministry is the channel – or the bottle-neck – through which the ministry of Christ is communicated to his people and through them to the world.'

It is interesting that one who is so often accused of selling the pass by trying to secularize the Christian faith should expound so high a doctrine of the priesthood. There is, in fact, still a great deal of the traditional churchman in John, and it is high time he was made a diocesan bishop. He was, I am told, disappointed not to have been made Dean of Canterbury when it fell vacant earlier this year, but I doubt whether that would have been a good idea and it was, I suspect, a hope born of desperation.

As I listened to his sermon, some parts of it seemed specially familiar, and when I looked again at the collection of articles and addresses published in his paperback *But That I Can't Believe* (1967), there was today's sermon. It was of course none the worse for being almost ten years old, but this may perhaps explain why it seemed to lack real fire. I can hardly bear even to look at my own sermons when they are just one year old.

Tuesday 21 December 1976

At today's Chapter Meeting it was reported that a performance by the English Chamber Orchestra in the Abbey next year is being sponsored by a tobacco company. But the Dean and Chapter has a firm policy that there shall be no advertising of tobacco products in the Abbey.

The organizers of the concert, who say that it is impossible to make alternative financial arrangements, asked us to reconsider our position, but after a brief discussion we decided unanimously to retain and enforce our current policy. This must be right, given the clear evidence now available about the threat to health posed by smoking.

Wednesday 22 December 1976

The attempt to secure the retirement of two of the three elderly Lay Vicars has occupied a great deal of negotiation and much Chapter discussion since it was first mooted in May and is still not settled.

One of them, the asthmatic Kenneth Tudor, is asking for a payment of twelve months' salary in compensation for relinquishing his freehold, a pension amounting to 7/12ths of his salary, and unlimited opportunity to deputize for other Lay Vicars at the normal deputy fees. Furthermore, he wishes to be given the title Lay Vicar Emeritus, to be allocated a stall and be allowed to continue wearing a scarlet cassock. All this for someone whom the Organist regards as now below the standard required for the choir of Westminster Abbey.

Harry Barnes, who has been associated with the Abbey since he came as a Chorister at the age of eight, is in a somewhat different position, inasmuch as he occupies, rent, insurance and exterior repairs free, a house at Carshalton owned by the Dean and Chapter. We thought that if he were to be allowed to continue in the house until the death of himself and of his wife it would not be necessary to give him a year's salary in return for his relinquishing this freehold. But no, he is demanding the same treatment as his colleague in this regard, and of course he expects the other perks, too, though it is doubtful if his health will permit him to do much deputizing.

He would, however, receive a pension supplement which, together with his state pension, would leave him better off in retirement than when working, so we are resisting the compensatory payment for his freehold. But Tudor has indicated that unless we give Barnes what he is asking for he will himself withdraw acceptance of his own deal.

Negotiations are continuing, with every prospect that the lawyers are going to do best out of this business.

Wednesday 29 December 1976

My first Christmas at the Abbey has been a wonderfully enriching experience, and it is certainly a great privilege to be ministering in a church where, in spite of all the behind-the-scenes problems, the music is so splendid and where the huge congregations help to create a very special atmosphere.

The doors had to be closed well before the start of the Midnight Eucharist on Christmas Eve and several hundred people had to be directed to an overflow service in St Margaret's. It is a pity, however, that the Abbey Choir refuses to sing at this midnight service and that we had to make do with a group of singers from Kensington who led the hymns and contributed some good carols during the communion of the people. I was interested to see that only about half of the huge congregation received communion – the other half being presumably unconfirmed or adherents of other religious faiths.

On Christmas morning the building was again full to capacity and a surprisingly large number attended Evensong at 3.00 p.m. The Lay Vicars sought to be excused this service in order that they might be at home with their families, but the Dean very properly reminded them of the significance for the Abbey of Christmas Day and also of the many other professions required to be on duty.

Duty required the Dean and Canons to attend the Choristers' Christmas Party after Evensong. This was a lively affair and obviously very important to the boys spending Christmas away from home, but the playing of party games after a short night and a heavy day's work was not quite what we ageing clergymen were looking for at five o'clock on Christmas afternoon, and it was almost 8.00 p.m. before we were able to escape.

Westminster is now the only choral foundation that remains in action beyond Christmas Day. The explanation of this is that King Edward the Confessor's first Abbey was dedicated on 28 December 1065, thus requiring us to observe the annual Dedication Festival three days after Christmas. Carol services were sung at 3.00 p.m. on each of these days and the crowds continued to come.

1977

Tuesday 4 January 1977

The New Year staff Communion and breakfast, held today in College Hall, was a jolly event, even though it was bitterly cold. Few staff parties can take place in such splendid and historic surroundings. College Hall was built by Abbot Litlyngton in the late fourteenth century as his state dining-room. The Minstrels' Gallery was added in Tudor or Jacobean times.

After the dissolution of the monastery in 1540 it became the Hall of the new collegiate body established to maintain the Abbey's life, and eventually it was made available to Westminster School as the dining hall of the Queen's Scholars and some other pupils. The huge oak refectory tables are said to have been made from ships of the Spanish Armada that were wrecked near English shores, and the eighteenth-century wainscoting is adorned with coats of arms and portraits.

Sadly, only about half of the 170 members of the Abbey's staff ever turn up for this annual event. Those who are not practising churchgoers seem reluctant to attend the service, and a surprising number are not very sociable. Or maybe experience has taught them that a building which has been without heating for three weeks at the turn of the year is not the kind of place to be having breakfast, even if the bacon, egg, sausage and tomato is piping hot. Which wasn't the case this morning.

Tuesday 25 January 1977

Better news from the financial front. Last year's deficit of £42,000 has been turned round, and for the year ended 29 September 1976 (we still keep the old Michaelmas year-ending) there was a surplus of about £40,000. The main reason for this was that income from visitors increased by 36% to a total of £469,536 – partly a benefit from the extension of the fee-paying Royal Chapels area, and partly because of a considerable increase in the number of tourists in London.

All of which was timely, since staff costs rose by 21.4% to £392,000.

National wage increases averaged 10% and we had to meet some unexpected costs arising from the Choir School debacle. The main problem, however, is that we have no machinery for controlling expenditure; nor have we an adequate staff structure, and a decision made some years ago to align Chapter Office salaries with those of the civil service has proved to be exceedingly expensive, since the civil service has been given massive pay increases in a catching-up operation. Many of our people are now overpaid.

Welcome though a £40,000 surplus most certainly is, it is too small for comfort in our vulnerable situation.

Wednesday 26 January 1977

During a fierce storm last evening a great deal of scaffolding, corrugated iron, tarpaulin and plastic sheeting was blown off the Chapter House and on to the roof of the Abbey and the road between the Abbey and the Houses of Parliament. The police had to close this for a time, and the noise of the wind and all the material being blown about was tremendous.

The Chapter House, which is undergoing restoration, belongs not to us, but to the state, because at the time of the dissolution of the monastery Parliament was meeting there. The restoration work is therefore being carried out by the Department of the Environment, and more than a year ago our Surveyor, Peter Foster, called attention to what he described as a scandalous and dangerous situation relating to the scaffolding and the construction of a temporary corrugated-iron roof.

Now the whole apparatus will need to be reconstructed properly and we shall have to claim compensation for the damage caused to the Abbey. It is a mercy that no one was killed.

Tuesday 8 February 1977

At noon we had a memorial service for Adam Fox, who was a Canon here from 1942 to 1964 and who died on the 17th of last month. He was a very remarkable man and I am glad that I had the opportunity (just) to get to know him, for he was still living in the Little Cloister when I arrived last May. By this time his prominent jaw was hidden by a flowing white beard and there were other signs that he was now ninety-three, but his mind was alert enough. Soon after we came he invited Jo and me for tea, and unfortunately involvement in a broadcast caused me to be about five minutes late. I apologized, of course, and after some general conversation I said, 'Dr Fox, what advice do you have for a new Canon of Westminster?' His reply was prompt: 'Do the job you are paid for.'

He came to the Abbey at a grim moment in its history. The Canonry was vacant because F.R. Barry had lost through wartime bombing not only the church of which he was Rector (St John's, Smith Square), but also his home in the Little Cloister, and it was considered important that he should be got out of London. He became Bishop of my home diocese of Southwell, and I was present at his enthronement in Southwell Minster.

At that time Adam Fox was in the relatively safe and comfortable post of Dean of Divinity at Magdalen College, Oxford, and he was also Professor of Poetry, having been elected in 1938 when the two chief contenders divided most of the votes. Before that he had been Warden of Radley College. It was therefore an act of heroism that brought him to London at the height of the Blitz and when the only accommodation available was in a nearby hotel. He was essentially a Platonist and, besides some useful introductory volumes on Plato, wrote an interesting biography of another Platonist – W. R. Inge.

We incorporated into the memorial service as much as we could from the instructions he compiled in poetic form in 1933 when he was at Magdalen.

There wasn't a huge crowd at the service because, obviously, he had outlived most of his contemporaries, but there were some representatives from the Skinners' Company, of which he had once been a keen member. Eric Abbott, our former Dean, read one of the lessons. We had all the music he asked for, and an admirable address (no mention of this possibility in the poem) was given by Edward Carpenter, who had been a fellow Canon for twelve years and a friend and neighbour during the fourteen years of his retirement.

Edward began by remarking that had Dr Fox been present today he would have noted that the service began one minute late. A number of other anecdotes followed. I liked the ones about how, on his 77th birthday, he travelled on the No 77 bus from one end of its route to the other, and how when, in the wake of a Billy Graham crusade, an earnest student at Ridley Hall, Cambridge, asked him why he had been ordained, he replied, 'Because they would not have me on the Great Western'. But the broad portrait was of a devout churchman who rarely missed Mattins and Evensong, an erudite scholar, and a tough Treasurer of the Abbey who would not permit any expenditure without his personal approval.

It seemed right to bury his ashes in Poets' Corner, but we felt unable to accept his suggestion that the gravestone be inscribed simply 'A FOX GONE TO EARTH'. Instead, it will catalogue his dates and appointments, which will be much less interesting and testify to our attachment to convention.

Wednesday 9 February 1977

At Chapter yesterday we decided to apply for a Royal Warrant to amend the section of our Statutes which lays down what academic qualifications are required of Deans and Canons. The Dean must be either a Doctor or a Bachelor of Divinity and the Canons must be Masters of Arts – a sixteenth-century requirement designed to ensure that the Canons should have a licence to teach and that the Dean, at least, should have a smattering of theology.

There was no problem about this when, until fairly recently, Canons were all Oxbridge men with MAs, and appointment to a Deanery was rewarded with an Honorary DD. But times have changed, and cathedrals with similar requirements in their Statutes had them removed in the 1960s. The Abbey was not, however, involved in the modest reforms of those days and this has created some embarrassments.

After my appointment was announced it was noted that I lacked an MA, so the Archbishop of Canterbury was prevailed upon to give me a Lambeth degree. There have been occasions when DDs have had to be found for new Deans, and it is clearly anomalous that a man with a first-degree BD could be appointed to the Deanery but not to a Canonry. When the Statutes were drafted, the only BDs were of the Oxbridge post-graduate sort.

So we are asking for this bit of nonsense to be changed, which doubtless it will be when we have agreed on the appropriate wording. In fact, the change is probably unnecessary, for if the Queen were to appoint someone without the requisite qualifications, as she did, no doubt inadvertently, in my case, this would over-rule the Statutes by virtue of her supreme power. Ah, well.

Wednesday 2 March 1977

It is not, I think, generally known, and certainly it has come as a surprise to me, that the great restoration programme on the Abbey, now under way and requiring at least £10 million – probably much more – is not the usual effort dealing with the decay of a mediaeval building. Most of the work involves the replacement of nineteenth-century stone.

In 1871, the then Surveyor of the Fabric, George Gilbert Scott, departed from what had become the accustomed practice of repairing with tough Portland stone and introduced instead Chilmark stone from a quarry near Salisbury. This policy was continued by his successor, John Loughborough Pearson, and between the two of them a huge amount of restoration was carried out, including the complete rebuilding of the North Front and the South Gable.

But the choice of Chilmark stone was an unmitigated disaster, since it has not stood up to attack by the sulphur in London's polluted atmosphere. In less than 100 years most of it has crumbled, and some of the statues created then look as if they have been standing on the Abbey since it was first built in the thirteenth century.

No one seems to know why Scott chose Chilmark or why Pearson followed his example. Nor is it certain that they were culpable. At the time of their restorations knowledge of the destructive power of London's pollution must have been quite limited, and there are, I dare say, examples of Chilmark wearing well outside London.

The same sort of question is raised by the condition of the Portland stone used by Nicholas Hawksmoor when he built the Western towers in the early years of the eighteenth century. The stone itself will stand up to most chemicals, but the introduction of iron clamps to reinforce the structure was apparently unnecessary and mistaken. The clamps have rusted and the consequent expansion of them has caused the stone to become spalled. When I first saw the effects of this on the towers and on some of the walls of St Margaret's Church I thought it must be the result of wartime bomb splinters.

Restoring defective work from the eighteenth and nineteenth centuries is not as romantic a task as that of dealing with the legacy of the Middle Ages, but in our case it is just as necessary.

Wednesday 30 March 1977

This evening's memorial service for Janani Luwum, Archbishop of Uganda, was an exceedingly solemn event, he being apparently the latest in the long line of Christian martyrs. He was a victim of the murderous regime of the present President of Uganda, Idi Amin – a monster of a man who is said to have killed 90–100,000 Ugandans during the first two years of his reign of terror.

It is understood that Archbishop Luwum, a courageous and much-loved leader of the Anglican Church in Uganda, and his fellow bishops, were summoned by Amin on 16 February to a kind of public trial in which they were accused of involvement in an arms deal with Milton Obote, the exiled former President. Of course there was not a grain of truth in this allegation, but after the bishops had been sent home the Archbishop was asked to stay behind.

At 6.30 that evening Radio Uganda announced that he and two government ministers had been arrested, and on the following day it was announced that they had been 'killed in a motor accident while trying to escape'. The truth is that they were shot. Radio Uganda ordered that there were to be no public prayers for the Archbishop. A memorial service for him that was to have been held in Namirembe Cathedral on 20 February was cancelled, though it is reported that many thousands attended Mattins in the cathedral that day.

Donald Coggan is naturally very upset by the death of one of his fellow-Primates, whom he knew and admired, and it was at his request that the memorial service in the Abbey was arranged. In spite of the short notice there was a large congregation which included many Ugandans and Commonwealth High Commissioners in London, and a good number of robed bishops.

I suppose that few, if any, of us had ever before been involved in the commemoration of so recent a martyr, and in spite of the clear note of resurrection hope sounded in the service, it remained a most poignant occasion. The rest of the world seems powerless to bring Amin to heel and at the moment the only hope seems to be that someone will assassinate him.

Thursday 7 April 1977

The Queen came this morning to distribute the Royal Maundy and I found this to be not only a magnificent spectacle but also a deeply moving occasion. The most impressive element in the whole ceremony is the movement of the Sovereign towards her subjects, 102 of them today, which is a reversal of the normal protocol. The Duke of Edinburgh read the section from John 13 which includes the feet-washing by Jesus and I read the 'Inasmuch as ye have done it to one of the least of these my brethren, ye have done it unto me' passage from Matthew 25. The six anthems sung by the Choir during the Distribution were breathtakingly beautiful.

Shortly before the service a courtier addressed the recipients of the Maundy money and warned them against falling into the hands of coin dealers who would be waiting outside the Abbey afterwards in the hope of buying sets for about £70. It seems that the coins are at their most valuable on the day of their presentation, because it is then that they are most rare. As time goes by the poverty or death of the recipients will cause more coins to be released on to the market and their value will fall. I am keeping the set handed to me in a small brown envelope as a fee for taking part in the service.

Wednesday 13 April 1977

A sad day indeed, for our much-loved cat Sidney has been put down – a victim of cat 'flu. He came to us not long before we left Ware, when a neighbour grew tired of caring for him. Large and pure white, he settled down immediately, and though he was none too pleased about the move to Westminster, he eventually came to accept it and, on the principle that a cat may look at a king, often took up a position at the foot of the statue of King George VI, immediately opposite the House of Lords. His colour blended rather well with the Portland stone of this statue.

His chief territory was, however, the Cloisters, where for some of most days he walked in a stately manner appropriate to his royal surroundings and attracted much attention from tourists. Sometimes he would accompany me into the Abbey, and on one occasion was found seated on the altar in St Margaret's, but he was not a regular church-goer, preferring – as do many others – to spend his leisure time fishing.

The pool beneath the fountain in the Little Cloister has for many years had a fine collection of goldfish, but following Sidney's arrival their number began to decline. As far as I am aware, he did not regard them as a supplement to the ample meals served to him in the kitchen, and was content to lay his catch on the front doorstep. Unfortunately, this was well within the sight of Marion Couchman, the Abbey gardener, whose devotion to cats is somewhat below that of my own.

Now the goldfish are safe again and we are in mourning. The vet at Ware was sharp enough to advise us to change the inherited name of Cindy to a masculine form, but neglected to advise an inoculation against the peril of cat 'flu. A short but memorable feline life that brought much pleasure and ended in this House of Kings.

Sunday 1 May 1977

I've now been here for twelve months, and this seems a good moment to take stock. It has been a happy year and I still find it hard to believe that I am in this most privileged place of Christian ministry. Friends often ask me if it was difficult to make the transition from a Hertfordshire parish to a great national shrine so closely associated with the Establishment; the truth is that it was quite easy.

The key factor was the four and half years I spent at Ware, as vicar of an ancient parish church with strong roots in its local community and an inclusive ministry that embraced virtually every aspect of the community's secular life. Moving to the Abbey seemed like a continuation of this, only on a much larger scale. Had I come here from my new housing-area parish in Stockton-on-Tees, where the ministry was of a pioneering sort, the contrast would have been much greater.

At first it seemed strange to be sharing in worship without having sole responsibility for its leadership. But I quickly adjusted to this, and the opportunity of sharing in worship three times every day in a glorious building and with marvellous music is what I most value in my life here. Less frequent preaching also gives opportunity for more careful preparation, and responsibility for preaching in the Abbey some twenty-five to thirty times a year is something I take very seriously. I am fortunate in my colleagues, whose company is always stimulating, and, as envisaged, I have considerable freedom to pursue my writing and broadcasting interests. The most difficult thing to adjust to, and I still have some way to go in accepting this, is the slow pace of getting things done. In the parish, if I thought a poster was needed to advertise something or other, I drafted a text, gave it to the printer, and within a week it was on the notice boards. But here, when I discern the need for a poster to encourage visitors to share in the daily worship or to advertise the fact that the Abbey is open on Wednesday evenings, I have to go through a complicated bureaucratic process and it is several weeks before the poster is exhibited. Maybe this is inevitable in so large an organization, though I doubt if large commercial enterprises function at this pace. Our procedures are more akin to those of the civil service.

Besides the daily worship, I greatly enjoy my daily round of the Abbey during visiting hours. I always wear my scarlet cassock and black gown, partly so that I may be identified by anyone who wishes to ask a question or to shake hands, and partly so that visitors may observe that this is an active church, with clergy on its staff, and not simply a national monument or museum. I generally devote about half an hour to this, and the contact with staff and voluntary helpers is, I think, useful too. Certainly I learn a good deal from them about what is going on below the surface of our community life.

I count myself fortunate therefore to be here, and if the remainder of my ministry is spent in Westminster, I am sure I shall find plenty of worthwhile things to do both within the Abbey and in other spheres outside its precincts.

Friday 6 May 1977

My confiscation on Tuesday of a football being used by boys from Westminster School on Green – the traditional name of the open space in Dean's Yard – seems to have caused consternation in the School and no little amusement in the Abbey community. This is one of those petty disputes which are always likely to arise when two historic bodies are sharing a limited amount of space.

Relations between the School and the Abbey are always delicate. The Dean and Chapter ran the School – no doubt very badly – until the 1868 Public Schools Act, when the link was severed. The division of property at that time was conducted acrimoniously, and this entered into the Abbey's corporate memory, not least because of its loss of Ashburnham – for many years the residence of the Sub-Dean and one of the finest houses in London.

Green is not generally available for games, though I gave permission recently for the School to use it for an American handball tournament. The erection of the goalposts for this on Tuesday, however, encouraged the boys to play association football, and when I was on my way to Evensong, I noticed the ball hit a number of cars parked nearby and also a passer-by. My request that play should cease was ignored, but then the ball conveniently came my way, so I gathered it up, carried it into the Abbey, and tossed it to a Verger as I joined the procession into Evensong.

Now the Headmaster, John Rae, who is not accustomed to having his, or the School's, authority challenged, has written me a letter of complaint, claiming that, in virtue of the Public Schools Act, the School has a legal right to use Green for whatever games it may wish and whenever it may wish. Please may they have the ball back? I have complied with his request, but rejected his claim.

Sunday 8 May 1977

Edward Knapp-Fisher, who is Canon-in-Residence, had a shock last evening when one of Jimmy Carter's security men telephoned to say that the President, who is on an official visit to London, would be attending the 8.30 a.m. Holy Communion in the Abbey today. It was explained that he required no special attention but would simply sit with the rest of the congregation; two security men would not be far away.

38

Naturally, Edward greeted him afterwards and in fact took him on a short tour of the Abbey, which apparently he much appreciated. He suggested that Dylan Thomas was worth a place in Poets' Corner, and although there has so far been no mention of this possibility, I dare say that we shall have a request before long.

I missed this encounter, as I was speaking at Marlborough College. Speaking is the word, because they have an enlightened arrangement which requires the boys to attend on Sunday morning either a service in the chapel or a meeting on some 'worthwhile' subject. I was asked to talk about some current issues in journalism and this provoked a lively response. I stayed for lunch with the Master, John Dancy, who is, I gather, considered something of a rebel by most of the public school fraternity. I found him likeable and interesting.

Tuesday 10 May 1977

The Dean and Chapter has backed me in my dispute with the Headmaster of Westminster School over the use of Green, the Receiver General having dug out an agreement made in 1959 which acknowledged that this space could no longer be used for organized games, such as football or cricket, because of the likelihood of damage to the grass. Any informal games must be played in soft shoes and only when, in the opinion of the Gardener, the ground is sufficiently dry. The fact that the School sought my permission for the American football tournament was of course an acknowledgment that it has no prescriptive rights over the use of Green.

In many ways this fuss is a silly business which ought not to be occupying the time of a Headmaster and a Canon, but there is something important at stake. John Rae is an ambitious man, and for many years now the School has been pursuing an expansionist policy which causes it to seek possible encroachment on Abbey territory. On his retirement in 1964 Adam Fox noted twenty-seven such encroachments during his time as a Canon.

There can be no more, and the School must learn that its current prosperity does not give it freedom to throw its weight about – at least, not in its relations with the Abbey.

Tuesday 24 May 1977

The congestion in the Abbey caused by visitors, especially in the morning, when as many as 100 coaches discharge their 53 passengers in the space of an hour, is now getting quite out of hand. There is a real danger that, quite apart from the general mayhem inappropriate to a church, some visitors may get hurt. The Vergers are unwilling to exercise any kind of control, and I think it has to be recognized that they are incapable of doing so.

After discussion of this problem with the Treasurer and the Receiver General, I have therefore proposed that the duties of the Vergers be redefined, to exclude any responsibility for visitors, and that their number be reduced from thirteen to seven. At the same time we shall recruit a Chief Marshal and six other marshals, who will wear distinctive red gowns and be responsible solely for visitors. This will involve them in controlling the numbers entering the more constricted areas of the building and, in extreme circumstances, closing the building until the congestion has eased.

It is important that those recruited for this task should be level-headed, good-natured people who are capable of firm action without recourse to methods and language that will make the visitors feel unwelcome. They will also need to be trained to answer questions about the history of the Abbey and its life today.

My paper on all this was warmly welcomed at today's Chapter Meeting. The Treasurer undertook to find the extra £1,600 per annum that the new arrangement will require and the Archdeacon made the very interesting suggestion that Dick Hutchings, our popular night gateman, should become the Chief Marshal. The crowds will continue to create problems, but we will be better able to solve these, and I am still trying to change attitudes so that visitors are seen not as a problem, but rather as a solution. It is empty churches, not crowded churches, that constitute a problem.

Wednesday 25 May 1977

The battle for the occupation of Green continues unabated. The Headmaster, with breathtaking but unsurprising arrogance, has unilaterally declared void the 1959 agreement between the Abbey and the School. He says, in his most recent letter, that he intends to allow occasional football provided that, in his opinion, the grass is unlikely to suffer.

The situation is not improved by his curtailing of the use of the School's Vincent Square playing field by our Choristers, in favour of Westminster Cathedral's Choristers, and by a somewhat aggressive letter from the Master of the Queen's Scholars to our Gardener about the use by the Scholars of the Abbey garden.

The Chapter has asked me to discuss all this with the Headmaster in the hope of reaching an amicable solution. If such a solution cannot be reached we may have to raise the matter officially with the School's Governing Body, but if possible this must be avoided, because matters of this sort are remembered for centuries in Westminster.

Sunday 5 June 1977

For no other reason than that I am Canon-in-Residence this month, I found myself preaching this morning at 'Mattins for Jubilee Sunday'. There was an official Service of Thanksgiving for the twenty-five years of the Queen's reign at 3.00 p.m., but a huge crowd came at 10.30 a.m. This is, I suppose, understandable, given that the Coronation actually took place here twenty-four years ago last Thursday.

We sang the National Anthem, had appropriate hymns, Bible readings and prayers, and I preached on one of my favourite texts, 'I will not offer to the Lord my God of that which costs me nothing' (II Samuel 24.24) – noting the sacrificial element involved in the Queen's dedicated service to the nation and Commonwealth. All straightforward stuff.

The Queen remains immensely popular, and deservedly so, I think, because she never seems to put a foot wrong. Since she came to the throne when she was only twenty-six, there is every likelihood that services will be held to mark her Golden Jubilee, and she may even reign for longer than Queen Victoria.

The only problem this may create concerns the Prince of Wales, who will be thirty later this year and have to wait another thirty to forty years before reaching the throne. 'What are we going to do with Prince Charles?' was the question put to me the other day by Robin Woods, who during his time as Dean of Windsor prepared the Prince for Confirmation and still seems close to the Royal Family. It was of course a rhetorical question, to which he could hardly have expected me to know the answer.

Thursday 9 June 1977

Peace has broken out over the use of Green. John Rae came to see me this morning and we had a friendly enough discussion of the problem. He confessed that he was unaware of the 1959 agreement until we had drawn his attention to it, and he agreed that nothing must be allowed to damage the appearance of Green. He thought, however, that occasional, controlled, use by the School was unlikely to cause damage and he

41

hoped that for an experimental period of twelve months this might be allowed. He undertook to stop games if there were any signs of damage.

I agreed to this proposal but added that there must be no games if the Gardener has signified, by means of a red disc, that the ground is too wet. My guess is that, apart from the annual American football tournament, the School will make no further use of Green – at least not for several years, when the issue will arise again and one of my successors may perhaps be observed carrying a football into the Abbey shortly before Evensong.

Tuesday 14 June 1977

I raised in Chapter a problem about the Reception for the Lord Mayor and members of Westminster City Council which is held every year after the Civic Service. It is an agreeable enough occasion and a valid expression of hospitality, but this year's reception cost £464 and, as usual, was attended only by Conservative Councillors. Evidently the Labour Councillors never attend the Civic Service because they are unwilling to wear the blue velvet robes prescribed, and provided, for official occasions such as this.

We are therefore spending a lot of money on an event which brings us into contact with only a part, albeit the larger part, of the organ of local government to which we relate. My suggestion was that we should reduce the cost by dispensing with professional caterers and, instead, purchase the wine in bulk and ask the Abbey ladies to serve it.

But Reg Pullen came up with what may be a better idea. This would involve abolishing the annual Reception and substituting a series of smaller parties at different times of the year. All the Councillors, together with their wives, would be invited to one of these and, hopefully, we would establish contact with the Labour members as well as the Tories. We could also organize in-house catering. We agreed to try this, provided the Party Leaders are happy with the idea.

Friday 1 July 1977

Today we, i.e. the Dean and Chapter plus the Receiver General and the Legal Secretary, went to Buckingham Palace to present the Queen with a Loyal Address on the occasion of her Silver Jubilee. We are one of the 'privileged bodies' allowed direct access to the Sovereign at significant points in a reign for the purpose of expressing our loyalty.

News of this reached us in April and, besides noting the date in our diaries, it was necessary to devise an appropriate message and then have this inscribed on vellum by a competent calligrapher. Copies of previous Loyal Addresses were extracted from the archives for guidance, but these seemed altogether too fulsome for the present age. So we produced something rather more prosaic, though it had its fulsome moments.

Robes for the occasion, following precedent, were scarlet cassock, preaching bands, gown, scarf and academic hood. At first we thought that we might walk to the Palace, but on further consideration it seemed that the sight of us crossing St James's Park in these robes might be a spectacle that would disturb the public. In any case it might rain.

We decided, therefore, to travel in the Choir School minibus. This created an equally strange spectacle. We were summoned for 9.30 a.m. in order to have a rehearsal, and on entering the Palace forecourt found ourselves in the company of many other privileged bodies who, sensing the importance of the occasion, had travelled in vehicles of considerable splendour – many of them hired, no doubt. In marked contrast, our minibus presented a woeful appearance. Shortage of cash has delayed its replacement for several years and it has accumulated a good deal of rust. Indeed, its condition is scarcely roadworthy. It was from this distressed vehicle that the Dean and Chapter of Westminster, in full fig, disembarked to express their loyalty to the Queen. It was comforting to believe that Her Majesty was unlikely to have been peeping through a window to watch our arrival.

The minibus having been parked between a huge Rolls-Royce and another limousine of the sort used by undertakers, we entered the Palace and were taken to a very splendid gallery hung with wonderful paintings – some of considerable importance. The place was crowded, for the number of privileged bodies is quite large. Harold Macmillan, the Chancellor of Oxford University, was there with a delegation, and I suppose that Cambridge is equally privileged. A number of bishops and other clergy represented the Convocations of Canterbury and York, but for the most part it was impossible to identify the other bodies.

We hung around for quite a long time, admiring the pictures, passing the time of day with others and gossiping among ourselves before being called to a rehearsal, and it was almost lunchtime before we were given the opportunity to express our loyalty. This took place in a room adjoining the gallery, at one end of which the Queen was seated on a throne, surmounted by a canopy. We bowed, advanced a few steps, bowed again, and the Legal Secretary unrolled the vellum and read our Address. We bowed once more, whereupon the Queen delivered her response. Unsurprisingly, this was a brief expression of thanks and thankfully included no reference to the minibus.

This ended, we bowed, walked backwards a few paces, made a final bow and went back through another door to the gallery. A courtier dismissed us and we returned to the Abbey in no less style than when we had embarked upon our historic mission some three hours earlier.

Tuesday 19 July 1977

I have never been one of Sir Arthur Bryant's greatest admirers, and my opinion of him slumped even further after hearing his One People Oration given in the Abbey last evening. This event was inaugurated in 1965 as part of the Abbey's 900th anniversary, and every year since then 900 people have been invited to hear a pronouncement from some notable figure, followed by a glass of wine in the garden.

It is, I gather, none too easy to obtain the services of orators who will occupy the pulpit for forty-five minutes or more, and it is tempting to suppose that this explains the presence of Sir Arthur Bryant. But, in fact, the Dean regards him as possibly the greatest living English historian and thought he would be a particularly appropriate orator during this Silver Jubilee year.

Never mind that he wrote approvingly of Hitler in the 1930s, and early in 1939 chose *Mein Kampf* as the National Book Association's Book of the Month, likening its author to John Bunyan. He changed his tune once the war started and thereafter wrote history as patriotic propaganda. But he continued to write disparagingly of the Jews, and in a series of articles in the *Illustrated London News* campaigned against the immigration of black people, whom he believed to be 'men and women of alien race'.

Last evening's oration was no more than a confection of pure jingoism and sickening royal toadyism, delivered with inflections of voice that not even the most fervent of evangelical preachers could ever hope to match. Sadly, most of those present thought it wonderful, though a great many were unable to hear because of a defect in the sound system. I was left wondering how such a man could ever have become a Companion of Honour, but on second thoughts the explanation is only too plain.

Saturday 23 July 1977

The opening and inspection of the Stuart Vault last evening was a singularly macabre, and in some ways distressing, experience. During the early part of the year, when accumulations of gas beneath buildings

44

in other parts of the country were causing devastating explosions, our Surveyor of the Fabric, Peter Foster, detected the smell of gas in the vicinity of Poets' Corner, not far from a series of royal vaults beneath the Henry VII Chapel.

He reported to the Dean and Chapter his fear that gas might be accumulating in one or more of these vaults and recommended that we seek the Queen's permission to open the Stuart Vault. This was granted without any fuss and yesterday at 8.30 p.m. the vault was entered. The inspecting party consisted of the Abbey clergy, the Receiver General, the Surveyor, the Librarian, the Keeper of the Muniments, the Lord Chamberlain and the Duke of Grafton, representing the Queen, the President of the Society of Antiquaries, and David Carpenter, the Dean's historian son.

Prior to our entry the Clerk of the Works and his son, Anthony Andrews, removed enough bricks from the vault roof to enable us to descend by means of a short ladder from the floor on the South side of the Henry VII Chapel monks' stalls. The vault was evidently constructed of brick during the sixteenth century and is rather like a cellar with plastered walls. Temporary lighting was provided by a long cable from the Chapel above.

On entering, one's eyes were drawn immediately to the five coffins – King Charles II, King William III, Queen Mary, Queen Anne and Prince George of Denmark. They are in fact lead linings; the original oak has disintegrated and fallen to the floor in a form rather like cork. This, together with grey dust, completely covers the floor. At the foot of each coffin is an 'urn of bowels'. It seems that the intestines were removed as part of the embalming process. Here, as with the coffins, the original oak has disintegrated, leaving only a round lead container. On each coffin is a royal insignia and a plate inscribed with the name of the occupant. Some of the velvet which originally covered the coffins and urns is still there, though it has faded to a dull, brownish colour. The contrast between the coffin-plates of William and Mary and the rest is striking. The latter, especially that of George of Denmark, have elaborate inscriptions, whereas the titles of the former are indicated simply by initials. I wonder why?

Charles II was obviously the first to be interred in the vault and his coffin is not a pretty sight. Unlike the others, some of the lead has also disintegrated, thus revealing the remains of the king. The benefits of the embalming have disappeared and the body is without recognizable form, having been reduced to its skeleton, some of which is visible, and to an unpleasant slimy, mud-like substance. Some of this is bright red, and Peter Foster thinks this may have been caused by the oxidization of the lead. Surprisingly, there was no unpleasant smell, though this may have been dealt with by the air-extractor that preceded our entry.

The sight of the mortal remains of a Stuart king who died almost 300 years ago produced emotions which I find impossible to describe. At the end of the inspection, which occupied about half an hour and revealed no trace of gas, I felt, however, that I had been involved in something that was intrusive and ought not have taken place. The testing for gas could have been carried out in another, more simple, way.

It is certain, of course, that the monarchs and their consorts were in no way inconvenienced by our visit, but regard for the dead, whether or not they be royal, seems to me to require that the final resting places of their bodies should never be exposed to prying eyes.

Tuesday 26 July 1977

We said Goodbye this morning to Major James Newton, who became Dean's Verger about eighteen months ago and is now leaving on health grounds. His appointment was a serious mistake and it is no fault of his that he was unable to cope.

When the irrepressible Algy Grieves retired from this post after thirty or more years in the Vergers' department, there was no obvious successor waiting in the wings. Neither the Canons' Verger nor the Sub-Sacrist were considered to be up to the job and, since they were at daggers drawn, there was, it was thought, no possibility of appointing either of them.

Instead, a recently retired army major, with an interest in military history, was recruited. And it did not work. The complexities of the Abbey's liturgical, ceremonial and organizational traditions take years to master, and there are obvious problems when a manager is for a long time dependent on his subordinates. When these subordinates constitute a very awkward squad the outcome is almost certain to be failure.

The accommodation provided for the Dean's Verger is suitable only for a single man, but James Newton is married and has several large dogs, so he camped out in No.2 until I arrived on the scene a year last May. He was then required to move into what is no more than a modest flat. Given the impossibility of the whole situation, it was no surprise when he succumbed to a heart attack last Christmas. A long period of convalescence left him still struggling, and now he is leaving to become Warden of a National Trust property in Scotland. As he goes, a lot of sympathy accompanies him.

In these circumstances there was no alternative but to appoint in his place the Canons' Verger, Gerald Powell, who was passed over last time. None of us is happy about this, and the only consolation is that the responsibilities of the Dean's Verger will be significantly reduced when a separate Marshals' department is established.

There were also official farewells today to the three elderly Lay Vicars who, after much hard bargaining and no little cost to the Dean and Chapter, have relinquished their freeholds and gone into retirement. What a difficult and unhappy business this has been.

But all was sweetness and light at the little ceremony held at the end of the Chapter Meeting. Which was right, because between them they must have given over 100 years of service to the Abbey's choral foundation, and it was only sad that they could not recognize the toll that age had taken of their voices.

The Dean naturally said nice things about them, and each was presented with a silver Tudor Rose dish. We then drank to their health, wished them long and happy retirements, and felt that we had been present at yet another historic occasion – the ending of freehold appointments in the Choir.

How long will it be before the Dean and Chapter relinquish theirs? These things are rarely done voluntarily and one day, I suppose, we, or our successors, will be forced into a corner about this.

Friday 19 August 1977

My little scheme for encouraging prayer at the shrine of St Edward the Confesor has been thwarted by souvenir hunters. Last month I placed near the shrine copies of some appropriate prayers in the hope that a few, at least, of our hundreds of thousands of visitors might pause to use them. Perhaps some have, but the original copies survived only two days and replacements have remained no longer. Doubtless they have been taken as souvenirs and perhaps they are now being used in private prayer in many different parts of the world; in which case we should keep replacing them at the shrine.

The same may be true of the 250 or so embroidered kneelers which have been taken from the Abbey since they were made by devout needle-women to mark the 900th anniversary in 1965. It would be good to believe that the souvenir hunters are now using these to aid their private devotions elsewhere. But I rather doubt it, and the few that remain have been chained to chairs.

On answering my door bell early this evening I found myself face to face with Roy Trevivian. 'So it is you, then,' he exclaimed. 'You've ratted.' Roy and I have known each other for about ten years, I suppose, and we used to meet fairly often when he was a producer at the BBC. But he had missed the announcement of my appointment to the Abbey and, when walking through the Little Cloister today, was shocked to find my name on the door of No. 2.

Being himself an arch-rebel, he regards my acceptance of a Westminster canonry as a complete sell-out to the Establishment enemy and a terrible betrayal of the liberal/radical cause. However, I got him inside the house, gave him a drink, told him about some of the things I am doing, and we ended up with him asking if he could bring some people from the Mayflower Centre in the East End on a special visit to the Abbey, with a personal tour by me. Of course I agreed, and said there would be special refreshments afterwards.

Thursday 22 September 1977

A pleasant little party in Jerusalem Chamber this evening for Barbara Harvey to mark the publication of her monumental volume, *Westminster Abbey and its Estates in the Middle Ages*. This is the product of twenty-seven years' work in our Muniment Room and a mine of readable information about the Abbey's extensive mediaeval estates and also about certain aspects of life in the monastery. It is a major contribution to the understanding of our history.

Barbara Harvey, a quiet blue-stocking, is a Fellow of Somerville College, Oxford and confessed that today was the first occasion on which she had addressed the Librarian, Howard Nixon, by his Christian name.

Wednesday 28 September 1977

We did not generally warm to former Prime Minister Ted Heath's suggestion, made towards the end of last year, that we should memorialize Sir Francis Chichester. Indeed, only one member of Chapter seemed to favour the idea. The Dean was quite keen, but the rest of us felt that while Chichester's single-handed circumnavigation of the world in a small sailing boat had certainly been heroic, the feat had not actually added to the sum total of human well-being. It was a sporting feat.

The Dean undertook to consult other sailing interests – the Royal Institute of Navigation, the Royal Ocean Yacht Squadron, and so on – who it seems generally favour the idea. Now there is the suggestion that we should instal a memorial to navigators, with special reference to Chichester and also to Sir Francis Drake, whose sword was used by the Queen when she knighted Chichester on the completion of his journey in *Gypsy Moth* in 1967.

I am not at all sure that the linking of these two totally different men makes any more sense, but we have encouraged the Dean, whose decision it is anyway, to pursue the idea a little further. If a suitable memorial materializes, we agree that it should be located in the Cloisters, rather than inside the Abbey.

Tuesday 11 October 1977

The idea of setting up a Friends of Westminster Abbey has had to be dropped for want of support. The Dean has hoped for such an organization for many years, and when I showed interest in developing our ministry to visitors he encouraged me to take the idea forward. George Dodson-Wells, our Press and Publicity Officer, was asked to visit a number of cathedrals to investigate the running of their Friends' organizations and to produce a report.

Which he did last year. As a result, a leaflet was produced and distributed among many thousands of visitors and others more closely associated with the Abbey. This explained the purpose of a Friends organization and asked them to indicate whether or not they would wish to join. After twelve months only seventeen affirmative responses have been received.

The explanation seems to be that whereas a cathedral is 'owned' by its diocese, is used for many local services and events, and attracts local support, the Abbey, while belonging in a sense to everyone, is 'owned' by no one. Its specialness, and not least its royal assocations, does not invite close involvement in its affairs.

This is the reality with which we must live; it indicates both the scope and the limitations of our ministry.

Thursday 13 October 1977

St Edward's Day was a good choice for the unveiling of the new memorial to those who, 'divided at the Reformation by convictions sincerely held, laid down their lives for Christ and conscience sake'. The idea for this came from the late Archbishop Geoffrey Fisher, who, back in the 1950s, expressed the hope that such a memorial might one day be installed in the Abbey. He added that he did not think this would be possible in the present century.

Geoffrey Fisher's suggestion was prompted by the very remarkable ecumenical inscription on the tomb of Queen Elizabeth I in the North aisle of the Henry VII Chapel. This tomb was erected by James I in 1606 and, while not quite as splendid as the one which he erected for his mother, Mary Queen of Scots, in the South aisle, is nonetheless very fine.

Beneath Elizabeth's coffin lies that of her half-sister, the Catholic Queen Mary Tudor, and King James marked her presence with a Latin inscription that reads: 'Consorts both in throne and grave, here lie the two sisters, Elizabeth and Mary, in the hope of one resurrection'. Given the atmosphere of the time, this must have caused astonishment and alarm when it appeared, and I am not the only person who finds it profoundly moving.

So the new memorial, appropriately unveiled by Lady Fisher, the former Archbishop's widow, has been placed on the floor near the united Tudors. All the British church leaders were there, apart from Cardinal Hume, who is in Rome for six weeks and sent Bishop Mahon to represent him. The Dean, whose baby this has very much been, preached a fine sermon, nicely blending the historical and the contemporary and expressing his own impatience at the slowness of current ecumenical progress.

Tuesday 6 December 1977

Our historians have been enjoying themselves over a request from the National Museum in Munich for the loan of the *Liber Regalis*. This is one of our most valuable treasures, being a beautifully illustrated manuscript of the Coronation service prepared for the crowning of Richard II in 1377. It was probably used by the boy-king himself and its main features have informed every Coronation service since.

The Munich museum people would like to borrow this item for an exhibition to be held next year in Nuremberg Castle to commemorate the 600th anniversary of the death of Charles IV, Holy Roman Emperor. The point is that Richard II married the Emperor's daughter, Anne of Bohemia, in 1382.

Howard Nixon, our Librarian, has pointed out, however, that there is no evidence that the *Liber Regalis* was used at Anne's Coronation, so we have accepted his recommendation that the loan request should be declined. In theory we are always ready to loan items for important exhibitions, but I think we are glad when there is a legitimate reason for saying No to a request for something as important as the *Liber Regalis*. The custody of such a national treasure is a frightening responsibility.

Tuesday 20 December 1977

Our dear pacifist Dean is bothered, as he has every right to be, by part of the ceremonial proposed for next year's service to mark the sixtieth anniversary of the foundation of the RAF. The Air Marshal who is in charge of the organization of this service has pointed out that RAF regulations, in common with those of the Navy and the Army, stipulate that when Colours are taken into church, the Colour Bearer and the Colour Warrant Officer should wear swords, while the Escorts should carry rifles with fixed bayonets.

Apparently this procedure goes back many centuries and the RAF simply adopted what was regarded as normal practice. But, leaving aside the particular problem of the pacifist, it does now feel altogether wrong that weapons designed to kill should become an element in an act of worship based on love and brotherhood. It may be argued, of course, that weapons are required for the keeping of peace and sometimes for the defeat of those who are intent on wreaking wholesale destruction on the earth.

Yet, even if this be accepted, as I do accept it, it still feels wrong to have swords and bayonets and other manifestations of sin paraded in church. So we have told the Air Marshal that we believe the time has come for the regulations to be reviewed. I wonder if they will be, or whether on this occasion they will simply be ignored?

Thursday 22 December 1977

The problem of the Lay Vicars' behaviour during services is rarely far away and is now firmly on our agenda, following a written complaint from a former Director of the Royal School of Church Music, Dr Gerald Knight, who was involved in an Abbey service on 6 December. He added that their bad behaviour dated back to at least 1959, when he first became acquainted with the Abbey.

What he was referring to is talking, laughing and general inattention during the spoken parts of services, lessons, sermons and prayers, and those of us who are present at the daily services are only too well aware that the Lay Clerks' conduct is often disgraceful. Obviously this makes it all the more difficult to keep the Choristers under control.

Responsibility for discipline lies clearly with the Precentor, and in practice with the Organist and Master of the Choristers, who has direct contact with the Choir. From time to time he calls the Lay Vicars to order, but the effect rarely lasts for more than a week; Douglas Guest's gentlemanly appeal to their better natures is too easily disregarded.

We have therefore decided to get tough. The Precentor has been instructed to call the Lay Vicars to a meeting at which they will be told that in the event of any further jusifiable complaints the individual(s) concerned will be brought before the Dean and Chapter and action will be taken under the official disciplinary procedure, which may eventually lead to dismissal.

Meanwhile one of their number, Rodney Williams, has written to the Dean about the proposal to abandon Choral Mattins on Fridays in such intemperate language that he has had to be officially rebuked and told, by the Dean, that this must never be repeated. In this instance of course Rodney is fighting for something he passionately cares about, i.e. the maintaining of the Abbey's choral worship, but he hardly advances his cause by insulting the Dean.

The Christmas festival of peace and goodwill is now only three days away.

Saturday 31 December 1977

This year ends sadly, with the decision of the Dean, supported by the other members of the Chapter apart from myself, that Mattins shall no longer be sung by the Choir on Fridays. Prior to 1939 virtually all the cathedrals and the Abbey had daily Choral Mattins as well as Choral Evensong, but the war ended this except at St Paul's and the Abbey, where Mattins continued to be sung on a few days of the week – in our case on Tuesdays and Fridays.

Now Friday has gone and Tuesday is sure to follow – sooner, rather than later, I fear. Several factors influenced this decision. The new Headmaster of the Choir School expressed unease at the degree of pressure being imposed on the Choristers by the increased number of special services, and wondered if they might be excused Mattins. The clash between the time of Mattins and the arrival of the first noisy visitors of the day has caused concern during the last two summers. The Organist and most (though by no means all) of the Lay Vicars find a

Friday morning service burdensome. And the clergy, apart from the Canon-in-Residence, the Precentor and myself, do not normally attend.

It has also to be acknowledged that the size of the congregation has normally been tiny – rarely more than a dozen, tho ƺh occasionally visitors have paused to join in. But I cannot believe that this really matters. The Abbey was built primarily as a place of worship, and over the course of nearly nine centuries first the Benedictine monks, then the Dean and Chapter and the Choral Foundation, offered daily worship within its walls without reference to the presence of any other people.

Daily worship will, of course, continue with said services and Choral Evensong, but it seems to me that to reduce, even in a small way, the commitment to choral worship is, in these increasingly secular times, sending out quite the wrong signal. We are bound to take account of change, but we must not allow ourselves to be absorbed by the spirit of any age.

1978

David Edwards, who is my closest friend on the Chapter, is to become Dean of Norwich and will be leaving Westminster after Easter. I shall miss him very much. He has been a supporter and encourager since *New Christian* days and it has been specially good to work together during these last eighteen months.

It was obvious that sooner rather than later David would become a dean. He has been here for about eight years, is not specially happy at St Margaret's, and has a remarkable combination of gifts that would adorn any deanery – or indeed almost any job in the Church of England.

I am not altogther certain, however, that Norwich is right for him. In many ways it would have made more sense for him to have been appointed Dean of Canterbury when this fell vacant in 1976. I don't believe that nothing of importance happens outside London and the Home Counties, but there is a lot to be said for keeping the most gifted people close to the centres of decision-making, and it feels strategically unsound to be despatching David to East Anglia.

On the other hand, writing occupies so central a place in his life that he may not wish to be responsible for the active management of a very busy cathedral – or of a diocese, for that matter. Norwich has gone through something of a revolution under the dynamic leadership of Alan Webster, who has moved to St Paul's, and it may be ready for a change of pace.

Sunday 15 January 1978

The Abbey is frequently used for the consecration of bishops, and these services are occasions of great solemnity and carefully choreographed ceremonial. Not so this evening – at least not as far as the ceremonial was concerned – when a young African priest, James Kauluma, was consecrated Bishop Suffragan of Damaraland, in what used to be known as South West Africa but now has the African name Namibia.

This must be one of the most difficult and dangerous jobs anywhere in the world church, and the new bishop was ordained to the priesthood only last year. The present diocesan bishop is the charismatic and courageous Colin Winter, who has been living in exile for the last few years, having played a major role in Namibia's continuing struggle to be free from the clutches of apartheid-ridden South Africa.

The English suffragan bishop having also been obliged to leave the country, Colin had no alternative but to choose an African to exercise an episcopal ministry on his behalf, so he selected James Kauluma, the most highly educated of his clergy. Naturally, Colin wished to be involved in the consecration service, and since he is denied admission to South Africa, where it would normally have taken place, he asked if it could be held in the Abbey.

The Dean readily assented and the planning began, but Edward Knapp-Fisher, who was Bishop of Pretoria until 1974 and is not, I think, particularly enamoured with Colin Winter's style and tactics, soon pointed out that consent for the consecration would need to be given by the Archbishop of Cape Town, in whose Province Damaraland lies. In the event of the Archbishop being unable to come to Westminster to preside over the ceremony, he would nominate a Commissary to take his place.

Contact was thereupon made with the Archbishop of Cape Town, who nominated none other than the former Bishop of Pretoria as his Commissary. Preparations for the service continued, and it seemed that it would be of the fairly traditional sort, though, being Sunday evening, the Choir would not be available and there would be more than normal participation by the congregation.

This congregation turned out to be quite large. A lot of friends of Namibia came together with a strong contingent of anti-apartheid campaigners. The Bishops of Guildford, St Albans, Rochester, Liverpool and Stepney were among the consecrating bishops, and of course Colin Winter presented the new Bishop.

More than this: before long Colin had vitually hi-jacked the service, introducing items and ceremonies that were not mentioned in the Order of Service or detailed in the Precentor's instructions. Namibians presented James Kauluma with episcopal robes, a pastoral staff and various other symbols of his office, and at the end of the service there was dancing.

Edward Knapp-Fisher, who was officially presiding over the occasion, was naturally surprised by all this, but he maintained his dignity and provided from his centrally-placed chair a stable centre around which everything else revolved. This proved to be a most valuable, even if unrehearsed, contribution and owed everything to his own highly disciplined spirituality.

The party afterwards was riotous, but one couldn't help thinking apprehensively of the young new bishop, who will soon be making a lonely journey to his homeland, beset by an increasingly violent struggle for freedom.

Tuesday 24 January 1978

John Baker, having resigned from the Treasurership in order to be able to give less interrupted attention to his theological work, has decided that he would like to succeed David Edwards as Rector of St Margaret's. This has surprised us all somewhat, but at the Chapter meeting this morning we readily agreed to appoint him. If John is ever to become a bishop it is important that he should gain some experience of running a parish church – untypical though St Margaret's certainly is.

I thought it necessary, however, to raise in Chapter a number of questions about the procedure for appointing a Rector, since this was the first ocasion on which it was in the hands of the Dean and Chapter, rather than of the Crown. The relationship between St Margaret's and the Abbey is now a tricky one. The congregational life of the parish church of the House of Commons is no longer strong enough to keep the place going unaided, and a great deal of money needs to be spent on the building. This is why it was taken back under the wing of the Abbey in 1972.

It might have seemed important therefore that on the first occasion of a vacancy in the Rectory after this move there would be a rather serious discussion about the future of St Margaret's and its relations with the Abbey. How can the two churches best exercise a complementary ministry? What sharing of clerical manpower, as well as financial resources, may be required? The views of representatives of St Margaret's and of the outgoing Rector would also have been worth hearing.

Instead of any of this, the appointment of John was engineered between himself and the Dean, with the rest of us simply invited to agree. I think that he will probably do this job very well, but an opportunity to consider wider strategy has been lost.

The memorial service for Clementine Churchill, Winston's widow, held at noon, on the thirteenth anniversary of her husband's death, was attended by a great throng. The Queen and the Royal Family were represented; there were about sixty High Commissioners and Ambassadors from other countries; the Prime Minister, the Speaker, the Leaders of the Conservative and Liberal Parties and many MPs were there, together with people from the various organizations in which she had been involved, and a lot of members of the general public. Officers and men from the submarine HMS Churchill and from The Queen's Royal Irish Hussars (Winston's old regiment) showed them to their seats.

I met her only once; that was a year last November when I chanced to be on one of my daily rounds of the Abbey at the same time as she was placing a pot of flowers on Winston's memorial stone near the Great West Door – something she did every year on the anniversaries of his birth and death. We had a short conversation and, though in a wheelchair, she seemed remarkably well for someone in her ninety-second year.

There was a nice touch at the beginning of today's service when, as the family started to move up the central aisle of the Nave, Mary Soames and Sarah Churchill, her daughters, paused to lay flowers on the memorial stone. The service was a quite simple one. The Archbishop of Canterbury and the Apostolic Delegate said prayers and Eric Abbott, our former Dean, returned to read I Corinthians 13.

Instead of a sermon, her grandson (also named Winston Spencer) read an extract from a sensitive and remarkably prescient address given by Bishop Welldon at her wedding in St Margaret's in 1908:

'The sun shines upon your union today; the happy faces of your friends surround you; good wishes are lavished upon you; many prayers ascend to Heaven on your behalf. Will you suffer me to remind you how much you may be to the other in the coming days? There must be in the statesman's life many times when he depends upon the love, the insight, the penetrating sympathy and devotion of his wife. The influences which the wives of our statesmen have exercised for good upon their husbands' lives is an unwritten chapter of English history, too sacred to be written in full . . . In the sunny hours of life, in the sombre hours, if they, too, come, may you recall the feelings and the resolves that were yours when you knelt today before the altar of God. So it is with deep feelings that I commend you to the blessings of the Eternal and Supreme. May your lives prove a blessing each to the other and both to the world, and may you pass in the Divine mercy from strength to strength and from joy to joy.'

Never can a bishop's words and prayers have been more amply fulfilled. Bishop Welldon had been Winston's headmaster at Harrow and later became Dean of Durham, where he is remembered for the occasion when, during a strike, the coal miners mistook him for Bishop Hensley Henson and pushed him into the River Wear. He deserved better.

Tuesday 14 February 1978

Colin Peterson, the Prime Minister's Secretary for Appointments, came to the Chapter Meeting to discuss the appointment of a successor to David Edwards. Since John Baker is to succeed him as Rector of St Margaret's, our need is for a Canon whose duties are confined to the Abbey.

If one were casting for a stage play that required a Secretary for Appointments, Colin Peterson would be the star choice. An introverted Wykehamist of the utmost discretion, courteous, well-informed, desirous of making the best possible decision, and never permitting an iota of space to come between his cards and his chest – that is Colin Peterson. And, it must be added, a thoroughly agreeable chap.

First we were asked to state the kind of person we thought would be most suitable. Since we had held a previous meeting to discuss this among ourselves, we were able to present a united front in requesting someone who would bring distinctive gifts to the Chapter and at the same time be willing to work as a member of a team. A preacher to make good use of the Abbey pulpit was mentioned, and also the possibility of another scholar to make up for the loss of David Edwards. It was thought desirable that the new Canon should have interests either in the wider church or in some other sphere beyond the confines of the Abbey.

We then raised the possibility of an appointment from the Commonwealth, since the Abbey has many links with the Commonwealth. In any case, in a multi-ethnic Britain it would be by no means inappropriate to have someone of another race and colour on the Westminster Chapter. We emphasized of course that such a priest would need to be otherwise qualified for the job.

Colin Peterson then produced a list of about eight possible names for consideration, though he warned us that it would be inappropriate and unfair for us to make a critical assessment of any of them, since none had asked to be considered and none was aware that his name was on the list.

The list, it has to be said, was not a distinguished one. Indeed the presence of some names astonished me, though I didn't say so, and there was really no one to match our profile. A number of additional names were thrown into the pool and I asked for further enquiries to be made about Wilfred Wood, the West Indian Vicar of Catford who used to be the Bishop of London's Chaplain for Community Relations. He is very well thought of and might well fill the bill here.

We shall hear the result of all this in due course and I expect that Colin Peterson will consult the Dean again before an announcement is made. All of which represents a considerable improvement on what happened until fairly recently, when there was no consultation at all with the Chapter about the filling of vacant Canonries. Eric Abbott, our former Dean, told me the other day that during his fifteen years at the Abbey the Crown appointed to Canonries a number of distinguished priests he was very pleased to have, but never anyone for whom he had specifically asked.

Tuesday 28 February 1978

Today the Chapter was provided for the first time with a quarterly financial statement – this one dealing with the three months ended 31 December. We have been asking for such statements ever since I arrived in May 1976, and David Edwards tells me that he was asking for regular financial information long before then. The financial situation is now so volatile that we really cannot do without close supervision of income and expenditure.

As it happens, the first statement presented a quite favourable position, explicable mainly by a considerable increase in income from admission fees to the paying area of the building and by a high turnover in the Bookshop during the Silver Jubilee year.

On the expenditure side we discussed our responsibility for insuring the Abbey against fire and other possible calamities. What would it cost to replace it? The chances of the entire building going up in smoke are obviously very remote indeed, but the insurers have pointed out to us that dealing with heavily damaged buildings can also be massively expensive. On the other hand, complete insurance cover would require us to pay enormous annual premiums.

If we were to increase our cover in line with the 25% increase in building repair costs which has taken place since a figure of £10 million was agreed in 1975 we should have to move to £12.5 million, but the Ecclesiastical Insurance Office will accept £11 million. This will cost us an additional £690 in the annual premium. Our cover is higher than for any cathedral in the country, where the insurance ranges from £1-5 million.

There was a nasty incident at this afternoon's Commonwealth Day Observance when, about half-way through the service, a woman rose from her seat, walked into the Choir and shouted at the Queen and the Duke of Edinburgh who were seated in two of the stalls. I couldn't make out what she said, and she was quickly seized by a couple of the Honorary Stewards and unceremoniously removed from the building. Apparently the police dealt with her under the Mental Health Acts, since she was obviously disturbed.

A number of questions are raised by this incident. How did the lady obtain a ticket for the occasion, and one that enabled her to get so close to the Queen? Why were the Honorary Stewards unable to restrain her before she had managed to get even closer and started to shout? The Queen raised a further question after the service about the degree of force used by the Honorary Stewards, which she thought to be excessive.

The problem of maintaining order at services extends beyond those attended by the Queen and other VIPs, for the Abbey attracts all sorts of people, including the mentally disturbed, and we have had incidents on Sundays. Not often, but enough to require the Honorary Stewards to be vigilant, while at the same time dealing sensitively with those who cause disturbance. A difficult balance to maintain.

Tuesday 14 March 1978

I have now succeeded John Baker as Treasurer. This is not, I must say, a job I was expecting to be given so soon after my arrival at the Abbey and certainly it is not one I was seeking. It is in fact the heaviest office in the Chapter, after that of the Dean, and its responsibilities have increased considerably during the last three to four years.

There are two main problems, the first of which is the unprecedented high rate of inflation which is affecting seriously all our costs, most especially wages and salaries, for we are a labour-intensive organization with 171 people on the payroll at the moment. The second is the unpredictable nature of our income. We have a surprisingly small amount of capital for an institution such as Westminster Abbey and the income from this source covers only a tiny proportion of costs.

We are therefore heavily reliant on income from visitors, and this is entirely unpredictable. At the present time we are doing well because the pound is low on the foreign exchange market and tourists are still flooding into London. Last year we had a surplus of almost £250,000. But a relatively small upward movement in the pound can change this, and an international crisis or terrorist activity in London could make the tourists disappear virtually overnight.

So everything needs careful watching, and the Receiver General, who carries the main administrative burden, needs a Treasurer who will take an active interest in the day-to-day problems which are now arising. Equally, because money has become so important in determining policy, the Chapter needs a Treasurer to ensure that financial and administrative factors do not dictate policy.

There is a certain irony in my appointment. Before joining the RAF in 1944 I spent two years on the staff of the Westminster Bank in Nottingham, but during my three and a half years in the RAF I decided that I was more interested in people than in money and that I would best serve God and my neighbour by seeking ordination.

Thirty years later I find myself the Treasurer of Westminster Abbey. Whose joke is this, I wonder?

Tuesday 21 March 1978

My good friend Nadir Dinshaw invited me to have lunch with him today at Boulestin's in Covent Garden. I found him in a state of considerable anxiety. He has for some years been a friend of Jeremy Thorpe, who until a couple of years ago was Leader of the Liberal Party and remains a well-known public figure. Nadir is godfather to his son, Rupert.

It seems that not long after the 1974 General Election Jeremy asked Nadir if he would handle for him a donation of £20,000 which Jack Hayward, a wealthy Liberal Party supporter who lives in the Bahamas, was making to help cover election expenses. Some of these were incurred during his national campaigning, others in his own constituency, and because of electoral law it was important that the donation should be kept separate from official Party funds. Nadir, whose main home and bank account are in Jersey, was requested to pay out the money, on demand, to David Holmes, a former Deputy Treasurer of the Liberal Party and Jeremy's great friend, who was dealing with this matter.

Nadir agreed, uneasily, and subsequently paid Holmes a cheque for £10,000 and, during 1975, a number of £500s in cash. These cash payments made him even more uneasy, and at one point he consulted Edward Carpenter, our Dean and a very close friend of his, who suggested that he return the balance of the money to Hayward. But because of his trusting friendship with Jeremy he continued to pay out money to Holmes until the £20,000 was exhausted. And that seemed to be that.

But now, apparently, the police are investigating Jeremy Thorpe's affairs and may wish to interview Nadir about the £20,000. His fear is that the police interest in this money may be related to a strange case that came before the Exeter Crown Court in the early part of 1976. Andrew Newton, an airline pilot, was sent to prison for two years for confronting with a gun a man named Norman Scott. This took place in an isolated place in North Devon and resulted in Scott's dog – a Great Dane – being shot dead. At an earlier hearing before magistrates in Barnstaple there was an outburst from Scott in which he alleged that he was being hunted down by Jeremy Thorpe because of a homosexual relationship he had had with him during the early 1960s, and he implied that Newton had been acting as Thorpe's agent.

Jeremy immediately issued a statement to the effect that Scott's allegations were without foundation and that he had not seen him for twelve years. But this did not prevent Scott from repeating them in the Exeter Court when he appeared as a witness. The police are obviously now following this up to see if there might be something really sinister behind the Newton trial.

Nadir did not of course have the slightest knowledge of any of this until he read the newspaper reports and speculation. As far as the £20,000 is concerned, he was told by Jeremy Thorpe that it was a gift from Jack Hayward for political purposes and it was on this understanding that he paid it over to David Holmes. I don't see how he can possibly be implicated in anything serious that may arise from the police enquiries, and I have tried to reassure him about this, but of course the prospect of being questioned about a transaction that had originally caused him anxiety is bound to be worrying. I hope it will soon blow over.

Sunday 2 April 1978

Canon Mary Michael Simpson of the Cathedral of St John the Divine in New York became the first woman priest to preach in Westminster Abbey when, at my invitation, she came to Evensong today. Her appearance in the pulpit was covered in all this evening's radio and television news bulletins, and doubtless there will be pictures and reports in tomorrow's newspapers.

Wisely, the preacher – who is also a nun – did not make a great thing of her appearance in the Abbey and concentrated instead on the nature and meaning of God's love. It was a first-class sermon. But her coming has created some local difficulties. The possibility of her preaching in the Abbey was first mooted in relation to a Sunday when Edward Knapp-Fisher was Canon-in-Residence and he, being strongly opposed to the ordination of women to the priesthood, did not feel able to extend an invitation to her.

Then, for totally unrelated reasons, her visit to England was postponed, and when the new dates were settled it turned out that she would be in London when I, who am deeply involved in the Movement for the Ordination of Women, was to be Canon-in-Residence. My decision to invite her to preach has not gone down well with my neighbour.

There is, however, an important principle at stake in this. Canons of Westminster are responsible for choosing the preachers at Mattins and Evensong on Sundays and they are entirely free to choose whom they wish. Among other things, this ensures that a wide variety of religious viewpoints are expressed (not always very adequately, it has to be said) from the Abbey's pulpit.

It is to be expected therefore that on matters such as the ordination of women, about which the Church of England is divided, some place will be found in the Abbey for women priests, if only to demonstrate that they are capable of preaching. They are not (yet) permitted to preside at the eucharist in any church in England, but since even lay people are allowed to preach, there really is no valid reason why a women priest should be debarred from our pulpit – provided of course that she has something to say which is worth hearing, as was certainly the case today.

Monday 17 April 1978

I have seen and had telephone conversations with Nadir Dinshaw several times during the last fortnight, and this evening I had dinner with him at the Chesterfield Hotel in Mayfair where he is staying. He told me that on Thursday of last week Jeremy Thorpe telephoned him at the hotel and suggested that they drive together round St James's Park. While in the car he told Nadir that certain people were out to destroy him and his political career and urged Nadir to tell the police that the £20,000 he had handled was part of a business deal between Hayward and Thorpe and that none of the money had gone to David Holmes.

Nadir replied that he could not possibly do this, and that he would have to tell the truth; whereupon Thorpe became upset and said that Nadir was being untrue to their friendship. The boot is of course entirely on the other foot, and there is not the slightest possibility of Nadir lying to the police. It was not a very happy dinner, because Nadir is naturally very upset by the wretched business, and I could do little more than listen to him recount his experience. I hope this helped.

With the benefit of hindsight he can see that it was, as he suspected at the time, very unwise to agree to handle the money, but it would have been difficult to say No to such a close friend as Jeremy has been, and there was not the slightest reason to suspect that anything sinister was afoot. I am afraid that Nadir's commitment to people leaves him vulnerable to exploitation.

Tuesday 25 April 1978

We have discussed in Chapter a number of issues arising from my invitation to Canon Mary Michael Simpson to preach in the Abbey on 2 April. The Dean circulated a paper last week in which he strongly emphasized the freedom of Canons to choose preachers, a right dating back to 1560, and also his own view that the Abbey ought to be a place where a wide variety of views are expressed.

There was no difficulty in obtaining agreement on these points, and the discussion focussed on two subsidiary points, the first of these being whether or not the Chapter should be advised if an invitation to a particular preacher was likely to cause controversy. I said that this could easily be dealt with if we all gave advance notice of all our preachers on a paper inserted in the services register. Such advance notice would also help to ensure that invitations were not sent to the same person at about the same time.

The second point, concerning publicity, was more tricky. Mary Michael Simpson's appearance in the pulpit attracted a good deal of media attention. Ought radio and television facilities to have been granted on this occasion? If so, who had authority to grant them? Broadcasters often come into the Abbey for 'Establishment' occasions, having first negotiated with the Receiver General the facilities required – a fairly leisurely process and one that involves no sort of controversy.

However, an item for news bulletins is an altogether different matter, since it is hardly ever clear until the very last minute whether or not news editors are interested. And since an Abbey sermon is a public event it is, in my view anyway, impossible to deny knowledge of such an event to the public at large. Censoring of the controversial could only encourage the already common belief that the Abbey is no more than the church of the Establishment.

In the end it was decided that on controversial occasions broadcasters will only be allowed in after the Dean or the Canon-in-Residence has obtained the agreement of the rest of the Chapter. I can't really see this working very satisfactorily, but there are unlikely to be many occasions requiring such consultation and when the next one occurs I dare say that today's new procedure will have been forgotten.

Earlier we had a long debate about a letter from Dr Una Kroll, on behalf of the Christian Parity Group, seeking permission for its members to hold a peaceful demonstration outside the West entrance to the Abbey from Sunday 30 July to Tuesday 1 August. The purpose of this is to draw attention to the case for women priests during the period when the bishops attending the Lambeth Conference in Canterbury will be debating this issue. The bishops will also be attending a service in the Abbey on 1 August, and it is intended that through the demonstration they will be made aware of the Group's feelings.

Not surprisingly, the Chapter was split over whether or not to give permission. Edward Knapp-Fisher thought it would be discourteous to bishops who had come to Westminster Abbey from all parts of the world for an act of worship if they were put under this sort of pressure, including the risk of their being personally confronted or even shouted at by the more militant element among the demonstrators. I argued for the freedom of individuals and groups to demonstrate on important matters such as the ordination of women.

In the end, the Dean proposed that permission be given for a peaceful demonstration starting on the Sunday but ending by 10 a.m. on the Tuesday, i.e. before the procession of bishops in the afternoon. However, for totally opposed reasons, this did not win support, and the Dean offered to discuss the matter with Una Kroll, the Sub-Dean also being present at this meeting. This was agreed.

Wednesday 26 April 1978

I had tea yesterday with Nadir to hear the latest in the Jeremy Thorpe saga. Quite a lot has happened – some of it bad, some of it good – during the past week.

Last Tuesday Jeremy Thorpe again telephoned him at the Chesterfield Hotel and told him that he was under no obligation to tell the police anything and that in any case he was himself quite uncertain about the disposal of the second £10,000. He couldn't really remember how it had been spent. Nadir replied that he would have to tell the truth, at which Jeremy retorted, 'In that case it will be curtains for me and you will be asked to move on.'

Nadir has taken this to mean that, because he is from Pakistan and now domiciled in Jersey, any official knowledge of his handling money in a highly publicized court case would, according to Jeremy, lead to his exclusion from Jersey and probably his deportation from Britain. Which is of course absurd. Nadir, immediately realizing this, was very sad that a friend should use such a tactic against him. As I know from personal experience, Nadir has a very high doctrine of friendship, and it was exceedingly cruel of Jeremy Thorpe to attempt to hit him on what he knows to be a vulnerable spot. That he should have done so is perhaps a sign of the desperate plight in which he now finds himself as a result of the police investigation.

The good news is that Nadir, having been interviewed very civilly by the police and given a full account of his handling of the £20,000, was told that they are entirely convinced that no shred of anything dishonourable or suspicious is attached to him.

So thankfully, this rules out any possibility of his being charged with anything that may have taken place. But the prospect of having to give evidence against a friend – if it comes to this – is not inviting and, although Nadir has been treated shockingly badly by Jeremy Thorpe, he still feels a sense of loyalty towards him and does not wish to do anything that will cause him harm.

Where love and morality conflict there are no painless answers and I, and Nadir's other close friends, can do no more than try to support him through whatever lies ahead. I still find it difficult to believe that there is any truth in the allegations against Jeremy Thorpe made by Norman Scott in the Barnstaple and Exeter courts. The story is simply too bizarre, but this is small comfort to Nadir.

Thursday 27 April 1978

The question of whether, and in what form, a Roman Catholic child might be baptized in the Henry VII Chapel has now been resolved. Members of the Order of the Bath are allowed to have a certain number of weddings and baptisms in this chapel every year, and about a month ago a member sought the Dean's permission to have a grandchild baptized there by a Roman Catholic priest and according to the rites of that church.

The Dean sought the advice of the Chapter and we strongly advised him to decline the request and to offer instead the possibility of baptism according to the rites of the Church of England but with a Roman Catholic priest participating in the service. Now we learn that the family concerned has consulted Cardinal Hume and been advised by him that the child can be baptized only by a Roman Catholic priest.

It is sad when baptism – the great sacrament of Christian unity – becomes a focus of disunity, but I don't really think it would further the cause of unity if we were to allow the Abbey to be used indiscriminately by the non-Anglican churches. There are occasions when it is appropriate for a Roman Catholic mass to be celebrated at the Shrine of St Edward, and it is normal for representatives of other churches, including the Cardinal, to be involved in big special services. But the administration of baptism is something different, as the Roman Catholics would doubtless point out if anyone requested an Anglican baptism in Westminster Cathedal.

Thursday 4 May 1978

I first attended a service in Westminster Abbey in RAF uniform on Ascension Day 1944. A few days earlier I had reported to the Air Crew Receiving Centre in Regents Park and this was my first taste of London. I have two abiding memories of that first encounter with the Abbey. The first is of how gloomy the interior of the building seemed. I now know that this was due to the accumulation of grime over many centuries, and the great cleaning operation carried out in the 1960s revealed glories that were then hidden.

My second memory is of the splendour of the ceremonial, for it was Festal Evensong and I can see now the wonderful array of banners being carried through the nave at the beginning and the end of the service. It was a truly celebratory occasion. I have seen, and taken part in, just such a procession many times since then, and they never cease to thrill as the mixture of rich colour and fine music enhances the wondrous beauty of the building.

The fact that I have no memory of the Bible readings or of the sermon (if there was one) illustrates the importance of the visual in worship. Some church ceremonial is over-fussy and distracting, but Jocelyn Perkins and Christopher Hildyard, who devised the Abbey's ceremonial during the 1930s, had a strong sense of drama and were more concerned with dignity and beauty of movement than they were with what might or might not be liturgically correct. I hope we shall always keep it that way.

Although Ascension Day does not attract the great crowds of Christmas and Easter, it is one of the most glorious days in the Abbey's year – and today was no exception. The triumphant affirmation of Christ as sharing in God's kingly rule over the universe and ever present in the lives of his followers is, for once, matched by hymnody and music that expresses powerfully a mystery which is the dynamic of the church's mission.

This evening I left the Abbey inspired and exhilarated, which is no bad thing after an act of Christian worship.

Wednesday 10 May 1978

We were visited today by the Patriarch of the ancient Coptic Church, otherwise known as the Pope of Alexandria, Shenouda III. He is in England on an official ecumenical visit and naturally the Abbey was included in his itinerary.

Apparently His Holiness is staying at a hotel in Park Lane, and he came to the Abbey with his entourage in a splendid Rolls-Royce. The Dean made a felicitous speech of welcome and there was a certain amount of conversation, couched inevitably in general terms, about the importance of tradition and unity.

It was harmless enough, and before he departed the Patriarch presented us all with rather fine medals commemorating his visit. These have the appearance of gold, but the reality must be different.

Thursday 25 May 1978

I returned from Rome last evening to learn that Sebastian Charles is to be our new Canon, in succession to David Edwards. I know him slightly, as he is the Secretary of the British Council of Churches Division of Community Affairs. He is of Burmese nationality, though he was born into an Indian Christian family and was largely educated in India.

I am not sure what brought him to Lincoln Theological College to prepare for ordination, but after three years as a curate at Portsea he returned to Asia as priest-in-charge of a church in Rangoon.

Then he came back to England to join the staff of the Manchester Industrial Mission, and before long was appointed Anglican Chaplain at Salford Technological University, where I believe he was highly effective.

The combination of nationality and experience made him an attractive proposition to the BCC when a new head of Community Affairs was needed in 1974, and now, after only just over three years in that post, he is coming to the Abbey – with an English wife, Frances, and four school-age children. Rumour has it that he has not coped very well with his BCC responsibilities and I hope this is not the reason for his leaving.

The Crown obviously took seriously what we said about having a Canon from the Commonwealth and someone in touch with the big social issues of our time. This will bring an entirely new element into the Chapter and should be very stimulating.

Tuesday 13 June 1978

Some strange requests before us today. An urn has been discovered in France which is believed to contain the entrails of King Henry V. Might it be possible therefore for the tomb of the great warrior king to be opened and tests made to see if there is any truth in this contention? If there is, ought not the urn to go with the rest of his remains?

Since this is an informal enquiry, nothing need be done about it, but if it becomes formal, the views of the Queen will need to be sought. It is highly unlikely that she will authorize something so undesirable. Henry V has had enough disturbance already, for the silver head of his effigy on the tomb, together with the sceptre and other regalia, were stolen in 1546, and a replacement head, this time in polyester resin, was only put on as recently as 1971.

Next, may the effigy of the head of Anne of Bohemia be loaned for an exhibition to be held in Cologne from next November until March 1979. Anne is buried, with her husband Richard II, in the Abbey and the bronze effigy on the tomb portrays them side by side. But the effigy of her head, almost certainly taken from a death mask, is in the museum. The Librarian advised us to decline the request for its loan. It seems that it went to an exhibition in Luxembourg in 1963, and soon afterwards it was noticed that its condition had deteriorated – due, it was thought, to temperature changes on the journey.

Much easier was the suggestion that William Shakespeare's name be inscribed on his statue in Poets' Corner. We readily agreed to do this and, for good measure, will add 'buried at Stratford-upon-Avon'.

When I came to the Abbey I entered a strange world, as far removed as can be imagined from the new housing area in Stockton-on-Tees where I ministered for eleven years in the 1950s and 1960s.

Wednesday 14 June 1978

Yesterday I shook hands with an unusually wicked man, namely Nicholae Ceausescu, the President of Romania. He is on a state visit to London, and a wreath-laying at the grave of the Unknown Warrior is part of the ceremonial procedure of these events.

It is not generally recognized, I think, just how repressively Ceausescu is ruling Romania. Attention is so much focussed on the Soviet Union that we tend to overlook the fact that the situation in Romania is every bit as bad. Church attendance there remains extraordinarily high, but the leadership of the Orthodox Church is very much in cahoots with the state, and dissident Baptists, in common with other dissidents, are severely treated.

Ceausescu looks a nasty, ruthless piece of work and the degree of compromise involved in welcoming such a man to Westminster Abbey is serious. But it is hard to see how we can avoid this because we, too, are in an alliance with the state – in some respects, anyway.

Wednesday 5 July 1978

Just back from South Africa and Romania, where I have been working on the BBC 'God and Caesar' programmes. I learn that the dispute with Una Kroll and the Christian Parity Group over their request for demonstration facilities at the time of the Lambeth Conference debate on women priests now seems to have been resolved.

In the end they asked only for an all-night vigil on the eve of the Conference service in the Abbey, and apparently readily accepted the offer of St Margaret's for this purpose. There are no problems about this, and the whole thing now seems some way removed from earlier press reports that Una and her friends intended to chain themselves to the railings at the West entrance to the Abbey.

No doubt they will turn up with banners and placards at the time of the bishops' procession and it will all be rather jolly.

Tuesday 11 July 1978

In the course of a discussion with the Receiver General the other day I was astonished and horrified to learn that Miss Groves, our dedicated seamstress who has cared for the Abbey's robes and vestments for as long as anyone can remember, is paid only 50p an hour – this figure having last been reviewed in 1974. She was trained in a convent for this important work, which involves handling copes that go back to the Coronation of Charles II, and the award of the British Empire Medal, which she was given on our recommendation last year, hardly compensates for such meagre pay. It also turned out that she had not asked for any increase in her travel costs from the East End for the last three years.

Today therefore we doubled the rate to £1 an hour and undertook to meet all her bus and underground fares. She won't get very rich on this, but it will bring her closer to our lower general pay level and it is doubtful if she would accept more. Now well into her eighties, she has decided views on most things and is not awed by Deans and Canons.

Saturday 29 July 1978

Catherine, our younger daughter, was married this afternoon to Anthony Andrews, the son of the Abbey's Clerk of the Works, who is following in his father's footsteps as a mason. He served his apprenticeship with the Abbey team, is now working for a firm that specializes in marble, and hopes one day to have responsibility for overseeing the restoration of large, historic buildings.

It was a splendid wedding, at which the Dean officiated, and since Catherine and Anthony both have large circles of friends, it was held at the High Altar. I gave her away and read the I Corinthians 13 lesson. For the anthem the Choir sang Parry's 'I was glad . . .', which never fails to thrill, not least in the Abbey, where it is memorably associated with the Coronations of this century.

Afterwards we had the reception in College Garden, in brilliant sunshine, and the evening was spent by the younger element, plus parents, dancing on a boat plying between Westminster Bridge and Greenwich. It is curious how wedding customs have changed: at one time bridegroom and bride could hardly get away quickly enough, but now the festivities are prolonged until midnight.

Catherine has been given a Council flat in a rough part of the East End in return for her commitment to teach RE in a comprehensive school in the Borough of Newham. Such heroism deserves a reward, but the contrast between such an abode and life in the Little Cloister is bound to be stark.

Tuesday 1 August 1978

We have had a jolly Lambeth Conference day. For the first time this gathering of the bishops of the Anglican Communion, which takes place every ten years, is being held in Canterbury, rather than in London. This is to enable the conference to be a residential affair and allow the bishops to meet informally outside the main sessions.

But there has to be one memorable day in the capital, so the 407 bishops, plus wives, and consultants and observers from other churches, came up to Lambeth for lunch in a marquee, then on to the Abbey for Festal Evensong, and finally to Buckingham Palace for a royal garden party.

We were invited to join in everything and it was good to meet quite a lot of the overseas bishops – a few of whom I knew already, but most of them only by name, famous names in some instances. Archbishop Moses Scott of West Africa gave a rousing sermon at an Evensong made specially colourful by the presence of so many robed bishops, and I recalled the 1948 Lambeth Conference, when I was one of the many King's College London students recruited as banner-bearers at a similar service in St Paul's.

Because the number was so much smaller than the 5,000 who attend the royal garden parties in July, this was an altogether more intimate affair, and the military band went so far as to play the song 'Consider yourself at home, consider yourself one of the family'. Disappointingly for all the overseas people, the Queen was absent on a state visit to Canada, so her place was taken by the Queen Mother. Princess Margaret, Princess Alice of Gloucester and the Duchess of Kent were also there. Fortunately the threatened rain did not materialize.

The informality of the occasion was clearly demonstrated in the tea tent when a woman leapt on to my scarlet-clad back. It turned out to be the wife of the Bishop of St Albans, Lindy Runcie – an old friend who can be guaranteed to enliven any occasion. It must have been the first time a Canon of Westminster has enjoyed such an experience in the garden of Buckingham Palace.

Serious conversation intervened at certain points, however. Many of the bishops feel that the preparatory work for the conference was weak. There is awareness, too, of an impending crisis over the ordination of women to the priesthood. Already New Zealand, the United States, Canada and Hong Kong have women priests; several other Provinces are moving quickly in this direction; and there is a fear that the dear old Church of England – the mother Church of the Anglican Communion – may find itself isolated on this issue.

Sunday 13 August 1978

In my sermon at Evensong I commented on an issue which has had some media attention this week. It concerns the refusal of the authorities at Heathrow to grant VIP facilities to a number of Anglican bishops who were attending the funeral of Pope Paul VI in Rome yesterday.

The airport people were not, I am sure, influenced by theological factors, but as I pointed out in my sermon, it was altogether wrong that bishops, who only a few days earlier at the Lambeth Conference had sought to identify themselves with the poor and oppressed, should seek special privileges when making the short air journey from London to Rome.

'The whole idea of the church's leaders being "very important people" who need special cosseting to protect them from the discomforts of the world is quite alien to the spirit of the gospel. Love requires identification, not separation.'

I feel very strongly about this at the moment, after my visit to South Africa last month, when I had the opportunity to visit Soweto and Cross Roads, and to hear the stories of two African priests in Johannesburg Cathedral, both of whom had spent several weeks in prison earlier this year.

But I was speaking basically about the need for the church not only to preach about love but also to show in its own community life what happens when love is allowed to be the controlling factor in human relationships. The VIP bishops and my South Africa experience were illustrative material.

Saturday 19 August 1978

I officiated this evening at the Unknown Warrior's grave when a Czechoslovak Occupation Anniversary Committee came to lay a wreath to mark the tenth anniversary of the invasion of their country by the Russian and other Warsaw Pact armies.

It was a simple, moving ceremony and I was glad to be involved, partly because of my interest in Eastern Europe, arising from the writing of *Discretion and Valour*, and partly because of a memorable lunch in Stockholm shortly before the 1968 invasion.

I was attending the Fourth Assembly of the World Council of Churches in Uppsala, and in the course of a visit to Stockholm I chanced to have lunch with Professor Josef Hromadka, the world-famous Czech theologian, who believed it was possible for Christians and Communists to co-exist and indeed to work together for justice and freedom.

His attempt to bring this about during the years of harsh repression were truly heroic, and when we met in July 1968 he was excited by the changes taking place in his homeland as a result of the so-called Prague Spring of that year. Alexander Dubcek had replaced the hard-line Novotny as leader of the Communist Party and was introducing reforms designed to offer the people 'socialism with a human face'.

Hromadka was deeply involved in all this, but expressed to me his concern that things were moving too quickly. Already representatives of Russia, Hungary, Poland, Bulgaria and East Germany had met in Warsaw and signed a letter condemning the Czechoslovak reforms. Dubcek rejected the criticisms and carried on with his policy, so on 21 August the Russian tanks rolled and the brief 'Spring' was over. A neo-Stalinist regime, installed by the Soviet Union, introduced a savage form of repression.

Apparently Josef Hromadka was shattered by this turn of events and in the following year he died. Had it been suggested to me at the end of our lunch that in ten years' time I would be remembering him at the Unknown Warrior's grave in Westminster Abbey this would have seemed utterly incredible.

Thursday 14 September 1978

Today, at Golders Green Crematorium, I conducted the funeral of someone who was not a Christian. Lucjan Blit was a member of the British Council of Churches working party on religious conditions in Russia and Eastern Europe which enabled me to write *Discretion and Valour* and we became firm friends. Although he had a special know-ledge of Polish Catholicism, he was never himself able to make the leap of faith and died an agnostic.

Lucjan was undoubtedly the most heroic friend I have ever had, and none has displayed greater integrity. Born in Warsaw in 1904, he was active in the Jewish Socialist Movement and by 1926 had become secretary of its youth section. In 1939, after the German and Russian invasions of Poland, he began underground work in Warsaw but was arrested by the Russians and sentenced to a year's imprisonment, followed by despatch to a labour camp beyond the Arctic circle. Only the assumption of a false name saved him from the fate of two close associates, who were shot on Stalin's orders. During this period his wife, his parents, his sister and almost all his relatives and friends were murdered in the Holocaust.

When the Soviet Union was drawn into the war against Hitler's Germany, Lucjan was allowed to leave Russia and was summoned to London by the exiled Polish Socialist leaders. A project to parachute him back into Poland for underground work had to be abandoned and he spent the rest of the war years trying to convince a disbelieving British public of the reality of the destruction of European Jewry.

After the war he remained in London, was happily remarried, to Barbara, and became a highly successful journalist specializing in Polish affairs and in social and political analysis from his left-wing position. In 1969, however, he was appointed to a joint teaching post at the London School of Economics and the School of Slavonic Studies and wrote two very good books: *The Eastern Pretender*, a biography of Baleslaw Pinsecki, a former Fascist who sought to subvert the Polish Catholic Church through a Stalinist association known as Pax, and *The Origins of Polish Socialism*.

I am not sure what it was that drew us together. He had a warm personality, a deep concern for humanity and an aversion to injustice and oppression of every kind. We just seemed to click. When I started on the *Discretion and Valour* project I knew nothing about Poland, but after the publication of the book the editor of a Polish newspaper wrote to me and said that he could not understand how any Englishman could possibly enter so fully into the life and outlook of the Polish nation. When I explained to him that Lucjan Blit had been my tutor, he replied, 'Now I understand'.

A lot of people from London's Polish community, the LSE and the world of international journalism came to the funeral. It was not a Christian occasion, but it involved no denial of Christian faith and was more truly religious than many a funeral I have conducted.

Sunday 17 September 1978

The annual Battle of Britain service at which, on the strength of my own RAF experience 1944–47, I preached this morning is one of the great events in the Abbey calendar and is always held on the Sunday nearest 15 September – the day on which the battle reached its climax in 1940.

The Abbey was filled with past and present RAF people, including the top brass, and immediately beneath the pulpit about 100 of the pilots who actually fought in the battle. The Central Band of the RAF filled the building with sound and there was a particular poignant moment when six of the Battle of Britain pilots – all of them decorated for their bravery – carried to the High Altar a Roll of Honour containing the names of the 1,495 men who were killed in the battle. As this little procession moved up the central aisle the band played the March Theme from William Walton's 'Spitfire Prelude'.

I explained that I was still a schoolboy in the summer of 1940 and had been absolutely enthralled by the reports of the battle – keeping a daily diary record of the number of aircraft lost on both sides. The pilots were my heroes and I was thrilled whenever a name or a photograph of any of them appeared in the newspapers. I marvelled at their exploits and their courage.

> 'But here you are, some of my boyhood heroes, sitting before me in Westminster Abbey, and I have to say that you all look rather ordinary sort of men – the sort of men who might after the war have gone on to become schoolmasters, or bank managers or wardens of National Trust properties' (I had ascertained earlier that these are some of the jobs they are now doing).

This introduction caused a good deal of amusement among the former pilots. I went on to say that we were grateful to them not only for what they had achieved in 1940 – 'Never in the field of human conflict was so much owed by so many to so few' – but also for the constant reminder that the stuff of history consists not of giants, but of little people: anonymous folk with limited gifts who applied themselves with diligence and dedication to a particular cause.

During the last few days a certain amount of controversy has arisen in the columns of *The Times* as a result of the suggestion of a military expert that the Battle of Britain was not specially significant and that the Royal Navy would in any case have prevented a German invasion. So I referred to this and said that the gratitude of the nation and of the free world sprang from the obvious fact, borne out by previous and subsequent experience, that without mastery of the air, land and sea forces were virtually powerless.

In the course of conversation with some of the men after the service one made the interesting observation that on the whole it was easier to be a fighter pilot than a bomber pilot, since the former normally engaged the enemy on more or less equal, one-to-one, terms, while the latter were flying a heavy, relatively slow, aircraft that was vulnerable to night fighters, concentrated anti-aircraft guns and other hazards on the long journeys to and from German cities. Hence the very heavy casualties among bomber crews.

I had not previously thought of this and, coming from a former fighter pilot, it could hardly be challenged.

There is, predictably, a sharp conflict of opinion over the Dean's suggestion that the cosmati mosaic work on the shrine of Edward the Confessor should be restored. The great shrine erected by King Henry III in the thirteenth century was, by all accounts, one of the finest in Europe. The basic structure was of Purbeck marble, and artists were brought from Italy to create the decoration: there were eleven golden images of kings and saints and many large jewels. It must have been a magnificent sight.

The shrine was despoiled at the dissolution of the monastery in 1540 and the body of the saint buried elsewhere in the Abbey. But during the reign of Mary Tudor enough pieces of the structure were recovered from the precincts to enable the lower half of the the shrine to be reconstructed, and Abbott Feckenham created a new Feretory. Edward's body was returned, and the Queen gave jewels to replace those that had been plundered. However, these were later removed, probably at the time of Oliver Cromwell, though the shrine itself was left intact.

This is how it stands today at the heart of the Abbey – a permanent reminder of the Abbey's founder and of its vocation as a place of worship and a school of sanctity. But of course it is nothing like its former glory, and all that remain of the thirteenth-century decoration are some fragments of the cosmati mosaic.

It is these that the Dean wishes to have restored and enhanced by the introduction of new mosaic to bring colour and warmth to this focal point of the building. But the Architectural Advisory Panel and the Surveyor of the Fabric are strongly opposed to this. They take the line, now the orthodoxy of historians and conservators, that the development of a building, whether good or bad, is an integral part of its history and should be accepted as it has become, rather than modified to eliminate some of the changes. The Librarian says that the only acceptable restoration would be to bring the shrine back to the glory of Henry III's time, which is obviously impossible.

I am strongly supporting the Dean and advising him to go ahead in spite of the opposition, but I doubt if this will happen, as he will not want to provoke public controversy or incur the disapproval of Buckingham Palace, which killed a 1960s scheme for replacing the Nave's stone floor with coloured marble.

The Chief Cashier is displeased because I have ordered the desks at which money is taken for entry to the East end of the building to be moved a few yards west into the Nave. We have had complaints that the desks were located so close to the memorial tablets to Elgar and Vaughan Williams as to obscure them from view.

This part of the Abbey is often known as Musicians' Aisle because it contains the grave of Henry Purcell, who was organist here from 1679–95, and also memorial stones to a number of other notable musicians. The complaint about the cash desks seemed a fair one, but unfortunately the Chief Cashier was prevented at the last moment from attending the site meeting I convened to consider the problem, and he believes that the new arrangement will increase the likelihood of robbery. So we must have another try: this time with the desks nearer the statesmen in the North Transept. The conflict between cash and credibility is never-ending.

Thursday 26 October 1978

Back in January a letter signed by Beryl Bainbridge, Alfie Bass and other notables appeared in *The Times* suggesting that a tablet to Charlie Chaplin should be placed in Westminster Abbey. They argued that history will show him 'to have marked this century more strongly than any other single British artist'.

The Dean, who is very keen on this, has been in touch with the man who organized the letter, and our Surveyor has now produced a drawing for a possible design which portrays the great star of silent films in his characteristic garb, with bowler hat, baggy trousers, a walking stick and splay feet. The idea, on which we are all agreed, is that this will go in the Cloisters, rather than in the Abbey. It should certainly make a jolly addition to an area where several famous eighteenth-century actors and actresses are buried. The only problem now is who is going to pay for it. The signatories to *The Times* letter seem the obvious people to raise the money, and this ought not to be too difficult.

Thursday 2 November 1978

As Treasurer I am now a member of the Westminster Abbey Trust, which was set up in 1972 under the Presidency of the Duke of Edinburgh in order to raise £5 million for the complete restoration of the

Abbey. Already inflation and the discovery of further decay has caused the target to be raised to £10 million, of which nearly £5 million has now been raised.

There has been no public appeal, nor is there likely to be one unless it is decided to use the restoration of the Western towers, the most familiar aspect of the Abbey, for this purpose. They are being left until the final phase. The method so far has involved the Trustees, all of them very high-powered businessmen apart from the Dean and the Treasurer, making very substantial gifts from the coffers of their own companies and persuading friends in other companies to do the same. It is done on a highly personal basis and doubtless there is an element of repaying debts and favours in the process.

The sight of the Duke of Edinburgh in action is instructive. He is no figurehead President but rather a very robust leader of the campaign who seems genuinely concerned to see the Abbey restored. He brooks no nonsense about policy matters and accepts no excuses for inaction; indeed he throws his weight about with considerable effect, and it is amusing to see how readily the tycoons fall into line. Once their companies have given as much as their shareholders are likely to approve, they are replaced by others who are ready to be milked.

It certainly is an enormous help to have an active royal president of this sort and today's meeting was held in Buckingham Palace, which usefully added to the glamour of involvement. We met in what is I believe known as the Chinese Dining Room – its decor consisting mainly of fabrics and furnishings culled from the Orient – and this is close to the balcony on which the Royal Family appears on great national occasions. So we were vouchsafed a view of the area around Queen Victoria's monument and along the Mall as seen through royal eyes.

Tea was served in wide china cups, more akin to soup bowls; this, I suppose, explains the description used in some social circles, 'a dish of tea'. The Duke was friendly enough and despatched the business very efficiently. The main discussion was about tactics for approaching potential donors, Tommy Thompson, the voluble Ulsterman who is our professional fund-raiser, spoke of a recent successful visit to America, and the Duke spoke of his concern that the rising level of pollution in London may well cause a newly-restored Abbey to decay even more rapidly than it has in the past. He has, I think, been to a recent conference on the subject and is keen to have the pollution level near the Abbey monitored. His opinion of the Department of the Environment is not high.

The memorial stone for Benjamin Britten was duly unveiled this evening in the course of a very splendid memorial concert in which we heard some of Britten's finest music. However, it was highly embarrassing to discover not long before the start of the concert that a mistake had been made over his dates on the stone. Instead of 1913–1976 it has 1913–1977.

Just how this came about no one seems to know; at least no one is prepared to accept responsibility for the error. The stone, which is close to those of Elgar and Vaughan Williams, will of course have to be taken up and completely re-done, at a cost to the Dean and Chapter of about £2,500, I fear.

The placing of this memorial has been by no means straightforward. At the time of Britten's death everyone was very enthusiastic about the prospect of an Abbey memorial and no one has ever questioned the rightness of this. But when it came to meeting the cost, the executors of the Britten estate, who must be handling a great deal of money, were unwilling to release any for this purpose, and in the end the Worshipful Company of Musicians found the money.

Then there was difficulty about who should carry out the unveiling of the stone. At first it was hoped that the Prince of Wales would honour the occasion, but he was either unable or unwilling to unveil. Next there was talk of entrusting the ceremony to Peter Pears, Britten's long-time love, but this idea did not find favour, and in the end it was done by Sir Lennox Berkeley – Britten's distinguished contemporary and friend.

The replacement stone will be slipped in quietly, and in future the designs for memorial stones must be carefully checked by the Library staff. They ought to be sound on dates.

Wednesday 13 December 1978

Bizarre though the allegations against Jeremy Thorpe and three other men still seem, the magistrates' court at Minehead has decided that there is sufficient evidence to justify their being charged in a higher court with conspiracy to murder.

The story that has unfolded is that Jeremy Thorpe did have a homosexual affair with Norman Scott during the early 1960s. This was apparently of quite brief duration, but throughout the 1960s Scott was begging money from Thorpe, with more than a hint that if he did not pay up he would make public the nature of their relationship. Thorpe

80

became Leader of the Liberal Party in 1967 and any disclosure would of course have been disastrous for him.

Scott was kept quiet for some years, without I think the payment of any large sum of money, but in 1971 he went to three senior people in the Liberal Party and told them his story. However, they were not convinced of its truth, because it seemed unlikely and Scott was quite evidently a shady character. Nonetheless they interviewed Thorpe, who strenuously denied the allegation, and the matter was dropped. Scott meanwhile was talking about the affair in the pubs of Thorpe's North Devon constituency.

After a time Thorpe and his friend David Holmes decided that Scott must in some way be silenced. Various attempts – including the purchase for £2,500 of some incriminating letters – having failed, they then determined (so the prosecution's story goes) to have him bumped off. The £20,000 donation extracted from Jack Hayward and channelled through Nadir Dinshaw's bank account to David Holmes would finance this.

Next, Holmes went to Port Talbot in South Wales to give tax advice to a carpet dealer named Le Mesurier, who subsequently put him in touch with a rough character named George Deakin who had made a lot of money from selling one-armed-bandit machines. He in turn introduced Holmes to the airline pilot Andrew Newton, who had a reputation for being able to solve inconvenient problems. Newton was thereupon engaged by Holmes to deal with Jeremy Thorpe's Scott problem in return for a payment of £10,000.

During the late evening of 23 October 1975 Newton lured Scott to a lonely place between Porlock and Combe Martin, in North Devon, where he threatened him with a gun, then fired some shots which killed Scott's dog. It is alleged that Scott survived only because the gun jammed following the shooting of the dog. Newton was subsequently arrested and his trial and conviction led in due course to the charging of Thorpe, Holmes, Le Mesurier and Deakin at Minehead.

Nadir was required to give evidence at Minehead, and this proved to be a very painful and upsetting experience for him, especially as Jeremy Thorpe was there to see and hear it. The newspapers have been full of the story with its lurid, and often unsavoury, details. There cannot surely have been such a case before.

Nadir is quite safe, but no doubt he will in due course have to repeat his evidence at the Old Bailey, or some other such court, and any kind of association with this case can only be painful. When a close and pre-viously trusted friend stands at the centre of it, the emotional element is bound to be excruciating. Fortunately, he has a deep Christian faith as well as other friends to sustain him.

Friday 15 December 1978

I chaired a meeting of the Security Committee this afternoon to deal with a curious, and in some ways disturbing, business. During the past week the Night Watchman told various members of the Clerk of Works staff, when coming on duty in the morning, that he had had a bad night because they left the Abbey doors open, that the alarm had gone off several times during the night, and that the police had come to the Abbey on three occasions. However, none of these alarms and visits is recorded by the security control firm or by the police.

The Chaplain, Neil Collings, has also reported a message from the headmistress of the school attended by the Night Watchman's son. She is worried because this parent sometimes turns up at the school dressed as a clergyman and claims to be involved in conducting services in the Abbey.

Our meeting with him lasted almost two hours but we didn't get very far. It is obvious that he has delusions arising from some psychiatric problem and he has agreed to see a Harley Street psychiatrist known to us. It is equally obvious that while he is in this condition he cannot be responsible for the Abbey's night-time security.

Tuesday 19 December 1978

The Dean is uneasy about a request for a service next year to mark the thirtieth anniversary of NATO. He doesn't believe that military alliances are suitable for Christian commemoration and this is of course entirely compatible with his strongly-held pacifist views. We had a useful discussion of the issues this morning, having received a short confidential memorandum from the Chaplain of the Fleet in which he pointed out that NATO collaboration extends beyond military matters.

The Sub-Dean thought it would be illogical to refuse NATO when permission had already been given to the RAF to commemorate its sixtieth anniversary next year. The Archdeacon suggested that instead of the special service, prayers for NATO should be said on 4 April and that maybe something special should be incorporated into Evensong on Remembrance Sunday.

Sebastian Charles and I took the line that permission should be given, but strict control should be exercised over the content of the service to ensure that NATO's wider objectives were emphasized. This was agreed. The Dean will, as usual, be involved in the compilation of the service and have the power to give or withhold final approval.

Wednesday 20 December 1978

We have a rather serious problem with Nicholas MacMichael, our Keeper of the Muniments. Last month he caused considerable embarrassment by going into the Bookshop and making a nuisance of himself both to customers and staff. He was hauled before the Dean and Chapter, apologized for his behaviour, explained that his condition was due to a limited amount of alcohol exacerbating a long-standing health problem (including asthma), and said that he had written a letter of apology to the Bookshop Manager. We gave him a formal written warning and said that any repetition of this sort of conduct would lead to his dismissal.

Now we learn that at 11.45 on Monday evening the Night Watchman found Nicholas lying on the pavement unwilling to move. The Clerk of the Works and the Receiver General were called out, and they in turn summoned the Custodian Caterer, who is experienced in these matters, having served in the Navy. Without undue difficulty, he got Nicholas to his flat, in the Little Cloister, and to bed.

Yesterday, at noon, therefore, Nicholas once again appeared before the Dean and Chapter. We had previously learned from the Librarian that on Monday he had returned from lunch incapable of work and been advised to go home. The Librarian also informed us that over the last twelve months he had not done more than one quarter of a normal day's work on any one day.

Nicholas was full of apologies, but the Dean told him that there was no alternative to suspending him from duty and that we would see him again on 23 January. He will go to stay with his sister, and we will use the time to see what help can be found to deal with his problem.

We all recognize that we have a tragic business on our hands. Nicholas is a lonely man who displays some of the eccentricities of the scholar. Although he never went to a university, his father, a Kent parson, got the great historian, Lawrence Tanner, who was at that time the Abbey's Keeper of the Muniments, to take him under his wing. The result was that Nicholas himself became an expert on the archives and succeeded Lawrence Tanner when the time came for him to retire.

There can be no doubting that he has an unrivalled knowledge of the Abbey's history and especially of the records of its Benedictine years, which are more complete than those of any other Benedictine community in Europe. Enquiring historians who are patient receive from him full and scholarly replies, and his revision of the Abbey's Official Guide, published last year, is a model of careful scholarship presented with remarkable economy of style. The cataloguing of the archives is, sadly, years behind schedule.

Nicholas is a member of our community and we are going to do everything we can to 'rescue' him, but we are only too well aware that his kind of problem is not easily solved.

Thursday 21 December 1978

Alec McCowen, the actor, gave a solo performance of St Mark's Gospel in the Abbey this evening. This is something he started doing earlier this year at the Mermaid Theatre, where he was soon playing to full houses, and several hundred people paid £10 and more to hear him in the Abbey.

Hearing the whole of a Gospel in one session is certainly illuminating and helps one to see much more clearly what Mark was trying to do. More than ever before, I was struck by the strong emphasis on suffering in his narrative.

The way in which Alec McCowen presented the material from the Authorized Version could hardly be faulted and it seemed to me, from the way in which he used his voice, that he had a good understanding of the Gospel's essential message.

I don't know how difficult it is for an experienced actor to learn by heart the whole of a Gospel, but the recital of it all without reference to the text was certainly impressive. As also was the fact that he could be clearly heard throughout the building without recourse to a microphone. I have often wondered how preachers made themselves heard in large buildings such as the Abbey before the days of sound reinforcement systems. Now I know: they learned how to project their voices.

Today we have a Sound Advisory Panel, made up of leading experts in acoustics and electronics, and we spend many thousands of pounds on sophisticated equipment, yet complaints about inaudibility are increasing.

1979

I don't normally stay up to welcome the New Year, but this time the weather decreed otherwise. There was heavy snow in the South of England yesterday and at about seven o'clock last evening the Dean telephoned from Groombridge on the Kent–Sussex border to say that the conditions were so severe that it would be impossible for him to return to London to conduct the midnight service in the Abbey. Would I, as Canon-in-Residence, please take his place?

A service of about thirty minutes is the requirement on this occasion, and fortunately I had preached on a New Year theme at Evensong yesterday, so without too much trouble I shortened this address, chose three hymns ('O God our help in ages past', 'Now thank we all our God' and 'Lead us, Heavenly Father, lead us'), and arranged some appropriate prayers. It worked out quite well, I think, and although the snow reduced the size of the normal midnight congregation I shook hands with above 200 people at the door afterwards. Saying 'A Happy New Year' so many times, and with conviction, is a special challenge.

I hope that Edward will now stay on at Groombridge, where the Abbey has a holiday home (generously donated by Sir William McKie, a former Organist), because the demands of Christmas left him very tired and there is nothing pressing in the diary for a few more days.

Thursday 25 January 1979

During the Week of Prayer for Christian Unity, just ended, we invite representatives of the non-Anglican churches to conduct the intercessions at daily Evensong. This seems a good way of demonstrating the degree of unity that already exists between us, and the other churches appreciate our invitation.

I am beginning to wonder, however, if the exercise does much to advance the cause of church unity. Naturally, our visitors pray in their accustomed manner, often at some length, and the style is sometimes so far removed from our Anglican tradition that it becomes difficult to participate. The prospect of more of this in a united church is not inviting, which is another reason for our seeking federal, rather than organic, unity.

Tuesday 30 January 1979

It was a happy coincidence that my first annual Treasurer's Report to the Chapter today contained much good news, not least the fact that the income and expenditure account for the year ended 29 September 1978 showed a surplus of £260,835 – a record, by a substantial amount.

None of this owes anything to me. John Baker, my predecessor, should take some credit, because the heavy losses sustained during the 1973–75 period drove him to overhaul the Abbey's accounting arrangements and bring financial matters under control. But the main reason for the surplus is that we have become more skilled in taking money from our visitors.

The number of visitors last year was in fact down – those entering the paying area declined from 1,502,898 to 1,410,574. Nonetheless, of the year's revenue of £1,031,148 – another record – no less than £738,000 came directly or indirectly from visitors. This included a net profit of £118,986 from the Bookshop and a commission of £22,000 from the Brass Rubbing Centre. The sale of Jubilee Year silver – ugly stuff, I thought – also brought in £34,000.

Running costs have, however, risen to £770,313, an increase of 11% over 1976–77 (due mainly to inflation), and the surplus does not take account of some £112,000 which needs to be spent on various maintenance projects. Indeed the Auditor believes that the cost of these projects should be met from revenue, and not be regarded as capital expenditure.

It is extraordinary, really, that the Abbey should have so prospered during a most serious economic breakdown in the nation as a whole. At this very moment industrial unrest is nearing crisis point and it remains to be seen what effects the new government policies will have. The explanation is that we are benefitting from a tourism boom which has been encouraged by a weak pound, but this is a dangerously unreliable source of income, since changes in this area would hit us at a point from which 75% of the money comes.

I therefore raised the question whether we should now be increasing our meagre reserves, lest we ever find ourselves in another financial crisis, and it was readily agreed that we shall discuss this, in the light of a number of major capital projects requiring consideration. The possibility of our giving say 10% of our surplus to outside charities is also to be considered.

I expressed my concern, too, about the level of wages paid to some of our staff. The take-home pay of the cleaners (all men) is no more than £50–55 per week; labourers on the Clerk of the Works staff average about £60 per week, including overtime payments; and the Vergers and Marshals have to work long hours – partly to meet the demands we lay upon them, but also to earn a reasonable salary. Again, this is to be looked into and remedied, though with a staff of over 170 we must be sure of a continuing steady income before we can commit ourselves to large wage increases. No doubt the Government's pay restraint policy will also have to be taken into account, but we cannot ignore the position of our lowest-paid employees.

Monday 5 February 1979

On my rounds I paused for a time, as I often do, at the tomb of Lady Margaret Beaufort in the south aisle of the Henry VII Chapel. Her recumbent figure in bronze is the masterpiece of the Florentine sculptor, Pietro Torrigiani, who achieved further fame by breaking Michelangelo's nose in a quarrel. It is quite the loveliest work of art in the Abbey and her hands, clasped in prayer, are marvellous – wrinkled, as with an old lady. The inscription, which extends all round the tomb, was composed by Erasmus and, as we can now see, marks the turning-point from the mediaeval to the modern world.

That she should have such a monument seems altogether appropriate because she was, by all accounts, a specially lovely person. She died in the Abbot's House, which is now the Deanery, on St Peter's Day 1509, and at the funeral her confessor, Bishop John Fisher of Rochester, later to be beheaded for refusing to acknowledge Henry VIII as supreme head of the church, said, 'Everyone that knew her loved her, and everything that she said or did became her'.

As mother of Henry VII she was the foundress of the Tudor dynasty, and during her later years she seems to have spent a lot of her time in and around the Abbey. We have her prayer book in the Library and still administer her charity for widows in Westminster. Her major benefactions include the founding of two Cambridge colleges – Christ's and St John's – and the Lady Margaret chairs of Divinity at Oxford and Cambridge.

The quality of her life, and its significance, ought to be more widely known.

Tuesday 13 February 1979

We have had to dispense with the services of the deluded Night Watchman. It is always difficult to terminate the employment of anyone in this community, even more so when they are ill, but there is no possibility of our employing a Night Watchman who cannot cope with the Abbey's security requirements. Sadly, there is no other job we can offer him.

In place of a Night Watchman, I have recommended that we employ a professional security firm, and the Chapter has agreed to this. It will cost us an additional £3,500 a year, but we shall have the benefit of men who have been vetted and trained, and we shall be covered for sickness and holidays.

There is an always-remembered occasion when King George VI sent his secretary to administer a rebuke to Dean Alan Don for allowing the Stone of Scone to be stolen from the Abbey, and while a repetition of this now seems unlikely, the possibility of other, more sinister, breaches of security seem only too likely. And there is of course the ever-present risk of fire, so we must spend the money.

We are also spending over £1,000 on medical treatment for the Keeper of the Muniments, whose medical condition was exacerbated by a slight stroke at the turn of the year. But he refuses to have in-patient treatment – like most of his sort, he is unwilling or unable to recognize that he has a problem – so we are not making much progress in that direction, though he claims to have abstained from alcohol since he appeared before us in December. That could be true, and we are permitting him to return to his flat in the Little Cloister, but not to his work in the Library.

Wednesday 14 February 1979

We have decided not to provide facilities for a jazz concert to be held in the Abbey in August as part of a London Jazz Festival sponsored by the Greater London Council. We were approached about this last month when it was proposed that Chic Coran, an American jazz composer, should write a religious work and perform it in the Abbey.

Although the Organist was strongly opposed to this, the Dean and Chapter agreed to the idea in principle, provided that Chic Coran, of whom none of us had heard, was of sufficient calibre to merit an Abbey setting for his performance. The Dean mentioned that some years ago Duke Ellington gave a much acclaimed performance in the Abbey.

Further enquiry has revealed that, although Chic Coran is well known in American jazz circles, he is not yet a Duke Ellington. Sebastian Charles has also ascertained that he is a teetotaller, a non-smoker and a Scientologist – which is not quite the point. In the end we thought that as the concert would take place during our 'closed season', when many of the staff will be on holiday, we had better say No. Had it been offered for another time of the year I think (hope) we would have chanced it.

Tuesday 27 February 1979

Today being Shrove Tuesday, Chapter proceedings were interrupted at 10.55 a.m. by the annual call to witness Westminster School's Pancake Greeze. Summoned by the Dean's Verger, we joined the Headmaster and the Chef (bearing a pan containing two pancakes) to form a small procession through the Cloisters to the hall known as Up School.

Here were assembled some thirty to forty senior boys in a variety of strange garb, but with rugby football kit predominating, and a large crowd of onlookers – members of the teaching staff and invited guests. It was the task of the Chef, on a signal from the Headmaster, to toss the pancake over a metal bar which runs the breadth of the hall, just below the ceiling.

His first attempt failed to reach the requisite height, but his second cleared the bar and as soon as the pancake reached the floor the contestants dived for it – the aim being to secure the largest portion. There being so many involved, the pancake immediately vanished from sight beneath a heap of flailing flesh. The violence employed by some seemed to threaten life and limb, and it was a miracle that no one was seriously hurt.

After about five minutes, Time was called and a number of boys emerged from the melée holding small pieces of pancake, which were then carefully weighed. The winning piece was something under two ounces, and the Dean presented its holder with a golden sovereign dating from the reign of George IV. This was returned almost immediately for use next year and a £5 note was substituted. The Dean then 'begged a play' (a half-day holiday later in the term) which the Headmaster granted; this was greeted with loud cheers.

Whereupon the members of the school repaired to College Hall to feast on unmolested pancakes, and the Dean and Chapter returned to

89

Jerusalem Chamber to consider a complaint from the Lay Vicars that they had not been paid a special service fee when the 200th anniversary of the death of Captain James Cook was commemorated in the course of a normal Evensong.

Friday 2 March 1979

It seems that we may be making a little progress towards allowing women to ring the Abbey's bells. The Ringers – a select self-perpetuating band – have hitherto rejected any suggestion that women might be invited to join them. The excuse has always been that the Ringers belong to the Ancient Society of College Youths (a ringing fraternity) which is by definition male. It is therefore impossible to admit women to the band.

The fact that the definition might also exclude middle-aged and elderly men has not occurred to them; the true explanation is that they are a highly conservative, as well as a dedicated, group of men. But now their secretary, who held office for many years and was given the OBE for his pains, has retired and his successor has indicated that he hopes, after consultation with the Ringers, occasionally to extend an invitation to women of sufficient competence to join the team for a particular occasion. There can be no question of women becoming permanent members because the rules of the Ancient Society of College Youths do not permit this.

Another possible concession, again to be discussed, is that visiting male ringers may sometimes be invited to join the team. The ringing world has apparently been complaining for years about the exclusive character of the Abbey tower, and even now the possibility of inviting visiting teams will not be considered.

The Dean is as unhappy as the rest of us about this situation, and we intend to apply further pressure.

Monday 26 March 1979

The Dean, Edward Knapp-Fisher, and I met an Air Commodore from the Ministry of Defence in the Deanery this afternoon in order to discuss the proposed NATO service to be held in May. The Hon. Diana Makgill, of the Foreign and Commonwealth Office, was also there.

The Dean has been very anxious about this request in case it suggests Christian approval of military might, but he was soon reassured. The Air Commodore readily agreed that the emphasis in the service should be on NATO's peace-keeping role, and he said that he was more than happy to leave the content of the service, including the choice of preacher, to the Dean.

We had some talk about the preacher. The Archbishop of Canterbury and the Archbishop of York were suggested, but I said that I thought the Bishop of Durham, John Habgood, would handle the subject better, and the Dean is to invite him.

Wednesday 25 April 1979

The appointment of a new Rector of St Bartholomew the Great, Smithfield, is causing a conflict that Anthony Trollope would have enjoyed. Prebendary Newell Eddius Wallbank, who became a Doctor of Music when he was only twenty-two, went to St Bartholomew's in 1937 as a curate to his godfather. When the godfather retired in 1945 he persuaded the patron to appoint the curate as his successor. This displeased the then Bishop of London, Geoffrey Fisher, who protested that Wallbank, at only thirty-three, was much too young for one of the City of London's richest livings. Wallbank was clever enough, however, to send a classic response in which he told the bishop that he agreed with everything he had written and desired earnestly to comply with his wishes, but unfortunately he had made a solemn oath to his godfather that he would succeed him, and his conscience would not permit him to break it.

He has been at St Bartholomew's – the oldest church in the City – ever since, and among his many achievements during the last thirty-four years was to persuade the patron to transfer her rights to the Dean and Chapter of Westminster. This is the first occasion on which we have been able to exercise these rights.

We are the patrons of about twenty-five parishes, most of them in rural areas where the Abbey once had great estates, and many are now amalgamated with other parishes in teams and groups. Whenever a parish falls vacant the Dean and Canons take it in turn to nominate the new rector or vicar. This brings a certain variety into our appointments and prevents dispute in Chapter.

Nowadays, Edward Knapp-Fisher, the Archdeacon, does all the preliminary work, but we each make the nomination. St Bartholomew's coincides with my turn and I had it in mind to nominate Eric James.

Eric and I have been close friends for over thirty years, but this was not the reason for my choice. He is at the moment a Canon Residentiary of St Alban's Abbey and also much involved in Christian Action. It would be a very good thing if he moved to London to become Director of Christian Action, but this can only happen if he is found a base from which to work. So, in the same way that John Collins was appointed to a Canonry of St Paul's in order to start Christian Action in 1948, I wanted to appoint Eric to St Bartholomew's, which is nothing like a full-time job for an able-bodied priest.

Unfortunately, a rumour of this proposal reached the ears of the Bishop of London, Gerald Ellison, who got into touch with Edward Knapp-Fisher and told him that Eric's appointment would be unacceptable. The reasons advanced for this included the alleged need for the church to be given a lot of attention, the certain unhappiness of the conservative congregation at the prospect of having a radical rector, and so on.

The truth is, however, that Gerald Ellison cannot stand Eric James. I am not sure if this is because Eric publicly criticized Gerald's translation from Chester to London, or if it is simply that he believes Eric's outlook to be incompatible with the traditions of the Church of England. Whatever the reason, and it may be a bit of both, he successfully blocked Eric's appointment as Dean of King's College London, and he has now effectively blocked his move to St Bartholomew's.

If the Dean and Chapter were prepared for a show-down with the Bishop I suppose that we might insist on appointing Eric, but he doesn't wish to start a new ministry in these conditions and has asked for his name to be withdrawn from consideration.

We have decided therefore to advertise the post, and I have myself withdrawn from the fray. The Bishop says that he has twelve names for consideration; one can be certain that none of them will be as able as Eric James.

Tuesday 1 May 1979

Eric Abbott, our former Dean, used to describe St Faith's Chapel as a 'thin spot', by which he meant that it is the place in the Abbey where it is most easy to become aware of the presence of God. Hidden away beyond a door at the end of the South Transept, it has not been a chapel for all that long. During the Middle Ages it was used as a vestry and later became a storeroom. Not until 1898 did it begin to be used for worship and prayer, and its location makes it the one place in the Abbey where peace and quiet is guaranteed.

The East end of the chapel, which seats about thirty people, is dominated by a magnificent mediaeval wall-painting in which St Faith is most beautifully represented in robes of dark green and red, wearing a crown and holding a grid-iron – the emblem of her martydom by burning. On the left of her a Benedictine monk kneels in prayer, and below her feet, just above the altar, is a small, exquisitely painted, portrayal of the crucifixion.

This is where we gather most mornings of the week at 7.40 for Mattins, followed at 8 o'clock by Holy Communion. The number attending is never large, but it is always sufficient to create a sense of representative community, and there could be no better start to the Abbey's busy day – and my own.

On the main saints' days we move to the Henry VII Chapel for Holy Communion. That offers a quite different experience, the altar surrounded by the greatest splendour, and today, the Feast of St Philip and St James, the morning sunshine was bursting through the East window with striking rays.

This is a magical time to be in the Abbey, and familiarity serves only to increase its power and the realization that one is worshipping and praying in a shrine. This is the third anniversary of my coming here.

Monday 21 May 1979

A happy weekend in Norwich – staying with David and Hilary Edwards, preaching at the Civic Service in the Cathedral, having lunch with old Durham friends, Gerald and Gwen Collier – ended in tragedy. When we arrived at Liverpool Street Station at about five o'clock last evening, Lilian Carpenter was waiting at the ticket barrier and she told us, in her characteristically gentle way, that Anthony, who married Catherine only last July, had been killed in a car accident at lunchtime.

We took a taxi to the Abbey and by this time Catherine had left her East End flat and was with Anthony's parents in their house in Dean's Yard. Utterly stunned by the news, I brought her across to the Little Cloister in a state of great distress, and gradually she told us what had happened.

She and Anthony were entertaining two other young couples for lunch. While the girls were preparing the meal, the boys went for a drink in a pub about a couple of miles away. This involved a short journey on a raised dual-carriageway and it was on a slip road from this, while on the way home, that the car, driven by Anthony, went out of control, and struck one of the upper road's supporting pillars. Anthony was killed instantly; David, who was seated behind him, was seriously injured; and Ian, who had not fastened his seat belt and was thrown clear, is in hospital with some injuries.

It is too early to say why the car went out of control. First indications are that it was not being driven specially quickly and that only modest amounts of alcohol were consumed in the pub. The police took the heavily damaged car away to test for mechanical failure – tyres or wheels – which seems the most likely explanation.

Meanwhile, we are simply trying to keep Catherine going, and indeed to keep going ourselves. It is hard to believe what has happened. Everyone in this community – itself in a state of considerable shock – is being very helpful, and I must try to get myself together for some BBC recordings of the 'God and Caesar' programmes this afternoon. These cannot easily be postponed as they are the first in a longish series of recording sessions.

Wednesday 30 May 1979

At six o'clock last evening most of the Abbey's inner community joined us for Anthony's funeral, conducted with great sensitivity by the Dean, and I conducted the committal at Putney Vale Crematorium early this morning. This was something Catherine wanted me to do, and indeed I was myself anxious to do it, but it was a harrowing experience. His ashes will be interred in the Cloisters.

The last ten days have been surreal. The violent death of a twenty-five-year-old lies beyond explanation and, naturally enough, Catherine cannot make any sense of it. Nor can Anthony's parents, who are deeply shocked and hurt by the death of their only son, who just ten months ago stood before the High Altar at a glorious Abbey marriage and last evening lay on virtually the same spot – his life on this earth ended.

I think that Christian faith is helpful in the long-term sense that everything will be all right in the end and that in God's providence nothing is ever wasted. But in the shorter term – in the grappling with grief and perplexity – it offers no immediate relief beyond (and I am learning to value this more than ever before) the support of friends who are, I believe, channels of God's love to us.

Yet we are left asking why a God of love allowed these tragedies to happen. I no longer find the traditional, orthodox answer – that suffering is a necessary price for our freedom – at all satisfying. Had I been able to prevent this accident happening I would have moved immediately to do so, and not felt that I was encroaching on anyone's freedom by my action. Is God less caring than I am?

94

Simply to ask this question feels close to blasphemy, and I am therefore drawn to conclude not that God chose to stand aside, as it were, but that because of the nature of his creation he was powerless to intervene. In the act of creation there was a 'letting go', a relinquishing of divine power, a self-limitation. This does not mean that God is absent. I believe that God is always alongside us and suffers with us, and that one day all our suffering will be taken up and transformed into something glorious. Meanwhile we must endure it and try to be open to God's grace to enable us to cope.

I am not sure that many of my friends who are professional theologians will like this way of thinking, but it feels right to me at the moment.

Monday 11 June 1979

Roger Job, our excellent Precentor, is to become Canon Precentor of Winchester Cathedral. He will be greatly missed here. Bernard Rose once described him as the best counter-tenor he had ever had at Magdalen College, Oxford, and he combines a beautiful singing voice with an unerring instinct for the kind of worship that suits Westminster Abbey.

Sadly, he is subject to attacks of disabling migraine which are liable to occur when he is under heavy pressure, and sometimes he has complained to Chapter about the increasing number of special services we are encouraging. He and Douglas Guest are of one mind over this – and much else.

So maybe he will find life somewhat less hectic at Winchester. Michael Stancliffe, the Dean there, snatched him from the hands of Norwich, which was about to claim him.

Friday 22 June 1979

The trial of Jeremy Thorpe and his three co-defendants ended today with verdicts of Not Guilty on the charges of conspiracy to murder Norman Scott, and in Jeremy's case the additional charge of inciting to murder. The case started at the Old Bailey on the 8th of last month, and there have been few days without some new twist to the drama.

Nadir Dinshaw gave his evidence about half-way through the trial, and in his summing up the Judge was kind enough to refer to him as 'a nice, respectable witness'. But it was a great ordeal for him to have to testify against a friend who was seated in the dock only a few feet from the witness stand, and more than a little embarrassing to have to acknowledge the handling of £20,000 which had, almost certainly, been used – unknown to him – for criminal purposes.

We had lunch together yesterday at the Reform Club while the jury was still out, and inevitably the trial dominated the conversation. There is, and has been, no denying that Newton, the airline pilot, confronted Scott with a gun, and the prosecution alleged that he was paid to do so by Holmes acting on behalf of Thorpe. Why only the dog, Rinka, was shot remains a mystery. The explanation of a jammed gun is not convincing, so Newton either lost his nerve or possibly never intended to shoot Scott. The question all along has therefore been, 'What did Thorpe intend?' He chose not to give evidence.

For the charge of murder to stick there would, as the Judge frequently pointed out, need to have been incontrovertible evidence of malign intention. But so many of the witnesses on both sides were such sleazy, untrustworthy characters that it must have been virtually impossible for the jury to determine who was, and was not, telling the truth. So Not Guilty became, it seems, the only possible verdict.

Naturally, Jeremy Thorpe is delighted, but he must know that his political career is now ended, and that is severe punishment for so ambitious a man. Nadir has survived it all, though at a heavy price, and now, following the tragic death of my son-in-law a month ago, it is his turn to prop me up. Which he does with great sensitivity and devotion.

Monday 25 June 1979

Tomorrow I must recommend that the Chapter spends just under £1,000 on the cleaning and conservation of the wax effigy of Charles II. The need for this has become urgent and the work will be carried out by the Textile Conservation Centre, as it is the king's clothes that require attention.

Which is hardly surprising, since they are almost 300 years old. The figure was made during Charles II's lifetime and is apparently a remarkable likeness of him. A contemporary wrote, not long after his death in 1685, ''tis to ye life, and truly to admiration', but unlike many of the effigies it wasn't carried at his funeral.

The king is dressed in his Garter robes, which include a hat with a plume of heron and ostrich feathers. His doublet and breeches are of cloth of silver and his sleeve ruffles and cravat are of Venetian lace. Altogether a splendid figure, and one that is going to need the most expert handling.

Good news today about the Keeper of Muniments. The Librarian reported that he seems to have made a real effort since the crisis shortly before Christmas and has apparently remained in control of himself since then. What is more, he has kept better hours and his output of work has improved. We must keep our fingers crossed.

Another Library item today concerned the possibility of our acquiring a Charter of King Edward the Confessor which was recently bought at Sotheby's by an American dealer for what was said to be a knock-down price of £58,000. This is what is known as a forged charter, in that it was drawn up by monks after the Confessor's death in order to give legitimacy to the land and privileges they already possessed. It dates from the first quarter of the twelfth century and was therefore regarded by mediaeval kings and popes as the Abbey's Foundation Charter – the most important document which the mediaeval Abbey possessed.

The difficulty over this is that we have an agreement with our own Trust that there will be no further appeals for the Abbey until the target for the restoration of our buildings has been reached. It is the case, however, that we can hardly stand in the way of another body raising money, publicly or otherwise, for something that the national interest requires to be retained in this country.

The Dean is to write to Sir John Davis, the Chairman of the Trust, explaining the position.

Thursday 12 July 1979

The Independence Day service for Kiribati – formerly the Gilbert Islands in the Pacific – was not a major Commonwealth event, but it was obviously important for its 67,000 inhabitants, spread over thirty-six small islands in two million square miles of ocean, and for its representatives and people in London.

So they had the usual splendid service for occasions such as this. We tried to avoid involving them in undue expense, but we were not helped in this by the attitude of the Lay Vicars. It was understood, of course, that they would be paid the normal special service fee, but when they heard that the High Commissioner for Australia wished to have a film of the occasion made for showing in the islands they asked for an additional, substantial fee. This was subsequently reduced on the understanding that the film would include only a small amount of the music contributed by the Choir.

The BBC also asked for recording facilities in order that the service might be broadcast on Kiribati local radio, but the Lay Clerks initially refused to accept a reduced fee for this, even though they were assured that the recording would not be used in Britain. Eventually they came round and agreed on a total fee of £30 for the service – not a huge sum, but when multiplied by twelve adding significantly to the total cost of the service.

We are pleased that agreement on these terms was reached, as it would have reflected badly on the Abbey's image had we been driven to submit an inflated account.

Thursday 19 July 1979

Anna Ford, the glamorous ITV news-reader, gave the One People Oration this evening. The presentation was, as one would expect, first-rate, but the content was a bit thin, being a kind of commentary on current affairs from the perspective of a *Guardian* reader. However, after the jingoistic rantings of Sir Arthur Bryant on this occasion two years ago one must not complain.

The choice of Anna Ford to give what is intended to be a substantial contribution to serious thought was somewhat odd. We were, I think, stumped for choice, and when Sebastian Charles suggested Anna, the Dean quickly invited her. Edward Knapp-Fisher was absent from that Chapter meeting, and although he protested against the choice on his return, by this time it was too late. The invitation had been sent and accepted.

To demonstrate just how unfair life can sometimes be, the austere Edward, being Canon-in-Residence, was required to escort the Orator in a procession through the crowded Abbey – she being clad in a see-through dress. I would not have missed this sight for worlds.

Wednesday 25 July 1979

We don't seem to be getting very far with the problem of our investment in Shell. In April we were approached by a Rhodesia Oil Sanctions Working Party to see if we would support a resolution which was to be moved at the Annual General Meeting of Shell on 17 May condemning the participation by the Company in the supply of oil to Rhodesia in contravention of a United Nations sanctions order made in December 1965. The resolution, which was sponsored by the British Council of Churches, the United Society for the Propagation of the Gospel, the

Methodist Overseas Division and the Roman Catholic Diocese of Westminster, also asked the Directors of Shell to give an assurance that the Company would not participate directly or indirectly in the supply of oil or oil products to Rhodesia while the UN sanctions were in force.

At the time of the AGM we were faced with two problems: 1. The Chapter was divided over support of the AGM resolution; 2. Our fund-raising Trust had fairly recently accepted a substantial donation from Shell. Regarding the first, the Dean felt that we could not really take public, controversial action if we were divided – and this was right. As for the second, there is an element of hypocrisy in accepting money from a particular source, then denouncing the means by which the money was obtained by the donor. The truth is of course that we were quite unaware of the Trust's action, and at the time the money was received probably would not have linked it with sanction-breaking. Shell are arguing that the oil is being sent into Rhodesia by their South African company, which is quite independent of the British company.

So we decided to write to Lord Armstrong of Sanderstead, a Director of Shell known to us, to seek a meeting at which we might express our concern and, hopefully, receive from him some reassurance, or at least a cogent explanation. Our first letter evoked no reply and the second, after a long delay, has brought a response from a Shell official in which he simply enclosed a copy of the discussion about sanctions held at his Company's AGM. He hoped this would answer our questions, which of course it doesn't.

Another letter is to go to Shell.

Thursday 23 August 1979

One of the most pleasant summer sights in London is provided by the band concerts given in College Garden at lunchtime on six consecutive Thursdays. The garden is thrown open to the public all day and some hundreds of people come from the surrounding offices with their picnic lunches. We offer soft drinks and provide chairs, though many prefer to sit on the grass.

Enclosed by the mediaeval monastery wall, and with the huge mass of the Abbey and the great Victoria Tower of the Palace of Westminster forming a dramatic background, it is difficult to believe that one is in the heart of a busy city – until, that is, a police or an ambulance siren on Millbank announces an emergency of some sort.

Today, however, heavy rain drove us into the Abbey for the concert and this is obviously a much less attractive setting. Not for the band, though. Many of them pray for rain in order that they may have an opportunity to play in the Abbey – for them the greatest of privileges.

The only problem about this is that a programme designed for the open air becomes ear-splitting when performed in the enclosed space of a building even as large as the Abbey. It can be very unpleasant, and after I had given my customary welcome at 12.30 I was glad to be able to retreat to the Cloisters for a spell. I think we must ask the bands – all of which are absolutely first-class – to bring alternative programmes for outside and inside performances.

Monday 27 August 1979

The jollity of this hot Bank Holiday Monday has given way to a deep sense of shock at the news of the assassination of Earl Mountbatten of Burma. Evidently he was on holiday in the fishing village of Mullaghmore, just south of the border between Northern Ireland and the Irish Republic – something he has done for many years past. Late this morning he set off on a fishing trip with several members of his family, and shortly after leaving the small harbour the boat was torn apart by an IRA bomb.

According to the latest BBC News, the Earl, his grandson Nicholas (aged fourteen), and a boatman (aged seventeen) were killed instantly. His daughter, Lady Brabourne, her son Timothy, and her mother-in-law, the Dowager Lady Brabourne, were seriously injured and are now in intensive care. The IRA has claimed responsibility for the murders and says that the bomb was detonated from the shore by remote control. Naturally, just what kind of security arrangements were in force has not been disclosed, but some reports suggest that the Earl refused to have any when he was on holiday. The IRA is now conducting a vicious campaign, and eighteen British soldiers were also killed yesterday by another remote-controlled bomb, again near the border, but in County Down on the eastern side of the island.

There will now have to be a great funeral in the Abbey. The service itself was, I know, planned in great detail several years ago, and the Earl was much involved in this. There should be a file in the Chapter Office safe. But the immediate requirement is to get the Dean back from his holiday in Jersey and the Receiver General from his holiday in France. Both will be key figures in the planning of what is bound to be a major state event.

I met the Earl a few times at parties and receptions after Abbey services he had attended in an official capacity, but although he is an impressive figure, I never found him an attractive man to talk to. Rather too much of the *haut en bas* attitude to make for easy conversation. There are, I know, those who believe that he was given to self-aggrandisement and that his merits have been much overrated, but we shall not hear much of this over the next few days, and a popular public figure will be widely mourned.

Monday 3 September 1979

Westminster Abbey and its precincts have been turned into a fortress. Such is the alarm created by the IRA's assassination of Earl Mountbatten, and the knowledge that the whole of the Royal Family, many Heads of State from other parts of the world, and leading politicians will be assembling here for the funeral on Wednesday, that the utmost security precautions are being taken.

We have all been issued with identity cards, and even Canons cannot enter the Abbey without scrutiny by soldiers and policemen. We have had to move our cars out of Dean's Yard, and the whole atmosphere is crisis-ridden. But soon after lunch today I went across to St Margaret's and on the way back decided to go into the Abbey through the nearby Poets' Corner entrance. There was no one on duty there and I walked to the centre of the building without even seeing anyone. Had I wished to plant a bomb, it would have been the easiest thing in the world to achieve.

The building will, of course, be searched and searched before the service, but my experience showed just how easily the tightest security can be relaxed. I reported this to the Receiver General, who called in the police and the military. Considerable consternation was expressed and disciplinary action is being taken.

Otherwise preparations for the funeral seem to be going well, and the television people are installing all their equipment. Allocating seats is something of a challenge, but the Lord Chamberlain's department knows everything that is to be known about procedure and protocol, so they have more or less taken over that side of things.

It seems that the Earl envisaged a state funeral, and his 'suggestions', which in the circumstances are tantamount to instructions, neglect no detail of ceremonial or of the people he wished to be involved. Only by advance planning is it possible to organize an event such as this at nine days' notice.

The funeral was, as anticipated, an extraordinary, dramatic occasion combining the tragedy of death by assassination and the panoply of state recognition and mourning. The Queen and the whole of the Royal Family came, together with some European royals of whom I had never previously heard – King Simeon of Bulgaria, King Umberto of Italy, King Michael and Queen Anne of Roumania, and King Constantine and Queen Anne-Marie of the Hellenes. I suppose the Earl must have known them all.

The Heads of State required a procession of their own and, naturally enough, there was a tremendous military presence and some martial music provided by the Royal Marines' School of Music. It was a curious experience, standing at the Great West Door immediately before the service and seeing on the television monitor screens the procession making its way along crowded streets, from the Queen's Chapel at St James's Palace to the Abbey. What seemed during this time to be a little distant and remote suddenly became real and immediate as the coffin was carried off the television screen, as it were, and into our close presence at the door. The sight of the Earl's young grandsons walking behind the coffin along with the Duke of Edinburgh, the Prince of Wales and other Royal Dukes, was a reminder of the family dimension of the occasion. We were also aware that other members of the family had been killed in company with the Earl, and these now include the Dowager Lady Brabourne, who has died of her injuries.

The service itself was quite simple. Hymns – 'God of our fathers, known of old'; 'I vow to thee, my country'; 'And did those feet in ancient time'; and 'Eternal Father, strong to save'. The Prince of Wales, obviously under great stress, read part of Psalm 107, 'They that go down to the sea in ships: and occupy their business in great waters'. The Choir sang William Harris's lovely anthem based on a poem by Edmund Spenser, 'Fair is the heaven', and the prayers were led by the Archbishop of Canterbury, the Archbishop of Westminster and a number of other church leaders, including the Chaplain of the Fleet.

There was no address. Apparently the Earl wished the service to be kept short and suggested that there should be no address unless the Prime Minister felt moved to say a word. In this case the address was to be short and to concentrate on Lord Mountbatten's efforts in the East and his personal leadership in helping to set a line on which the British Empire changed itself into a Commonwealth of sovereign states.

It seems that the Prime Minister did not feel so moved, which is perhaps just as well, and in any case she probably would not have wished to have the content of her address dictated to her. It is also fair to assume that the Earl did not envisage the possibility of a woman giving the address at his funeral.

Immediately after the service there was a most poignant scene as we stood outside the Great West Door, in company with the Royal Family and the Earl's family, watching the coffin being carried away on a Land Rover, with an escort of Life Guards, to Waterloo Station. It then went by train for interment in Romsey Abbey – the Earl's parish church.

Friday 7 September 1979

The announcement that Bob Runcie of St Albans is to be the next Archbishop of Canterbury occasioned no great surprise. On the strength of the Military Cross he won in 1944, the *Evening Standard* billboards said 'War hero to be Archbishop'.

I was accidentally involved in a minor kerfuffle over this morning's announcement which led to charges of breach of embargo against the BBC. Some three to four weeks ago a news reporter asked me to record a speculative interview about the likely identity of the next Archbishop. In the course of the interview I suggested that Robert Runcie was almost certain to be appointed, he being the best in a rather mediocre field. For some reason unknown to me, the recording was put on one side and not immediately used.

Last evening, however, while dining with Nadir Dinshaw in the Reform Club, I heard a rumour that an announcement about the new Archbishop was imminent. So I telephoned the BBC newsroom and told them that if they intended to use the interview with me they had better do so quickly, otherwise it would become out of date.

The recording was broadcast at 7.45 this morning, by which time the official announcement of Bob Runcie's appointment was in the hands of the media with an 11 a.m. embargo. This was not known to the producer who put out my piece, but the resulting impression was that the interview had been contrived in order to make the BBC first with the news. It was in fact a sheer accident of timing.

Monday 10 September 1979

Edward Knapp-Fisher and I had a private meeting with the Dean last evening to express our concern at the marked deterioration in our community life over the last twelve months. Until David Edwards moved to

Norwich in April 1978 the Dean and Canons saw a good deal of one another – at the daily services and at various other formal and informal events. Before and after these occasions there were opportunities for conversation while walking through the Cloister to and from the Abbey or the Deanery. But much of this has now gone and we are together relatively infrequently, apart from Chapter meetings.

The reason for this is twofold. John Baker is throwing himself – very effectively – into his responsibilties as Rector of St Margaret's and he is, of course, also Speaker's Chaplain. Inevitably, this is now absorbing a great deal of his time, though it may be that he will eventually redress the balance somewhat and give a little more to the Abbey.

Far more worrying is the position of Sebastian Charles, who has none of these additional responsibilities but of whom we see very little, except when he is actually on duty in the Abbey, either as Canon-in-Residence or officiating at one of the daily eucharists. Before he came here his work at the British Council of Churches, and before that as an industrial and university chaplain, obviously did not involve him in the disciplines of daily worship, and it seems that he is unwilling to embrace these now that he is part of a community in which worship is paramount. Nor does he apparently recognize much responsibility for supporting other elements in our corporate life, and I gather that he spends most evenings in his former haunts in South East London.

All of this has been an anxiety for some time, but the tackling of the problem is made more urgent by the impending arrival of a new Precentor and a new Chaplain. The holders of these two, more junior, appointments are bound to be influenced sooner or later by the example of the Dean and Chapter, and this could lead to further deterioration in the quality of our life.

We had a frank discussion with the Dean, who sees the problem just as clearly as we do and is troubled by it. The only point of divergence is that his marvellous liberalism leads him to have such respect for the freedom of the individual that he never wishes to impose anything upon anyone. I think it may also be the case that he has been here so long – twenty-seven years now – that he has grown accustomed to a certain ebb and flow in the Chapter's commitment to worship and community.

Anyway, he has agreed to convene a meeting at which these matters can be discussed – frankly but charitably.

Monday 24 September 1979

We had an informal meeting at the Deanery this evening to discuss the anxieties about the deteriorating quality of our community life which Edward Knapp-Fisher and I expressed to the Dean a fortnight ago. I am not sure that we got very far.

John Baker explained what pressure he is under, coping with three different jobs and also trying to do some work for the wider church. This is of course fully understood and we were grateful for his undertaking to try to attend the daily services in the Abbey a little more frequently.

The position of Sebastian Charles is altogether different, since he has no other special responsibilities, and although we raised the issue of our rarely being together at worship in the most delicate way, he reacted by accusing us of launching a personal attack on him.

It is difficult to know how to interpret this. Possibly he feels guilty about his absences, which sometimes extend over several weeks, and can only cope with this by lashing out at those who call attention to the problem. Or it may be that he does not have the faintest notion of what is involved in the creating and maintaining of a Christian community such as this.

Either way, it seems unlikely that things are going to be very different in the future, which is very depressing, because the very basis of what we are about is undermined.

Monday 8 October 1979

Mystery surrounds the disappearance from the wall of the West Cloister of a monument to Frances Louisa Parnell, a five-year-old child who was buried under the pavement beneath it in 1812. We were quite unaware that it had ever existed until a member of the family wrote to the Dean last month to complain that it was no longer there.

Reference to the Monuments' Register indicated that it had been erected by the child's 'afflicted and disconsolate mother' and was certainly still in place at the end of the nineteenth century. Peter Foster, the Surveyor of the Fabric, believes that it may have disappeared some time between 1963 and 1967 when restoration work was being undertaken in that Cloister.

But monuments, and this one was fairly large, are not normally stolen, since they have no market value and hardly make an attractive decoration in a home. One possible explanation is that the monument fell from the wall and broke into many pieces. The workmen, noting perhaps that the lettering was no longer clear, simply dumped the fragments and kept quiet about it, expecting, or at least hoping, that no one would notice. Little did they realize that few activities are more hazardous than the removal of monuments and tombstones, since aggrieved relatives always turn up sooner or later.

The Surveyor tells us that a smaller replacement, incorporating some but not all of its elaborate inscription, will cost about £1,500. Question: who is to pay for this? The relative may well think it is our responsibility, but I am afraid he will have to be told that it is impossible for the Dean and Chapter to maintain the 700–800 memorials in the Abbey.

Wednesday 24 October 1979

The position over the acquisition of the King Edward the Confessor Charter has become complicated inasmuch as the American dealer who purchased this at Sotheby's has withdrawn his application for an export licence. This means that the Friends of the National Libraries no longer feel that they can launch a successful appeal to secure the Charter for the Abbey. The chief aim of such an appeal would be to retain it in this country, and if there is no risk of it going abroad, no money will be forthcoming.

We are therefore on our own over this and and in urgent need of a benefactor, since we cannot ourselves launch an appeal because of our agreement with the Abbey Trust.

Tuesday 13 November 1979

The Organist and Master of the Choristers has received a telephone call from America inviting the Choir to spend Christmas over there, giving recitals and singing in various churches during the festival.

This ties in with a question sometimes asked by American visitors to the Abbey – Are worship services still held here? They are astonished to learn that twenty-five such services are held every week, and apparently the telephone enquirer was equally astonished to be told that the Choir will be leading the Abbey's worship at Christmas.

1980

Tuesday 1 January 1980

The Christmas services, extending from Christmas Eve until Holy Innocents Day, once again attracted huge crowds and met a wide variety of needs, though the present pattern – established many years ago – shows some signs of tiredness. Having said that, however, it has to be recognized that a high proportion of those who come are visitors, experiencing the Abbey's worship for the first, and perhaps the only time, in their lives. Any 'tiredness' is more likely to be felt by those of us who are regulars, but this may influence the atmosphere as a whole.

The chief problem continues to be the Midnight Eucharist on Christmas Eve. The building was full to capacity soon after 11.15 p.m., and some hundreds of people had to be directed to St Margaret's. There was a great sense of expectation, but without the Choir it was impossible to create the kind of vibrant worship necessary to a large crowd in a large building. A small group of singers from Kensington sang carols beautifully during the Communion, but for the rest it was simply a 'said' service with hymns.

This year the Blessing of the Crib at the beginning of the service was a helpful innovation, but the introduction of a commentary at various points in the service was, I thought, disastrous. The last thing required in an act of worship is interruption with didactic material. Liturgy is a form of drama, and no one would dream of breaking into a stage play or an opera with explanations of what it was all about. So we had better not have this again.

There are two reasons why we cannot field the Choir at midnight. The Organist and Headmaster tell us that it is too late for the Choristers and the Lay Vicars are prepared to turn out only if we will let them off Evensong on Christmas Day. At the moment this seems an intractable problem. Curiously enough, those who are diverted from the Abbey to St Margaret's do much better, since there they find a professional choir (men and women) singing a Mozart or a Haydn Mass.

Lawrence Tanner, whose memorial service was held this afternoon, must, I think, have been Britain's most distinguished local historian – local for him being Westminster Abbey and its immediate environs. He was born in 1890 in a house just outside the precincts at the time when his father was Senior Assistant Master at Westminster School and, apart from seven years spent at Cambridge and in the wartime army, he continued to live just around the corner until his death, shortly before Christmas.

Naturally, he attended Westminster School and, having read history at Pembroke College, Cambridge and served as a Lieutenant in the 1914–18 war, returned to the School to teach history until 1932. In 1926, however, he took on the additional duties of Keeper of the Muniments at the Abbey and by 1932 had become so absorbed by its archival history that he gave up teaching in order to concentrate on his work in the Muniments Room and the Library. He was also Librarian from 1956–72, and at the time of his retirement was probably the oldest librarian in the country.

There was apparently nothing about the recorded history of the Abbey that he did not know. He loved the place and for nearly half a century placed his impeccable scholarship at its disposal. This proved to be invaluable when the Coronations of King George VI and the present Queen were being planned, since he knew all the precedents for the various rites and ceremonies. On both occasions he held the title Gold Staff Officer.

His learned books about the Abbey were widely acclaimed, honours were heaped upon him by the historical societies, and the Queen gave him a CVO. But he was never happier than when showing visitors the archives or taking them on what proved to be an unforgettable tour of the Abbey. And he was responsible for opening up of the muniments to scholars from all over the world.

The sight of his venerable figure in the Cloisters and his friendly, albeit brief, conversations with a newly-arrived Canon I shall always remember.

Thursday 24 January 1980

Although I am firmly wedded to the church's sacramental life and am at the altar every day, except on Saturday morning when I have a lie-in, Evensong remains very special for me. It is, I think, the Church of

England's greatest contribution to the worshipping life of the world church, though I dare say it may not seem like this to Christians in Central Africa and Latin America.

The opportunity to share in daily Evensong, led by a choir such as our own in a building of great beauty where worship has been offered without a break for over 900 years, is a rare privilege that I would not have missed for the world, though there are of course occasions when other commitments keep me away.

Hence the joy of being Canon-in-Residence, as I am this month, when duty requires me to be present every day of the month. The congregation today was only small – a dozen or so, I suppose, besides the choir and the clergy – and outside it was cold and wet, with sleet mixed in the rain. But the singing of the Psalms (the first four sections of the wonderful No.119) and the Canticles (Byrd's Second Service), together with Byrd's anthem 'Sing joyfully', was, in turn, thrilling, challenging and consoling. I read the First Lesson and the Dean the Second, while the Precentor led some apposite prayers.

As with all true worship, there was the sense of being caught up into something infinitely greater than one's self. The Abbey was virtually empty, yet in a sense it felt as if it were full – every nook and cranny suffused with the divine. Because of this, I don't think it much matters if one's mind sometimes strays, as mine does, from the actual words being used. The worship still goes on, and when concentration returns there is not the slightest sense of discontinuity.

At the end we processed into the empty Nave, the Dean bowed to the Choir, and after a brief word with members of the dispersing congregation, I walked slowly through the gas-lit Cloisters, sheltered from the rain and conscious of having shared in a true *Opus Dei*.

Tuesday 29 January 1980

In my Annual Report today it was necessary to point out a number of financial problems that have arisen during the last year and which look seriously threatening for the current year. The number of visitors paying for entry to the Royal Chapels fell from 1,410,600 to 1,220,300 – this 15.5% decline corresponding almost exactly with the general decline in the number of visitors to London.

Since we rely on visitors for 75% of our income, such a decline is bound to have serious repercussions, and during the first quarter of the current year, October–December, there has been a further fall of 14%. If this continues throughout the year, the projected surplus of £40,000 will become a deficit of £10,000 unless remedial action is taken. The contrast between this and the £250,000 surpluses we had in 1977 and 1979 shows the near impossibility of accounts budgetting.

There is at the moment no sign of inflation being brought under control and we have been obliged to allow 15% for this in the current year's budget. The salaries of our senior and office staff have had to be increased by no less than 25% – partly because of cost-of-living needs but mainly because of a substantial upward movement in the Civil Service scales to which their pay is linked.

Last November, after long discussions with the Heads of all departments, I presented the Chapter with alternative budget proposals in case we are ever faced with a desperate financial situation. These indicated that across the board cuts of 5% and 10% would result in savings of the order of £40,000 and £80,000 respectively, but none of these could be achieved without seriously damaging the Abbey's ministry and many of the individuals involved in its life.

I offered five options for dealing with the immediate situation, but it was decided – rightly, I think – to monitor things for a further three months in the hope that the spring will show an upturn in the number of visitors. A working party is also to examine what would be involved in charging visitors for entrance to the Abbey, exemption being offered to those entering for worship and prayer. I am strongly against this, but recognize the need to think the unthinkable in times of crisis.

Thursday 31 January 1980

During the course of the now concluded Audit Chapter I raised in my report the thorny problem of the Treasurer's responsibilities:

'It has become clear to me during the last year that the demands made of the Treasurer himself, in the areas of information, planning and decision-making, have changed the character of the Canonry he is honoured to hold. I suspect that the Treasurership has never been a sinecure office, but during the present century at least there has developed the tradition that the Canons of Westminster might have time for reflection and the opportunity to make some *substantial* contribution to the wider life of the Church through their scholarship and writing. I would, I believe, be failing in my duty if I did not place on record what is already obvious to sensitive observers, namely that the responsibilities of the Treasurer, as these have evolved and seem certain to be continued, are now in serious conflict with this tradition.'

John Baker resigned from the Treasurership because its duties were not compatible with his work as a scholar, and although he immediately took on the responsibilities of the Rector of St Margaret's, this does not undermine the validity of the point he was making.

We had a good discussion about this without reaching any real conclusions, and we are to discuss it again next month. The only solution I can envisage is that the Treasurer should hold office for only a limited period, say three to four years, but this would only work if we had a supply of Canons capable of doing this job.

Wednesday 27 February 1980

The Byron Society has been pressing us to accept a bust of Lord Byron for installation in Poets' Corner, but we have declined it, though not for the reason that led to the great man being denied burial in the Abbey in 1824.

That was at the time, and for some years following, a *cause célèbre*, for the then Dean not only denied him burial but also refused a statue of him – in both cases because of Byron's immoral way of life. On the day of his funeral the hearse passed by the Abbey, and this led Macaulay to write:

'We cannot even now retrace the close of the brilliant and miserable career of the most celebrated Englishman of the nineteenth century, without feeling something of what was felt by those who saw the hearse with its long train of coaches turn slowly northwards, leaving behind it that cemetery which had been consecrated by the dust of so many great poets, but of which the doors were closed against all that remained of Byron.'

He was buried in the village church at Hucknall, not far from where I was brought up in Nottinghamshire, but he was given recognition almost 150 years later when, on 8 May 1969, a white marble memorial was placed in the floor of Poets' Corner – the gift of the Poetry Society.

It is the existence of this memorial that has led us to decline the bust. Not even Byron can be permitted two memorials in Westminster Abbey, but the Dean, who is one of his great admirers, hopes that the bust may find a place in the Deanery. I doubt, however, whether this is what the Byron Society has in mind.

The Chapter has agreed to my proposal that we should explore the possibility of the Norman Undercroft being turned into a coffee shop. This only remaining part of Edward the Confessor's Abbey now houses the Museum, and although some important items are displayed there – most notably the wax effigies – it is not really of a standard appropriate to the late twentieth century. The best items could well be moved to a refurbished Infirmer's Hall in the Little Cloister or to the neglected Cheyneygates rooms which form part of the Deanery.

I have made this proposal for two reasons. First, because there is nowhere in the immediate vicinity of the Abbey where visitors can obtain refreshments. Two ice-cream vans are permitted to operate on the Parliament Square side of our site, and unauthorized villains, operating barrows, charge extortionate prices for cans of lemonade. Apart from Grandma Lee's, opposite Big Ben and some distance from the Abbey, there is no possibility of buying a cup of tea or coffee. A number of cathedrals report that the provision of refreshment facilities is helping to strengthen what they call their ministry of welcome.

Then, of course, there is an urgent need for us to increase our regular income and it seems obvious that a well-run coffee shop, selling light refreshments, would make a great deal of money. I explained to the Chapter that there would be no point in exploring any of this if they were absolutely opposed to the idea. But, thankfully, they are not.

Wednesday 12 March 1980

Some Westminster School boys who have their meals in College Hall have taken to throwing banana skins and orange peel down in the Deanery Courtyard and the Cloisters. The cleaners recently gathered up 4 lbs of roast potatoes and other foodstuffs which had been scattered in the Courtyard. The newly lime-washed walls of the Dark Cloister are also being used as a 'dart board' for apple cores.

All of which is, of course, tiresome and in the case of the fruit skins potentially dangerous, not least for the Dean, whose sight is limited. A strong letter of protest is to go to the Headmaster.

Although I have not researched the matter, I suspect that incidents of this sort are a recurring theme in the long history of the Abbey and the School. It is just the kind of thing that is likely to happen when two such institutions are co-existing in a limited space. And in the hot-house atmosphere of these communities the significance of most things tends to be exaggerated.

Which is not to say that the misbehaviour of the Westminster boys is to be tolerated: simply that it should not surprise us.

Tuesday 25 March 1980

To Canterbury today for the Enthronement of Bob Runcie as Archbishop. Jo and I spent the night in our house in Sandwich, partly to keep an eye on the place and partly to avoid the inconvenience of travelling from Victoria this morning in a train full of clergymen.

During the late morning we met our friends, Lawrence and Faith Jackson, who had come down from Blackburn, and together we had the most appalling of lunches in the dreariest of pubs. A number of people stopped me in the streets near the cathedral to say that they were watching and enjoying my television series 'The Controversialists', but this momentary fame will soon fade. 'Once seen, never remembered' are Oscar Wilde's reassuring words.

Shortly before entering the cathedral we heard the news of the murder of Archbishop Oscar Romero and it was a strange experience to be seated a few moments later within sight of the spot where another archbishop, Thomas Becket, was murdered eight centuries ago. Quite a thought for a new Archbishop on the day of his Enthronement.

The cathedral was crowded with familiar faces and Bob looked a splendid sight in a white and gold cope and mitre – the work no doubt of Jennie Boyd-Carpenter. It is obviously an advantage for an archbishop to be tall, as it was for Michael Ramsey to look venerable.

Bob preached a fine sermon on Christian Authority and he has a remarkable capacity for the striking, memorable phrase:

'If the Church acts as if it possessed its answers to life's problems tied up in neat packages, it may be heard for a time. It may rally some waverers; but its influence will not last. It will confirm others in their suspicions and hostility. To them it will mean that the Church, like every other human institution, is making a bid for power.'

He spoke of a forthcoming visit to Central Africa for the enthronement of an archbishop for a new French-speaking province and said,

'This service in Canterbury, so carefully prepared, so magnificently beautiful, speaks eloquently of the glory of God and the dignity which God gives to men by loving them. But it may be that the simple service

113

to which I shall go in Africa will prove more eloquent about the uncluttered way in which the Church should live now, about the unpretentious character of real Christian authority.'

All good stuff, and encouraging that the 102nd Archbishop of Canterbury should be thinking in these terms. But one cannot help believing that it has become an impossible job for any man to do adequately. Small wonder that it took Bob six weeks to decide whether or not to accept it.

Monday 21 April 1980

There was a nasty incident in St Margaret's today. A man came into the church, ordered all the visitors out and then locked himself in. The police were sent for, and when the man heard them forcing entry he took the cross and candlesticks from the altar and threw them to the floor. He also damaged the altar frontal. The police naturally arrested him, but all the signs suggest mental disturbance rather than criminality.

The security of St Margaret's is a serious problem, since it is proving exceedingly difficult to recruit a Verger of adequate calibre. John Baker, the Rector, was obliged to dismiss the latest recruit just over a fortnight ago and until another is found, improvisation is the only option.

We, and I suspect this is also true of all the cathedrals, have yet to tackle the issue of what kind of presence is required in the Abbey and St Margaret's during opening hours. The traditional concept of the Verger's role, reflected in both his or her pay and status, is that of someone who performs fairly menial tasks. Yet the Verger is the church's front-line representative in its encounter with huge numbers of visitors, and maintaining a proper balance between welcome and security calls for great skill.

The image of the Verger (possibly the name Verger) needs to be changed and a different kind of person recuited – at great cost, no doubt.

Thursday 1 May 1980

Robert Runcie, the new Archbishop of Canterbury, came this morning to consecrate some bishops. Since it was his first official visit to the Abbey since he became Archbishop, we read the 'Protest'. This, in so many words, challenged his right to come to the Abbey and required him, as a condition of entering the building, to acknowledge that he has here no rights, jurisdiction or precedence.

The origin of the 'Protest' goes back to the Middle Ages, when the Pope exempted some of the major Benedictine abbeys in Europe from local episcopal jurisdiction. These communities were therefore answerable directly to the Pope, which gave him useful power bases in every country. It also gave the communities freedom to develop their own religious life without undue interference.

Westminster was among the exempt abbeys, and when the monastery was suppressed at the sixteenth-century Reformation the exemption was retained – the only difference being that the Abbey related directly to the Crown, rather than to the Pope. Hence the description of the Abbey as a Royal Peculiar, placing it outside the jurisdiction of either the Bishop of London or the Archbishop of Canterbury. The 'Protest' was retained also in order to assert the Abbey's independence at the beginning of every new archiepiscopal ministry.

But it has now become something of an anomaly and is a little embarrassing. While we are certainly keen to protect the Abbey's independence, our relations with the Archbishop of Canterbury are invariably cordial, and whenever he comes here we are generally pleased to see him.

We discussed this at some length in Chapter earlier this year and decided to modify the wording of the 'Protest' – removing its bleakest phraseology – and to follow it with an expression of warm welcome to the new Archbishop.

When the moment for this came today the Archbishop seemed distinctly unamused. He was surrounded by the many other bishops who were taking part in the consecration service, and a couple of lawyers, in wigs, were on hand to see that the document of disclaimer was duly signed.

I cannot believe that the Archbishop was annoyed by this reminder that his writ does not run everywhere. He has quite enough responsibility beyond these precincts to keep him occupied. I suspect that he was a little irritated by what he may well have regarded as the nonsense factor in the ceremony. It hardly expresses the spiritual warmth that comes with fellowship in the gospel.

The 'Protest' should also be read whenever a new Bishop of London appears on the Abbey scene, but for some reason this was dropped many years ago. If, as is often predicted, Graham Leonard of Truro is translated to London when Gerald Ellison retires next year, I would strongly favour its revival.

We now have an opportunity to secure the Charter of Edward the Confessor which came on to the market last year but for which we could not find the necessary money. I attended a meeting last month with the Dean, the Librarian, the Receiver General and a Mr Jack Lunzer – a noted Jewish bibliophile who is both rich and generous.

He is anxious to acquire the copy of the Babylonian Talmud, in nine volumes, which we have in our Library. This is an early sixteenth-century copy and, as far as I am aware, is never consulted. His suggestion is therefore that he should buy the Charter from the American dealer (who bought it for £58,000 plus commission at Sothebys and is now prepared to sell it for £63,000) and present it to the Abbey. In return for this we will give him the Talmud.

My only reservation about this proposal was related to the possibility that the Talmud might be worth considerably more than £63,000, but a number of experts have advised us that it would be unlikely to fetch more than £50,000 at auction, and from this the auctioneers would claim 10% commission. A Hebrew expert at the British Library believes it would be in our best interests to accept Mr Lunzer's offer.

The Chapter has agreed to do so and it will be wonderful to restore the Charter to the place where it belongs.

As anticipated, a very large number of applications have been received for the post of Organist and Master of the Choristers, though a good many of these could hardly have expected to get the job. Today we met our advisers, Sir David Willcocks, Dr Bernard Rose, Dr Francis Jackson, and our own Douglas Guest, to consider their suggested short list.

First, however, Douglas Guest gave us his opinion about the nature of the job, based on his own experience since he came here in 1963. This was a rather depressing statement, reflecting more of his own predilection and offering no sort of vision of what the Abbey's music might become under new leadership. He suggested that if the Organist made the Abbey his true priority he would have no time to undertake overseas visits with the Choir, or even as a recitalist. Furthermore, commercial recordings were ruled out by the difficulty of bringing together the Lay Vicars, who had many other professional engagements. Nor would it be possible to do much broadcasting, because the Lay Vicars' fees, determined by Equity, always frightened away the BBC and ITV. In any case, the Choristers could not undertake any more work without risking their education or their health.

I am not sure if this was offered as a defence of Douglas's own inactivity or whether it was an attempt to dissuade us from appointing Simon Preston, but Simon's name is on the short list, along with John Birch of Chichester, Martin Neary of Winchester, Christopher Robinson of St George's, Windsor and Roy Massey of Hereford.

David Willcocks advised us that any of these five would be capable of doing the job well and after lunch he and the other advisers suggested that we should add to the short list the name of Gerre Hancock – the highly-thought-of Organist of St Thomas's, Fifth Avenue, New York. We decided not to accept this suggestion but left it that if, when the choir of St Thomas's gives a short recital in the Abbey next month, we are sufficiently impressed with Mr Hancock, we shall invite him to join the short list.

The interviews will be held on 16 June.

Thursday 8 May 1980

The Receiver General and I have been to the Treasury to discuss with one of its senior officials a delicate problem arising from Lord Mountbatten's funeral last September. There were of course certain costs to the Abbey involved in this major event, and these have been fully reimbursed by the Treasury.

But the closure of the Abbey for several days before the funeral caused us to lose a significant amount of revenue – about £9,000 – from visitors. In my view, we ought to be compensated for this loss.

The Chapter recognizes that this is a tricky matter inasmuch as a dispute between ourselves and the Treasury over a tragic event that greatly moved the nation would not win much public sympathy. But quite apart from the £9,000, which we can ill afford to lose, there is a question of principle which needs to be established.

The preparations for the Coronation in 1953 required the Abbey to be closed for nine months. All the services were held in St Margaret's, and eventually most of the revenue lost by the Dean and Chapter because of the closure was recouped from entrance fees charged to people who wished to see the Abbey as it had been on the day of the Coronation.

But the financing of the Abbey in those days was on an entirely different scale from what it will be at the next Coronation – an event which we hope and pray lies in the distant future. A nine-months' closure then will lead to a revenue loss of millions of pounds and spell catastrophe.

All this Reg Pullen and I put to the Treasury Accountant. Regarding the funeral he took the line that it was impossible for him to authorize payment for anything that had not previously been agreed. Nor could there be reimbursement for something that was incapable of being precisely quantified, i.e. the number of people who might have paid fees or bought guide books during the period of the Abbey's closure.

This seemed to me to be a typical Treasury approach, and I dare say that we could get his decision overturned if we went to the top. But we don't wish to create a fuss and are content to let the matter rest. What emerged from the discussion at the Treasury, however, is that just as soon as the plans for a major event, such as a Coronation, are being made, the Dean and Chapter must raise the issue of revenue loss during any period of closure that may be needed.

Tuesday 27 May 1980

The Chapter has strongly advised the Dean to refuse permission for the Richard III Society to examine by modern scientific methods the sarcophagus which is believed to contain the bones of Edward V and his brother, Richard, Duke of York, 'The Princes in the Tower'. They are alleged to have been murdered on the orders of their uncle, Richard III, in 1483.

The bones were evidently found at the foot of a staircase in the Tower of London in 1674 and Charles II, presuming them to be the bones of the sons of Edward IV, had them placed in a sarcophagus which was inserted into the East wall of the North aisle of Henry VII's Chapel.

No one knows for sure whose bones they are, and doubtless the Richard III Society would dearly love to be able to demonstrate that their hero was not a murderer. But, as the Dean readily acknowledges, it simply is not on for royal tombs in Westminster Abbey to be opened and subjected to scientific investigation in the hope of solving historical conundrums. Where would this stop?

Even if we were willing, the Queen would have to give her consent – a most unlikely eventuality. After our experience of opening, for quite different reasons, the Stuart vault in 1977 it will, I think, be a very long time before anything similar is authorized.

When the history of Westminster Abbey in the second half of the twentieth century comes to be written it will need to be recorded that it was under my Treasurership that the Abbey ceased to have any stonemasons on its staff – possibly for the first time ever.

Which is not to say, of course, that stonemasons are no longer at work on the building. On the contrary, a large team of masons is engaged on a major restoration programme that will encompass the entire building and cost at least £10 million. But virtually all of this is being carried out by specialist contractors, and our team of a foreman, three masons and three apprentices spends 75% of its time working with the contractors.

My recommendation that the teams should be fully integrated was stimulated by the knowledge that the contractors were about to give their masons substantial pay increases – bringing them up to £8,000 per annum – which we simply could not match. So now the paymaster will be the Abbey Trust, and we shall pay only for any work undertaken by the contractors outside the restoration programme.

From the point of view of tradition this is a sad move, but when the restoration is completed, hopefully before the year 2000, the Abbey will doubtless re-establish its masons' department for the never-ending work of conservation.

If ever I find myself on the wrong side of the law, I hope that Edward Carpenter, our Dean, will be available to speak for me in court.

One Friday afternoon some weeks ago, shortly before the Choir was due to start its weekly rehearsal in the Choir stalls, a Verger noticed an apparently sleeping figure in a stall immediately behind those to be occupied by the musicians. It turned out to be the director of another London choir – a flamboyant figure, well known to us – who had evidently had a very good lunch. The Verger judged that it would be best to leave him undisturbed.

The strains of the Abbey Choir in rehearsal, however, soon woke him up and he staggered to the side of Douglas Guest, the Organist, and began to point out various errors he believed to have discerned in his conducting technique. Dr Guest was not amused and called for the Vergers to remove the intruder.

This they accomplished without too much of a struggle, and shortly after setting foot in Victoria Street, Dr Guest's erstwhile tutor was arrested by the police and escorted to Cannon Row Police Station where he was charged with being drunk and disorderly. All this was reported to me, as Canon-in-Residence, and twice during the evening I telephoned the police station to enquire about the well-being of the musician in the cell. At about nine o'clock I was informed that he had been released.

This morning, well before lunch, he appeared in the Bow Street Court and the Dean was in court to speak on his behalf. And so eloquently and so convincingly did Edward speak that the Magistrate returned a verdict of Not Guilty.

Tuesday 17 June 1980

Simon Preston is to be our next Organist and Master of the Choristers. Most of yesterday was spent in the exhausting task of interviewing the five short-listed candidates and it was a remarkable array of talent – I suppose the best there is in church music today.

All interviewed well. John Birch came through as the highly professional musician that he is and Ray Massey as the very nice chap that he is. Martin Neary was, I suspect, the most hungry for the post and Christopher Robinson, obviously a sensitive man, seemed a little nervous. Simon Preston, who had not actually applied but indicated that if invited he would be interested, displayed some keenness to return to the Abbey, where he was Sub-Organist from 1962–67, but it was the muted enthusiasm of someone with sufficient confidence in his own outstanding ability not to mind overmuch if he failed to be appointed.

In the early stages of the selection process I thought the choice would be between Martin Neary and Christopher Robinson, which is what Bernard Rose and Douglas Guest (close friends) wished. But once Simon Preston appeared on the scene there was really no choice, because he is reckoned to be one of the world's best organists and combines this with unusual gifts as a choir director.

Until the interview I had not met him, but I found him to be an engagingly attractive character, and although we have been warned against a degree of prima donna-ism in him, we all feel that the risk is worth taking. Since he is not only the Organist but also a Lecturer in Music at Christ Church, he is going to cost us more than we had bargained for, but we are agreed that if we are to have the best we must be ready to pay its price.

The glass porch erected inside the Great West Door is now complete and operational, though a number of teething problems still need to be sorted out. In fact, the whole scheme has been beset with problems.

Its origin goes back to the Mountbatten funeral last September when, for ceremonial purposes, the Victorian/Edwardian wooden porch had to be removed. This was an unworthy, depressing object and once it had been taken away it was clear that it should never be returned. The magnificent view of the Abbey through the open, unobstructed door which we had at the time of the funeral needed to be preserved. A glass porch was the answer.

But the making and installation of this proved to be more easily ordered than constructed. The very considerable weight of the glass created structural problems and at one stage the District Surveyor – a difficult man – declared it to be unsafe. The necessary adjustments then left the doors ill-fitting and certain to admit blasts of cold air in the winter.

Painted panels were prescribed to protect users from colliding with the clear glass and doing themselves much harm. It seemed a good idea to incorporate into these certain coats of arms – Edward the Confessor, Henry III, Earl Mountbatten and the present Dean – but there was disagreement about the choice and Sir Anthony Wagner, who is Garter King of Arms and a member of our Architectural Advisory Committee, wrote an intemperate letter in which he described the proposals as half-baked.

This was eventually settled to no one's real satisfaction and the painted panels bearing the arms were installed. However, they were immediately found to be unsafe. The Superintendent of the Cleaners refused to allow his men to touch them and the Chief Marshal, who has to supervise the entrance and exit of visitors, asked the Dean and Chapter to give him personal indemnity against possible injury.

After all this, a great ceremonial opening seemed out of place. Nonetheless the porch is a splendid addition, the only disappointment being that during daylight hours the visitor approaching the Great West Door sees, not a wonderfully uplifting view of the interior of a great thirteenth-century abbey, but the reflection of a modern building across the road which is marked Barclays Bank.

Over 400 Anglican and Roman Catholic monks and nuns came this evening to sing Vespers in commemoration of the 1500th anniversary of the birth of St Benedict. A similar number came on the day of Cardinal Basil Hume's ordination as Archbishop of Westminster in 1976.

The sight of Benedict's twentieth-century followers processing through the Cloisters, as they did in much smaller numbers for almost 500 years prior to the Reformation, was deeply moving. As was their presence in the Abbey, singing the plainsong of a monastic Office. Such expressions of our Benedictine past serve as a powerful reminder of the way of life that we, in our different circumstances and with over 400 years of a different history behind us, are called to lead today.

It is unhelpfully romantic to suppose, however, that the re-establishing of a Westminster community living under the Benedictine rule would further the Christian mission. The Abbey is the most secular church I know. It stands at the intersection of church and state, of the sacred and the secular, and this requires expressions of Christian discipleship which spring from recognition of the divinity that infuses every part of life, rather than from the ancient disciplines of the cloister.

The reintroduction here of monks would represent a serious step backward in every way.

Wednesday 23 July 1980

A most almighty row is raging between the Senior Lay Vicar and the Clerk of the Works – two of the most fractious people on the staff. It started when Roland Tatnell wrote a very rude letter to Bob Andrews complaining that although the regular flooding of the Lay Clerks' Vestry had been frequently reported, nothing had ever been done about it. The last redecoration of the Vestry had, it was alleged, been ruined within months.

But Tatnell also wrote to the Receiver General suggesting that as the Clerk of the Works was inefficient, it would be advisable to bring in an outside contractor to deal with the flooding. When Andrews was acquainted with this letter he went immediately to a solicitor, who advised him that he might well have a case against Tatnell for defamation of character.

Our own Legal Secretary informed us that the letter might be regarded as defamatory by implication, so he suggested that we get the Senior Lay Vicar to write to the Clerk of the Works assuring him that he had no intention of casting doubt on his competence. But Tatnell, who has also consulted a solicitor, will have none of this and has refused to sign a letter drafted by the Receiver General. He is taking the line that if Bob Andrews wishes to take the matter to court he is free to do so.

The whole thing is pretty childish, and mercifully the summer break is almost upon us, so I doubt whether any legal action will be taken. But it is sad when a conflict of this sort arises in a community which purports to be Christian. July often seems to be a bad month for personal relationships in the Abbey.

Monday 11 August 1980

The longer I am here the more I seem to value, even enjoy, all the monuments. At first sight they seem to clutter the building and destroy the symmetry and purity of the thirteenth-century Gothic architecture, but daily encounter with the individual items and increasing knowledge of the people they memorialize makes for a fascinating study of English history through the lives of those who made it.

Recently I have noticed how the posture of the effigies changed with the passage of the centuries. The mediaeval kings and queens are all portrayed recumbent. During the sixteenth century, however, the figures are showing signs of life – still lying, but with head and shoulders raised, supported by an elbow.

Gabriel Goodman, the Elizabethan Dean, goes further and is shown kneeling devoutly in prayer, which is only proper for a Dean, but so also are Thomas Cecil, Earl of Exeter, and his first wife. By the end of the seventeenth century Dr Richard Busby, a famously ferocious Head-master of Westminster School, is portrayed reclining – weary perhaps after flogging so many boys – and the large figure of Sir Isaac Newton (1731) on the Choir Screen shows him equally at ease.

Move on a century and the great men are seated: William Wilberforce with his legs crossed and William Wordsworth rather more decorously. Towards the end of the nineteenth century the statesmen – Gladstone, Disraeli, Canning, Palmerston and others – were not only on their feet but also on pedestals, in a variety of classical poses that make them look anything but humble in the presence of their Maker.

Since then, however, modesty and shortage of cash have combined to reduce many of the great poets to second-rate busts – Epstein's portrait of William Blake excepted – and even Winston Churchill has no more than a simple slab in the floor.

The act of prayer conducted from the Abbey pulpit every hour between 10 a.m. and 4 p.m. is, I think, an important part of our witness. When I first came here I thought that it might well be an undesirable imposition on our thousands of visitors who do not come to the Abbey to pray, but to admire its architecture, to see the Coronation Chair and the royal tombs, and possibly to ponder its history.

Three years later, however, and having myself conducted the prayers on many occasions, I can see that they act as a valuable reminder of the Abbey's main purpose and also serve as a focus of prayer in which visitors are often pleased to share. Visitors – usually Americans – frequently thank us for the prayers, and maybe more would do this if we were clever enough to utter them in languages other than English.

It is essential that the prayers should be preceded by a brief word of welcome and that the whole exercise should last no more than two or three minutes. It is equally important that the Vergers should remember to switch on the microphone every hour – something that cannot, by any means, be guaranteed.

We have now been driven to bribe the registered Guides who bring parties into the Abbey. At least, that is what our decision to give them commission amounts to.

The Guides have parties of twenty to thirty tourists for half a day, sometimes a full day, and take them to see the Tower of London, St Paul's, Buckingham Palace and other 'sights', besides the Abbey. Along the way there are a number of shops selling guide books, postcards and souvenirs, and the Guide decides at which of these his or her party will stop. The benefit to the chosen shop is obvious.

Recently we learned that a shop near Lambeth Palace offers Guides a commission for every party taken into their premises and, perhaps not surprisingly, the Guides are now moving in that direction – to the detriment of our own Gift Shop. A party of between twenty and thirty can easily spend £100 or more.

There seems no alternative but to win the Guides back by offering them £2 for every group of tourists they bring into the shop. This will be in the form of a voucher which can be cashed at the end of the month.

All of which goes against the grain, but it is very much in line with the competitive spirit which, we are told by the new Government, is necessary to the country's salvation.

Monday 10 November 1980

Towards the end of last month our quirky Senior Lay Vicar, Roland Tatnell, wrote to the Dean complaining about the left-wing content of many of the sermons preached in the Abbey. He enclosed the draft of a letter on this subject – couched in the most rude terms, and containing several inaccuracies – which he proposed to send to *The Daily Telegraph*.

The Dean brought the two letters to a Chapter Meeting for corporate consideration. My initial reaction was to express surprise that any of the Lay Vicars had ever heard an Abbey sermon, since their behaviour at this point in the service indicated otherwise.

It was recognized, of course, that Roland Tatnell is perfectly entitled to write to any newspaper on any subject, though not in his capacity as Senior Lay Vicar. We asked the Dean to see him in order to point this out and to suggest that the letter be toned down and its inaccuracies corrected. Indeed Mr Tatnell would be well advised not to despatch the letter.

This led to a general discussion about the content of Abbey sermons. It is utterly absurd to suggest that more than a few of these express opinions that might be construed as politically left-wing. But it is the case that some of us, and some of our visiting preachers, have sometimes commented critically on the actions of the very right-wing government over which Mrs Margaret Thatcher now presides.

It is a sign of our times that such comments, which are generally based on an exposition of biblical truth, are regarded – probably by most of our ultra-conservative Lay Vicars and Honorary Stewards – as signs of Marxist sympathies. When that can truly be said of Westminster Abbey's pulpit the revolution really will have started. It still seems some way off.

A point which even the Senior Lay Vicar recognized after his interview with the Dean. The letter has not been sent.

Tuesday 11 November 1980

The Coffee Shop project is making good progress. The Surveyor of the Fabric sees no problem in adapting the Norman Undercroft to this purpose and has some good ideas about how this can be done imaginatively. Planning permission has been given and it is fortunate that we are not required to install lavatories, since there is no space for additional building.

Five catering firms have submitted schemes for managing the facility once it is completed; easily the best of these is Clark Paterson, who already runs the Brass Rubbing Centre in the Cloisters. He has visited eighty-three other refreshment places of a similar sort and promises us 15% of our Coffee Shop income, with £23,500 guaranteed.

The outlay will be about £100,000 for the adaptation of the Under-croft, of which £50,000 would in any case have to be spent on a new floor and ventilation, and £50,000 on the re-siting of the museum exhibits. This is of course a large sum for us to take out of our reserves, but if the project is as successful as most of us believe it will be, with about two million visitors a year within reach, the money will soon be repaid.

There are two outstanding problems. We have not yet settled on a site for the royal effigies and other museum items that will be displaced. Cheneygates is one possibility, and although the escape facilities for the public are limited, the District Surveyor believes they can be made adequate. Another possibility is the remarkable Pyx Chamber which, like the nearby Chapter House, is administered by the Department of the Environment. They are quite happy for the Chapel to be used in this way and it would give it a new purpose. The Dean and Chapter says, very properly, that the project cannot go ahead until the future of the museum has been settled.

The other problem relates to objections within the Chapter. John Baker believes that the Abbey is already over-commercialized, as he would put it, and that our financial problems would be better solved by dismantling the expensive Choir. The prospect of a coffee shop is, for him, the last straw. Edward Knapp-Fisher shares some of these views, though not those relating to the Choir, and believes that the proximity of the Coffee Shop to the Little Cloister would destroy the peace and tranquillity of the beautiful part of the Abbey where most of us are fortunate enough to live.

The Dean, Sebastian Charles and I are very keen to go ahead once the museum problem is solved, but it will not be a happy situation if we have to move on the basis of a 3–2 vote.

Tuesday 25 November 1980

The Coffee Shop project has been abandoned. After a long and some-what heated discussion in Chapter today Sebastian Charles announced that he had changed his mind and no longer favoured the proposal. This left only the Dean and myself backing it and we were obliged to acknowledge defeat. The fact that the Receiver General and the Surveyor of the Fabric were strongly in favour made no difference, since they have no votes, and even when Reg Pullen said he thought that he might be able to secure a gift of £100,000 to help with the financing, this made no difference. The objections are fundamental.

It is, I think, a bad business, partly because the benefits – pastoral and financial – to the Abbey would have been considerable, and also because a great deal of planning has gone into the project. Leaving aside my own time and that of the Receiver General, Clark Paterson (the caterer) has incurred costs of £50–60,000, a consulting engineer has done about £750 of work, and the Surveyor of the Fabric has put in a great deal of time, for which he is entitled to be paid at going architects' rates.

If, at a much earlier stage, the Chapter objectors had pulled the plug on the whole thing, some of us would have been very disappointed, but much frustration and unnecessary cost would have been avoided. Just why Sebastian Charles changed his mind at the last minute is not at all clear, and he gave no reasons.

Thursday 27 November 1980

Queen Elizabeth, the Queen Mother, came last evening to a party given by the Collegiate Body to mark her eightieth birthday and this turned out to be a most relaxed, indeed quite a jolly, occasion. She arrived at six o'clock, and first we took her into the Abbey – at its most magical in the evening when all the visitors have long departed and the mixtures of light and shadow on the vaulted roof and the royal tombs is specially evocative.

We visited the spots where she was married in 1922 and crowned in 1937, and we showed her the silver candlesticks which she and the then Duke of York gave to the Abbey to mark their wedding. These stand on the small altar in the Shrine of St Edward, and recently they have been joined by a matching silver crucifix – the gift of a private donor. 'I love the Abbey,' she said, 'Everything happened to us here.' The Choristers sang a short anthem and she spent some time talking to them after-wards.

We then repaired to the Jerusalem Chamber for drinks and bits. The Queen Mother spoke to everyone and in due course was handed, on a silver tray, a glass of gin and tonic – the desired proportion having previously been ascertained from her private secretary.

As the Dean began his speech, she stood at his side and placed her glass on a nearby table. It was a felicitous, albeit lengthy, utterance in which Edward said many nice things about our royal guest. As anticipated, it ended with a call to us to raise our glasses and drink to the health of Her Majesty, Queen Elizabeth, the Queen Mother.

Which we all did enthusiastically. Indeed so great was the Dean's enthusiasm, and so limited his sight, that he seized our guest's glass and downed its contents.

The Queen Mother led the uproarious laughter at this act of pure *lèse-majesté*, and the beauty of it was that Edward seemed in no way embarrassed. It says a lot about the Queen Mother that the atmosphere was warm enough for the incident to add to everyone's enjoyment, and it was a classic example of the way in which Edward treats everyone alike and is quite unfazed by the status of those whose company he keeps.

After seeing our guest to her car at about 7.30 p.m. with handbells ringing, we went to our houses chuckling, and wondering if, under an earlier Queen Elizabeth, the gin-and-tonic incident would have seemed so amusing.

Friday 28 November 1980

The meeting with the Lay Vicars this evening was useful for settling various matters related to fees, but it did nothing to resolve the fundamental problem that the men who sing in the Choir see the Abbey in a light quite different from that which illuminates the vision of the Dean and Chapter.

They believe, for example, that on those Sundays (two in every month) when there is a Sung Eucharist as well as Mattins in the morning they should be allowed to withdraw from Evensong before the sermon. They would also like to see Choral Evensong abolished on Christmas Day, and their interest in special services, when we welcome various organizations to celebrate something or other, is confined exclusively to the level of fees payable to them.

This is a great pity, for many of them have a great affection for the Abbey and delight in the daily services, which they sing so well, but I suppose that money is a problem for some. They are also heirs of a long tradition of relating music to money.

An eminent Oxford musicologist has been driven to conclude that during the mediaeval period the church's liturgy was never accompanied by instruments. The evidence for this is that none of the archives indicate payments to instrumentalists, and, since musicians will never play without a fee, it must be that none ever played at services.

Wednesday 10 December 1980

The Human Rights Day service organized by the British Council of Churches and held this evening was a good occasion and it is right that the Abbey should be involved in an event of this kind. Sheila Cassidy spoke movingly about the appalling situation in Chile and reminded us that the denial of human rights in countries of any political persuasion is actually increasing.

The service was not, however, without its problems. First, a group of Irish campaigners for the IRA's Maze prisoners requested permission to state their case during the service. This we refused on the grounds that the granting of such a request would require us to give an equal opportunity to those who might wish to speak on behalf of the victims of IRA violence.

Next came a request from Amnesty International to leave literature about Chile in the Abbey during the service. This was also refused, because it was obvious that Sheila Cassidy would refer to Chile and it did not seem right to focus attention on one particular country.

Then we were asked by the BBC to allow the filming of certain parts of the service for use on television. The Receiver General, who hates the thought of the Abbey being involved in anything controversial, said that our electrician was otherwise engaged this evening and that in previous years it had not been regarded as necessary to film the service.

Two members of the Chapter supported his view that filming should not be permitted, but three of us, including the Dean, thought otherwise, so the cameras were there. The fear of the Receiver General and the police that there might be disturbances during the service proved to be unfounded.

Friday 19 December 1980

It is sad that the Christmas lunch of the Clerk of the Works Department is never characterized by the spirit of goodwill and joy that belongs to this season. Today's gathering was no exception.

Some, perhaps most, of the problem is with the Clerk of the Works himself. He is a highly skilled mason, with much experience of managing large buildings, but he has little idea of how to manage people. Thus his speech at this lunch is something we all dread.

Instead of a short utterance devoted to thanking his staff for their work during the past year and wishing everyone a happy Christmas, it always consists of a catalogue of complaints and a depressing account of the hardships he has suffered – most of these imposed by the Dean and Chapter.

Some of the men now refuse to attend the lunch on the grounds that they have no wish to be hectored on such an occasion. And one of them, the redoubtable Joe Bloomfield, Foreman of the Attendant Cleaners, gave me an additional reason for non-attendance. At last year's lunch, he claimed, tinned turkey was served.

This was quite untrue, but it is, I suppose, a sign of how low morale has sunk when such an accusation can be made. I don't think anyone would much mind if we were to abandon this event. After a break of two or three years we could then make a fresh start, with the Dean or the Treasurer in the chair.

1981

The Dean – that kindest and most enthusiastic of men – wants us to join the chorus of praise for Fred Housego, the winner of the recent BBC Mastermind contest. Housego and his wife were invited to have drinks and bits with the Dean and Chapter and their wives at lunchtime today and Edward presented him with an inscribed copy of Dean Stanley's *Memorials of Westminster Abbey*.

He is to open an exhibition in the Library in July to mark the centenary of the death of Dean Stanley and there is even talk of his presenting the prizes at the Choir School speech day. All of which is part of a lionizing process encouraged by the BBC, who have gone as far as employing him as a radio presenter.

The reason for Fred Housego's current fame is that he won the Mastermind contest as a mere taxi-driver with no sort of intellectual pretensions. It was, in other words, a victory by the common man over professors and other clever competitors who were tried and found wanting. At least that is how it has been made to appear.

This is not, however, quite the whole truth. Mr Housego certainly drives a taxi, sometimes, but he is also a London Tourist Board Blue Badge Guide who specializes in Westminster Abbey. Naturally, he chose the Abbey as the special subject on which to be quizzed and, equally naturally, he found the questions easy to answer. The other part of the contest which involved general knowledge questions was altogether more difficult, but he did well enough – and this is certainly to his credit – to accumulate sufficient points to win the day and create a sensation.

It is no doubt a symptom of our times that a reputation as a 'Mastermind' comes from answering questions in a television quiz show. But I don't see why Westminster Abbey should collude in this – I complain haughtily.

My annual Treasurer's Report, just completed, indicates a useful surplus of about £82,000 for the year ended 29 September 1980. This is a surprisingly good result because there were several anxious periods during the year, and what we have achieved is due to tight control of expenditure and a certain amount of luck.

The number of visitors entering the Royal Chapels' paying area once again declined – this time by 141,907 to 1,078,383 – and over the course of two years we have lost 332,207 entry fees. It is fortunate that we decided in good time to increase the charge from 60p to 80p, and although the decline in visitor numbers is undoubtedly due to the highly valued pound, the high interest rates have increased our investment income by £21,950.

The cost of running the Abbey totalled just over £1 million, and if inflation continues at 10% we shall need an additional £100,000 during the current year simply to stand still. Admission charges must go up to 90p. The cost of the Choir continues to be a problem. The Choir is of course a central, indispensable part of our life, but the net cost last year rose from £145,595 to £167,377; each of our thirty-six Choristers costs us £2,248 after an endowment contribution of £1,067 and a parental contribution of £573.

Towards the end of last year we closed the Museum, which has for some time been losing money, and when it re-opens in March it will be staffed by volunteers, with just one paid supervisor. This will save money, but not help to solve the growing problem of unemployment.

Monday 23 February 1981

The natural rejoicing over the engagement of the Prince of Wales to Lady Diana Spencer is somewhat muted here. Shortly before the official announcement the Prince's Private Secretary, Edward Adeane, called on the Dean to inform him, in a none too courteous manner, that the wedding was to be held at St Paul's. He explained that the Prince has nothing against the Abbey but prefers St Paul's and believes that its vast space, with an unrestricted view, will be more suitable for the large number of guests who are to be invited. He had been much impressed by the Service of Thanksgiving for the Queen Mother's eightieth birthday held there.

The Dean is deeply shocked by this decision – not because he would have enjoyed the glamour of being responsible for arranging the marriage service (no one is less concerned than Edward about such things), but rather because he believes that the Abbey itself has in some way been slighted. For the Royal Family to turn away from this Royal Peculiar, with which it has such an intimate relationship because of Coronations and other special events, seems like some form of rejection. And for Edward, the historian who has been here for almost thirty years and loves every stone of the place, this is almost too much to bear.

As a relatively recent arrival at the Abbey I don't share this sense of shock. It is disappointing, of course, and, since the *raison d'être* of the Abbey is that it should serve the Royal Family's spiritual needs, the maintaining of this tradition is important. But the holding of royal weddings here goes back only to the marriage in 1922 of the Duke and Duchess of York (later to become King George VI and Queen Elizabeth). Before then royal weddings took place more or less privately in the Chapel Royal.

As the Dean himself recognizes, the Prince of Wales is perfectly entitled to be married wherever he wishes. St Paul's will certainly accommodate more guests, but it is an illusion that they will see more than they would in the Abbey, since the great distance between the chief participants and the majority of the congregation will restrict visibility to the processions to and from the West door.

Wednesday 25 February 1981

Last evening's concert by SKY, a high calibre rock band, was a spectacular success. The Abbey was crowded with young people and, although I am no expert in the field, the music seemed to be of a very high quality. And the lighting, mainly in shades of blue, illuminated not only the performers but the whole of the sanctuary area and the surrounding arches in a remarkably beautiful way. The noise was at times ear-shattering, though not in an unbearable way, and at the end all the people I talked to seemed delighted with the whole thing. It should make an impressive television programme.

The only people who were not delighted were the Surveyor and the Clerk of the Works, who this morning discovered the triforium area of the building to be littered with cigarette ends and other debris. These had apparently been left by television lighting and camera crews acting in defiance of our regulations.

There is no part of a great abbey or cathedral more vulnerable to fire than the roof space. Above the stone vaulting is a vast amount of dry timber that supports the pitched roof, and if a fire starts in any part of this space it will almost certainly sweep the length of the building as if through a tunnel.

All smoking, indeed any form of ignition, is therefore strictly forbidden, so now there must be strong words with the BBC and the organizer of the concert.

Wednesday 11 March 1981

The death of Bob Andrews, the Clerk of the Works, has come as a great shock to our community. Until he went into hospital about a month ago he seemed quite fit, and although there have been ominous reports of 'brain inflammation', it seemed reasonable to suppose that he would recover. He was sixty-three.

I suspect that his death was not entirely unrelated to the tragic death of his son, Anthony, in a motoring accident less than two years ago. He had trained Anthony, his only son, to follow in his own footsteps as a mason who would one day take charge of the conservation of a great building such as Westminster Abbey. It was a source of great pride to him when Anthony was married to Catherine, our younger daughter, in the Abbey in 1979.

The fatal accident just ten months later was a blow from which he seemed never really to recover, and I think that early retirement became his primary objective from that point. Naturally, his death has added to Catherine's agony, for although irascible, he had a great affection for her, and this increased when Anthony was killed.

As Clerk of the Works during a period of major Abbey restoration Bob was certainly highly competent. He had a profound knowledge of stone, acquired over many years of first-hand experience, and demanded the highest standards of workmanship. He took great pride in his position at the Abbey.

But he was undoubtedly better with stone than with people and, as our Security Officer, became obsessed with safety matters, particularly those related to possible terrorist attacks. For a time this seemed amusing, but in the end it became somewhat tiresome and we rather dreaded his annual report to the Audit Chapter, when we were hectored mercilessly.

I think we shall remember him as a zealous Clerk of the Works and that should please him.

Tuesday 24 March 1981

The Dean is keen that a letter should go to the Queen expressing our concern at the decision of the Prince of Wales to be married in St Paul's, rather than in the Abbey, and making one or two points about the role of the Abbey as the Coronation Church and as a Royal Peculiar.

The Receiver General has had a conversation with the Lord Chamberlain in which it was indicated that such a letter would not be unwelcome at Buckingham Palace. There was apparently a broad hint that the Queen would have preferred the wedding to take place in the Abbey.

The drafting of a letter agreeable to the whole Chapter has, however, proved to be impossible. Edward Knapp-Fisher feels very strongly that no such letter should be sent and he would not be willing to sign one. I am nervous, too, since it is difficult to avoid giving the impression that we are motivated by personal disappointment, even resentment, rather than by an objective concern for wider issues.

We had a long discussion about all this this morning and in the end my suggestion that the letter should go only in the name of the Dean was accepted, though I think he believes this will weaken its impact. We shall see.

Sunday 29 March 1981

When I heard that Desmond Tutu was in London this weekend and free this morning I invited him to take my place in the pulpit at Mattins. It isn't often that we get a preacher straight from the front line, and the opportunity to hear at first hand about the situation in South Africa was too good to miss.

Desmond is now a key figure, perhaps *the* key figure, in the struggle against apartheid. I have never quite understood why he left Johannesburg in 1976 to become Bishop of Lesotho, but within two years he was back as the first black General Secretary of the South Africa Council of Churches. This body now enables the black and the white churches to speak to each other and, with the exception of the Dutch Reformed Churches, present a united front in opposition to government policy. It is a prime target of the Afrikaaner government's assault on the churches, but in Desmond Tutu the Government has a formidable adversary.

Desmond and his wife Leah came to the house for a cup of coffee before the service and in characteristic fashion threw their arms around Jo and me as soon as they entered the door – lovingly uninhibited.

The sermon was electrifying. Powerful statements delivered in Desmond's high-pitched voice rang throughout the Abbey memorably, and the congregation, which is always made up entirely of visitors, must have wondered what was going on in this royal church, this symbol of the English establishment.

His theme was liberation, and drew heavily on biblical material relating to the God who is ever seeking to liberate his people – from the destructive power of personal sin and also from the destructive power of structural sin expressed through oppressive political regimes. In South Africa, he told us, the white man is as much in need of liberation as is the black man, for he is bedevilled by anxiety and fear and is driven to invest resources to protect himself against change that would be better used creatively in other spheres.

'The greatest need at the moment,' he concluded, 'is the development of black consciousness, sustained by an authentic black theology. We rely on our white fellow-Christians to understand the significance of what we are doing. But we cannot await your approval.'

Freedom to provide the opportunity for these things to be said in Westminster Abbey is precious indeed, and I am thankful that I recognized the need to make way for a prophet.

Tuesday 31 March 1981

It seems, indeed is, extraordinary that a Dean and four Canons should have to spend time dealing with the fact that some of the Lay Vicars appear at services wearing brown shoes. Yet, so were we occupied this morning and not for the first time: the subject was on the Chapter agenda in mid-January.

This is a trivial matter in one sense, but important in another, inasmuch as the appearance of the Choir makes an impact in the Abbey's worship. Thus the Lay Vicars' contracts specify black shoes, partly for the sake of uniformity and partly because black accords best with scarlet and white robes.

The annoying element is that this disciplinary matter is not being dealt with at the level to which it belongs, namely the Music Department, where the Precentor and the Organist are in charge and have sufficient authority to deal with shoes. Indeed, it is their responsibility to see that both the music and the appearance of the Choir is up to Westminster Abbey standards.

Sadly, however, the Precentor, Alan Luff, is not respected by the men and the Organist, who retires in a fortnight's time, has for some time been untroubled by breaches of discipline. We must expect better of his successor. In the meantime, the Dean is going to lay down the law about the colour of shoes.

Thursday 2 April 1981

A very pleasant farewell party this evening for Douglas and Peggy Guest, who are retiring to Gloucestershire. It is, we think and some of us hope, the end of an era in the Abbey's music. Douglas has represented at its most elegant the immediate post-war generation of organists who achieved a very great deal in reviving cathedral music in difficult times – in his case at Salisbury and Worcester. But they lacked the dynamism that would not only restore but also take forward, and it has needed their successors, of whom our incoming Simon Preston is one, to move the church's choral tradition into the demanding musical world of the late twentieth century. Douglas has always scorned broadcasting, recordings and tours and it is many years since he gave a public recital.

He has in fact exuded the air of a country gentleman, and certainly during my time here has displayed much enthusiasm for salmon fishing in Scotland. The war affected him greatly. As a battery commander in the Royal Artillery, he was wounded during the Italian campaign, mentioned in despatches, and left the army as a major – a title he continued to use for several years afterwards. It is perhaps significant that one of his few compositions is the beautiful, and widely used, setting of Laurence Binyon's 'They shall not grow old' for Remembrance Sunday.

By the time he came here, in 1963, he was I dare say past his best as a musician, for earlier he had been much involved in the direction of the Three Choirs' Festival and as a conductor in Birmingham. Responsibility for the music at the wedding of Princess Anne and at the funeral of Earl Mountbatten led to an expectation of high honour, but a knighthood did not materialize, and he had to be content with a CVO and a Lambeth D.Mus.

The Choristers, for whom he has been a grandfather figure, are very upset at his leaving, and we shall all miss the most generous hospitality dispensed at 8 Little Cloister, for Douglas knows about wine and Peggy is a wonderful cook.

Wednesday 15 April 1981

The request from St Matthew's Meeting Place, Brixton for a loan of £5,000 could not have been more timely. Last weekend there were serious racial riots in central Brixton which caused some casualties and immense damage to property. It seems to be the usual mixture of poverty, racial discrimination, and insensitive (some say brutal) policing. Apparently there is still tension in the area.

The Victorian St Matthew's Church, which has for many years – maybe always – been far too large for its congregation, is now being converted into an ecumenical, multi-racial centre with a wide variety of community activities, as well as a place of worship. Under the leadership of its able vicar, Bob Nind, it is already making a significant contribution to racial understanding in Brixton, though it can only be a contribution when the problems are so great.

They are about to start the second phase of the conversion of the building and need an interest-free loan of £5,000 for three years to add to funds from other sources. I recommended to the Chapter yesterday that we should not offer a loan, but rather undertake to raise the money for them as a gift before the end of next March.

Sadly, we are not – for cash-flow reasons – in a position to make an immediate grant from our corporate funds, but the collecting boxes within the paying area of the Abbey can be used for the Brixton project, and if these have not yielded £5,000 in time we can make up the balance from our One People Fund.

This was readily agreed and we intend to keep in touch with the project. No doubt more money will be needed later.

Thursday 16 April 1981

We have been told that the Distribution of the Royal Maundy, which took place this morning, will be the last to be held in the Abbey for at least another fourteen or fifteen years. The ceremony, which can be traced back to the twelfth century and records of which are continuous from the reign of Edward I, was for several centuries held wherever the Sovereign chanced to be in residence. Then it was confined to the old Chapel Royal (now the Banqueting Hall) in Whitehall, and from 1890–1951 it was always held in Westminster Abbey.

But during the 1950s the ceremony started to be taken occasionally to cathedrals and abbeys in other parts of the country, and this has now proved to be so popular that it is to become the normal practice. Obviously it is good that as many different people as possible should have the opportunity to witness a ceremony which is both spectacular and deeply moving. We shall greatly miss it.

Originally, the Sovereign washed the feet of poor people and gave them gifts of clothing, food and money, and at the party in the Deanery after today's ceremony I dared the Dean's wife, Lilian, to suggest to the Queen that it might be a good idea to return to the practice of summoning the poor to receive the Maundy money.

I should have known better, for Lilian, being totally unselfconscious and irrepressible, immediately went to the Queen and put my suggestion to her. The Queen thought for a moment then replied, 'Yes, that is a good idea; my only doubt is whether they would get here on time.' Which was, I think, a pretty smart off-the-cuff response.

Friday 17 April 1981

The Dean is worried about the attendance at Chapter Meetings. He has calculated that thirty-nine meetings have been held during the last two years and that at least one member of the Chapter was absent from twenty of these. Since there are only five of us, including the Dean, and we try to move forward on a consensus view, this level of absence is creating some problems – partly on decision-making but also on our sense of community.

It is, as with most other things, a question of priorities. Canons of Westminster are not appointed to serve only the Abbey and St Margaret's. It is expected that they will be of service to the wider church. Sometimes this involves travelling abroad and an absence of more than two weeks. There are also occasions of sickness, and the Rector of St Margaret's, who is Speaker's Chaplain and tied by Parliamentary sessions, may have to take holiday outside the Abbey's own summer recess.

Edward recognizes all this and makes the valid point that, because there will be those inevitable absences, it is all the more important that we should not accept other commitments on Chapter days unless it is absolutely clear that what we are being asked to do deserves priority over our Abbey responsibilities. Sebastian Charles's apparent lack of commitment to our corporate life is a continuing worry.

As Treasurer, I cannot really miss any Chapter meetings, and problems arise only when some broadcasting opportunity conflicts with one of our regular dates and cannot be changed. Edward suggests that if we ever need to be absent we should report this at the previous Chapter meeting and explain the reason. This is a good idea.

Thursday 23 April 1981

This evening's farewell party to Ernest Browning, a long-serving Verger who has now retired, was notable for an astonishing speech made by the Deputy Dean's Verger. The Dean's Verger, who should have made the speech, is on holiday, so his Deputy, who rejoices in the name of Jack Whissell, took the opportunity to denounce his boss.

He did this by expressing deep sympathy with his colleague Browning for the way in which he had been 'badly treated and victimized' by the Dean's Verger during his years at the Abbey. Since he is not a gifted speech-maker, Whissell's attack was quite without subtlety and, having dealt with his boss, he turned on the rest of his colleagues, alleging that only Browning and himself were capable of conducting tours of the Abbey. He did not mention Ernest's most memorable custom of bowing on every conceivable and inconceivable occasion, after the manner of a Chinese mandarin.

In some ways it was exceedingly funny, but it was yet another sign of the low morale in the Vergers' department and it can only undermine relations even further.

Wednesday 29 April 1981

After some delay, the Dean received a letter from Robert Fellowes, the Queen's Assistant Private Secretary, replying to his letter about the forthcoming royal wedding. This was, as might have been expected, of a bland, non-committal nature, but affirming the Queen's awareness of the special role of the Abbey in the life of the nation.

Now, following last week's Royal Maundy service, another letter has come, expressing the Queen's appreciation of this service and couched in the warmest of terms. The Choir's 'outstanding contribution' is mentioned and also the Queen's recognition of the immense work and planning that went into the ceremony. We are assured that the Queen is 'never less than highly impressed by the beauty and precision with which the ceremony turns out at Westminster Abbey'.

The Dean believes this to represent a coded reassurance to the Abbey, following the decision about the wedding, and this could be true. But there is no way of knowing.

Wednesday 13 May 1981

An eventful day. The President of Ghana came to lay a wreath on the grave of the Unknown Warrior this morning, and he and his entourage were given a brief tour of the Abbey. Lunchtime was occupied with a lively session of 'Come and Sing', followed by a lunch for the chief participants – provided by Jo in our house. Later Evensong – without music because Wednesday is the Choir's day off, and conducted by me as Canon-in-Residence. About half way through the service a Verger handed me a scrap of paper on which was written in red ink: 'Message from the Dean. The Pope has been shot (not dead). Could a prayer be said?' Indeed it could, and was, though the prayer book I was using contained nothing for such an occasion and I was driven to extemporize.

For the congregation my prayer constituted a shocking announcement, but it now seems that, although the Pope was seriously wounded by his would-be assassin, his life is not in danger. It must have been the action of a madman.

Monday 25 May 1981

John Baker is to succeed George Reindorp as Bishop of Salisbury and will be leaving us early next year. This is, I think, a good appointment, provided that John's health will stand the racket of a modern diocesan bishop's punishing way of life. He will take to Salisbury strong gifts of pastoral leadership and to the bench of bishops much-needed theological skill.

But he will be greatly missed here, and ideally he should have spent a few more years at St Margaret's, where he has put in a tremendous amount of work since he took over as Rector in 1978 and has been leading something of a revival of its congregational life and public witness. It is clear, however, that the demands of the Salisbury bishopric and of the wider church have much greater priority than any of this.

Like the rest of us, John came here in order to be free to serve the church in some special way, in his case as a scholar, but the great changes that have taken place in the life of the Abbey since 1974 have claimed much of his time and he has not been able to produce any substantial books. Over the last two years, however, he has chaired a General Synod Board of Social Responsibility working party on nuclear warfare and in the course of this work seems to have become a nuclear pacifist. We have had a number of conversations on this issue but got nowhere near agreement.

Jill, who was the Receiver General's secretary until she married John in 1974, has contributed a great deal to our community life, and her love of animals should have more scope in the wide open spaces of Wiltshire and Dorset.

The Flower Festival organized by the National Association of Flower Arrangement Societies is quite stunning, and throughout the day there have been long queues of people, extending down Great Smith Street and along the adjoining streets, waiting for admission to the Abbey. The entire interior is a riot of colour, and the banners of flowers hanging from the pillars in the Nave are particularly striking.

I don't think that I had previously recognized the degree to which flower arranging has become a sophisticated art form. The displays – all assembled in a very short time and related to the Festival's overall theme – are works of considerable sensitivity and skill. The arrangers have come from all parts of the country and the organizers are expecting even larger crowds of visitors tomorrow and Friday.

The Queen came to the preview yesterday afternoon and stayed quite a long time. She was obviously very impressed, and when we reached the display related to the Coronation Chair made the interesting observation that the seat is so high that at the Coronation her feet could not reach the floor.

Monday 22 June 1981

Simon Preston's Installation as Organist and Master of the Choristers on the 15th of last month was an astonishing experience. It took place near the beginning of Evensong, and as soon as the ceremony was completed he stepped forward and conducted the Choir for the rest of the service. The impression was that we not only had a new Organist but also a new Choir. Inspection revealed that the same Choristers and Lay Vicars were in the stalls, but the sound coming from them was different – more confident, more vibrant, indeed thrilling. And this on Simon's first appearance.

When we appointed him we realized that we had secured an outstandingly gifted musician and we knew that under his leadership the choir of Christ Church, Oxford, had won golden opinions in the world of music. But none of us expected so dramatic an improvement in the Abbey Choir so soon. It was extraordinary, and daily Evensong, with Simon in charge, has become an exciting experience.

Not exciting enough for him, however. He came to the Chapter meeting this morning and told us frankly that the Choir is sub-standard and that we are not getting value for the £250,000 per annum spent on the Choral Foundation. He identified two fundamental problems:

insufficient rehearsal time and poor discipline among both the men and the boys.

At Christ Church, Oxford the Choir evidently rehearses for eleven hours each week, whereas at Westminster only nine hours are available, much of which is spent correcting the boys, to the intense irritation of the men. The men recognize the need for more rehearsal time to improve the standard but feel that they should be rewarded for this with a salary increase of between £300 and £500 per annum. It doesn't need much mathematical skill to calculate that this would add something in the region of £5,000 to our annual expenditure.

A bonus scheme to provide pocket money for the boys is another Christ Church idea that was apparently very successful. Good and bad points are awarded, and each boy can earn up to a maximum of £3 per term. This would cost up to £300 per annum, which is altogether more manageable.

We are to consider these ideas again at our next meeting, and doubtless we shall have to find more money to maintain the impetus that Simon Preston has created. He is also talking about the need for the organ to be given a major renovation, and this can only cost hundreds of thousands of pounds. Hardly music to a Treasurer's ears.

Tuesday 23 June 1981

The widow of a man killed by a terrorist bomb in Northern Ireland has asked us to accept his wedding ring as a gift. It is of course a symbolic offering and therefore a tricky one to handle. She doesn't say whether her husband was a victim of the IRA or of one of Protestant paramilitary groups, but it was probably the former.

Would acceptance of the ring imply that we were taking sides in the conflict? We do in fact support the view that Northern Ireland is an integral part of the United Kingdom and that the problems this creates in Ireland as a whole cannot be settled by bombs. But inasmuch as we are praying for reconciliation and trying to encourage those on both sides who are working to this end, it seems best that we should not publicly identify the Abbey with one side in the conflict.

In any case, we lack any place where the ring might appropriately be displayed, so we have decided to decline the offer and to tell the widow what we are doing in the cause of reconciliation and peace.

We met this morning in the Jerusalem Chamber to discuss the points we shall make to the Prime Minister's Appointments Secretary about John Baker's successor and, mainly, the future of St Margaret's and its relationship with the Abbey.

The Dean had already had a meeting with the St Margaret's Churchwardens, who asked that the traditional Book of Common Prayer services be maintained, along with the present high standard of music. The preaching and pastoral ministry was also deemed to be very important, and they believed it to be essential for the Rector to continue as Speaker's Chaplain in order to maintain the link between the church and the House of Commons.

We talked about the need for St Margaret's to become rather more integrated with the Abbey. John Baker's noble effort to breathe new life into the church's dry bones has, perhaps inevitably, tended to strengthen its separate identity, and we have certainly seen much less of John in and around the Abbey than we would have liked.

This raised the question of just how, or even whether, the three jobs of Canon of the Abbey, Rector of St Margaret's and Speaker's Chaplain can be adequately combined. I suspect not, and the answer, we agreed, was that the Abbey clergy as a whole should become more involved in St Margaret's.

There is also the anomaly of Sunday morning Mattins taking place at more or less the same time in both churches, and Edward Knapp-Fisher would like to see this rationalized, so that there is Mattins in one church and a Sung Eucharist in the other. But sensible though this may seem, I cannot see it working in the particular circumstances of the two churches. St Margaret's congregation would not tolerate a Sung Eucharist every Sunday, and the Abbey needs Mattins for its many visitors from all kinds of non-sacramental traditions.

We agreed that the new Rector must have a strong parish experience, for although John Baker, the scholar, has done well, another appointment to St Margaret's of this sort would be far too risky. In any case, it is doubtful if an academic would want to take on this job. The Appointments Secretary is to be asked to get on with finding a Rector as quickly as he can, as we are anxious that the momentum established by John should not be lost during a long interregnum.

The Dalai Lama left today after spending five days at the Deanery. Besides his evident holiness, he has left other memories. His arrival last Monday afternoon in a convoy of Land Rovers was quite dramatic, and the entourage included a number of burly security guards who immediately took up positions inside the Deanery front door and outside the guest's bedroom. Lady Redcliffe-Maud, who was in the Deanery later in the day, moved in the direction of the bedroom and was unceremoniously diverted by the guards, who are obviously expecting attempts to abduct a leader who has a political as well as a religious role. Jean Redcliffe-Maud seems an unlikely kidnapper.

The Deanery's devotion to the Dalai Lama is matched only by its commitment to vegetarianism. Even Hadrian, the dog, is confined to a vegetarian diet, though rumour has it that he is a frequent visitor to the Choir School kitchen, where non-vegetarian scraps are sometimes available. What consternation therefore when a message to His Holiness's room about his breakfast requirements elicited the response, 'Bacon, eggs, liver and sausage'. Not all Buddhists are, it seems, vegetarians. In this instance courtesy was given priority over conviction.

Yesterday morning we were invited to the Deanery drawing-room to meet His Holiness or, as it turned out, to have an audience with him. He was seated in a large chair near the centre of the room and we took it in turns to occupy a chair alongside him. Conversation was by no means easy. I put to him the by no means original question, 'What do you believe to be the most important issue facing the world today?' After a long pause came the reply, 'Peace.' 'How does your Holiness believe this can be achieved?' Another long pause. 'By seeking unity.' 'How is unity to be achieved?' A longer pause. 'Through compassion and tolerance.'

Recognizing that I was unlikely to get any of the quick, off-the-cuff, comments to which I am accustomed in television studies, I gladly made way for one of my more patient colleagues. On Thursday evening the Dalai Lama addressed 2,000 people in Central Hall across the road and I am told that most were entranced by his presence and message.

Monday 6 July 1981

I have had a long conversation with the Dean about the possibility of my succeeding John Baker as Rector of St Margaret's and Speaker's Chaplain. Such a possibility was as far removed from my mind when I came here in 1976 as anything could ever be. Indeed, I am on record, in my book *The Church of England in Crisis*, as advocating the pulling down of St Margaret's (*a*) because it was a redundant church, and (*b*) because its removal could improve the view of the Abbey. What then has happened to raise the possibility of my having to eat my words?

1. John Baker has demonstrated during his short time as Rector that St Margaret's has a distinctive and important ministry complementary to that of the Abbey.

2. This ministry is closely related to its role as the official church of the House of Commons and to the tradition, developed largely during the present century, that the Rector is also Speaker's Chaplain.

3. It seems right that I should stay at the Abbey for some more years; there are strong rumours that I am to be offered the bishopric of Worcester, a position I do not covet, and in any case it is highly undesirable that John Baker and I should leave at about the same time.

4. There is a personal reason for my staying, inasmuch as Catherine is experiencing a delayed bereavement following the tragic death of her husband so soon after their marriage, and it seems very important that Jo and I should remain here to provide her with a home and close support until she is through this.

5. If I am to stay at Westminster, there is not much sense in my being trapped in the office of Treasurer. This is an important job, but not one that ought to occupy any member of the Chapter for more than three or four years.

6. I am strongly attracted to the work of Speaker's Chaplain. As far as I can tell, no one has ever attempted to develop this beyond its ceremonial role and in the direction of a dynamic pastoral/frontier ministry in the House of Commons. The conjunction of the religious and the political has always been one of my special interests, and there is the opportunity to do something about this at the heart of the nation's political life.

Taken together, these considerations seem to point firmly towards my moving over to St Margaret's – provided of course that everyone else involved is in agreement. Certainly the Dean is very enthusiastic about it, partly, I suspect, because he is anxious that I should stay at Westminster and also because he himself wanted to move to St Margaret's in 1957 to do the kind of things I have in mind, but was not considered on account of his pacifist views.

So he is going to see George Thomas, the Speaker, and Patrick Cormack and Bill Stead, the Churchwardens, to see how they feel about the proposal. And of course it will need to be discussed with the others on the Chapter.

Tuesday 14 July 1981

For the second time since I came here we have been to Buckingham Palace to present a Loyal Address to the Queen. It turned out that the betrothal of the Sovereign's eldest son is always an occasion when the Privileged Bodies are expected to demonstrate their loyalty in this archaic way. So off we went this morning with our carefully prepared and beautifully inscribed Address, the only difference this time being that the Choir School mini-bus was a more recent model, and therefore of less disgraceful appearance, and the waiting time in the great gallery was shorter.

The Address, which was chiefly the work of the Dean and contained, of course, no hint of our disappointment at the location of the forthcoming wedding, read as follows:

TO THE QUEEN'S MOST EXCELLENT MAJESTY THE HUMBLE ADDRESS OF THE DEAN AND CHAPTER OF THE COLLEGIATE CHURCH OF ST PETER IN WESTMINSTER

MOST GRACIOUS SOVEREIGN

We, Your Majesty's most dutiful and loyal subjects, express our delight and deep satisfaction at the engagement of His Royal Highness The Prince of Wales to the Lady Diana Spencer. We wish them every blessing, happiness and fulfilment, and we are confident that through the grace of God their relationship of mutual trust and sacrificial self-giving will encourage the younger generation to build a world more compassionate and caring.

In wishing them well we express our gratitude for the unique contribution made by Your Majesty to the well-being of the Nation and Commonwealth at a time when social change and the weakening of older authorities have tended to erode domestic loyalties and a sense of belonging. The Royal Family has significantly provided a stabilizing influence and example.

We are not unaware that the complexity of modern life has inevitably led to Government becoming more remote and impersonal. The Royal Family gives a human face to the historic identity of the nation, thus enabling it to evoke a truly moral and personal allegiance.

To advance the cause of 'One People' in a society where many different faiths and cultures co-exist is now recognized as being every day more urgent. The leadership of Your Majesty in transcending such distinctions and in ministering to the common humanity which binds us together is, we hope, a happy augury of things to come and of the kind of world to which the best of our young people will increasingly desire to belong.

In a spirit of gratitude, and confident that the example Your Majesty has given will be followed by The Prince of Wales and his bride, we assure you that we share the joy, enthusiasm and eagerness with which the Nation awaits their marriage.

(Signed & Sealed)
EDWARD CARPENTER
Dean

Our bewigged Legal Secretary, Clifford Hodgetts, was entrusted with the reading of the document and the Queen responded with a brief, formal Thank you.

Within a matter of minutes we were back at the Abbey and meeting in Chapter. The first item on the agenda was a new catering contract for the Choir School and the next was a complaint about Evensong.

Saturday 18 July 1981

A remarkable service this afternoon was attended by over 600 guide dogs and their blind owners, together with 1,000 or more friends and supporters of the Guide Dogs for the Blind Association which was celebrating the Golden Jubilee of its foundation. Princess Alexandra, who is the Association's patron, also came.

The nave of the Abbey was a wonderful sight. Yellow and white Labradors were in the majority, but there were quite a large number of Alsatians (or German Shepherds, as I think we are now supposed to call them) and this surprised me, as I hadn't realized that these were used as guide dogs. Many of the dogs sported red, white and blue rosettes – one was flying a Union Flag – and it was strangely moving to see them sitting quietly at their owners' feet during the lessons and prayers, then rising with their owners for the singing of the hymns. Not one made an audible sound throughout the hour-long service.

The address was given by George Thomas, the Speaker of the House of Commons, and he began by remarking that the congregation to

Alan Luff (Precentor), Trevor Beeson (Treasurer), Edward Carpenter
(Dean), Edward Knapp-Fisher (Archdeacon), Charles Taylor
(Chaplain) with the Abbey Servers and the Dean's Verger

The Jerusalem Chamber where Henry IV died in 1413, the translation
of the Authorised Version of the Bible was master-minded 1607–11,
and the meetings of the Dean and Chapter are held today

Noeline Kelly

Trevor Beeson with Princess Anne after a concert in aid of the Women's Caring Trust for the victims of violence in Northern Ireland

Press Association Photos

Farewell to Earl Mountbatten of Burma. The Queen and other members of the Royal Family, together with the Dean and Chapter, watch the coffin leave the Abbey after the funeral

Trevor Beeson with the Queen Mother after the Blessing of the Field of Remembrance

Alfred Hepworth

Trevor Beeson greets Dr Herbert Howells at a
party to mark the composer's 90th birthday

The Prince of Wales with officers of the Order of the Bath and
Trevor Beeson after an Installation of Knights

Trevor Beeson escorting the Princess of Wales from the Abbey after the General Synod House of Laity centenary service

THE HOUSE *magazine*

The Weekly Journal of the Houses of Parliament   No 360 Vol 12 December 15, 1986

The cover of the Christmas 1986 edition of the *House Magazine*. Trevor Beeson is portrayed with the Leaders of the main political parties — Margaret Thatcher, David Owen, David Steel and Neil Kinnock

The Speaker of the House of Commons, George Thomas, with Trevor
Beeson and other members of his procession before a State Opening
of Parliament

Trevor Beeson with the Prime Minister at a Reception in 10 Downing
Street for the Speaker's Appeal for St. Margaret's Church. Also in the
picture the Speaker and his wife, and Jo Beeson

Trevor Beeson's daughter, Catherine, and Charles Taylor leaving the High Altar after their marriage

Tomas Jaski

which he was speaking was much better behaved than the one he normally addressed 'across the road'. From that point onwards he had rapt attention and went on to say the usual helpful things, 'We are treading where the saints have trod, yet even here history has been enriched today. Even this ancient Abbey has not, I believe, hitherto ever known such an experience as we enjoy.'

After the service the congregation, together with the dogs, marched behind the band of the Irish Guards along Birdcage Walk to the Royal Mews of Buckingham Palace for tea. I haven't heard whether the dogs were fed.

Tuesday 28 July 1981

Tuesday Choral Mattins has been lost and I feel pretty sore about it, even though the decision was made for the best of reasons, namely the quality of the Abbey's music.

Soon after his arrival in May, Simon Preston told the Chapter that the music was sub-standard and that the only solution was more Choir rehearsal time – seventy minutes per week was prescribed. The need for this was agreed all round, but of course the Lay Vicars soon made it plain that they could not give an extra ten minutes per day, even to bring the Choir up to standard, without a salary increase. £300–£500 per annum was mentioned.

Then Michael Keale, the Headmaster of the Choir School, complained that the additional rehearsal time would eat further into the Choristers' school time-table. He told us of his belief that the Choristers were already withdrawn from school too frequently for special services and the like and that the loss of another seventy minutes would make it impossible to give them an adequate education.

So Choral Mattins on Tuesdays is to go. This will deal with most of the 'time' problem and enable us to settle with the Lay Vicars for an affordable salary increase. But, in my view, this decision will lead to a serious diminution of the Abbey's life.

For most people, I suppose, the loss of a service attended only by the Choir, a few of the clergy and a congregation numbering no more than a handful, may not seem very important. But the Abbey was built over 900 years ago primarily as a place where daily worship would be offered. The suppression of the monastery in 1540 inevitably led to a reduction in the number of daily services, but a Choral Foundation was established to ensure that Mattins and Evensong would be sung daily.

And so they were until the outbreak of war in 1939. In the changed circumstances of the postwar era, Mattins was sung only on Tuesdays and Fridays, but the Friday service was lost owing to time and financial pressures in 1977, and now the Tuesday Service has gone the same way. All of which suggests to me that daily worship is no longer considered our highest priority.

I can, and do, argue that daily Evensong, except on Wednesdays, together with three choral services on Sundays, is keeping the tradition fully alive. But I regard even the slightest reduction in choral worship as a dangerous erosion of something which, in our increasingly secularized world, needs to be maintained at all costs. If money and time-tables are to dictate the quantity and quality of the Abbey's worship, we are caving in to things that need to be resisted.

Wednesday 29 July 1981

Westminster and its Abbey have been eerily quiet today, with all attention focussed on St Paul's and the Royal Wedding. I went across to the Mall to watch the splendid procession on its way to St Paul's and managed to get a good view from a conveniently placed mound in St James's Park.

On my return I was horrified to discover no flag flying from the Abbey's mast – almost certainly the only public building in London without one. With the flagman and the rest of the Clerk of the Works staff all having the day off, and myself utterly ignorant of the location of our flags and the method of raising them, there was no way of remedying this, and it can only have seemed to passers-by that we were feeling miffed by the Prince of Wales's decision. It was of course no more than a monumental cock-up – something at which we are becoming quite adept. Mercifully the Ringers remembered to ring the bells between 1.30 p.m. and 2.30 p.m.

I watched the service on television and was not surprised to find it very well done. Bob Runcie presides over big occasions with a good combination of dignity and humanity, and his address was superb. Edwin Muir's definition of a good marriage as a life,

> Where each asks from each
> What each wants to give;
> And each awakes in each
> What else would never be,

will, I am sure, be quoted in a million other wedding addresses.

During the late afternoon the Receiver General went to Buckingham

Palace to collect the bridal bouquet, which now lies on the grave of the Unknown Warrior – at the request of the new Princess.

Friday 31 July 1981

I went to see George Thomas this morning about the possibility of my becoming his Chaplain. We already know each other quite well, because I have sometimes deputized for John Baker at House of Commons Prayers and George often comes to services and receptions at the Abbey.

Speaker's House, which is an integral part of the Palace of Westminster, is certainly palatial. We met in a beautiful room overlooking the Thames and among the personal items I noticed a portrait of an elderly lady – his mother, 'Mam' – and a miner's lamp, a symbol of his origins in the Welsh valleys.

We got on very well. George has a warm, almost effusive, personality and the fact that I had worked in a coal-mining parish in the North East of England and, as he put it, come from the same humble background, established an immediate bond.

He told me that he is very keen for me to become his Chaplain and intends to ignore the advice of a group of MPs who, having heard rumours of my possible move to St Margaret's, warned him against appointing a Chaplain who shared his own political convictions. They thought this would not be 'wise', but we agreed that they would have no anxiety if a Conservative Speaker appointed a Conservative Chaplain.

Edward Carpenter had mentioned to George my idea of developing the Chaplain's role and spending more time in the House of Commons, and when I began to spell this out a little he became positively enthusiastic. 'It is just what is needed,' he said, 'and you can count on my full support.'

He promised a letter offering me the job, we shook hands, and I found my way, with guidance, through the labyrinthine corridors of the House of Commons to St Margaret's Street, which separates the Houses of Parliament from the Abbey. An exciting prospect lies ahead of me.

Sandwich   **Monday 3 August 1981**

Edward Carpenter telephoned me this morning at our holiday home to say that on Saturday there had been a special meeting of Chapter at which it was unanimously agreed that I should be offered the appointment of Rector of St Margaret's. An announcement will be made on Thursday.

Apparently the Chapter, and especially John Baker, is very pleased that I am taking this on and it is suggested that I should be officially Installed at the beginning of February. A few eyebrows will, I'm sure, be raised, but the opportunity to occupy every Sunday a pulpit on the edge of Parliament Square and to minister in the House of Commons, as well as a continuing ministry in Westminster Abbey, is not lightly to be dismissed.

The only problem from my own point of view, and it is a serious one, is that I shall have virtually no free time for writing and broadcasting, and, in any event, the kind of things I have been accustomed to saying in broadcasts on social-political issues will not be possible for me as Speaker's Chaplain. Publicly, I must share in the Speaker's political neutrality.

Still, one cannot do everything, and the Christian life is about choices.

Wednesday 23 September 1981

The weakest feature of the Abbey's architecture is the space above the 'crossing' where the original builders must have intended to erect a central tower. For some reason, probably shortage of money, this was never built, and all that we have is a tower base rising no more than a few feet above the ridge of the roof.

Recognizing that this was incomplete, later architects had the base covered with only a temporary roof. This turned out to be providential on the night of 10 May 1941 when German incendiary bombs landed on it and the whole thing fell to the 'crossing' floor where the blaze was easily extinguished. Had the roof not collapsed in this way, the fire might well have spread to the nave roof and destroyed it.

During the early part of the eighteenth century Sir Christopher Wren was the Surveyor of the Fabric and, although over eighty, was still full of bright ideas, including the building of a spire on the central tower base. He thought this would give the Abbey 'a proper grace' and went as far as producing a model to show the Dean and Chapter how it would look.

Of course the spire was never built, but the model was retained. Later it was rather badly damaged, but a Mr J. G. O'Neilly has patiently restored it and, following its exhibition by the Royal Institution of Chartered Surveyors, it has been returned to us.

Very fine it is, too, made of oak and pearwood, standing six foot high, and presenting a tall graceful spire that would certainly have matched Hawksmoor's Western towers and completed the building. We have decided to display the model in the North Transept and, who knows, it may one day inspire a wealthy benefactor to pay for the spire to be built. What will the planners say then, I wonder?

Tuesday 13 October 1981

We have turned down a request from a promoter of 'pop' concerts that we should provide facilities for a concert starring Stevie Wonder to be held in the Abbey. Stevie Wonder, a blind American singer, is apparently one of the best in the 'pop' world and we are, after the hugely successful SKY concert, certainly ready to encourage styles of music other than classical.

But the Deputy Head of Harlech Television, who is knowledgeable about the 'pop' world, and Nicholas Wright, who organized the SKY concert, both advised against a 'pop' concert because they believed it would attract the sort of audience that could not easily be controlled in Westminster Abbey.

There is another point: we are not in the business of providing concert-hall facilities. As a church, whatever we promote or facilitate must have a recognizable connection, even if oblique, with our overall mission. To bring 2,000 young people into the building simply to enjoy themselves is not enough. The SKY concert had a religious dimension which gave it a certain validity, whereas the Stevie Wonder programme would have been entirely secular.

Monday 19 October 1981

We petitioned today for a Supplementary Charter that will require future Deans and Canons to retire on reaching the age of seventy. When I came here in 1976 I was aware that the 1974 Synodical Measure, which introduced a compulsory retirement age of seventy for Church of England clergy, did not apply to Westminster Abbey, since we are a Royal Peculiar and outside the jurisdiction of the General Synod. The Royal mandate for my appointment included the phrase 'for the period of your natural life'.

What I was not aware of until July was that in 1973, while the Synodical Measure was under discussion, the then Dean and Chapter undertook to take steps to bring the Abbey clergy into line with the new rule. The Dean and Canons of Windsor, another Royal Peculiar, agreed to do likewise and in 1978 applied to the Queen for a Supplementary

Charter to modify the section of their Statutes dealing with appointments.

Nothing was done about this at the Abbey, and it is not altogether clear whether the Dean and the Receiver General, both of whom were here in 1973, forgot about the undertaking or thought it best to leave the issue on one side. But the Receiver General has now brought it to our attention. There is nothing contentious about it. Clergymen ought not to remain in office beyond the age of seventy, though one has to be a little careful in saying this here since the Dean will be seventy-one in December and has, I think, no intention of retiring for some years. In his case, however, it can be argued that as he did not become Dean until he was almost sixty-five, and as it would be quite impossible to do anything useful in that office in a mere five years, there was always an expectation that he would go on beyond the age of seventy. The problem with this argument, however, is that the responsibilities of the Dean of Westminster are exceedingly heavy and it may become increasingly difficult for a man in his seventies to carry them out efficiently.

Tuesday 24 November 1981

Two curious little matters relating to the tower of St Margaret's were on the Chapter agenda today. First the clock: Smiths of Derby, who are responsible for its maintenance, have advised us that its electrical striking mechanism requires renewal at an estimated cost of £1,000. But, as the Surveyor of the Fabric has pointed out, this would be a waste of money, because if the St Margaret's clock were to be on time the sound of its striking would always be drowned by Big Ben. It would only be heard if it were running either slow or fast. The clock is to remain silent.

Then the flagpole, which has been the subject of discussion for several months. Because we are short of money and cannot afford an expensive metal pole, the Surveyor of the Fabric suggested, very sensibly, that we invest in a well-creosoted wooden pole. His own experience is that such flagpoles last for many years.

The said flagpole having been erected a couple of weeks ago, the District Surveyor has written to the contractors expressing surprise that they had put it up without first giving formal notice as required by Section 83 of the London Buildings Act. He went on to warn them that they were liable to be prosecuted and, if convicted, fined for this offence, and invited them to give reasons why proceedings should not be taken against them.

The facts are, however, that our own Surveyor has been in constant consultation with the District Surveyor – a notoriously difficult man whose powers are far too wide – and, after much huffing and puffing, finally obtained his approval for the wooden flagpole. The latest fuss is probably because some bureaucratic procedures have not been carried out to the letter, so we must now fight to smooth this out and keep the flag flying.

Friday 11 December 1981

We were expecting to welcome the new Bishop of London, Graham Leonard, to the Abbey today, but earlier this week he told the Dean that he would be unable to come because of another engagement. The plan was that he would attend Evensong, read a lesson, and join us afterwards at a welcome party in the Jerusalem Chamber.

We do not need to welcome a new Bishop of London since we are outside his jurisdiction and should, by rights, read a 'Protest' on his first appearance at the Abbey's door. But he is a near neighbour in Barton Street and it seems only decent that we should establish friendly relations. Indeed, with Gerald Ellison, his predecessor, there were bonds of warm friendship, and we gave him a key to College Garden as the episcopal residence is without a garden.

Graham Leonard is, however, a totally different kind of bishop and I suspect that the establishment character of the Abbey does not appeal to his neo-Roman Catholic view of the church as a body untainted by the world. This hardly excuses discourtesy, however, and the Dean has already sent a number of letters (all unanswered) and made several telephone calls to his office in the hope of settling on a mutually convenient date.

My own view is that we should cease trying.

1982

Tuesday 12 January 1982

At today's Chapter Meeting I initiated a discussion about the style of the memorials we have been placing in Poets' Corner and elsewhere in the building. A fair number of these have appeared during the last four years, and invariably the Surveyor of the Fabric's design has consisted of no more than white lettering inlaid in black stone. They might almost have been bought in as standardized items and they make no contribution to the artistic aspects of the building.

We were discussing the design of the memorial to Dylan Thomas which is to be unveiled on 1 March – St David's Day. This project has been attended by a certain amount of disquiet and some controversy, for there are those who believe that a man whose way of life was characterized, for some of the time anyway, by hard drinking and wild behaviour, ought not to be commemorated in a Christian shrine such as Westminster Abbey. But the Dean takes the line, and I am sure this must be right, that the only criterion for a place in Poets' Corner is the quality of the individual's poetry.

The proposed memorial stone is to be the work of a Welsh sculptor, Jonah Jones, and his design is pleasant enough. So much so that an enquiry has been made about the possibility of a duplicate of it being installed in Laugharne, in Wales, where Dylan Thomas is buried – not an idea that appeals to us. It is of course unrealistic to suppose that every poet might have something as memorable as Epstein's magnificent head of William Blake, but we ought to have a rule that nothing goes into the Abbey that will not in some way enhance its beauty, or at the very least not detract from it.

Monday 18 January 1982

Today the House of Commons returned from its Christmas recess and I conducted Prayers for the first time in my capacity as Chaplain. It is a singular ceremony and was a curious experience.

I went across the road to my room in the Commons soon after 2.00 p.m. and was soon joined by my 'dresser' – one of the House messengers, clad in white tie and tails. The Chaplain's robes begin with a cassock of black, silk-like material, over which goes a heavy Geneva gown and a black scarf bearing a coat of arms. Decoration includes preaching bands, white gloves, and a handkerchief on the left wrist – originally this was scented to counteract the stench from the Thames. Patent-leather shoes with silver buckles and a tricorn hat, carried under the right arm, complete a garb that dates back to 1661.

Thus attired, I was then led by the 'dresser' to the Speaker's Office where, already assembled, were the Serjeant-at-Arms, in court dress and holding the mace, and a senior messenger in white tie and tails who was to lead the procession. At 2.24 p.m. the Speaker, in court dress, black gown and full-bottomed wig, emerged through the door from his house, accompanied by his train-bearer, in court dress, and his secretary in black jacket and striped trousers.

George welcomed me in his exuberantly friendly style and we had some small talk until the messenger announced 'Time to go, Sir'. So off we went in solemn procession, though at a much faster pace than ecclesiastical processions, along the Library corridor, through the Central Lobby, where many people were assembled, then through the Members' Lobby, and so to the Chamber. From time to time the messenger who led the way cried out 'Speaker. Hats off, strangers.' He was followed by the Serjeant-at-Arms, with the mace on his shoulder, then came the Speaker and his train-bearer, with the Secretary and myself bringing up the rear. As we passed, Members and others stood respectfully to one side and bowed to the Speaker.

On entering the Chamber (how small it seems on first acquaintance) the procession came to a halt at the Bar of the House, just as Big Ben struck 2.30 p.m. We all bowed and everyone but the Speaker, the Serjeant and myself peeled off and returned to the Lobby. The three of us then advanced a few paces and bowed again, before the Serjeant placed the mace on a rack in front of the Clerk's table, while the Speaker and I went to the Chair and stood side by side facing the House.

The Prayers were printed in large type and contained in a folder. First, Psalm 67, without a Gloria, said by me; next, 'Let us pray', whereupon the Members (there were, I suppose, fifty or so present) turned to face the walls on either side of the Chamber. We then had 'Lord, have mercy upon us, Christ, have mercy upon us, Lord, have mercy upon us', followed by the Lord's Prayer said together. I then recited prayers for the Queen and for the Royal Family, after which came a long, and somewhat convoluted, prayer for Parliament, and this was followed by the Collect 'Prevent us, O Lord' and the Grace.

A doorkeeper then called out 'Prayers over' and a crowd of Members who had been waiting outside surged in to claim seats. Meanwhile the Speaker moved to the Chair and I, having taken up a position near the mace, bowed to him and walked backwards – no more than seven or eight paces, I suppose – to the Bar of the House, bowed again, and was immediately picked up by the 'dresser', who escorted me back to my room. On the way I was greeted by several Members, some of whom I knew; others shook my hand and welcomed me.

This is to be my daily assignment whenever the House is sitting, which is for about thirty-five weeks of the year, and the timing of the procedure is so exact that I must always be within easy reach of the House for 2.30 p.m. Monday–Thursday, and 9.30 a.m. Friday.

Tuesday 19 January 1982

My belief, confirmed by the Speaker and other Members, that the role of the Chaplain can extend far beyond the conducting of daily Prayers was amply confirmed this afternoon when Jim Callaghan, a former Prime Minister, came to see me. During the Easter recess he is visiting India and, among other things, has been asked to make a speech on religion and science. He wondered if I might lend him a hand, so I have undertaken to prepare him a draft and also let him have a paperback by an Australian priest-scientist named Birch, which he should find helpful.

I am of course still finding my feet in the House, and only with difficulty am I discovering the way through its intricate network of corridors, but everyone is exceedingly friendly, and unlike an industrial chaplain, who has patiently to win acceptance in a secular institution, the Chaplain, because of history and tradition I suppose, is regarded as an integral part of the community.

That it is a community often (always?) under stress is obvious. I am astonished to discover that besides the 650 Members there are no fewer than 2,500 on the staff, including well over 100 employed in the Library on research work of one kind or another. I am to have a regular weekly meeting with the Speaker so that we can compare notes and share a few things. He has a very considerable pastoral role in addition to his official duties in the Chair because Members with personal as well as political problems often turn to him for guidance. In his position, however, there are few people with whom he can himself talk frankly and confidentially.

At the annual Audit Chapter today I reported a surplus in last year's accounts of a mere £5,748. From a total income of £1,118,399 this was of course totally inadequate, but in a year of world trade recession and serious economic and social problems in the United Kingdom we must be thankful that the Abbey has been kept going without a major deficit being incurred.

The decline in the number of visitors entering the Royal Chapels' paying area shows no sign of bottoming out and a 16% reduction took us down to 893,548. In 1977 we had 1,502,898. The instability of the stock market, reflected in wide fluctuations, caused a fall of £84,000 in the value of our assets on the day of their valuation.

But in spite of high inflation, we managed, by a most stringent economy, to keep the increase in costs down to 8.3%. The transfer of stonemasons from the Clerk of Works department to the staff of the contractors responsible for the Abbey's restoration helped, and the death of Bob Andrews caused delay in much maintenance work. Little capital work was carried out.

Because of uncertainty about visitors, the size of our income this year can only be a matter of guesswork, so constant vigilance must continue. The £8,666 deficit sustained by St Margaret's is a worry and will have to be discussed with the Churchwardens. The main difficulty, however, is that virtually all the 'easy' cuts in expenditure have now been made, and should further cuts be needed these will be painful – not least because we are so labour-intensive: more than 60% of our expenditure is on staff costs.

What we need to be doing is maximizing our income, rather than cutting costs, and in the current situation of uncertainly, which may become a permanent feature of the economic situation, we need to plan for four to five years, rather than treat each year as a single entity.

Friday 29 January 1982

The Precentor, Alan Luff, who joined us just over a year ago, has made a good point about the planning of memorial services. At the moment we meet with the widow, and sometimes other members of the family, in the Jerusalem Chamber. It is a very formal, almost ceremonial, setting and for some at least of the relations of the deceased a daunting experience. They face, across the long table, a dozen or more representatives of the Abbey – the Dean, the Canon-in-Residence, the Precentor, the Organist, the Receiver General, the Dean's Verger and various other people who will in some way be involved in the service.

The Receiver General hands everyone a thirty-point questionnaire requiring information, ranging from the date and time of the service to the choice of hymns and name of the person who is to give the address. It is highly efficient and leaves no possibility of error of protocol or organization. The result is invariably good and after the service many letters of gratitude are received.

But, as the Precentor says, the services could often be better, and he believes this would be achieved (a) if the family representatives were better prepared for the meeting and encouraged to bring to it ideas and material, and (b) if the meeting itself were less formal, with a different configuration of the seating arrangements. Both would encourage greater family involvement. Who, after all, knew the subject of the service better?

It is not, of course, always possible to give the family precisely what they want. What will work well in a small village church is sometimes lost in a huge building such as the Abbey. Music is a highly sensitive ingredient and the choice of hymns and anthems can make or mar a service. So there needs to be close collaboration. I think it would be best if the Dean and the Precentor were to meet the family representatives privately to plan the content of a service and then use the Jerusalem Chamber meeting to deal with the nuts and bolts of administration – seating arrangements, press announcements, flowers, printing and so forth. The Dean is going to think about this suggestion.

Sunday 14 February 1982

My Installation as Rector of St Margaret's took place this morning in a full church and I think that the new phase in its mission got off to a promising start. A good number of Parliamentarians came, including the Lord Chancellor, Quintin Hailsham, and two former Prime Ministers: Alec Douglas-Home and Ted Heath. The Speaker read the Second Lesson.

In my sermon, based on Psalm 133.1, 'Behold how good and joyful a thing it is, brethren, to dwell together in unity', I took the opportunity to outline my view of the relationship between St Margaret's and the Abbey and between St Margaret's and the House of Commons; also between the Christian faith and the realm of politics:

'What I shall seek to do in this pulpit is to speak of those things that make for true unity – of the God whose all-embracing love draws us to himself and to each other, of the God who offers forgiveness and the possibility of new beginnings, of the God who cares for each and every one of his children. And in speaking of such a God it will of course be necessary to speak of those eternal values of justice and freedom, of acceptance and endurance, of trust and compassion which are essential to wholeness and peace.

And what is spoken from the pulpit needs to be authenticated and expressed in compassionate concern for individuals – not least those who have heavy responsibilities in public life and whose personal lives are sometimes placed under great strain in consequence. In any parish preaching has to be accompanied by pastoral care, and my first month as Speaker's Chaplain has already indicated to me that a parish which embraces the House of Commons will be no exception to this rule.'

Within the congregation of St Margaret's there are, however, quite a lot of people, many of them elderly, some former MPs, who are not involved in Parliament. They will need nurturing, too, though I don't see how I shall find time for much of a pastoral ministry among those who travel to the church from all parts of London and beyond. James Mansel, the retired Sub-Dean of the Chapels Royal and a skilled pastor, is already undertaking some of this work in his capacity as our Honorary Assistant Curate, and I shall encourage him to do more.

Tuesday 16 February 1982

The unexpected death of Gilbert Beach, the St Margaret's Vestry Clerk, has a curious element to it. My predecessor recruited him about three years ago and his duties, part-time, included manning the church telephone, dealing with enquiries about baptisms, weddings, funerals and memorial services, maintaining the church registers and accounting for the petty cash.

Before coming to St Margaret's Gilbert – a man in his mid-sixties – had been the secretary of a London club, so he had some administrative skills and the job here was well below his capacity. For a time he proved to be a useful acquisition. He had a good, albeit somewhat effusive, telephone manner, got on well with the fussy mothers of 'society' brides, kept the registers meticulously and generally made himself useful. It was unfortunate that he and the Head Sidesman were at daggers drawn, but the fault was by no means entirely his.

During the last twelve months, however, other problems arose. Gilbert spent an increasing amount of time in and around the church and tried unsuccessfully to persuade John Baker to make his job full-time. The petty cash accounts were not accurately kept and the vestry became the repository of many wine bottles – some empty, some not.

Shortly after the announcement of my appointment as Rector he became ill and was eventually admitted to hospital for an operation, not of a particularly dangerous sort. When I visited his wife, Eunice, in Putney last week to see how things were going it emerged that previously unopened bank statements and several 'final notice' accounts pointed to a man living well beyond his means. It also turned out that he was a racegoer.

This was to be a part of my St Margaret's inheritance and I was certainly not looking forward to sorting out a situation that would inevitably involve Gilbert's departure. But lo and behold, on the day following my Installation as Rector he died – a most remarkable coincidence and a most improbable solution of my problem.

His wife, who attends St Margaret's, is going to need a lot of help – perhaps financial as well as emotional – and we must do everything possible to support her. I think we can manage without a Vestry Clerk if we establish good co-ordination between the work of my secretary and that of the Verger.

Wednesday 24 February 1982

I am grappling with a knotty problem over an anti-nuclear warfare vigil which has been taking place for some months, on a daily basis, in St Margaret's Churchyard. My predecessor, John Baker, who has been chairing a Church of England working party on the nuclear issue, is convinced that the British Government should give a lead by declaring unilaterally that it will abandon all nuclear weapons. He was therefore quite happy for a well-organized consortium of nuclear disarmers to demonstrate, with placards, speeches and so forth, every day at lunch-time from a position in the churchyard immediately opposite the St Stephen's entrance to Parliament.

The point at issue, however, is that St Margaret's is the official parish church of the House of Commons and a place in which the Speaker has an acknowledged role. It is therefore impossible for us to take, or allow others facilities to take, a partisan position over a political matter, and, inasmuch as the Government is opposed to unilateral nuclear disarmament, the demonstrators are making a strong political statement.

One of the first things the Speaker raised with me after my appointment as Rector had been announced was the difficult position in which he found himself as a result of the vigil. He had received representations from members of the main parties and there was, he told me, a general feeling that the position of St Margaret's *vis-à-vis* the House of Commons was being compromised.

I have discussed this problem with the Chapter and we have agreed that there shall be no demonstration of a political complexion in the precincts of St Margaret's. It will be acceptable for them to be held near the Abbey, but this is bound to be much less attractive to would-be demonstrators, as the site is not visible from Parliament.

Since the organizers of the present vigil were given permission until June, we have decided that they may stay, provided that they reduce their visual material to a single banner with the words 'Pray for Peace'. They will, however, be at liberty to distribute leaflets arguing the case for unilateral nuclear disarmament.

This is, I think, a reasonable compromise in the circumstances, but the unilateralists don't think so and they are generally blaming me – a known radical – for modifying a decision of my predecessor. Emotions are running high at the moment.

Sunday 28 February 1982

The Horse Rangers Association came to St Margaret's this morning for their annual birthday parade service and I can now see, only too clearly, why the overwhelming majority of the regular congregation takes a Sunday off whenever they come.

The Association, let it be said, is an admirable young people's organization. It was founded some years ago by Raymond Gordon, who once saw a small girl gazing enviously at his daughter's pony and thereupon decided to raise money and create an organization that would enable the children of relatively poor parents to learn to ride and care for a pony. This took off and the HRA now has some hundreds of members and instructors, mainly in the Home Counties but with some further afield, and a few branches for disabled children.

The founder also decided that the Association should have a uniform and, having recently attended a performance of the musical *Annie Get Your Gun*, had one designed in a similar cowboy style. This colourful garb looks attractive on the children, but the skin-tight breeches which may well have suited the sylph-like figures of actresses do nothing for the often portly middle-aged women who serve as riding instructors.

Indeed my Honorary Assistant Curate, James Mansel, asked to be excused attendance this morning on the grounds that the sight of these ladies is a hindrance to his spiritual life. The male instructors wear a military-style uniform closely akin to that of the cavalry.

Besides wearing the uniform, the members are encouraged to demonstrate their loyalty to Queen and Country in a somewhat jingoistic fashion, and at one point in the service I was required to read out telegrams from various members of the Royal Family and other notables – all in response to loyal greetings sent to them by the bossy second wife of the founder, so a little phoney. The service itself had to be arranged in a form suitable for children, who packed the church to capacity. There was no problem about it, except that we had to have the National Anthem and hymns such as 'I vow to thee my country'. There was also a curious ceremony in which representatives of the members presented the founder with birthday presents, for it was his birthday that was being celebrated. He, being now well into his eighties and not fully aware of what was going on, could only grunt an acknowledgment of the gifts. It must have been a weird and possibly frightening experience for the children.

They will come again in November, not long after Remembrance Sunday, when they will also march past the Cenotaph.

Thursday 4 March 1982

Richard Hickox, the St Margaret's Organist and Master of the Music, came to see me this morning to explain that he must resign, following his appointment as Artistic Director of the Northern Sinfonia. He was almost in tears, for his ten years at St Margaret's – he was appointed when he was only twenty-four – have been very important to him and certainly he has served the church magnificently.

It is something of a miracle that St Margaret's has been able to claim his allegiance for so long. He is a hugely talented musician who is already Music Director of the City of London Sinfonia and the London Symphony Chorus, as well as Artistic Director of a number of provincial festivals. A great career as a conductor obviously lies before him and he must move on.

Yet week by week he has found time to conduct a mid-week choir practice with boys from Westminster City School, who adore him, and to direct the morning service on Sundays. Until Evensong was abandoned a few years ago, he turned out for that, too, and when financial problems threatened the survival of St Margaret's music he and the adult

164

members of the choir offered to take a cut in their salaries to enable it to continue. Fortunately, this proved to be unnecessary, but the attitude was in marked contrast to that of the Abbey's choral foundation.

For some reason I don't quite understand – I suppose it is personal preference – Richard takes the Psalms and Canticles much more slowly than is customary these days. This greatly irritated my predecessor, John Baker, who was anxious to contain Mattins to sixty minutes, in order that the following Holy Communion might always start on time. It led to some friction, and I dare say that eventually it might have irritated me, but there will be no possibility of this now – sadly.

Monday 8 March 1982

At today's Chapter Meeting I resigned from the office of Treasurer and a generous resolution was passed thanking me for what were described as my 'outstanding services to the Abbey at a vital period in its financial history'.

Normally my resignation would have followed my appointment as Rector of St Margaret's and Speaker's Chaplain as a matter of course. But there is a problem inasmuch as Sebastian Charles, who is the only possible successor, seems to be quite incapable of coping with the Treasurer's heavy responsibilities. Paradoxically, he is the only Canon of Westminster ever to have taken a degree in Commerce (in his case at Madras University), but he is without the intellectual capacity and the energy to take on any major responsibility.

At first the Receiver General, who relies very much on the Treasurer's involvement in financial and administrative matters, wondered if I might carry on for a time, but after less than a month at St Margaret's it is evident that the opportunities for developing work both there and in the House of Commons make this impossible. Hence my resignation and the election of Sebastian as my successor.

The financial situation needs constant attention, but Reg Pullen, the Receiver General, is highly dedicated and competent, so nothing should go seriously wrong. The need for us to entrust him with so much responsibility raises other questions, however, about the locus of power in our community.

Wednesday 10 March 1982

Edward Knapp-Fisher, Sebastian Charles and I have registered our great displeasure at the news that Anthony Harvey, our new Canon who will join the Chapter from Oxford in September, is to be absent for three months next year because of his commitment to a lecture tour in Australia and New Zealand.

We welcomed Anthony's appointment, since he is a very good New Testament scholar and we were hoping for a scholar of some sort to replace John Baker. But the long delay over his appointment and his arrival at Westminster was already causing us disquiet. The announcement that John was to be the next Bishop of Salisbury was made last May, Anthony Harvey's appointment to succeed him was made in December, and he will be Installed in September – sixteen months after the impending vacancy became public knowledge. There is of course often a price to be paid for appointing an academic to any post inasmuch as he generally cannot move until the end of the academic year, but any system that requires sixteen months to put someone in place on a Chapter cannot be described as efficient.

It is this delay that has made us angry about the new Canon's three months absence next year. When someone accepts a new appointment his existing commitments should be subordinated to his new responsibilities and, if necessary, abandoned or revised. It is not good enough to demand that their future colleagues should alter their diaries to cover a three months' absence, but the Dean is unwilling for us to dig in our heels over this, lest it gets our relationship with Anthony Harvey off to a bad start.

Tuesday 23 March 1982

An odd, probably absurd, issue of protocol has arisen over the status of the Archbishop of Canterbury when he comes on Thursday to preach at the unveiling of a memorial stone to all who have died in this century in the causes of justice, freedom and peace.

When the Archbishop last attended a special service he brought with him his chaplain, who went before him in the procession carrying his primatial cross. But the presence of a chaplain and a primatial cross imply some sort of seniority and jurisdiction, which the Archbishop does not have in the Abbey.

So the Dean is to contact him about the Thursday arrangements and tell him to come unaccompanied. In the procession he will either walk with the Senior Canon, which the Preacher normally does, or be conducted by a Verger ahead of the members of the Collegiate body.

Viewed in the light of the world's problems, this is plain nonsense, but if the Abbey's life has distinctive traditions, which have made it the place it is, and if we wish to continue to assert our independence of external authority, apart from that of the Crown, I suppose we must insist on the details that express our special position.

Saturday 3 April 1982

For the first time since Suez Parliament met today in emergency session, the Argentinian forces having invaded and occupied the Falkland Islands yesterday. I went across this morning to conduct Prayers and found the corridors buzzing with shock and outrage. When I joined the Speaker's procession, however, the Serjeant-at-Arms merely murmured 'We are living in stirring times', while the Speaker, who looked anxious, confined himself to 'This is going to be an historic day'.

The chamber was packed to capacity, with some members sitting on the floor, and many others occupying seats in the gallery. The Opposition Front Bench members stood aside to let me through and, crisis or no crisis, I read Prayers which have been unaltered since 1661. I sometimes wonder if it is helpful that the content of the Prayers should be so constrained, but most Members feel it better that they should be free to carry into a traditional and familiar act of prayer their own concerns, rather than have these imposed by the Chaplain. They are probably right.

By the time Prayers were over and I had deposited my robes in my room, the gallery seats reserved for Officers of the House were all occupied, so I stood behind the Speaker's chair for the debate. The Prime Minister was surprisingly nervous and seemed unsure of herself. She is of course carrying a heavy responsibliity and is, I suppose, trapped between the need to assert Britain's intention to retain sovereignty over the Falkland Islands, whatever the cost, and the recognition that this crisis would not have arisen had her Government taken action as soon as the Argentinians made their intentions clear.

Michael Foot, the Leader of the Opposition, made a surprisingly belligerent speech for someone whose outlook had always seemed close to pacifism, and the Opposition is generally supporting vigorous action against Argentina. Under no circumstances will the House of Commons accept the possibility of transferring the sovereignty of a territory without the consent of its inhabitants. There was in fact a markedly jingoistic element in many of the speeches and anger was turned not so much on Margaret Thatcher as on the Foreign and Commonwealth Office and John Nott, the Defence Secretary.

John Nott's own speech was very poor indeed and he made a serious mistake when he tried to turn the crisis to Party advantage. This didn't come off and was entirely inappropriate in a House that was, temporarily no doubt, united in crisis. Enoch Powell referred to Margaret Thatcher's reputation as the 'Iron Lady' and ended in his most ominous tones, 'Now we shall see of what metal this lady is made'.

This evening the Bishop of London, Graham Leonard, conducted a confirmation of adults in the Abbey, and I couldn't help contrasting this event with what I had been experiencing earlier across the road in Parliament. A confirmation is not of course an occasion for discussing foreign policy but, at a moment when the nation is facing an acute crisis, an address to adults entering into a new Christian commitment that includes not a single reference to the existence of such a crisis seems to me to be gravely deficient.

Sunday 4 April 1982

When I woke up this morning I realized that it would be quite impossible to preach the sermon I had prepared for Mattins and that, in the parish church of the House of Commons of all places, it was necessary to attempt a Christian evaluation of the war that has now broken out. So I had a quick breakfast and prepared something different.

I began by saying that the Christian faith offers us no *direct* instructions on what to do in the present, or indeed any other international crisis, not because Christianity is unconcerned about political matters but because it is concerned with eternal values and leaves every generation of Christian people to work out for itself how these values are to be expressed in local, national and international communities. So we have no direct word of the Lord; there can be no leaping straight from the Bible to the current situation in the South Atlantic. The issue for us is: How is love best expressed in our present relations with the people of the Falkland Islands and Argentina?

I then examined briefly the pacifist position in the light of the need to love our neighbours as ourselves – such love involving practical matters, including seeing that our neighbours have the freedom to make their own decisions and to determine the course their lives shall take.

This brought me to consider the case for intervention in the Falklands Islands. The people of those islands have been subjected to naked aggression and, since all negotiations have failed, we have a duty to set them free. We have to be sure, however, that any action we take now will serve the long-term interests of those we are trying to help. This is not an easy calculation: it involves risks.

Another argument for intervention is that the cause of justice and freedom in the world requires that acts of aggression should always be resisted and shown not to pay. I cited the example of other aggressive acts by other nations in our own century and the disastrous consequences of failing to check them in their early stages.

Against this, however, it can be argued that the Falkland Islands situation is a special one. The occupation of these islands by Argentinian forces will not necessarily lead to acts of aggression elsewhere, and the introduction of open warfare between Britain and a Latin American nation may have serious consequences for long-term peace and stability in the world as a whole. Therefore love requires us to get the best deal we can for the Falkland Islanders and minimize our and the world's losses.

This, I went on, is the dilemma in which we find ourselves and, since there is no direct word from God, we must agonize over the issues and do what we believe to be right, i.e. the most loving, recognizing always that we may be mistaken. I then made four specific suggestions:

1. We must continue to hope and pray for a negotiated settlement. There will have to be a settlement sooner or later, so let it be sooner.
2. We must resist the temptation to indulge in the wrong kind of patriotism and suppose that British pride and dignity are the most important things at stake. Now that ships and aircraft are in action it will be easy to become over-excited and forget that the ultimate aim must be to establish justice and freedom in both the Falkland Islands and Argentina. Military action must be kept to the minimum.
3. We must remember that Argentina is a nation of Christian people – far more devout than most of us here in Britain. Its government is an appalling Fascist dictatorship, but its people are our fellow Christians who, like us, are struggling to travel along the way of love. So, vindictiveness and hatred on our part cannot be squared with the Gospel.
4. We must remember those who are carrying terrible burdens of responsibility on our behalf – members of the armed forces, who are risking life and limb, and their relations and friends at home; the Prime Minister, members of the Government, and Members of Parliament, so many of whom worship from time to time in this church, and who now have to make the most appallingly difficult decisions. They should be able to count on our prayers.

I concluded:

'Just what the future holds for us all is, as always, far from clear. But this is God's world, and if we try to follow the way of love, uncertain though this may be, I believe that His will will triumph – even though we may make some mistakes along the way.'

There were quite a lot of MPs in the large congregation, and a number of them thanked me afterwards for what they decribed as 'a very helpful sermon'. Some MPs have clearly been very shaken by the events of this past week.

Monday 5 April 1982

There was, as anticipated, a full turn-out this afternoon for Rab Butler's memorial service in the Abbey, but there were some notable absentees, including the Speaker, because the service was arranged for 2.30 p.m. – the precise time at which the House of Commons meets. I slipped in a little late after Prayers. The Speaker and some Government ministers who were on Front Bench duty were annoyed by the timing and asked me to request that the Speaker's Office be consulted about the days and times of big Parliamentary occasions such as this. Today, however, the Prince of Wales's diary seems to have been the controlling factor.

The address was given, not by an eminent Parliamentarian, but by a Mirfield monk – none other than Harry Williams, who was Dean of Trinity College, Cambridge when Rab was the Master and evidently forged a close friendship both with him and with Mollie his wife. So we didn't get much politics in the address: rather was it, in true Harry Williams fashion, a deep and affectionate analysis of Rab's characer. I liked his summing up:

'Behind that immense subtlety of mind and manoeuvre, so charac-teristic of Rab, there lay a conviction, simple yet profound, to which I believe he totally dedicated himself. It could be summed up in some well-known words from the Gospels: "A house divided against itself cannot stand."'

This also won the approval of the Prime Minister, Margaret Thatcher, who managed to be there in spite of the Falklands crisis and after the service asked me to convey to Harry her best thanks not only for his address but also for his books. This astonished me greatly, but in further conversation with her it turned out that she has read virtually all his books and, she said, derived a good deal from them. There was no opportunity to pursue this with her, so I can only guess that, while much of Harry's exceedingly liberal ethical stance may not appeal to her, his deeply personalized interpretation of Christianity fits very well with her own highly individualistic view of life and deep distrust of any corporate approach to human problems. Harry is, I suppose, himself a high Tory, though I have not previously thought of him as such.

I passed on the message. Harry was chuffed and said that he would write to thank her for it.

The task force of ships and commandos that was assembled during the weekend has sailed today for the South Atlantic and, if further attempts at a negotiated settlement fail, will be ready to go into action in two to three weeks time. Apparently large crowds gathered at Portsmouth to see the ships leave and there was much flag-waving and military music.

Meanwhile the Foreign Secretary, Lord Carrington, has resigned, along with two other Foreign Office ministers, Humphrey Atkins and Richard Luce. The crisis stems from a bad misreading of the South Atlantic situation by the Foreign Office. John Nott offered his resignation but this was refused. Francis Pym, the Leader of the House, is now Foreign Secretary.

The Speaker asked to see me this evening to discuss this and that – in particular the reaction of Members to the events of the last few days. His own view is that, although a united front is being displayed at the moment, this will quickly disappear if and when any British ships are sunk or any servicemen are killed.

On the way into his room I bumped into John Biffen, who has left his job as Secretary of State for Trade in order to succeed Francis Pym as Leader of the House. He had been discussing with George the forthcoming business of the House and, I suppose, the need to clear the deck should any further crisis develop. He wasn't in a very cheerful mood and I gather that in Cabinet he voted against sending the task force.

Tuesday 6 April 1982

A letter today from Charles Smyth, who was here from 1946–56 and by all accounts was a hugely effective Rector. Unfortunately, he fell out with all his colleagues on the Chapter and had several rows with Westminster School, so he returned to Corpus Christi College, Cambridge, whence he had come, and wrote a devastatingly candid biography of Archbishop Cyril Garbett. Curiously, his most widely read book was entitled *The Friendship of Christ*.

My dear Rector,

Will you allow your oldest surviving predecessor as Rector of St Margaret's (I have just entered upon the eightieth year of my life) to send you his best wishes as you embark upon your first Holy Week and Easter as Rector of the church where I spent the happiest years that I have ever known?

I can claim to have known many of my predecessors in that office, going back to Armitage Robinson (whom I knew as Dean of Wells when I was a student at Wells Theological College), Hensley Henson, Vernon Storr (the first Canon of Westminster to invite me to preach in the Abbey) and, of course, Alan Don. But I am now in the sear and yellow leaf – R.A.Butler and I were elected Fellows of Corpus on the same day, he to teach Modern Languages and I to teach History, when we were both very young – and I doubt if there is anyone left in your congregation who would remember my wife and me, unless possibly Dr Lloyd Rusby.

I came to St M's shortly after World War 2, when the church was in a sad condition, having been hit by an oil bomb (and consequently closed for twelve months): many of the windows had been blown out, and the Sunday congregation was little more than a handful. But we still had 'fashionable weddings', beginning with that of Mary Churchill and Christopher Soames; and it was a great challenge to get the church back 'on the map'.

I am now painfully crippled by a leg ulcer, and there can be few traces of my ten years as Rector, apart from *Church and Parish* and a small paperback collection of sermons (*Good Friday at St Margaret's*) which I edited. But I have many memories to treasure in my old age, and even if we never meet I can at least send you my best wishes, and my hope that you will find your work at St M's as happy and rewarding as I found mine.

Yours very sincerely,

Charles Smyth

I must tell him in my reply that when I was a student in London in the late 1940s I sometimes used to attend St Margaret's to hear him preach to what had by then become a very large congregation. His sermons, which were more like lectures with a considerable historical content, always lasted for half an hour and were very demanding, intellectually. I never dreamt that I would one day occupy the same pulpit.

After Evensong a wreath was laid on the grave of Charles Darwin in the North Aisle of the Nave, and some special prayers were said – this being the centenary of his death.

The presence of Darwin's grave in the Abbey often causes comment and some surprise. Visitors from the Soviet Union, especially, cannot understand how someone whom they regard as a pillar of atheism has found his way into a great Christian shrine such as this. The truth is that Darwin, who in his early years felt drawn to ordination in the Church of England, was not an atheist. Towards the end of his life, apparently, he came increasingly agnostic about matters of Christian belief, which was hardly surprising considering the response to his work by people like Bishop Samuel Wilberforce, but I don't think that he ever saw his theory of evolution through natural selection as incompatible with religion. Nor is it.

The Victorians evidently thought sufficiently well of him to have his body interred near the grave of Isaac Newton. Around them both are the graves or memorials of other leading scientists, including William Herschel, the 'father' of modern astronomy; Joseph Lister, the pioneer of antiseptic treatment; and Joseph Dalton Hooker, the botanist friend of Darwin.

Monday 24 May 1982

At the Chapter Meeting the Dean initiated a discussion on the Falklands crisis. There was plenty to discuss, for although British forces have established a beachhead in San Carlos Bay on the main island, there have already been casualties on both sides. The sinking of the destroyer HMS Sheffield by an Exocet missile three weeks ago killed 21 sailors, and HMS Ardent was sunk during the landings three days ago. The torpedoing of the Argentinian cruiser Belgrano on 2 May left 362 feared dead and this is causing a lot of controversy, nationally and inter-nationally, since the ship was clearly well outside the 200-mile exclusion zone which the British Government has declared to be the sphere of hostile action.

The Dean wondered if the Chapter ought to take what he called 'some positive line' and he mentioned the possibility of our sending a letter to *The Times*. As an avowed pacifist, he is himself strongly opposed to the war. During the discussion it soon became evident that we were divided on the matter, and that it would be impossible to draft a letter for publication which all could sign.

I expressed surprise that no one had so much as mentioned the war in a sermon from the Abbey's pulpit, and that my own sermon in St Margaret's on the day before the task force sailed had been the only attempt to evaluate the crisis in a Christian perspective. The Dean said that preachers were entirely free to express their views on this and other matters, without in any way committing the Dean and Chapter to a particular position.

It was agreed that special posters should be exhibited inviting people entering the Abbey to offer special prayers for peace, and that two minutes silence will be observed every day at 1.00 p.m. for as long as the crisis persists.

Thursday 27 May 1982

This morning we had in the Abbey the service and ceremony of the Installation of the Knights Grand Cross of the Order of the Bath – a very colourful occasion held every four years and attended this year by the Queen as well as by the Prince of Wales, who always comes as the Great Master of the Order.

The preparations and rehearsals for this event required the Abbey to be closed to the public on the day before and the demand for tickets, restricted to members of the Order, is so great that only a small proportion of them can ever be admitted. The procession, captured so dramatically in Canaletto's famous painting, is certainly something to behold and the Canons were provided with cream and pink mantles to match those of the knights, but without their elaborate decoration.

The service itself was fairly brief: a couple of hymns, 'Praise to the Lord, the Almighty, the King of creation' at the beginning and 'For all the Saints' at the end; Psalm 68, 'Let God arise, and let his enemies be scattered'; one lesson, Philippians 4.4–8; some special prayers; and Elgar's Imperial March for the procession to the King Henry VII Chapel.

The actual Installation of the Knights in stalls in the Chapel is a highly elaborate ceremony, carried out by the Prince of Wales, and is witnessed only by the other senior Knights and the Dean and Chapter – also on this occasion by the Queen. The long rehearsals paid off in precision on the day and there were successfully installed two Admirals, four Generals, two Air Marshals, and Lord Adeane, formerly Private Secretary to the Queen and father of the present Private Secretary to the Prince of Wales.

The degree of compromise involved in ministering in the Abbey was,

I thought, vividly and poignantly expressed when the Dean, a life-long, 100% pacifist was required to receive the sword of the senior newly-installed Knight, lay it on the altar, and then return it to him with the admonition:

> 'I exhort and admonish you to use your Sword to the Glory of God, the Defence of the Gospel, the maintenance of your Sovereign's Right and Honour, and of all Equity and Justice to the utmost of your Power.'

I suggested some time ago that the final procession should go outside the Abbey, as it obviously did in Canaletto's time, and thus allow the public some sight of its splendour. But the hierarchy of the Order turned this suggestion down, chiefly I suspect because of the security problems that would attend the public appearance together of so many senior officers of the armed forces.

Saturday 29 May 1982

This evening Jo and I went to a reception at Archbishop's House, a dark, red-brick building located behind the Roman Catholic cathedral. We were to see and hear Pope John Paul II, back in London after the very remarkable ecumenical service in which he shared in Canterbury Cathedral this morning.

Virtually every room in Archbishop's House was packed with people who felt privileged and honoured to have been invited to an unprecedented occasion in English history. We were in a large room that seemed to have been allocated to leaders from other churches, people prominent in public life, and representatives of the media. The wine flowed freely, the canapés were substantial and I spoke to Mary Whitehouse, Lord Longford and many others whose company I do not normally keep.

Inevitably, I suppose, the Pope's arrival was delayed, but no one cared, and in due course we fell silent as Cardinal Hume led His Holiness into the room. He was, as always, wearing a white soutane and skull cap which, together with his strong, yet gentle, features, makes a commanding presence. After seeing so much of him over the years through the media it seemed slightly odd to encounter him in person and to find him no different from the pictures.

The Cardinal bade him welcome on our behalf and invited him to address us. Which he did in the kind of broken English that commands attention because of its imperfections. But we were bemused by the nature of his utterance. He spoke of the need to raise money for the furthering of the church's mission, of the privilege of sacrificial giving, of the importance of church schools, and of the vocation to manage the church's finances. With this the successor of Peter moved on.

What he had said was all true, but why had the man whom many believe to be the holder of the keys to the Kingdom of Heaven chosen to speak to us about cash? There is certainly a spiritual element in money-raising, but this was surely pressing the point too far in this company. We were greatly mystified until on the way out we learned that on entering our room the Pope had been handed the wrong speech.

Evidently the room next to ours was occupied by the treasurers of Roman Catholic schools and others connected with the finances of the dioceses of England and Wales, and the speech was intended for them. Instead, no doubt, they heard about the witness of Christians separated from the see of Rome and of the need for us all to work together in opposition to abortion, euthanasia and the other 'evils' of our time. Perhaps, after all, the mistake was providential.

Monday 7 June 1982

The saga of the weather vanes for Henry VII's Chapel now seems to have ended, but not without the mixture of confusion, acrimony and unforeseen cost that often accompanies new projects in this place.

The early sixteenth-century Chapel, a truly glorious building, is known to have had gilded weather vanes on the twelve finials of its roof, but over the course of time these were lost and never replaced. Now that the roof is under restoration the Surveyor wondered if we might think of making good what our predecessors had neglected, and the Royal Institution of Chartered Surveyors whose headquarters is nearby very generously offered to meet the cost of the new weather vanes – something in excess of £25,000.

A prototype was submitted for the Dean and Chapter's approval and then remitted to the Architecture Advisory Panel. The vane was in the form of a lion rampant, which is the symbol of the RICS, and seemed eminently suitable. But when it reached the Panel one of the members, Sir Anthony Wagner, who is Garter King of Arms, apparently went up in smoke, threatened to resign, and declared that since Henry VII's Chapel is a royal foundation it may be ornamented only with royal symbols approved by his section of the College of Arms. A lion rampant, such as used by the RICS, does not fall into that category.

He had a point, which we readily conceded, and he and the Surveyor then sought out royal devices within the Chapel itself. There were more than enough of these from which a choice might be made, but at this stage Sir Anthony informed us that he could not give further advice as a member of the Architectural Advisory Panel but only as Garter King of Arms, for which fees would have to be paid.

Again, he had a point, though we rather wished that he had not made it, and since we were anxious not to burden the RICS with extra costs we met them ourselves. The Prince of Wales was also brought into the discussion, since the Order of the Bath, of which he is the Great Master, has a special interest in the Chapel, but fortunately he did not charge a fee for his opinion.

Now the designs have been chosen, everyone is happy, and as work on the roof progresses the weather vanes will be installed. They should look very jolly on days that are both windy and sunny.

Tuesday 8 June 1982

This morning for the first time ever a President of the United States has addressed a joint session of the Houses of Parliament. He didn't say anything particularly striking – mainly generalities about the historic bonds that unite our two countries, the need to strengthen these bonds for the benefit of the whole world, and how much he values his friendship and collaboration with Margaret Thatcher – but it was of course a great Parliamentary occasion and there were few absentees. I went in as part of the Speaker's procession.

I was specially struck by Ronald Reagan's eloquence. He spoke at some length without any sign of a script or even a few notes and as a performance it was a *tour de force*. But as we were leaving at the end I noticed two small, mirror-like objects suspended from the roof above the rostrum. These were, I learned later, auto-cues, and the President had in fact delivered his speech from a full script transmitted on to these screens.

Even so, it was a masterly performance, since I know from personal experience that auto-cues in television studios are by no means easy to use convincingly, and very few people in the audience could have been aware of the President's method. The fact that he was once an actor must help.

Monday 14 June 1982

The Prime Minister interrupted a debate in the House of Commons this afternoon to announce that a report had just been received indicating that Argentinian forces were flying the white flag over Port Stanley. The war was now ended. The House cheered, there was much waving of order papers, and a general feeling of relief that a war which could and should have been avoided had been brought to a satisfactory conclusion relatively speedily – though not without the loss of over 250 British and, it is said, more than 600 Argentinian lives.

When Margaret Thatcher returned to Downing Street she was greeted by cheering crowds which sang 'Rule Britannia', 'For she's a jolly good fellow' and the National Anthem. In response she said, 'We had to do what we had to do. Great Britain is great again.'

No doubt there will in due course be a national service of thanks-giving, but I expect this will take place in St Paul's Cathedral, where the military associations are much stronger than those of the Abbey. I hope so, anyway, though I shall have to say something more about the issues in my sermon in St Margaret's next Sunday. The defeat of a Third-World power by the sophisticated British military machine, aided by the United States, doesn't warrant much of a celebration.

Sunday 20 June 1982

There was a large congregation in St Margaret's this morning, inflated no doubt by some who came to give thanks for the end of the fighting in the Falkland Islands.

In my sermon I said that since, as Christians, we are committed to the cause of peace we are bound to wonder if we should ever have entered into this particular conflict. And if we conclude that the action of Britain was justified we must try to see how it squares with the gospel. 'Each of us must answer this question for himself and it is no part of my duty as a preacher to lay down the law about this matter.'

I devoted the rest of the sermon to our examination of the place of compromise in the actions of those who are seeking to live in the light of God's love revealed in Jesus Christ. Whatever the Government's decision over the Falklands Islands, for Christians committed to the way of love, there was bound to be an element of compromise. There was no possibility of translating the Sermon on the Mount directly into the situation that blew up in the South Atlantic. All we could, and can, say is, 'Given the position in which we now find ourselves, what compro-mise with the absolute demand of love will enable us to achieve the most just result?'

'Decisions of this sort, however, can never be made with absolute certainty, for our judgment has to be made in an atmosphere befouled by sin, and by people like ourselves who are still in the process of discovering what it means to live fully in the ambit of love. Yet, in spite of the uncertainty, decisions have to be made and compromises accepted.

These compromises are a reflection of the truth that because we belong to a world in which good and evil are mixed, we live within a massive compromise. The Kingdom of God is a kingdom of love, and it is generally advanced not by simple choices or noisy slogans, but by our courage, faith and skill in distinguishing between Christian and un-Christian compromises. May the God of love guide and sustain us as we seek to do just that, and may the same God of love forgive us when we make wrong choices.'

Wednesday 14 July 1982

Pigeons are a problem. They get into the Abbey, are quite often to be seen flying in the Choir area during Evensong, and sometimes trigger off the burglar and fire alarms. They also make a mess, and this displeases the Surveyor of the Fabric, who raised the matter when he attended yesterday's Chapter meeting.

Various remedies have been tried. Motor-car headlights projected into the darkened building one evening failed to draw them out, and corn-seed soaked in whisky left them stone-cold sober. The advice of the Royal Society for the Protection of Birds is now being sought, and the Surveyor has ordered a recording of a kestrel hawk in the hope that this may drive them back to Trafalgar Square.

We are subject to some constraints, however, since the Dean and his wife have a great attachment to all forms of wild life and would be distressed by violence towards pigeons. During the discussion yesterday the Dean ventured to suggest that the presence of pigeons would have presented no problem for the mediaeval monks of Westminster, and I could not forbear to respond that far from regarding them as a problem the monks would have seen them as a solution. The monastic records indicate that they were very partial to pigeon pie.

Saturday 17 July 1982

The St Margaret's Summer Fête held on the Dean's Yard green today was a happy occasion, though the estimated total proceeds, about

£1,700, has disappointed the Fête committee and is really a rather poor return on the immense amount of work, extending over several months, that went into the event.

The last Fête, held two years ago after a long interval, was very successful and raised £3,000. This led the committee to become over-ambitious and to incur expenses that reduced considerably the potential profit. They decided, for example, to insure the event against rain – at a premium of £500. But it was a gloriously sunny day, with not a cloud in the sky from start to finish. It was also decided to hire an expensive herd of donkeys from Hampstead, but few children were tempted by the prospect of a ride around Dean's Yard.

The Duke of Westminster was a disappointment, too. He was invited to open the Fête, which he did admirably, but, although reputed to be one of the richest men in Britain, he gave no donation, nor did he purchase a single item from any of the stalls.

If only it had poured with rain for most of the day, we would have made £5,000.

Thursday 22 July 1982

Scarlet cassocks were the chief excitement at today's Chapter meeting. Although most people believe the Abbey clergy to have been wearing those for centuries, they were in fact prescribed for this Royal Peculiar and for Royal Chaplains by King Edward VII, as part of a campaign to brighten up royal ceremonies.

Since then, however, quite a lot of other churches and institutions, claiming royal foundation, have taken to clothing their clergy in scarlet, and many parish choirs are also in scarlet – chiefly because it is thought to be a nice colour. But the Queen, who is a stickler for protocol, doesn't approve of this. After visiting Winchester for the Royal Maundy three years ago, she enquired why the clergy and choir of that cathedral were wearing the Royal livery. An explanation that Winchester had been a royal church and a place of coronations long before Westminster Abbey was even thought of did not satisfy Her Majesty, but to show there was no ill-feeling, she paid for the scarlet cassocks to be replaced by others in a different shade of red. This must have cost her all of £3,000.

Now the Receiver General has seen a confidential letter sent by the Lord Chamberlain to the main ecclesiastical outfitters asking them to point out to would-be purchasers of scarlet the restrictions on its use. Since the edict mentions only clergy, we wondered if the Abbey Choir and the Lay Officers were entitled to be in scarlet, but Johnnie Johnson, the No. 2 in the Lord Chamberlain's office, has assured us that they are.

Meanwhile another problem, as to where and in what circumstances scarlet cassocks may be worn, claimed our attention. It was reported that one of the Priest Vicars – these are musical clergy who come in from their parishes to sing Evensong when neither the Precentor nor the Chaplain is available – has been observed riding to the Abbey on his motor cycle wearing a crash helmet and a scarlet cassock. Only one of the Chapter had witnessed this remarkable sight, but we readily agreed that such flamboyance was inappropriate and that the miscreant should be advised to leave his cassock at the Abbey and wear it only when on duty.

I never cease to marvel at the subjects which the Dean and Canons of Westminster are called upon to consider.

Friday 23 July 1982

The Speaker gave a splendid dinner last evening in honour of the Queen Mother and it turned out to be a very good occasion. The Queen Mother obviously enjoyed herself because she stayed quite late – until well after 11 o'clock – and at the time of departure looked much less tired than I felt, even though she is more than a quarter of a century older than I am.

Apart from the late ending, the normal pattern of Speaker's dinners was followed, though the menu was upgraded a little. Vichyssoise was followed by salmon trout, then came a marvellous concoction of strawberries, cream and Grande Chartreuse. Very good wines accompanied each course and there was a 1966 brandy afterwards.

George chose his guests from among the Privy Counsellors in the main parties: Michael Foot, Merlyn Rees, Alan Williams and Walter Harrison (Labour); John Biffen and Norman St John-Stevas (Conservative); Roy Jenkins (Social Democrat); Donald Stewart (Scottish Nationalist). Charles Irving (Conservative) was there presumably because he is chairman of the House of Commons catering committee; Bryant Godman Irvine is a Deputy Speaker; and I was there to say Grace.

The Queen Mother brought with her, no doubt by agreement, a considerable entourage of courtiers: Sir Martin Gilliat, her private secretary; Ruth, Lady Fermoy and the Dowager Duchess of Abercorn, Ladies of the Bedchamber (what does that involve?); Sir Eric Penn; the Duke and Duchess of Grafton; and the Lord Chamberlain – so there was no shortage of people of 'quality'.

George, who clearly gets on very well with the Queen Mother, made a characteristically 'George' speech – 'A memorable occasion . . . a wonderful servant of the nation and Commonwealth .. . a privilege to be in her company . . . so much to be grateful for . . . the Queen Mother in the Mother of Parliaments' and so on, with a little joke inserted here and there. George's combination of dignity and warmth is unbeatable.

After the meal I had some interesting talk with Michael Foot about the effect of the Falklands War on the political situation in Britain. He, like almost everyone else, believes it saved Margaret Thatcher's bacon and was in a sense her war. On a sofa Norman St John-Stevas and Charles Irving were keeping the Queen Mother happy – 'three queens in a row' someone wickedly whispered to me.

Walking through the gaslit Cloisters on the way home Jo remarked that the evening had been some way removed from the pie and peas suppers we attended when I was a curate in a North West Durham mining parish.

Monday 27 September 1982

The Dean told me this afternoon that his hope of having a memorial to George Bernard Shaw in Poets' Corner has been dashed by opposition from the Bernard Shaw Society. For Edward the matter of a man's religious beliefs, or lack of them, is neither here nor there when a possible relationship with Westminster Abbey is concerned. The only question is whether or not an individual merits national recognition – in this case for his contribution to literature. Edward also admires his vegetarianism and other unorthodox views, which is not quite the point. I share this general approach, but of course memorialization cannot really take place if a candidate's chief supporters are against it, and since Shaw left specific instructions that he was not to have a memorial in Westminster Abbey it is difficult to see how he can ever be allocated a place in Poets' Corner among his peers. The bust of General Booth, the founder of the Salvation Army, in St George's Chapel is, however, often mistaken for him.

Tuesday 12 October 1982

Chapter discussed today a paper I had circulated on my problem of trying to combine the responsibilities of being a Canon of the Abbey,

Rector of St Margaret's and Speaker's Chaplain. The last two of these are developing jobs since St Margaret's is, more than ever before, being used for special services (some of which are transferred from the Abbey) and the scope for ministry in the House of Commons (never before seriously attempted) seems to be limitless. I find myself chasing about like a scalded cat and the quality of my ministry is bound, sooner or later, to suffer.

I pointed out, however, that a significant amount of my time is taken up with routine discussions and consultations with those organizing special services, and that if the Chaplain of the Abbey were to take over responsibility for this liturgical work the Rector would have much more time for his other concerns. The Chaplain's current pastoral work would have to be handled differently.

This suggestion was sympathetically received, though the Sub-Dean wondered if the best solution might not be to release the Rector from some of his responsibility for St Margaret's by appointing the Dean as Rector and letting the four Canons take a period of Residence in St Margaret's. The difficulty over this suggestion, however, is that the Dean simply could not exercise a dynamic leadership in both churches and responsibility might well fall between several stools. Furthermore, a move in this direction would need an Act of Parliament modifying the requirement that one of the Canons must be put in charge of St Margaret's and designated Rector.

In the end it was decided that as soon as financial circumstances permit we shall recruit a second Chaplain whose prime responsibility will be to me and to St Margaret's, with any surplus time going to work in the Abbey. It was deemed unwise to divert the present Abbey Chaplain from his current work. The cost is likely to be about £10,000 plus accommodation in the Precincts or nearby, and this is a considerable difficulty in our straitened financial circumstances. However, it was agreed that it is a question of priorities and that an attempt to find the necessary money will be made at next month's Budget meetings.

31 October 1982

The end of October has arrived and still there is no sign of an end to the Dean and Chapter's negotiations with the Lay Vicars over their terms of service. I think it is the case that none of our fortnightly Chapter Meetings this year has been without this item on the agenda, and there have been many other smaller, and sometimes bitter, meetings besides.

The basic problem is that Simon Preston, who has already worked wonders with the Choir since he succeeded Douglas Guest as Organist and Master of the Choristers in 1981, believes that the Abbey's music is still not up to the required standard and that this is due to the overall performance of the Lay Vicars.

Some of this problem relates to the fact that the best singers among them are frequently absent, because of other more lucrative commitments, and employ Deputies of an inferior standard. Our proposal therefore is that absences be restricted to no more than one in each part (Bass, Tenor, Alto) and that the choice of Deputies be restricted to a relatively small group of competent singers approved by the Organist.

We are also proposing that voice testing be introduced in order that a degree of control can be exercised over the quality of performance. If a Lay Vicar appears to be falling below the required standard he could then be required to undertake further training or, if his voice had permanently declined, be asked to leave.

Simon Preston is also keen that we should move towards fixed-term contracts, in place of the present retirement at sixty agreement, but I think this is unrealistic except in the case of young recruits from the Oxford and Cambridge college choirs.

We propose, too, that the Dean should have the authority to require the presence of all the Lay Vicars on certain important occasions, e.g. major services at which the Queen is present. At the Order of the Bath Installation in May four or five Deputies were employed and the music suffered in consequence.

Inevitably financial considerations enter into all these matters and the whole business has become exceedingly wearying and often unpleasant. It is a poor way to run the music of a place like Westminster Abbey, and the public would be astonished to know what underlies the great acts of worship they attend or see on television.

Part of the trouble, undoubtedly, is the financial insecurity felt by musicians who are not in the top bracket of their profession. But over the course of many years a culture of conflict has developed and we now seem to be at a point where nothing can be done without recourse to lawyers, by both sides.

I shall be surprised if the present dispute is settled by the end of the year.

Wednesday 10 November 1982

Pressure is mounting to have Noel Coward memorialized in the Abbey. During the past few weeks the Dean has received some thirty letters asking for this to be considered – most of them from influential people in the theatrical world – and since many of the letters are couched in identical terms it seems that an organized campaign has started. Sir John Tilney appears to be master-minding it and probably drafted the letter. An approach for support has also been made to the Queen Mother and possibly to the Queen, though it is unlikely that either of them will wish to be involved with a pressure group.

The case for memorializing Noel Coward is, I suppose, quite a strong one and there are ample precedents for honouring stage celebrities in this way. David Garrick and Henry Irving are actually in Poets' Corner, but this wouldn't be the place for Noel Coward. The Dean is thinking more in terms of the South Quire Aisle, near the memorial to Sybil Thorndike – if, that is, it is decided to go ahead.

Thursday 11 November 1982

There has been a great fuss about a new hymn book, *Hymns for Today's Church*, which was launched at a special service held in St Margaret's last evening. It has been produced by an evangelical group meeting under the chairmanship of the Bishop of Chester, Michael Baughen, and it not only includes many new hymns, which was to be expected, but also substantial alterations to traditional, established hymns.

If the committee did not approve of the doctrinal emphasis of a particular hymn they changed it – in some instances making it say the precise opposite of what its original author intended. Which raises, of course, questions about artistic integrity, but this has not been the cause of the controversy.

The great crime has been to provide an alternative to the traditional National Anthem. And this to be associated with St Margaret's – the parish church of the House of Commons. MPs have protested vociferously and the media have taken it up with a vengeance. Many, not realizing that we were doing no more than hire out the building to the proprietors of the hymn book, supposed that I was responsible for the wretched compilation.

In the end I denied facilities to the television people who wanted to cover the launching service and heighten the controversy. The service itself was innocent enough, though of inordinate length, and afterwards the Bishop of Chester – not one of the most sensitive members of the episcopal bench – presented me with a copy of the book and expressed the hope that we might introduce it at St Margaret's. Some hope.

At St Margaret's this afternoon we had a Memorial Service for Lord Rupert Nevill – the Duke of Edinburgh's private secretary who died quite young. The Queen and several other members of the Royal Family came and there was a very large congregation, consisting of most of the great and the good of the land.

The service, which I had compiled after a number of visits to Lady Rupert Nevill, the widow, at her home in St James's Palace, went well enough, but curiously the Duke of Edinburgh's address lasted for barely five minutes. Often the addresses at memorial services are far too long, but on this occasion one felt that more could and should have been said about the man whose life was being commemorated.

Lady Rupert Nevill – a woman of considerable charm – is naturally anxious about where she is going to live, since the apartment in St James's Palace was tied to her husband's job. But she is a close friend of the Queen, who may well wish to have her continue close by, so I doubt if she will be turned out on to the street. I hope that she will be given an early reassurance on this point.

The Speaker's Breakfast Group met again this morning and we followed the usual pattern, gathering in St Margaret's at 8.15 a.m. for Holy Communion (1662 service, with the Speaker reading the Epistle), then across to Speaker's House for breakfast, followed by a talk and discussion, ending just before 10.00 a.m. Today someone spoke about Christian work in prisons, and there were about fifteen of us; sometimes the number goes up to about twenty-five.

It is, I am sure, very worthwhile, but the composition of the group highlights a serious problem. Because my predecessors were, for various reasons, unable to give much time to the House of Commons, apart from the daily Prayers and the Speaker's Dinners, some evangelical MPs took the initiative and started a number of groups, of which the Speaker's Breakfast, held twice in every Parliamentary session, is just one.

Those who attend the meetings are not all evangelicals – Patrick Cormack, the Rector's Warden at St Margaret's, is something of a high churchman – but these predominate and nearly all are Conservatives. This is fair enough: they are a good influence in the House and do valuable pastoral work among their fellow MPs. George Thomas has a kind of evangelical background, stemming from his background in Welsh Methodism, though his outlook, and of course his style, is different from theirs.

The difficulty for me is that because the ethos of the group is so evidently evangelical and the membership politically Conservative, many other MPs who are Christians of one sort or another will not become involved. Frank Field, for example, who is an Anglo-Catholic and prominent Labour back-bencher, feels unable to join the group, and there are others like him.

It is also a little tricky for the Speaker who, because of his position, cannot be identified with anything that appears to be the preserve of any one political party. He would, I know, be very pleased if more from all parties came to his breakfast, but I don't see this happening.

Tuesday 7 December 1982

It is obvious that a world-famous building such as Westminster Abbey should be floodlit by night. The City Council, recognizing its responsibility for tourism in this part of London, paid for the installation of floodlighting in 1966 and until a couple of years ago met the cost of the electricity – about £2,000 per annum.

This came to an end during a period of local government spending cuts, caused by a reduction in grants from central government and the need to deal with the problem of high inflation. Since then the cost of the electricity has been met by a number of oil companies whose head-quarters are located in Victoria Street, but they have indicated that no further support will be possible after the end of next March.

A new offer of £500 from the Westminster Chamber of Commerce will help a little, but only a little, and unless we can lay hold of another £1,500 the Abbey will be in darkness for most of the year. The Treasurer has suggested that floodlighting should be confined to the summer months, including June – the anniversary of the Coronation – but the Archdeacon thinks it would be best to put on the lights during the evenings of the most important church festivals.

We could of course find the money from our own corporate funds, but a deficit of over £60,000 is anticipated during the current financial year and it would be irresponsible of us to increase this.

It all makes a sorry story. Westminster, the seat of government, probably the richest local authority in the country, and the prestige location of the headquarters of some of the biggest national and international companies, cannot find £2,000 to illuminate the church which embodies the whole of English history since William the Conqueror was crowned in it on Christmas Day 1066.

The failure is short-sighted, too, because tourism is to become a primary source of revenue in the future and Westminster must make itself attractive by night as well as by day. Rome, which is always beautifully floodlit, cannot be richer than London, but I suspect that the Italian government accepts responsibility for dealing with the major buildings, and that may be the answer here.

Tuesday 14 December 1982

At noon I baptized in the Crypt Chapel the son of Jonathan and Lolicia Aitken. Jonathan is the MP for Thanet South and a Director of TV-am, the recently formed breakfast television company. His great-uncle was the famous Lord Beaverbrook, and he and his family live in a very splendid house in Lord North Street, just beyond the College Garden wall. I see quite a lot of them.

The baptism was straightforward enough. We had the traditional service, and Princess Michael of Kent was a godmother. The only departure from tradition came with a short anthem composed and conducted by Ian Hall, an exuberant West Indian, who knew Jonathan at Oxford and now directs the London University Choir. The subject of the anthem, in a sort of negro spiritual idiom, was 'Little William', and its ending was signalled by the singers leaping in the air, then stamping the floor. Another Parliamentary first, I suspect.

Friday 17 December 1982

At lunchtime I conducted as harrowing a service as I have ever experienced. A twenty-three-year-old Westminster Medical School student, having completed his training, volunteered – as so many of them do – to spend a year engaged in medical work in the Third World. He was one of the ablest and most popular graduates of the School for several years.

While swimming off the coast of Sri Lanka, however, he was attacked by sharks; since his body was never recovered, it is presumed that he was eaten by them. Thus we were driven to hold a funeral/memorial service without a body present. St Margaret's was crowded, mainly with students, and two of them spoke about their friend.

The atmosphere could hardly have been more intense, and one can only have the greatest admiration and sympathy for the victim's father (also a doctor) and mother who, with Christmas only eight days away, endured what must have been a terrible public ordeal. They told me afterwards that the service had been of the greatest help.

1983

The Organist and the Headmaster of the Choir School are in conflict again and both are appealing to the Dean and Chapter for support. There is, I suppose, an inevitability about this and now that we have strong characters, both unmarried and totally dedicated to their professions, tensions are bound to increase.

The Organist is complaining that the Choristers were permitted to stay up late on Christmas night, and again on 27 December, which left them tired and lacking in concentration when they reached the choir stalls on the following days. He is also annoyed that school sports fixtures sometimes get in the way of rehearsals and even lead to the rescheduling of choral services. He believes, too, that excessive educational demands on the boys are incompatible with their musical responsibilities in the Abbey.

The Headmaster, for his part, points out that he is responsible for ensuring that the boys get the best possible education and are equipped to gain places at public schools when they leave the choir. Himself an ex-King's College, Cambridge chorister, he is sympathetic to the Choral Foundation's requirements, but he is ambitious for the school's reputation and is answerable to parents for their sons' achievements, or lack of them.

Compromise must be the name of this game but, for some unknown reason, the Headmaster is no longer willing to have a weekly meeting with the Organist at which conflicting interests can be resolved and advance notice of important dates shared.

We are now insisting that these weekly meetings be reinstated and I don't doubt that they will without the application of too much Chapter pressure. The last time a breakdown of relations seemed imminent the two men were seen dining together in a Westminster restaurant like long-lost brothers. The crisis had, it seemed, been no more than a tiff.

Although last year's budget indicated a surplus of only just over £1,000, the final accounts show a surplus of £53,873, indicating once again the sheer impossibility of forecasting in an institution so heavily dependent on visitors for its income. An increase or decrease of 150 visitors (three busloads) a day makes the difference between a useful surplus and a threatening deficit.

My successor as Treasurer, Sebastian Charles, has sensibly suggested that some £30,000 of last year's surplus should be retained against a projected deficit of £64,000 in the current year, but no one can tell if it will be needed. The remainder is to be spent on urgent repairs to houses in the Little Cloister and College Hall.

It is pleasing to note that the St Margaret's deficit has been reduced to £860 and I hope that we can move into surplus this year, though some aspects of the church's life will continue to be heavily subsidized by the Abbey.

The Dean is keen to establish a small fund to assist those organizations, usually representing minority interests, that may wish to hold a service in the Abbey, but cannot meet our charges, which are necessary to cover staff costs and overheads. This is a good idea, which has the Chapter's full support, and if, say, £2,000 is put into the fund every year it should mean that no group will be excluded from the Abbey for financial reasons.

Such a modest allocation of funds will not seriously affect our attempts to find £80,000 for the final stage of the rebuilding of the Abbey's organ and the £200,000 needed for the re-roofing and refurbishment of No.4 Little Cloister.

Wednesday 16 February 1983

Howard Nixon, our distinguished Librarian, died suddenly today – presumably of a heart attack. This is a great blow to the Abbey community, not only because of his high professional skill but also on account of his warm friendship, wisdom and commitment.

He was born and brought up in the Abbey precincts during the early years of this century when his father was the Precentor. His professional career was spent at the British Library, where he became one of the world's leading authorities on book-binding – for which only recently he was made an Honorary Fellow of his old Oxford college (Keble) and awarded an OBE.

Returning to the Abbey in 1974 to serve as its Librarian was a retirement job, supposedly two or three days a week, though in fact he worked more or less full-time. The problems of the Keeper of the Muniments, which he encountered daily, were a considerable burden to him, but he handled this unhappy situation with charity and pastoral sensitivity. He will not easily be replaced.

Enid, his much younger wife, who is also a professional librarian, is naturally devastated by Howard's death, but we all hope that it may be possible for her to remain in the Little Cloister, for she is an invaluable member of our community and no one is more highly regarded.

Monday 21 February 1983

Several Christian MPs are arguing about the way Jesus might or might not have voted had he been on a British electoral register today. Among them, Harry Greenway, the ex-schoolmaster Member for Ealing North, believes 'Jesus called us to be Conservatives, not Socialists', but Eric Heffer, the devout Anglo-Catholic Member for Liverpool Walton, says it is 'a racing certainty' that he did nothing of the kind. So far, no one has claimed Jesus for the Liberal/SDP Alliance, though there are certainly Christians in this party, including Simon Hughes, the new Member for Bermondsey.

I am therefore going to devote my editorial in the March St Margaret's Newsletter to this question. I must begin by pointing out that the problems surrounding the detection of what Jesus actually said and did in the world of the New Testament are formidable enough, and that there is no way of knowing how he might have reacted to the great social and political issues of the twentieth century.

What is true, however, is that Christians are called to 'have the mind of Christ', that is to say, we are to approach the personal and social issues of our day in the light of the insights and values disclosed by Jesus. This leads some of us to detect a close connection between his commitment to the way of love and his evident concern for the underdog, but it does not give us direct help with our political decision-making.

All the main parties in Britain claim to have a concern for the poor either through their commitment to the enlarging of the national 'cake' or through their policy of more equitable sharing. The problem for the politician and the voter is that of deciding which approach is most likely to have the desired result, and there is no specifically Christian guidance on this crucial point. How could there be?

With Holy Week and Easter just a month away it is nonetheless worth recalling the central place of self-sacrifice in the Christian life. This suggests to us that human society as a whole requires the spirit of sacrifice, rather than of selfish ambition, if there is to be justice and freedom for all. Yet no politician could hope to be elected or any party returned to power with a manifesto based mainly on a call to self-sacrifice.

The conclusion must be, therefore, that the Man on the Cross would have the utmost difficulty in aligning himself with any of our political parties. Which is not to say of course that there is no Christian concern for political issues: simply that all of us are under judgment, and in the end all of us are unworthy servants of the God who loves and rules over his people, irrespective of their political allegiances.

I wonder what they will make of this?

Thursday 24 February 1983

An exciting meeting this morning in the Chapter Office strongroom with Colonel Robert Blott – a silver expert. Towards the end of last month I discovered in the safe at St Margaret's a safe deposit receipt issued by Williams & Deacons Bank in Victoria Street. This bank is now Williams & Glyn's, but the St Margaret's accounts have for some years been with Barclays Bank across the road.

I telephoned Williams & Glyn's to ask if I might call to collect the items they were holding, but after the clerk had been to the safe he told me that the items consisted of several large wooden boxes and that I would need a van to carry them away. Intrigued, I went to the bank to inspect the boxes and found them full of superb silver Communion plate – chalices, pattens, flagons and other items of the highest quality.

The requirement now was Securicor transport, and this brought the boxes to our strongroom. Many of the items, some of them very large, bear inscriptions indicating that they were gifts to the church from wealthy duchesses and the like. Quite a number date back to the reign of Charles II, when attempts were being made everywhere to replace silver lost at the time of the Reformation. Colonel Blott, equipped with scales, proved to be very knowledgable and is to submit a report and valuation. His first impression is that the silver cannot be worth much less than £400,000.

This is going to create a problem – a very nice problem, of course – that will need careful handling. We do not need all this silver for regular use. The chalices and flagons are of a size that suggests they were used, probably infrequently, when very large numbers of communicants were present, maybe on those occasions in the seventeenth and eighteenth centuries when Members of Parliament were required to receive Holy Communion in St Margaret's before they were permitted to take their seats in the House of Commons. This was to demonstrate that they were not Roman Catholics.

Once removed from the strongroom the silver will become a considerable security risk, and if it were to be exhibited in the church, very expensive display cases would be needed to provide the necessary protection. Another possibility is to sell some or all of it, but to release so much fine church plate on to the market could hardly fail to attract the attention of the media and we would soon be embroiled in controversy.

So, for the time being, it must remain unused and out of sight – as it has been for many years past. 'Lay not up for yourselves treasures on earth,' Jesus wisely warns us. It is a warning the church has seldom heeded.

Wednesday 16 March 1983

The Trustees are expressing considerable anxiety about the future of the appeal for the restoration of the Abbey. Launched in 1974 with a target of £5 million, the fund-raising has been very successful, and over the last five years about £1 million has been spent every year. But chronic inflation, high wage settlements for stonemasons, and the discovery of much additional decay has led the Surveyor of the Fabric to calculate that with nil inflation a further £6.7 million will be needed to bring the work to completion; with 4% inflation £7.7 million will be needed, and with 8% inflation a further £8.9 million.

The chances of raising this sort of money at a rate of £1 million a year are not deemed high, partly because many companies have already given major donations and others are feeling the effects of the recent economic instability. Some of the Trustees suggested that the Appeal should be closed down for three years and a new start made in 1986. Others thought that the present work on the largely unseen South side of the Abbey should be abandoned for a time and a public appeal for £4 million be launched to deal with the prominent Western towers. The Duke of Edinburgh has been worried about the expenditure of money on carved stones and statues in high and largely invisible parts of the building – an attitude unlikely to have won the approval of Henry III when he embarked on the rebuilding of the Abbey in the thirteenth century and almost bankrupted the nation in the process. It would not, in any case, save much.

In the end it has been decided to scale down the restoration to £500,000 a year and review the situation in 1985. This seems a sensible solution, and there is no reason why the work should not be carried out over a much longer period than originally envisaged. The Abbey isn't going to fall down, but in normal circumstances the maintaining of an appeal over a prolonged period is fraught with difficulty, and it is obviously more economical to deal with the restoration fairly quickly.

The Dean and Chapter is fortunate to have this aspect of the Abbey's life dealt with by a lay Trust. In most cathedrals, the Dean and the Canons have to be the fund-raisers.

Sunday 20 March 1983

Enoch Powell stayed behind after this morning's 8.15 a.m. Holy Communion at St Margaret's and asked if he might speak to me about my intercessions. With great courtesy, he pointed out that I had prayed for an end to violence and a new spirit of reconciliation in Poland, in Northern Ireland and in the countries of the Middle East – in that order.

He had nothing against the subjects of the prayers, but he thought my sandwiching of Northern Ireland between Poland and the Middle East implied that this province of the United Kingdom was a foreign country. This, he asserted, was untrue and, in the context of the present troubles in Northern Ireland, likely to be unhelpful.

He obviously felt strongly about this, but was almost apologetic in raising it with me, and I readily conceded that he had a point. It is, I think, the case that most of us tend to think of Northern Ireland as a foreign country – part of the Commonwealth, of course, but not integrated in the same way that Scotland and Wales are. And this, I dare say, is an important factor in the now seemingly intractable Irish problem.

In future I shall be careful to include Northern Ireland among the prayers for 'our own country'.

Tuesday 22 March 1983

Kenneth Kaunda, the President of Zambia, came this afternoon to lay a wreath on the grave of the Unknown Warrior. He is here on an official state visit. It was a particularly warm encounter for us, partly because this President combines dignity and friendliness in a rather special way, but also because of his interest in the Abbey and its life. He let it be known last month that he would, if possible, like to hear the Choristers sing, so we arranged for the normal Choir rehearsal before Evensong to take place in the Abbey instead of in the Song School. So, as we took him on a brief tour of the building, following the wreath-laying, he was able to stop and listen to the Choir. He is obviously very interested in music and was impressed.

These wreath-layings are usually very formal affairs, and only occasionally are we able to make any real contact with our distinguished visitors. So today was particularly pleasurable and enhanced our admiration for a President who has played such a vital part in the liberation and development of his country and who, like most of his kind, spent some time in prison during the early stages of the rebellion against colonialism.

Tuesday 29 March 1983

I have just completed a course on Liberation Theology for the Parliamentary Christian Wives Group. It has about fifty members, and meets in Speaker's House every Tuesday lunchtime for sandwiches, coffee and, usually, a speaker. Elizabeth Home, the former Prime Minister's wife, and Lyn Weatherill, the Deputy Speaker's wife, are mother figures to the MPs' wives but the leadership is in Evangelical hands: Sylvia Mary Alison, wife of the Prime Minister's Parliamentary Private Secretary; Susan Stanley, wife of the Minister of State for the Armed Forces; and Susan Sainsbury, wife of the Member for Hove and of the grocers' dynasty.

They invite me quite often to conduct Bible studies, and in this context it is possible to introduce them to all manner of things they have not previously considered. Thus Liberation Theology, with its strong biblical roots, has excited them greatly, though this may not be unrelated to the fact that its chief exponents are confined to far-away Latin America.

But the group's most important function is to provide support for women whose lives are lonely and whose marriages are sometimes under great strain because their husbands are so busy running the country. The wife of one middle-ranking minister told me last week that she and her husband meet once a week (for lunch on Saturday), but she is intensely loyal to him and their marriage remains happy. However, not all are so lucky, and without the support of the group many others would, I feel sure, be in trouble.

It is a pity therefore that the Evangelical atmosphere deters some from joining, and hardly any Labour wives attend. This may have something to do with the fact that few of them can afford to live in London.

Wednesday 30 March 1983

A good attendance at today's Parliamentary Holy Week service in St Margaret's. I preached on Ambition, taking my cue from the feet-washing incident before the Last Supper and the declaration of Jesus that true leadership involves humble service.

I drew some implications from this for the political realm, emphasizing in particular the honoured place in the tradition of the House of Commons of the ordinary back-bench Member who never aspires to high office but who gives unstinted service to the House and to his or her constituency.

There are, it has to be said, far fewer of these than there used to be. The recent intakes have included many highly ambitious Conservatives – 'no longer estate owners, but estate agents', someone has said – and these seem anxious to keep on the right side of the Whips in order to improve, or at least not diminish, their chances of promotion.

But, by and large, I find MPs to be a dedicated group of people who are in politics because of a desire to serve the community, to improve the quality of its life, and to defend the interests of their constituents. The level of their commitment and the quality of their service is not less than that exhibited by the clergy, and in many cases it is noticeably higher.

It is no part of my job to pass judgment on those who work in the House of Commons, but I find more to admire and encourage than I do to deplore and condemn.

Friday 29 April 1983

The Bible readings at Evensong are, I think, a considerable problem. Large numbers attend this service: they are visitors from all parts of the world and for some it may be their first encounter with Christian worship. The music is rarely less than superb and for many this is a considerable attraction. Evensong in Westminster Abbey is a lovely service.

But the readings from the Old and New Testaments, which are prescribed by the Lectionary, often make no sort of sense to the uninitiated, and even to those of us who are theologically educated they are sometimes puzzling. This is partly because they come from a world radically different from our own, and partly because we often read between twenty and thirty verses from the Old Testament, which can only be understood if they are related to their context.

In response to this problem, John Baker and Neil Collings, the then Chaplain, compiled a Lectionary special to Westminster Abbey. This is certainly an improvement on the official version approved by the General Synod, but by largely maintaining the tradition of continuous readings from the various books of the Bible it retains a lot of material which really ought not to be read in public.

We have for some time now prefaced the readings with one or two introductory sentences in the hope that this may help the congregation to understand more easily what follows. I am not sure, however, what the congregation made the other day of the Dean's introduction to I Corinthians 14. 26–40 about the place of women in the church. He said 'St Paul got this quite wrong'. It was a brave assertion, but left unanswered my question: If St Paul was mistaken, why read his erroneous words at Evensong?

Thursday 12 May 1983

Today being Ascension Day, Harry Swainston marked the seventy-second anniversary of his admission as an altar server by serving at this morning's Holy Communion at St Margaret's. It was as a thirteen-year-old boy that he became an altar server at an Anglo-Catholic church in Newcastle-upon-Tyne, and it was on Tyneside that he trained as an engineer after active service in the 1914–18 war.

During the 1930s, however, he moved into the world of commerce and earned his living by devising ingenious sales ploys – the first of which involved linking a *London Evening News* weekly competition with reduced-price books in Foyle's bookshop. During the 1950s he ran what he called the Dron Plan – a mail order business that enabled the middle class to obtain the benefit of bulk-order terms on household items such as toilet rolls, electric light bulbs, and bed linen. He also helped to found the Henley Staff College for the training of managers.

A Pickwickian figure, Harry is the ultimate entrepreneur and on our first meeting offered to let me have 144 toilet rolls at a knock-down price – an offer I had to decline for want of storage space. David Edwards brought him to St Margaret's in the early 1970s in the hope that he might be able to solve the church's financial problems: in particular, raise £500,000 for the church's restoration. Much to Harry's chagrin, however, this was stymied by the Dean and Chapter's decision to set up a Trust, under the Presidency of the Duke of Edinburgh, to raise several million pounds for the restoration of the Abbey and ultimately St Margaret's.

I find him hugely amusing, for his conversation is dominated by what he regards as enterprising ways of making money. Sometimes these are related to his personal convictions, and his intense, jingoistic nationalism led him to have printed several thousand copies of a small book containing pictures of all the kings and heroes of England. Most of these remain unsold in St Margaret's vestry. His latest idea, pressed with engaging enthusiasm, has to do with his deep attachment to the Book of Common Prayer. Believing that London is full of people like himself who are unhappy with the new services, he wants the weekly advertisement of St Margaret's services in *The Daily Telegraph* and *The Times* to include a bold indication that the 1662 Prayer Book will be used. This will, he asserts, attract worshippers from all over London and visitors from the provinces. More people in the pews equals more money on the collection plate and the doubling or trebling of our income.

He has now made this proposal several times and on each occasion, when I have told him that we are not in the business of trying to attract refugees from other churches, he has looked puzzled. 'Surely we are all competing in the same market-place,' he responds, with a twinkle in his eye. But he is a devout and generous man and, having noticed that our copies of the Prayer Book are getting somewhat tattered and worn, has undertaken to present us with 150 new copies. 'A good investment,' he assures me.

Friday 13 May 1983

George Thomas has just retired from the Speakership following the dissolution of Parliament, consequent upon the calling of a General Election on 9 June. He is going to be greatly missed, not least by me, for he has been a good friend since he appointed me as Chaplain of the House of Commons at the beginning of last year. Besides our daily brief encounters before the Procession and Prayers, we have usually met once a week to discuss various issues – mostly of the pastoral sort – that have arisen in the life of the House, and I think he has valued the opportunity to let his hair down with someone who has no political axe to grind. He has also appeared frequently in St Margaret's, and I have been summoned to a multitude of social occasions in Speaker's House.

By common consent, George has been a great Speaker, and the introduction of broadcasting from Parliament has made him a national figure. His Welsh intonation of 'Order, Order' is recognized and often imitated everywhere. He is a great performer and this, combined with the style of the schoolmaster he once was, enabled him to maintain order and facilitate business very attractively. His ability to defuse potentially ugly situations with a touch of humour – often directed against himself – has also been invaluable. What is not generally recognized, I think, is the pastoral, caring ministry he has exercised among Members; I have sometimes said, 'The Speaker is the real Chaplain of the House, and I just lend him a hand.'

There are nonetheless quite a number of Opposition Members – former Labour Party colleagues – who believe that George toadied too much to the Government and did not always display the impartiality required in a Speaker. I have of course never been in a position to judge this, but there may be something in it, for George adores Margaret Thatcher as a person. I don't think he has much room for her political views, but it seems almost as if, following the death of his revered mother, 'Mam', she has provided a necessary feminine element in his life. Nothing wrong with this, but it may sometimes have affected his judgment in the Chair.

I think it must also be recognized that there is another side to the warm, effusive friendliness he normally displays. He can be suspicious of people almost to the point of paranoia and tends to harbour grudges. This has cost him some friendships. But it has to be remembered that he is unmarried and, although surrounded constantly by people, experiences an inner loneliness that can affect relationships.

He is perhaps the last notable politician to have found his way into public life via the Methodist chapel. It was his involvement in Welsh Methodism that enabled him – from the poorest of mining homes – to develop his oratorical gifts and to win recognition by the local Labour Party. His Christian faith is of the warm evangelical sort – not to be confused with its contemporary 'happy-clappy' manifestations – and although he is prepared to preach and speak anywhere, he has a deep distrust of Anglican bishops and of the Roman Catholic Church in general. His Methodism does not, however, prevent him from indulging in a glass of whisky at bedtime. I shall always be grateful that I had the opportunity to work closely with him in the last eighteen months of his time as Speaker.

I raised in Chapter today what seems to me to be a very important issue relating to the quality of the furnishings and other items being introduced into the Abbey. This arose from my reporting on the Dedication last Sunday of the new hangings in the Chapel of Christ the Intercessor in St Margaret's. These were commissioned during the time of my predecessor and have been paid for by a generous American couple. They are in no way offensive and the workmanship is of a high order, but the design – which has some resemblance to the illustrations in an old-fashioned Sunday School book – is second-, or probably third-rate.

Similar problems have arisen recently in the Abbey. The engraving of the glass which encloses St George's Chapel is thoroughly unsatisfactory and the painted glass decoration of the Great West Door porch remains incomplete, even though the porch was dedicated three years ago. A Paschal candlestick designed by the Surveyor of the Fabric for the High Altar sanctuary is quite out of scale and its form is incongruous. I have frequently complained about the unimaginative design of most of the recently installed memorial stones.

All in all, it adds up to a dreary story – and this is one of the world's great churches where only the best is supposed to be good enough. Part of the problem is that we have no real visual-arts expert to keep us up to the mark. The Dean, who is ultimately responsible for what goes into the Abbey, has very poor sight and, in any case, is a literary, rather than a visual-arts, man. I am interested, but have neither the time nor the expertise to do more than complain about what is being commissioned, and the rest of the Canons are not specially concerned. The Surveyor is a specialist in mediaeval buildings, and the Architectural Advisory Committee, packed with mediaevalists, has no specialist in contemporary art.

We had a good discussion about this problem and there is, I think, a general recognition that we need to do better in this important area of the Abbey's life. But under the present dispensation there is not much prospect of our recruiting the kind of help we need.

Sunday 5 June 1983

After preaching this morning in Croydon Parish Church at a service to mark the 100th anniversary of the Borough of Croydon, I returned to Westminster with Bernard ('Jack') Weatherill, who is MP for Croydon North East and a leading contender for the Speakership, following the retirement of George Thomas. Jo and I had a pleasant lunch with Jack and his wife Lyn in their Lupus Street home, but inevitably conversation was dominated by Jack's prospects at the election of the Speaker in ten days' time and especially by his fear that the prize may elude him.

Whoever follows George Thomas will have some difficulty, and Jack's personality is so different from George's that there are those who wonder if this quiet, self-effacing man will be able to rule the House and deal effectively with its rebels. Margaret Thatcher evidently thinks not and is said to favour Humphrey Atkins, an elegant man who was Conservative Chief Whip when the party was last in Opposition and since then has done sterling work as Secretary of State for Northern Ireland. The Prime Minister would like to reward him.

The fact that Jack has been Deputy Speaker since 1979 may also tell against him, because the House has not in the past been disposed to elect Deputies to the Chair. And, sadly, George Thomas conducted something of a campaign against Jack during the closing weeks of his reign and let it be known that he hoped someone different would follow him. I don't know what lay behind this, but George turned against a number of his close associates as retirement drew ever closer.

I hope that Jack will get it. He is a good man and would be absolutely fair to all sides of the House. Just how well he would control the debates, without George's charisma, isn't easy to tell. As Deputy Speaker he has had some problems, but the office of Speaker has its own aura and I am told that the House always cherishes and supports the occupant of the Chair, so that it is virtually impossible to be a bad Speaker. That said, it has to be acknowledged that the alcoholic Horace King had a good try.

I tried to reassure Jack and Lyn, who are going to be very disappointed if the vote goes another way on the 15th, but of course I am not in a position to know the intentions of the Members – about 150 of whom will be new, anyway. So I could be only pastoral.

Tuesday 7 June 1983

Although by no means unexpected, for he had been in failing health for some time, the death of Eric Abbott, our former Dean, yesterday has brought great sadness to the Abbey community and to me personally. I never worked with him – he retired two years before I came here – but I knew him for forty years, and he played a large part both in my decision to seek ordination and in my subsequent training.

When I was wondering about ordination, the curate of my local parish in Nottinghamshire sent me to see Eric, who was at that time Warden of the theological college at Lincoln. I stayed the night, and in the course of two longish converstions I was astonished by his insights and perception of the way I was moving. Later I chanced to be serving on an RAF station near Lincoln, and from time to time he again invited me to stay at the college.

Soon after the end of the war he moved to be Dean of King's College London, and when I was demobilized I went there as a student. So for the next four years I was under his direct influence, and it was a very considerable influence, for he exercised a great, yet gentle, power over all who recognized his authority.

King's was at that time teeming with ex-service ordination candidates, and although it is impossible to tell just how many future priests and bishops passed through his hands during his years in Lincoln, London, then in Oxford, where he was Warden of Keble College, it cannot be fewer than about 1,500. In this way, and some others, his influence on the Church of England was enormous.

I never belonged to his inner circle of 'boys', with whom he seemed to have quite intense relationships, but we kept in touch after I was ordained, and when he moved to the Abbey and I was in London editing *New Christian* I was in and out of the Deanery fairly often. It seems that he related much more easily to his former pupils than to his colleagues, for during his time as Dean the Canons got into the Deanery only rarely.

Eric's special contribution to the life of the Abbey, apart from the massive celebration of its 900th anniversary in 1966, was to re-establish it as a place of prayer and devotion. This was his great gift, and his constant emphasis on the priority of worship and prayer brought new light and warmth to a shrine that, all too easily, can become formal and cold.

He was really nature's own Dean, for his appearance was elegant, his voice beautifully modulated and his involvement in worship combined dignity and spirituality in a measure I have experienced in no one else. Apparently he got on very well with the Royal Family and presided over three royal weddings, as well as preparing some of its younger members for confirmation.

When I came here in 1976 he was living in retirement in Vincent Square and would every now and then invite Jo and me over for dinner – surprisingly gossipy occasions. His last written communication with me was one of his famous postcards when I became Rector of St Margaret's and Speaker's Chaplain, and our last personal encounter was on Low Sunday last year, when he came to St Margaret's on the day before he moved to sheltered accommodation in Surrey and received Holy Communion at my hands – thirty-nine years after my first visit to Lincoln and his final appearance at a service in Westminster.

Friday 10 June 1983

The General Election has given the Conservatives a landslide victory and a majority of 144 – the largest since the famous Labour victory in 1945. I don't think that anyone is in the least surprised, because the Labour Party, under the leadership of Michael Foot, has been in disarray for some time and there was never any possibility of the electorate returning so divided and so confused a Party to power. I like Michael Foot, and he is a great Parliamentarian, but it was a disastrous mistake to make him, rather than Denis Healey, Leader. I expect that Neil Kinnock, the fiery but not I think very substantial Member for Bedwellty, will shortly take his place.

Jo and I had the unusual experience of seeing the results announced from within the Palace of Westminster itself. Victor Le Fanu, the Serjeant-at-Arms, and his wife, Elizabeth, have an official residence in the Palace and they very kindly invited us, together with Bill Beaumont, the Speaker's Secretary and his wife Kythé, to have supper with them, then watch the results on television.

They especially, and I to some extent, knew all the sitting Members, so the successes and failures merited appropriate comments and the sense of personal involvement was strong. The temptation to stay up 'for just one more result' was therefore all the more powerful, and it was daylight when we returned to Little Cloister.

The Liberal/Social Democrat challenge came to nothing, and its leaders are naturally complaining that a return of 23 seats for 25% of the total votes is a reflection of the unfairness of the 'first past the post' electoral system. A Government with a majority of 144 is unlikely to share this sense of injustice.

Soon there will be a new Speaker, and I shall have a new boss – assuming that I am reappointed Chaplain. The chances of this seem fairly high, for, although the Speaker is entirely free to appoint whomever he wishes, the tradition of reappointment is virtually unbroken.

In 1874 Speaker Brand chose not to continue Henry White, preferring Francis Byng, who was said to have at one time been 'fond of horse-racing and an admirer of the ladies'. But when Byng succeeded his brother as Earl of Stafford in 1889 a new Speaker, Arthur Peel, invited White back. The only other instance of anything of this sort was in

1906, when Speaker Lowther decided not to reappoint Basil Wilberforce, but the Prime Minister, Campbell Bannerman, leaned on him and he reversed his decision.

What would happen, I wonder, if Norman St John Stevas were to be elected Speaker? He has been mooted as a candidate, would I am sure like the job, and is a prominent Roman Catholic. The general opinion is that, since he is a staunch champion of the traditions of the House, he would be quite happy for me to remain as Chaplain.

Wednesday 15 June 1983

Jack Weatherill was, after all, elected Speaker this afternoon – and unanimously. Jim Callaghan, the Father of the House, took the Chair and called for nominations. Jack was proposed by Humphrey Atkins, who had until yesterday been considered Jack's chief opponent, and seconded by Jack Dormand – a salt-of-the-earth Labour Member who is respected by all sides.

Both made gracious speeches, lauding Jack's qualities, and when no other nominations were forthcoming he was elected without dissent and to the accompaniment of loud cheers. In accordance with tradition, he displayed some (but not too much) reluctance to assume the Chair, then made a good speech of acceptance, putting himself at the service of the House. Specially touching was his reference (made to me on a number of previous occasions) to the tailor's thimble which he always carries with him – a gift from his grandmother, to remind him of his humble origins.

After the Queen had formally approved Jack's election – secured in lightning time – the bells of St Margaret's rang out, again in accordance with tradition, and it seemed with special joy, because he is one of our most faithful worshippers and a stalwart supporter. The link between the House of Commons and St Margaret's can only be strengthened by his election, and he is the first Anglican to be Speaker for some years, as George Thomas, Selwyn Lloyd and Horace King were all Methodists.

What evidently swung the vote decisively in Jack's favour was the knowledge that Margaret Thatcher wanted someone else. Backbench MPs are very conscious of their rights and privileges and are also aware that ultimately he is the protector of their freedom of opinion. So even Conservative MPs who normally do the Prime Minister's bidding without question were not prepared to allow her to determine the choice of Speaker. Her advocacy of Humphrey Atkins actually assisted Jack Weatherill, and it was entirely characteristic of the House tradition that when the views of Members became known the chief adversary became the chief sponsor. I suspect that only in Britain could this happen.

Thursday 23 June 1983

The Service of Dedication and Commitment in St Margaret's at midday attracted a large congregation of MPs, Peers and members of the staff of both Houses to mark the beginning of the new Parliament. The new Speaker and the Prime Minister read lessons, and prayers were led by the Moderator of the General Assembly of the Church of Scotland, the Moderator of the Free Church Federal Council and a representative of Cardinal Hume. The Leaders of the Liberal and Social Democratic Parties were there, and three former Prime Ministers – Lord Home, Edward Heath and James Callaghan – but, sadly, no one from the hierarchy of the Labour Party.

Robert Runcie, the Archbishop of Canterbury, gave the sermon. He is really very good at this kind of thing. He began by reminding us of an occasion in 1772 when the Regius Professor of Modern History at Oxford delivered a sermon in St Margaret's to the House of Commons. The professor was later accused of uttering some 'arbitrary Tory, high-flown doctrines' and it was proposed that his sermon should be burnt by the common hangman. Fortunately, someone remembered just in time that a formal vote of thanks to the preacher had already been passed and an order made for the sermon to be printed.

That was a good start, which put today's congregation in fine humour, and the rest of the sermon was devoted to emphasizing the importance of worshipping the God revealed in Jesus Christ, rather than human beings or impersonal objects and ideologies. It was all sound stuff which many MPs spoke well of afterwards, so I doubt whether there will be any call for this sermon to be burnt.

Monday 27 June 1983

A very sad sight in the House of Commons at the moment is that of former Members who, having failed to be re-elected, are now collecting their belongings from the lockers and rooms they have used, sometimes for a decade and more. They are departing from the political scene – possibly for ever.

The House of Commons is a deceptive place. For much, perhaps most, of the time it has the atmosphere of a comfortable club. Fine furniture, deep carpets, book-lined rooms and corridors, valuable paintings, a wonderful library, elegant dining rooms, an intimate debating chamber, and a warm friendliness that extends across party boundaries. It is marvellous really.

Yet the *raison d'être* of Parliament is power, and all of a sudden individuals and groups are hurt, and sometimes destroyed. The cost of the privilege of being here as an elected Member is that one can be thrown out unceremoniously, at a very short notice, and without having broken any rules or done any other wrong. It is, I am sure, good that the ruthless element in political life should mostly be tempered by warmth and friendship, but when the instruments of power strike the result is shocking for the victims.

I had some talk this morning in the corridor between the Central and Members Lobbies with Joe Dean, the former Member for Leeds West, who had just packed his bags and was about to leave. He was elected in 1974 after some years in the Trade Unions and Local Government, and he was, I am sure, a most diligent constituency Member, but he is one of the many victims of the Conservative landslide and now has nowhere to go. Unlike most displaced Tory MPs, he is without directorships and consultancies to fall back on, and, although he served in the Whips Office for two short spells, he has no immediate claim on a seat in the House of Lords. I feel sorry for him and will miss the chats we had most days of the week.

Another victim of the General Election, though of a different sort, is Ernest Armstrong, who has been returned as Member for North West Durham, a seat he has held since 1964, but been denied the expected opportunity to become the Deputy Speaker and Chairman of Ways and Means. I knew him slightly before I became Chaplain, but since I took over from John Baker we have become good friends – partly because of the North West Durham connection, partly because he is a past Vice-Chairman of the Methodist Conference and a strong supporter of what I am trying to do, and also because our paths have crossed frequently in the Speaker's Office.

He was for some years one of the Speaker's deputies, and there was every reason to suppose that, after the General Election when George Thomas would be succeeded by a Conservative Speaker, the Labour Party would nominate Ernest for the number two position, which has considerable prestige and influence. But there was a row in the Labour Party when, following a revision of constituency boundaries in Durham, he refused to fight a new constituency which had become fairly marginal and chose instead to remain in the safe seat he had occupied for nearly twenty years.

Many people in the House sympathized with him over this, for there is ample precedent for senior Members having safe seats, but when the Durham marginal was lost great fury was directed towards him, and the powers that be in the Labour Party decreed that he should forfeit the chance to hold one of the great Parliamentary offices which he had coveted and which he would have discharged exceedingly well. The job has gone instead to Harold Walker, the Member for Doncaster, who has held a number of junior posts in Government and Opposition.

Naturally, Ernest is very distressed about all this, but he is not considering resignation or anything of that sort. As he told me the other day, 'Politics is a rough old game and I have been very fortunate and privileged over the years.' He has, I think, fallen victim to the general disarray that now encompasses the Labour Party.

Sunday 3 July 1983

Yesterday was what must have been one of the most joyful days in the long history of Westminster Abbey – at least, at the level of personal celebration. Catherine, our younger daughter, whose marriage in 1978 ended so tragically when, after only ten months, her husband, Anthony, was killed in a car accident, was married again – this time to Charles Taylor, the lively young Chaplain of the Abbey.

Charles has been our neighbour in the Little Cloister since 1979, and although we were aware that he and Catherine had been seeing something of each other, Jo and I were as surprised as we were delighted when they announced their engagement last Christmas. For Catherine, some of the journey to that point had been, as one might have expected, dark and painful. But she soldiered on – teaching Religious Education in the toughest of comprehensive schools in London's East End, taking a diploma in Pastoral Studies at London University Institute of Education, and all the time wonderfully supported by a group of friends whom she came to know during her schooldays in North London.

As I stood with her, once again, at the Great West Door of the Abbey, waiting to join the procession to the High Altar, it really seemed too good to be true, and I couldn't help wondering if this was the first time ever that anyone had been married twice at the High Altar of Westminster Abbey.

Although Charles left her entirely free to choose, Catherine decided to have a 'big' wedding, rather than a quieter, smaller-scale ceremony in, say, the Henry VII Chapel. This was partly because she was conscious of the fact that it was the first time for Charles who, as Chaplain and therefore much involved in the ordering of the Abbey's worship, would naturally enjoy using its full liturgical resources at his own wedding. But I think she also felt that, having emerged from the dark tunnel of bereavement and been given the opportunity to embark again on the married life, she wanted to celebrate this as joyously as possible.

Certainly the Abbey community wanted to celebrate it that way. There were over 300 guests and, as I said in my address, it was a resurrection experience for us all. Charles's father, who is a parish priest in Lichfield diocese, officiated at the marriage and the Dean celebrated the Eucharist. The music was out of this world.

It was a perfect summer evening for the reception in College Garden and we all recognized how courageous and generous it was of Kay Andrews and her daughters, Marica and Judy, to share with us in the great day. Like Jo and me they had been there before and, as a result of a cruel accident, had lost a son and a brother, and indirectly a husband and a father. I was deeply moved by their presence.

Edward, the Dean, proposed the health of the bride and bridegroom in his usual felicitous way, Charles responded with a mixture of sensitive reflection and good jokes, and now he and Catherine are on their way to a honeymoon in Yugoslavia.

Friday 22 July 1983

The General Synod, representing I suppose the general outlook of the Church of England, is in a fearful muddle over its attitude to the remarriage in church of people who have been divorced. At its meeting earlier this month it reaffirmed the Christian view of marriage as a life-long commitment and its unwillingness to give a general *carte blanche* to church weddings after divorce, but said that 'in certain circumstances' remarriage in church might be allowed.

The present legal position is that a clergyman is at liberty to officiate at the remarriage of divorcees without any by your leave from anyone, and an increasing number are exercising their freedom in this matter. But the practice is frowned on by bishops and others because it runs contrary to what hitherto has been the expressed view of the church.

It is now proposed that in every diocese there shall be panels to which parish clergy can refer requests for remarriage, if they wish to do so, and the expectation is that, except in cases involving serious scandal, permission for a church wedding will be given. Such weddings will, however, have to be prefaced by a statement that one or both of the partners has been previously married – a thoroughly undesirable requirement, it seems to me.

Once this new arrangement is implemented, whether or not a couple with a background of a previous marriage can be married in their parish church will be something of a lottery. Everything will depend on the willingness or otherwise of the local parson to accept them and remit their request to the diocesan bishop and his panel. In some parishes this will happen, in others not – and the result can only be confusion and some resentment.

As far as we are concerned, at the Abbey and St Margaret's our hands are tied, except in the case of anyone who lives in the precincts. Everyone else requires an Archbishop of Canterbury's licence, and we gather that, because of the divided state of the church, the Archbishop will not grant licences to anyone who has been previously married and whose former partner is still alive.

Although St Margaret's is no longer the premier London church for fashionable weddings, we still have quite a number of marriages, fashionable and otherwise, usually through a Parliamentary connection. Some of these involve people who have been divorced. It would be good if these could have the full marriage service in order to give them the best possible start in their new commitment. I don't believe that the institution of marriage is well served by the pretence that previous, but broken, marriages still exist simply because the partners to them are still alive. Marriages as well as people can die.

But there is no way forward for us in this direction at the moment, so at St Margaret's and in the Crypt Chapel of the Palace of Westminster we shall continue to offer a Service of Blessing arranged in the best possible way, with most of the traditional ceremonies and appropriate music. This is not entirely satisfactory, but it works quite well, and many of those who attend such services believe them to be simply another officially revised marriage rite.

Saturday 27 August 1983

The extensive restoration of the Abbey and of the Palace of Westminster is making St Margaret's look grubbier every day and the building is a sad sight. The fabric has hardly been touched in the present century, and when David Edwards became Rector in 1970 his first sermon was published in pamphlet form under the title 'A national disgrace on the doorstep of the House of Commons'. But this evoked little response apart from a certain amount of grumbling from MPs – all of whom were sent a copy.

The present position is that the restoration of St Margaret's will be financed by the Westminster Abbey Trust when the work on the Abbey is completed. This can hardly be before the mid-1990s, and may be even later if there are hiccups in the Abbey programme. Rather than wait almost indefinitely, therefore, the suggestion has been made that we should simply clean St Margaret's so that it ceases to look dismal and neglected.

This would be relatively inexpensive, but it would involve some duplication of costs because a thorough cleaning of the stone will be necessary when the restoration work eventually starts. I am going to air this problem in next month's St Margaret's Newsletter and talk to the Speaker about it. The Surveyor of the Fabric thinks a complete restoration of the building will cost about £1 million at present-day prices.

Tuesday 30 August 1983

Intensive physiotherapy, extending over several weeks, has failed to alleviate my lower-back problem, so today I had an appointment with the Westminster Hospital consultant whom I saw in the spring. He told me that chronic back conditions are never easy to cure and that regular muscle-strengthening exercises over a long period, perhaps for ever, are my best hope. But he also asked about my life-style and wondered if I might be subject to special, tension-making, pressures. He hastened to add that any such pressures would not have created my problem, but might well be hindering its solution.

The truth is, of course, that I am working under considerable tension-creating pressure. The three jobs I am trying to do in the Abbey, St Margaret's and the House of Commons are, as is now generally recognized, one job too many for anyone to carry out effectively, and it is, I am sure, the case that a combination of responsibilities, each making its own demands, is more tension-creating and therefore more exhausting than most single-focussed jobs.

The consultant suggested that I should reduce my workload, but I am so deeply involved in a rapidly developing ministry which I certainly do not want to reduce in any way. The back pain is hardly life-threatening. Structural change is the real answer, and I must keep going until this becomes possible.

The appointment of Thomas Trotter, the brilliant young organist of St Margaret's, as Birmingham City Organist has led to a flutter of controversy in some parts of the music world. It is being said that he is far too young for such a post and that the choice was unduly influenced by the presence on the selection panel of people from King's College, Cambridge, where he was once the Organ Scholar.

Young he certainly is, and in comparison with Sir George Thalben-Ball, whom he will succeed, he must be regarded as a mere infant. The real issue must be, however, Can he play the organ? And the answer, as anyone who has heard him will testify, is, Yes, brilliantly. He is undoubtedly in the same class as Simon Preston, and his burgeoning national and international engagements point to a future of the greatest distinction.

Jealousy is the reason for the fuss. The Birmingham post is much coveted because it is not specially demanding and is well paid. A weekly lunchtime recital in the City Hall, to an audience made up mainly of old-age pensioners, is the basic requirement, and the salary is £6,000 per annum.

Such a guaranteed income is wealth indeed to a free-lance musician and provides a sound financial base to which recital fees can be added. Small wonder that a number of other leading organists were in contention, and even less wonder that George Thalben-Ball hung on to the post for so long.

We are all delighted by Thomas's success. He is the most modest and generous of performers and, mercifully, his Birmingham commitment will not get in the way of his strong commitment to St Margaret's. Large numbers will continue to stay behind after Mattins and to applaud his final piece.

Wednesday 28 September 1983

The Dean, who is President of the Anglican Society for the Welfare of Animals, has been thwarted in his desire that a small-scale 'protest' gathering of animal rights people should be held in the Abbey precincts on St Francis Day – 4 October. The original idea, it seems, was that the protesters should march from St Martin-in-the-Fields to the Abbey, but the police refused permission for this on the extraordinary grounds that the Law Lords will be sitting on that day. Just how 100 people marching down Whitehall could possibly interfere with or influence a handful of judges ensconced in the House of Lords is beyond comprehension, but I suppose it has to do with a blanket regulation of some sort.

A similar bureaucratic mentality will keep the Dean and his friends away from the Abbey. Having been denied the opportunity to march, they decided to walk quietly to our precincts, display placards and posters, and distribute leaflets to passers-by. A small group, including the Dean, would then walk across to the House of Commons and hand in a petition. All harmless enough.

But we have a rule that there shall be no demonstrations in the precincts without the express permission of the Dean and Chapter, and when the matter was raised on Tuesday two of us voted in favour of granting permission and two against. The Dean could easily have used his casting vote to settle the matter, and in my view should have done so, but Edward, being Edward, would not force his wishes on anyone, so he withdrew the request.

The two colleagues who opposed are, I am sure, all in favour of animal welfare, but they were more concerned with a legalistic interpretation of an earlier decision. It seems wrong, however, that the Dean of Westminster cannot have one of his concerns modestly ventilated in the precincts of the Abbey he has now served for over thirty-two years. He is to seek the assistance of another Westminster church.

Thursday 13 October 1983

The Dean is keen that part of the South Choir Aisle shall be developed as a place where eminent people connected with the theatre have memorial stones. The musicians are in the North Choir Aisle, many of the statesmen are in the North Transept, the scientists are near Newton at the East end of the Nave and the poets are in the South Transept.

The idea of a special area for theatrical stars has sprung from the decision to memorialize Sybil Thorndike in 1976. Noel Coward, who was refused a memorial service in the Abbey in 1973, is to have a stone near Sybil Thorndike's, and this will be unveiled by the Queen Mother next April. The inscription has just been agreed:

> Noel Coward
> Playwright and Actor
> 1899 – 1973
> A Talent to Amuse
> Buried in Jamaica

Now the question has arisen as to whether Sir Ralph Richardson, who died on Monday, might one day have a memorial. It is too early to say, but if stage people are to be welcomed there will be no shortage of candidates because they are, by the very nature of their work, 'famous'. The idea of an amusing memorial to Charlie Chaplin in the Cloisters has fallen through, as those who would have paid for it now believe that a statue in Leicester Square, in the cinema world, would be more appropriate. I think they are right.

Tuesday 18 October 1983

The resignation of Cecil Parkinson as Trade and Industry Secretary and from the chairmanship of the Conservative Party, following the revelations of his love affair with the now-pregnant Sarah Keays, has naturally led to a lot of heated discussion both inside and outside the House of Commons. It seems that the Prime Minister was not at all keen to accept the resignation of one of her favourites, who was almost certainly destined to become the next Foreign and Commonwealth Secretary, but backbench and media pressures have won the day. John Gummer is to be the new Party Chairman and Norman Tebbit is taking over Trade and Industry. This seems an excessive price to pay for morality.

Herein lies the problem, which I had better address in the November Newsletter, as there is a common belief that the church has some sort of vested interest in the demand for resignation in these situations. But does the holding of high office in the nation, especially political office, require of the individuals concerned exemplary personal behaviour as well as skill for a particular task?

The main point I must make is that Christianity has no direct guidance to offer in the current debate. Far from prescribing that government should be the prerogative of the virtuous, the Christian religion roundly declares that all men and women, even the best, are 'miserable sinners' in desperate need of forgiveness. If personal sanctity ever became an essential qualification for membership of Parliament or of the Cabinet, or of the church for that matter, there would be many places unfilled.

It is unreasonable and un-Christian, therefore, to look for perfection in politicians or their policies. What degree of imperfection is intolerable must always be a *political* decision based on judgment concerning what is acceptable to the electorate and what will stand in the way of individual politicians or their governments carrying out the tasks for which they have been elected.

In no sense, therefore (I shall argue), was the resignation of the Secretary of State for Trade and Industry required by religious or moral considerations. It was a political issue and the Christian task was – and remains – to show understanding and compassion to all concerned in the sad business.

Friday 21 October 1983

The Crypt Chapel – or, more correctly, the Chapel of St Mary Undercroft – in the Palace of Westminster is a place where I frequently officiate. During Parliamentary sessions there is Holy Communion at 12.30 p.m., attended by only a handful of people, and there are also baptisms, weddings and, occasionally, memorial services which attract large numbers. It is the one place in the Palace that offers peace and quiet for prayer and reflection.

Built in the thirteenth century beneath the chapel of the old Royal Palace, it was damaged in the 1834 fire, but when Charles Barry's great replacement Palace was completed his son, Edward, masterminded its renewal as a place of worship. Previously it had been used as a cellar, stables and the Speaker's state dining-room.

Taking his cue from the colour that remained on some of the wonderfully carved bosses at the conjunctions of the lierne vaulting, Barry the younger decorated in red, green and gold every inch of the surfaces of the roof and walls. Paintings of saints fill the wall behind the altar and painted glass the windows. The sanctuary floor is of marble and the remaining floor has coloured tiles. The octagonal Baptistry is also highly decorated and the Font has a huge cover of elaborate design in various metals.

The chapel is a monument to high Victorian Gothic and, because of the low cavernous nature of the building itself, is somewhat gloomy and oppressive. But the mere fact of its existence within the Houses of Parliament is remarkable and its importance as a place of worship and prayer undergirding the business of Government cannot, I believe, be exaggerated.

Roman Catholic masses are sometimes celebrated in the chapel, much to the chagrin of Ian Paisley, the Democratic Unionist MP for North Antrim. The Moderator of the General Assembly of the Church of Scotland has held services for Scottish Members and the other day we had an Orthodox baptism. The only problem is the organ, which is quite the worst instrument I have encountered in any place of worship. I have pointed out to the Speaker and the Lord Chancellor the incongruity of this in the 'Mother of Parliaments', and they are going to raise the matter with the Lord Great Chamberlain, who is responsible to the Queen for the Palace and controls the purse strings. Meanwhile I have asked Simon Preston to advise on the chapel's requirements.

Saturday 29 October 1983

The Day of Prayer for Peace, organized by the Quakers and held in St Margaret's, attracted strong support and is deemed to have been very successful. Throughout the day, from 10.30 a.m. – 6.00 p.m., there were rarely less than fifty to sixty in the church praying for peace, and the building was crowded for the act of worship at the end.

I was in and out of the church most of the day, and it was good to have a powerful witness to the importance of world peace that for once did not involve controversy, violence and arrests. There is, I am sure, a place for demonstrations of a more dramatic sort, but quite a lot of people who are concerned for peace don't feel able to join in these, and today's event provided them with an alternative close to the heart of Government.

Friday 11 November 1983

Quite unprompted by me, the Speaker and the Rector's Warden, Patrick Cormack, have written to the Dean in the following terms:

'We are sure that you are already aware of the widespread appreciation at the Commons of the work being undertaken by Mr Speaker's Chaplain. In addition to the regular and occasional Services held within the Palace, he has readily made himself available for pastoral work amongst the Members and staff of the House. He has developed the connection with St Margaret's, and encouraged Members to use it as their London church. A recent meeting to welcome newly-elected Members was attended by over one-third of those elected this year. As Speaker and Rector's Warden of St Margaret's we are anxious that this work should be continued and developed, and that the link between the Commons and St Margaret's should be sustained. Our purpose in writing to you is to invite you to consider the possibility of Mr Speaker's Chaplain being helped to devote the greater part of his time to these tasks, since we feel that the three roles of Chaplain, Rector and Canon of Westminster with full Residential duties impose burdens that no one individual should be asked to carry. We should be grateful for any thought you could give to this question.'

The Dean has discussed this with me and we are agreed that the problem is more easily stated than solved, since it is constitutionally impossible for a Canon of Westminster to be relieved of his responsibilities in and for the Abbey. This is the task to which he was appointed and at the end of the day it must have priority.

What may be possible is a reorganization of duties that will free me of responsibilities that are not integral to my role as a Canon and thus enable me to concentrate more on the work of the Chaplain and Rector. The Dean is to raise this in Chapter to see what, if anything, can be done.

Saturday 26 November 1983

Many of the survivors of HMS Barham and their families came to Evensong this afternoon, as they always do on the Saturday following 25 November – the day on which their ship was sunk in 1941. After so many years it might have been expected that their number would dwindle, but in fact it seems to be increasing, and attendance at the Abbey is part of an annual reunion. Some are widows and other dependants and the two standard candlesticks at the Nave altar were given in memory of those who were lost.

We had a short act of remembrance at these candlesticks immediately after Evensong; it is an occasion which I always find specially moving. A fleet comprising the battleships Queen Elizabeth, Barham and Valiant, and eight destroyers, was sailing in the Eastern Mediterranean when the Barham was hit by three torpedoes fired from a U-boat. The ship rolled over and the crew could be seen massing on her upturned side. A minute or two later the main magazine blew up, and when the smoke cleared the Barham had disappeared.

Realizing what had happened, the chaplain of the Queen Elizabeth, Lancelot Fleming, who later became Bishop of Portsmouth, then of Norwich, obtained permission to say prayers for the dying and the dead, and for the whole fleet, over the ship's loudspeaker system. The captain of the Barham and 861 other members of the ship's crew died, and there were about 450 survivors who, when the war was over, formed an association to look after the welfare of the bereaved families.

Among others who have poignant memories of this tragic wartime event is Gerald Ellison, the former Bishop of London, who had been chaplain of the Barham but left the ship, following a disagreement with its captain, a few days before it sailed from Alexandria. His replacement was among those killed.

Monday 28 November 1983

George Wigg's memorial service at St Margaret's this morning was something of a challenge. I did not know him personally, as he had left the House of Commons long before I arrived on the scene, but I had of course heard of him and a little research revealed much more.

A newspaper's description of him as 'Parliament's Punch-up Man' seems to have been not far wrong, though other papers described him as 'People's Champion' and 'Kind Breaker of Idols'. Certainly he was a colourful personality and, by all accounts, a master of political intrigue. Hence 'wiggery pokery' – a phrase still used in the House of Commons.

Largely self-educated, he served in the ranks of the army for eighteen years, where he came under the influence of William Temple, A. D. Lindsay and others involved in the Workers' Educational Movement. During World War II he rose to the rank of Colonel in the Army Education Corps, and in 1945 became Labour MP for Dudley, which he represented until 1967.

He managed Harold Wilson's campaign for the Leadership of the Labour Party after the death of Hugh Gaitskell, and when Labour returned to power in 1964 was rewarded with appointment as Paymaster General and special advisor to the Prime Minister. Just before the General Election he had been relentless in pursuing John Profumo over the Christine Keeler affair and succeeded in bringing him down. It was ironic, therefore, that he was himself much later charged with kerb-crawling near Marble Arch and was generally thought to have been lucky to escape conviction.

Harold Wilson soon tired of George Wigg's advice, and after three years had the bright idea of offering him the chairmanship of the Horserace Betting Levy Board and a Life Peerage – a combination of jobs he could not resist because he was madly keen on racing. Over the years he made many enemies, but was intensely loyal to his friends and was sustained by a strong Unitarian faith.

How does one adequately reflect such a life and character in a memorial service? The only answer is: with the greatest difficulty. It is the responsibility of the person who gives the address to decide what to say and what to leave out, but the Bidding at the beginning of the service should in some way encapsulate the life of the one who is being remembered.

I did my best, and a lawyer from the world of horse racing who gave the address drew the congregation's attention to 'the delicate manner in which the Rector described George Wigg's personality'. This raised a good laugh and evidently the family were well pleased, for Lady Wigg sent me an antique silver salt-cellar this evening, along with a letter of warm thanks.

Thursday 1 December 1983

A fascinating meeting this evening in the Jerusalem Chamber between members of the Westminster Abbey Trust, led by the Duke of Edinburgh, and influential members of the Jewish community, including the Chief Rabbi. Although arranged as a social gathering, it was understood by everyone that the purpose of the encounter was to acquaint the Jewish visitors with the great restoration programme now being carried out on the Abbey and the need for more money to keep this programme going.

Earlier, Edward Carpenter, who is a leading light on the Council for Christians and Jews, expressed serious doubt as to the wisdom of arranging such an occasion, since it would not be possible for Jews to give money for the restoration of an Anglican church. They might conceivably give to the Library, but not to anything specifically Christian.

However, Sir John Davis, the chairman of the Trust executive, was determined to have a try, and by issuing the invitations in the name of the Duke of Edinburgh secured a response sufficient to crowd the Jerusalem Chamber. Half-way through the evening the Duke welcomed his guests and Sir John Davis spoke about the restoration and the progress of the Appeal.

The Chief Rabbi responded with a fairly lengthy speech which, after the expected words of thanks, clearly indicated that there was no reason why Jews should not support the Appeal. 'The Abbey is not only a Christian church but also a national shrine,' he said, 'and we Jews belong to this nation. It is therefore entirely appropriate that we should support a project of this kind and I hope that many members of my community will do so.'

All of which was music to our ears. It has opened the way for the Trust to approach wealthy Jews for donations. But there was, I think, more to it than money, for the Chief Rabbi was asserting that the Jews have now ceased to think of themselves as a beleaguered minority in

Britain. Rather are they an integral part of our national life, which brings privileges and also responsibilities.

Edward Carpenter was both astonished and delighted, and we all feel that the evening marked a breakthrough at a particular level – national, rather than religious, but at Westminster Abbey it is impossible to separate the two.

Tuesday 6 December 1983

At long last the design and wording for Eric Abbott's memorial stone in the Nave sanctuary has been agreed. It has been a laborious process. Eric himself left behind some modest suggestions about this, but these – consisting mainly of career details – did not seem right, so the Dean invited the Chapter to make alternative suggestions.

Inevitably this led to disagreement, sometimes about single words and even about the size of letters, but now everyone is happy and the result is good:

> ERIC SYMES ABBOTT
> K.C.V.O. 1906 – 1983
> Dean of Westminster 1959 – 1974
> Friend and counsellor of many
> he loved the Church of England
> striving to make this House of Kings
> a place of pilgrimage and prayer
> for all peoples
> PASTOR PASTORUM

It would be nice to think that future generations will pause to wonder why it was necessary for a Dean to strive to make this great church a place of pilgrimage and prayer, but I dare say that the tension between the sacred and the secular will always be here.

Wednesday 7 December 1983

The death of John Robinson on Monday night, after a long battle against cancer, was a sad end to a life which has been tinged with sadness for as long as I had known him, some twenty years, I suppose. His name will always be associated with *Honest to God* – a brilliant distillation and popularization of the work of Bultmann, Bonhoeffer and Tillich – which became a symbol of the movement for Christian renewal in the 1960s.

Had John not been a bishop, the book would hardly have been noticed, and the initial print-run was for no more than a few thousand copies, but in the event it created near-panic among the hierarchy of the Church of England and left its author marked as something akin to a heretic. Even Michael Ramsey, one of the few theologians to have occupied the Archbishopric of Canterbury in recent centuries, joined in the chorus of denunciation, though he came to regret this later.

The consequence of this was that the Church of England never had the benefit of what could have been an excitingly creative episcopal ministry. Although few people outside the Diocese of Southwark knew it, John was a highly effective suffragan Bishop of Woolwich. He had a strong pastoral sense, was a great encourager, forged links between the church and the secular community, and was a gifted preacher and teacher.

All of which should have been carried forward into a major diocesan bishopric, but neither Lambeth nor Downing Street would countenance this, so John was in effect sidelined. He could not have stayed at Woolwich for ever and for the want of anything better coveted the Deanery of Canterbury, which he failed to get, finishing up as Dean of Chapel at Trinity College, Cambridge. Even here his teaching gifts were nowhere near fully exploited.

With less than enough to do, therefore, he began to explore some of the strange byways of religious thought. It seemed distinctly odd that a man who had hit the headlines with 'Our image of God must go' should have believed the supposed image of Christ on the Turin Shroud to be credible. And, although he had never been numbered among the most radical of New Testament scholars, there is a quirkiness about his soon-to-be-published final book which argues for the priority of St John's Gospel. It was a sad waste of a huge talent.

I shall always be grateful to John for his friendship, encouragement and support during the time I was editing *New Christian*. He was the contributor whom I, and the readers, most valued and he was extraordinary generous in writing and reviewing – and delivering his copy on time – whenever asked.

We first met in 1963 when we were both involved in the negotiations that led to the merging of Parish and People and the Keble Conference Group. From the North East of England where I had been working for the past ten years, I had always imagined him to be something of an extrovert firebrand, so it was a great surprise to encounter a shy and sensitive man whose stimulating ideas were the expression of deep pastoral concern.

In other words, he bore the hallmarks of the best kind of English theologian and bishop – and there are too few of these about to justify the gross wastage of such gifts.

Friday 9 December 1983

Jo was rushed into Westminster Hospital this afternoon with acute pancreatitis. She has been ill in bed for the last six weeks with what was diagnosed, mistakenly it would seem, as hepatitis. Recovery from this is always a protracted affair, with little treatment apart from rest, so the fact that she wasn't making any perceptible improvement did not seem significant – certainly not alarming.

But her condition took a marked turn for the worse during the night and the senior partner in our local medical practice who visited her this morning ordered her to hospital immediately. When I went in this evening she was being given large doses of antibiotic and vitamin E intravenously, but of course it is too soon for this to have had any noticeable effect.

I don't know if her condition should have been picked up earlier. She has been in the hands of a recently recruited young woman doctor who certainly seems capable enough, but it could be that she has not seen a case of this sort before. One of the problems of living in the heart of London is that, although there are superb hospitals close at hand, there are hardly any GPs – at least not working in the National Health Service. The cost of maintaining premises is too high and our nearest practice, on the far side of Pimlico, seems to have so many people on its books that it has difficulty in providing an efficient service.

I think some kind of subsidy for medical and dental surgeries in areas such as this is called for, but this is hardly likely when the decision-makers have opted for private medicine and have little first-hand experience of the NHS.

Saturday 10 December 1983

The problems attending the memorial to Earl and Countess Mountbatten are not yet resolved. They involve both its design and its location.

The design itself, the work of Christopher Ironside, portrays the Earl and the Countess in profile, in brass and in a somewhat elaborate setting with various coats of arms. The Architectural Advisory Panel is not very happy about this, and some of its members asked for their objections to be minuted. Sir Anthony Wagner, Garter King of Arms, has predictably objected to some of the heraldry. He says that the use of dolphins is 'improper'. But the Mountbatten family like it and they have shown it to the Queen, who has also declared herself pleased with the design, so we don't think it can now be changed.

As for the location, we argued that it should be placed on the floor at the West end of the Nave, near St George's Chapel. But now the Surveyor and the designer would like it to go centrally between the grave of the Unknown Warrior and the Winston Churchill memorial. Doubtless this would please the Earl, though the family have not asked for this more prominent position.

There are two problems about this proposal, the first being that in the central position the memorial would be constantly walked on, and indeed on great occasions, when the Queen and others were being officially received at the Great West Door, people would be standing on it.

I also made the point in Chapter last Tuesday that it is by no means certain that history will assess Lord Mountbatten as being in the same category as Winston Churchill and the Unknown Warrior. To place his memorial between the two would be to assert something that ought not to be asserted and that could not easily be revised. There is an additional fact that the elaborate Mountbatten memorial would not sit easily between the austere stones of the Unknown Warrior and Churchill.

The Dean, who is the ultimate authority in these matters, and the rest of the Chapter, see this clearly, so the memorial will go in the place already allocated to it.

Friday 23 December 1983

Jo has returned home from hospital just in time for Christmas, but she will not be able to take much active part in the festivities, and certainly won't do any cooking. Eight weeks in bed, and for some of this time quite seriously ill, has inevitably left her very weak and I have been warned that it will be some time before she is back to normal.

The Speaker has suggested that we might go to Bermuda for a couple of weeks as soon as Jo is well enough to make the long flight. Apparently the Speaker of the Bermudan Assembly is the chairman of an hotel out there and he has generously told Jack Weatherill that if anyone associated with the Westminster Parliament is ever in need of a recuperative break he will be pleased to provide the hospitality of the hotel. Jack is confident that he can find the money to pay for the flights. So we must see how things stand a month from now.

Meanwhile there is Christmas to be celebrated, and it is part of the craziness of our arrangements that the Rector of St Margaret's is Canon-in-Residence at the Abbey during December, of all months, when both churches are functioning at full stretch. It is fortunate that Catherine and Charles are living just next door and can lend a hand with the domestic arrangements, including the Christmas Day lunch for a few people who would otherwise be on their own.

1984

Saturday 21 January 1984

A very remarkable service in the Abbey at midday to mark the fortieth anniversary of the ordination to the priesthood of Florence Tim Oi Li – the first woman priest in the Anglican church, who was ordained by Bishop R.O.Hall of Hong Kong to meet a wartime emergency.

The service was arranged by the Movement for the Ordination of Women and well over a thousand people came. Most important among them of course was Florence herself – a tiny woman who now lives in Canada and who came over specially for the occasion. One couldn't help marvelling at the courage and dedication embodied in that tiny frame: for many years after the war the validity of her ordination was denied by the rest of the Anglican Communion, and between 1958 and 1978 the Communist rulers of China forced her to work, first on a chicken farm, then as a manual worker in various factories in Canton.

The service itself, a eucharist, was imaginatively ordered by MOW. The president was Gilbert Baker, the present Bishop of Hong Kong, who regularized Florence's ordination in 1970, and the preacher was Joyce Bennett, the first Englishwoman to be ordained priest, also in Hong Kong. All the male priests processed into the Abbey first and a chair was left empty beside each of them. The women deaconesses and some women priests from overseas then came in and occupied these empty chairs – symbolizing first the incompleteness of the church's existing ministry, then the partnership that we are working to bring about.

The Dean read a message from the Archbishop of Canterbury to Florence which many thought encouraging:

'Sometimes you have suffered from misunderstandings about your ministry. You have never been eager to promote yourself, but only to build up the life of the church and serve its mission in places of desperate human need. Your selfless ministry is an example to us all.'

Later she read the Gospel in Chinese and, along with the other women priests present, administered the sacrament to the very joyful congregation. My own joy was reduced somewhat by a recurrence of my back problem and the onset of a vicious muscular spasm which would have driven me out of the building had I been able to move.

Eventually, however, it subsided and I couldn't help feeling that if a service such as this could be held in Westminster Abbey the ordination of women to the priesthood cannot be delayed for very much longer.

Monday 23 January 1984

A long discussion in Chapter today about the letter from the Speaker and the Rector's Warden about the difficulties I am experiencing in trying to cope with three demanding jobs – the Abbey, St Margaret's, and the House of Commons. We didn't get very far, partly because everyone has different ideas as to how this problem might be solved, and partly because we have, in the short term, very little room for manoeuvre.

The general view, which I do not share, is that I should have a full-time assistant priest who would shoulder the responsibility for organizing special services and undertake some pastoral work. This would certainly be helpful up to a point, but would not deal with the main problem. There would not in fact be enough work to keep a full-time assistant usefully occupied.

The fact of the matter is that a high proportion of the people with whom the Rector of St Margaret's deals are men and women of some seniority in their own walks of life, and whenever they are doing business with the church in Westminster they expect to encounter someone of equivalent seniority – not a junior curate. Equally, the Sunday morning pulpit at St Margaret's could not be handed over to such a priest, so quite a lot of my work simply cannot be delegated.

Good part-time assistance would, however, be useful, and to this end I made a fairly radical solution. It was that when next a Canonry falls vacant the Crown should be asked to appoint a musician to fill the position and that he should be given the title Canon Precentor. He would have full responsibility for the musical side of the Abbey's life, which would be desirable in itself, since many of the apparently intractable problems with the Choral Foundation spring from the fact that no one of sufficient seniority is in charge. The Precentor ought to be a member of the Chapter and have the authority to crack the whip when necessary.

Under this proposal the present Precentor post would be redesignated Sacrist, and this priest would assist the Canon Precentor with the Abbey services and the Rector with the St Margaret's services. The Chaplain, who would have fewer liturgical responsibilities, would concentrate on pastoral work in both church communities.

There was, however, no support for this idea. The Receiver General pointed out that the appointment of a Canon Precentor would substantially reduce the involvement and influence of the Dean over the ordering of the Abbey's worship. Sebastian Charles and the others thought that so radical a solution was undesirable for what could be a short-term problem, inasmuch as my successor might not wish to devote so much of his time to the House of Commons. I found this attitude specially depressing as it is clear to me that, now the door to significant pastoral and other opportunities in the House of Commons is open, it ought to be kept permanently open by the appointment of Canons who will always regard this work as a high priority.

The only other long-term solution I can see would be for the responsibilities to be shared by two Canons, one as Rector of St Margaret's, the other as Speaker's Chaplain, the latter collaborating with the former over the use of St Margaret's for Parliamentary purposes. But I did not raise this as a possibility, since it is hardly likely to be a realistic option for several years.

Meanwhile, it was agreed that Charles Taylor, the able Chaplain of the Abbey, will during his remaining time in Westminster devote as much time as can be spared from his other duties to liturgical matters at St Margaret's. Apart from the immediate practical assistance this will provide, it will help us to see how a musical/liturgical priest might operate in both churches.

Tuesday 24 January 1984

It has happened again: an anticipated deficit of £64,000 has become a surplus of over £160,000. All because of a great upsurge of visitors since last Easter, caused chiefly, it would seem, by the strength of the American dollar in relation to the pound. The Abbey was full of Americans throughout the summer and the autumn, and St Paul's and St George's, Windsor have had similar experiences.

The hope is, of course, that this will continue, but one IRA bomb in London could change the situation overnight. The Treasurer is therefore recommending that we continue to keep £100,000 in a deposit acount as a hedge against unexpected cash-flow problems. He is also warning against the submission of items of capital expenditure for approval by Chapter without previous subjection to normal budgetary procedures.

This is, I suspect, directed against Anthony Harvey's grand scheme for the refurbishment of the Museum and the establishing of a Treasury.

Of last year's surplus, £65,000 is to be spent on the completion of the rebuilding of the organ, £21,000 on the internal re-decoration of the Choir School, £11,000 on the Abbey lighting, £25,000 on the repair of official houses, £23,000 on the repair of College Hall, and a number of smaller items. 'Cautious optimism' is the Treasurer's reaction to our present situation, but we were unhappy with his suggestion that the staff should be given a 2.5% bonus of their basic salaries. This would cost £10,000 and set a difficult precedent.

Wednesday 25 January 1984

Simon Preston's annual report tells us that 'the Choir's tour of Paris last summer, with its concerts in outlying towns, culminating in the High Mass at Notre Dame, was without doubt the greatest success imaginable', but it concludes, ominously:

> 'I would like to say how difficult it is to work in Westminster Abbey
> . . . I now have no ready access to the Chapter over difficult matters,
> indeed I feel the Chapter do not really wish to know the views of
> people who hold contrary opinions to their own. In this respect I
> include the state of our services in Westminster Abbey, towards which
> I feel an increasing alienation: the Advent Carol Service, the Sung
> Eucharist on Sundays and the mounting number of hymns which are
> being sung to the detriment of the choral tradition in Westminster
> Abbey. Furthermore I am horrified to discover that the plans to intro-
> duce yet more electronic sound equipment are still alive; this can only
> lead to a further deterioration in the aesthetic quality of our services.
> Is it small wonder that so many of the people who work on the
> musical side in Westminster Abbey feel that their efforts are not
> worthwhile and that they are working in a vacuum?'

One is tempted to point out to Simon that the vacuum would have been even larger had the Dean and Chapter not spent over £235,000 on the music in 1983 and embarked on the rebuilding of the organ at a cost of about £400,000. But this would not get us very far. Simon has the single-mindedness of the genius he undoubtedly is and is quite incapable of seeing the great contribution he makes through music in the context of the Abbey's overall mission. Our rejection of his views about hymn-singing, liturgical change, attempts to lift the sound of worship above the choir screen so that it may be heard by the congregation in the Nave, and so on, are interpreted as unwillingness to listen or to maintain high standards.

None of which is remotely true, but accepting his complaints is the price we must pay for his gifts, and fortunately they don't affect personal relationships in the slightest.

Thursday 2 February 1984

An important meeting with the Speaker this evening to discuss the possibility of launching in his name an appeal for the restoration of St Margaret's. Strictly speaking such an appeal ought not to be necessary, as the Westminster Abbey Trust is committed to dealing with the church when the restoration of the Abbey is completed. But this seems to be a very long way off, as the restoration programme is only just reaching its half-way stage, after ten years of work, and the raising of funds is becoming increasingly difficult. There has even been talk of 'resting' the Trust for a time, or maybe switching the programme to the Western towers and launching a public appeal.

As St Margaret's becomes more active, so those associated with its life, especially on the Parliamentary side, have become more impatient with the delay in tackling a building which is coated with grime and presents a sad sight. Tim Rathbone, the Member for Lewes whose father, also an MP, was Rector's Warden until he was killed in the RAF during the early days of World War II, suggested an appeal. The Speaker and some others first wondered if it might be possible to spend a limited amount of money on simply cleaning the building. There are specialist firms ready to tackle this, but the Surveyor of the Fabric has advised us that this would be wasteful, since the building is not only dirty but also has much decayed stone and a serious problem with the roof. Scaffolding erected for cleaning purposes needs to be used also for restoration work.

The Surveyor thinks that the cost of full restoration may be about £1 million. The Speaker is ready to launch an appeal provided that I am prepared to supervise its day-to-day running. Obviously he doesn't have the time for major involvement, neither have I for that matter, but someone will need to do it and I think that a once-in-a-century effort of this sort deserves priority.

The only real problem, and it may be an intractable one, is that the Dean and Chapter gave an undertaking to the Trust, back in 1974, not to engage in any fund-raising efforts until the money for the Abbey's restoration had been raised. This was by no means an unreasonable demand by the Trust, though no-one realized at that time just how much money was going to be needed for the Abbey and how long it was going to take to raise it and complete the work.

I am therefore to discuss the possibility of an appeal for St Margaret's with the Dean and Chapter, and suggest that it should be a rather private affair, confined almost entirely to members of the House of Commons and the House of Lords and their personal contacts. There should be enough money in those quarters to restore half a dozen St Margaret's, and such an appeal would not conflict with the efforts of the Trust.

Monday 13 February 1984

Westminster Abbey has never held a high view of bishops, and from the time of Elizabeth I its polity has been essentially presbyterian. It was perhaps inevitable, therefore, that when we departed from tradition by commissioning a bishop's chair things would go badly wrong.

The starting point was unsound. The admirable Purcell Club wished to purchase something as a gift to the Abbey and the equally admirable Metropolitan Police Special Constabulary offered to pay for a lesser gift, but one that would bear its crest. Put the two together and the result was a special chair for visiting bishops, complete with a fine cushion and a comfortable kneeler.

The Surveyor of the Fabric was asked to design this furniture and the result is now to hand. It looks fine – appropriately modest, rather than magnificent – but it is apparent that the Surveyor has never measured an episcopal bottom. The seat is altogether too narrow, so that even the most austere member of the physically weighty bench of bishops would have difficulty in compressing himself into it. And even if he succeeded, a couple of Vergers would be needed to prise him out. Add elaborate robes to natural episcopal bulk and the apparatus becomes impossible.

What is the explanation of this miscalculation? No one quite knows, least of all the Surveyor, and a wise Chapter, taking it as an ill omen, might have abandoned the project. But sadly the Purcell Club and the Police have been promised a bishop's chair, so we must meet the cost of a re-designed version. This will leave us with a chair to spare, which may one day bear the crest of the Weight Watchers organization.

Tuesday 6 March 1984

The Joint Council for the Welfare of Immigrants held one of its regular lunchtime meetings in the Jerusalem Chamber today. I became involved in these meetings through the influence of my friend Nadir Dinshaw, who is one of its strongest behind-the-scenes supporters, and, although I have no expertise in race relations and immigration issues, making the Jerusalem Chamber available to the Council and organizing a sandwich lunch seems to be a valued contribution. I sometimes chair the meetings.

Ann Dummett, the wife of Michael Dummett, the Oxford philospher, is the leading light in the Council, and its thirty or so members are all professionals working the the race-relations field. All are uniformly depressed by the Thatcher government's attitude to immigrants and I am myself appalled by the degree of sheer cruelty being experienced by the victims in many of the cases reported to the Council.

There is, I am sure, widespread ignorance of what is actually taking place in our cities.

Thursday 8 March 1984

The Chapter is ready to support the idea of an appeal for St Margaret's provided that the Abbey's Trust is willing to release us from the 1974 undertaking not to engage in any fund-raising until the restoration of the Abbey is completed.

The Dean is very enthusiastic about the idea and the Canons are pre-pared to back me, even though they don't regard the restoration of St Margaret's as a very high priority. The most apprehensive is Reg Pullen, the Receiver General, who believes that approaching the Trust at this particular time when its own fund-raising is in the doldrums and its chairman, Sir John Davies, feels threatened, may be disastrous. Reg is always very nervous about anything that may jeopardize the well-being of the Abbey, for his whole life is so closely bound up with it. Although he has given me strong support since I took over St Margaret's, his loyalty will always be to the Abbey if a choice has to be made.

Friday 9 March 1984

Sebastian Charles, our Treasurer, was once again absent from the Chapter because of unspecified indisposition. These absences, combined with failure to keep engagements and an apparent inability on some occasions to grasp the essentials of a discussion, are becoming a great worry. In his own interests, as well as those of the Abbey, this problem – which seems to have a health dimension – needs to be tackled. But the Dean, who is the only member of the Chapter who can do this, evidently feels unable to grasp the nettle.

This is understandable, but I am not sure it is excusable, because the well-being of our community is at stake. And the same is true of decisions about the Dean's own future at the Abbey. Edward is now almost seventy-four – four years older than any of his successors in office can ever be. He is a most remarkable man who has made a very special contribution to the Abbey's life since he came here as a Canon in 1951. He is greatly loved and the last person on earth one would wish to hurt.

Yet his powers are fading quite rapidly. This became noticeable soon after the disappointment over the wedding of the Prince of Wales and is accelerating. Leadership of Westminster Abbey is now a very demanding responsibility. The sheer volume of work is enormous; some of the Dean's tasks are unique and call for special sensitivity, and, in common with other institutions of this sort, it has a propensity to develop tricky problems.

Most of this Edward is still capable of handling, but an increasing amount lacks a firm grip and, when combined with the weakness in the Treasurer's department, leaves us very vulnerable to mishap. There is the further point that the Sub-Dean, Edward Knapp-Fisher, wishes to retire when he becomes seventy next year, but recognizes that he needs to be here to manage the interregnum when the Dean finally retires. The fact that he has no idea when this might be makes it impossible for him to plan.

Yet none of us feels able to raise the issue with the Dean and suggest, even in the gentlest possible way, that the time has come for him to go. The Sub-Dean has tried to discuss it in terms of his own retirement, and seemed at one stage to have obtained a tacit agreement about dates, but the final decision appears to have been postponed.

I am close to Edward and might well be the best person to speak to him, but for some reason – I suppose it is cowardice – I don't feel able to do so. This is partly for fear of hurting someone who has himself always avoided painful confrontation with others, and partly because Lilian, who is some years younger than her husband, is by no means ready to leave the Deanery and would, I think, resent any suggestion that the time for this is now close.

On the whole it seems best to let things run a little longer and hope that Edward will make an unaided decision before he becomes seventy-five. Shortly before his own retirement, Gerald Ellison, the last Bishop of London, said, 'It is better to go while people are saying "Why is he retiring?", rather than wait until they are saying "When is he retiring?".'

The case for fixed retirement ages is, I believe, unanswerable – for the sake of everyone.

Thursday 26 April 1984

I had three visitors from Hungary this morning. They came via the British Council of Churches and constituted an official ecumenical delegation. Bishop Karoly Toth is a leader of the Reformed Church and also President of the Christian Peace Conference. Janos Pastor is a distinguished theologian and Bishop Messzarof is a Roman Catholic auxiliary bishop.

Before touring the Abbey we had some talk over coffee. Fortunately, they had reasonable English and I was able to ask a few questions about the present position of church/state relations in Hungary. They were rather defensive, as these official delegations tend to be, and unless one already knew otherwise, it might be supposed that they had no very serious problems.

When compared with some other parts of Eastern Europe they have a fair degree of freedom, but still need to tread very carefully. Bishop Toth could not have become a bishop without the approval of the Communist government, and the largely discredited Christian Peace Conference, over which he presides, still tends to support the Soviet Union's foreign policy.

What now seems to be the case is that all the mainline Hungarian churches support their government's socialist programmes, and in return for this are allowed to order their own lives without overmuch interference. The Roman Catholics are, apparently, taking advantage of this and developing large numbers of what they call 'base communities', comprised of lay people, many of them young, who are working out the ecclesiological and social implications of Vatican II. This sometimes makes them highly critical of their own bishops.

Criticism of the government is not permitted, however, and the Reformed Church, while involved in much social work, does not apparently see church reform as a continuous process. The recent development of the ecumenical movement in Hungary, of which my visitors were a clear sign, may be the herald of wider change.

They seemed to enjoy their tour of the Abbey, and the sight of the Coronation Chair and the Royal Tombs rang bells with them, for in Hungary until the Communist era the crown had – and maybe still has – a deeply religious significance. For almost a thousand years it was a symbol of the nation's allegiance to Mary, the Mother of God.

Wednesday 2 May 1984

The St Margaret's Annual General Meeting must be the only one of its kind at which those attending are first subjected to a thorough security check. The reason for this is that the meeting is, by long tradition, held in one of the House of Commons committee rooms, and there is no avoiding the police with their electronic equipment at the St Stephen's entrance to Parliament.

This year the attendance was so large that the committee room allocated to us could not accommodate everyone and another had to be found. Even there, venerable figures such as Enoch Powell were obliged to sit on the floor.

It was a lively occasion, too, with plenty of participation from the floor, though, as is usual on these occasions, a lot of time was taken up with reports. My own report included the information that during the year there had been twenty-two weddings, fourteen baptisms, nine memorial services and funerals and sixteen other special services in St Margaret's, besides a number of weddings and baptisms in the Crypt Chapel. I also expressed my view that relations between St Margaret's and the Abbey were probably better than at any time since the Reformation.

The Treasurer reported a small surplus – the first for many years – though the church remains heavily subsidized by the Abbey in some major areas of its life. There was competition for the twelve places on the Church Council and tribute was paid to Bill Stead, who has been an excellent People's Warden and, sadly for us, is retiring to Somerset.

All was ended by 7.30 p.m., as one of the advantages of meeting in the House of Commons is that committee rooms can be booked for no more than one hour. This leaves little scope for dawdling.

Tuesday 8 May 1984

As anticipated, Sir John Davis, the chairman of the Abbey Trust Executive Committee, is very unhappy about the prospect of a St

Margaret's appeal and says that he is unable to release the Dean and Chapter from its commitment not to have any appeals until the restoration of the Abbey is completed.

Fortunately, the decision is not his alone, and the matter is to be considered fully by the Trustees when they meet under the chairmanship of the Duke of Edinburgh next Tuesday. The Speaker has used his position to send a private briefing on the subject to the Duke, and the other Trustees are also to be briefed in advance of the meeting. I am to attend the meeting to present the St Margaret's case.

It may also be to our advantage that efforts are now being made behind the scenes to remove Sir John Davis from the chairmanship of the Executive Committee. He has done a very good job for us, albeit in a somewhat overbearing manner, over the last ten years, but now that he has retired from the Rank Organization he no longer has much influence in the City, where the remainder of the Abbey's restoration money still lies. This is, I suppose, partly because he is regarded as a 'has been', but also, and perhaps chiefly, because he is himself no longer in a position to provide support for other appeals. There is quite a lot of 'I'll support your appeal if you'll support mine' in this business.

Tuesday 15 May 1984

This evening's meeting of the Abbey Trustees went surprisingly well, and we were given permission to go ahead with a St Margaret's Appeal.

I made the point – indeed laid it on very heavily – that the position of the Trustees was fully understood and that as a Canon of Westminster I had not the slightest desire to hamper their work for the Abbey. It was proposed therefore that any appeal for St Margaret's should be of a semi-private character. We hoped that a successful appeal would be encouraging to the Trustees at this half-way stage in their efforts for the Abbey and also be a relief at the end of the day, when it would no longer be necessary to raise £1 million for St Margaret's.

The Duke of Edinburgh, in his down-to-earth, practical way, thought there was quite a lot to be said for this, and, although Sir John Davis and Tommy Thompson, the Trust's fund-raising manager, spluttered a bit, the rest of the Trustees fell in behind the Duke. Indeed they went further and said that they would be quite happy for the Speaker to approach anyone for money, provided they were not already on the Trust's own target list. I undertook to clear with the fund-raising manager the names of anyone outside Parliament whom we wished to approach. It was recognized that members of the St Margaret's congregation would be asked for support.

So now we are in business, or at least soon will be, and this is good.

Saturday 19 May 1984

I was happily engaged this afternoon in the Crypt Chapel wedding of Harold Walker, the Chairman of Ways and Means and Deputy Speaker, to Mary Griffin, who held a number of senior jobs at Labour Party headquarters before qualifying recently as a solicitor. Harold, the Member for Doncaster, was a widower, and since Mary is a Tipperary-born Roman Catholic, we had a nuptial mass. The Speaker read one of the lessons and I gave the address, in which I ventured to express the hope that the bridegroom would set a good example to his colleagues by not permitting devotion to the House of Commons to have priority over devotion to his wife. I urged Mary to ensure that he kept to this.

There is a major problem here, for many Parliamentary wives are sorely neglected by husbands who are so committed to politics that they have little time left for their families. I mentioned in my address that clergy wives often find themselves in a similar position.

These serious considerations were soon followed by champagne at the Speaker's House reception, though I had first to conduct another wedding in St Margaret's. The Speaker told the assembled company that this was the first occasion on which a Deputy Speaker had been married in the Crypt and also the first time a Speaker's Chaplain had given the address at a Roman Catholic mass in the Chapel.

Tuesday 22 May 1984

Billy Graham is in town again. During the next few weeks he will be addressing some hundreds of thousands of people assembled in football grounds and other meeting places up and down the country. The organizers of this campaign confidently assert that 30,000 people will make new confessions of Christian faith by the time it ends and that many more will have their faith renewed.

I went, as a journalist, to one of Billy Graham's first British crusades, held in Harringay Stadium in about 1967, and was absolutely horrified. Not so much by the content of the worship, but rather by the emotional pressure applied by the preacher, especially on the young people present. We were told of a pop star who had recently been killed, indeed decapitated, in a road accident, and we were warned that something like this could easily happen to any of us. We had therefore better repent and embrace the Christian faith while there was still time.

At the time I deplored and dismissed all this as an ephemeral expression of revivalism that would make no lasting impact on the British religious scene. I could not have been more mistaken, for I did not anticipate that a significant number of those who came under Billy Graham's power would go on to seek ordination and become leaders in the burgeoning evangelical movement that is now gaining much influence in the Church of England and in other churches.

Last evening, after an interval of more than a quarter of a century, I had another encounter with Billy Graham when he addressed an open meeting in Speaker's House. After the usual sumptuous buffet supper, provided by the members of the Parliamentary Christian Wives' Group (who are specially good on puddings), the great evangelist spoke to us – about 150 in all – and I was struck by two things.

First, removed from all the razzmatazz of a crusade meeting, his speech was not specially compelling. In fact, he spoke fairly quietly, from prepared notes, and at times was, I thought, rather boring. I suppose this kind of orator is so integrated into his main public setting that he is much less effective when operating in the more intimate, even if palatial, surroundings of a room in Speaker's House.

The other thing that surprised me was that his message now has a social content that seemed entirely absent in the 1960s. The old intensely personal interpretation of the gospel was still there, of course, but he talked quite a lot about the need for justice and righteousness in the ordering of society, and about Christian concern for the poor and hungry in the Third World and elsewhere. I don't think this was added simply because he was speaking to politicians in Westminster. It seemed to be an important part of his whole message, and to this extent his thinking must have moved on since the early crusades.

There was, however, nothing specific enough in his address to disturb the almost entirely Conservative audience.

Monday 4 June 1984

Today marks the beginning of the Speaker's Appeal for St Margaret's. though the official launch will not be until 22 November. Things have moved quickly since we were given the go-ahead by the Abbey Trust three weeks ago. A strong committee has been formed consisting of Tim Rathbone MP; Tim Sainsbury MP; Patrick Cormack MP (who is also

Rector's Warden); Clifford Dann, a Past President of the Royal Institution of Chartered Surveyors, which has strong associations with St Margaret's; Clifford Boulton, Clerk Assistant of the House of Commons and Deputy Rector's Warden; Freddie Hetherington-Sims, an Inland Revenue tax lawyer and Deputy People's Warden; and myself. The Speaker, who has been designated President of the Appeal, will attend meetings whenever he can and Tim Rathbone will chair all meetings in his absence.

From the outset it was recognized that the help of a professional fund-raising consultant would be needed, and Tim Sainsbury introduced us to Bernard Ashford, who had impressed him in the course of a school appeal. He in turn brought along Patricia Jennings-Bramley, an able organizer who will be in charge of the day-to-day administration. I spent the whole of this morning installing them in my room in the House of Commons, from where the Appeal is to be run.

The Surveyor of the Fabric and the Abbey's Quantity Surveyor have been asked to draw up a detailed restoration programme, fully costed, and to let us know precisely how much we have to raise. The Speaker says that he wants the Appeal completed in twelve months, as he is very busy now and will have other things to do from 1986 onwards. This may be a little optimistic, but it gives us a stimulating challenge. The main task now is to compile a list of potential donors, and also to plan a number of fund-raising events.

Tuesday 26 June 1984

Grim news indeed last evening, and even worse today. Towards the end of the Bible Study Group Jo answered the telephone and called me into the study to tell me that Madeleine, one of my closest friends, had died suddenly. This morning Anne, the Prioress of the Carmelite Monastery in Wales where Madeleine was a novice, telephoned to tell me in the strictest confidence that she had taken her own life. I am devastated.

Madeleine and I came to know each other in 1968 when I was editing *New Christian* from an office near the Augustinian Convent in Highgate where she was Novice Mistress. She became one of the leading lights in the movement for the reform of the religious life, following Vatican II, was in great demand as a lecturer, and wrote a very good book, *Solitary Refinement*.

Eventually she became Mother Superior of her convent and began to put some of her ideas into practice. But this created problems in her community, which was the English house of a French nursing order.

Complaints that she had more time for the drop-outs and problem people who came in increasing number to the convent than she had for her Sisters became frequent and, although I tried to help her through the various crises that arose, in the end she was driven to resign as Superior.

Then, after a period of reflection, she moved to Presteign, where a Carmelite community was looking for someone to run, experimentally, a house for people with problems of various sorts. This was successful up to a point, but the supply of 'problems' dried up and she entered the main Carmelite monastery to test her vocation to the contemplative life. It was a lively community with a number of interesting nuns from a variety of backgrounds.

Inevitably this reduced the contact between us, but some telephone calls were allowed, I went to Presteign a few times to give talks to the nuns, and Madeleine, not yet fully professed, was permitted to travel to London occasionally.

All seemed to be going well and last Sunday, St John Baptist's Day, she was due to be professed as a Carmelite nun. It was to have been a very happy occasion. But what I did not know was that the community was deeply divided over whether or not Madeleine should be admitted. They suspected, with good reason, that she would be a reforming Carmelite and a disturbing influence.

Nonetheless, arrangements for the profession and a celebratory party went ahead. But on Sunday morning the Prioress called Madeleine into her room and told her that after much agonized thought and prayer she had reached her conclusion that it would not be right for her to be admitted to the community.

Apparently Madeleine asked for time on her own to consider the implications of this decision and retired to the caravan in which she had spent some days in Retreat preparing for her profession. When she failed to appear in Chapel and at breakfast yesterday morning, the Prioress and another nun went to the caravan, which they found locked, and having forced the door they discovered her lying dead – empty bottles of pain-killers and sherry by her side.

It is quite unbelievable, but I can see clearly that, having left the Augustinians and committed herself to the Carmelites, only to be rejected by them just a few hours before this commitment was sealed, it must have seemed to her that there was nowhere else to go. Her commitment to the religious life ran so deep that there was really no possibility of her creating a new life in the secular world. So, tragically, she took the only way forward she could see at that moment.

The Prioress is naturally shattered by the consequences of her decision, and in two telephone conversations I have tried to reassure her by telling her that if she believes her decision to have been the right one she cannot be blamed for what followed. Questions remain, however, about the way in which the whole situation was handled; and it is at this level that the Prioress is going to need most help.

I was celebrating the Eucharist in the Abbey this morning and prayed for both Madeleine and Anne.

Tuesday 3 July 1984

A long and tiring day at Presteign yesterday for Madeleine's funeral and Requiem. I collected three of the Augustinian sisters from the Highgate convent at 8.00 a.m., and the drive through the Cotswolds and across Worcestershire and Herefordshire to the Welsh border took just over three hours. Conversation was a little tricky, since the Highgate community has not yet been told how Madeleine died.

The Requiem combined the traditional and the informal in the way that she liked, and someone played the guitar. I gave the address – a difficult task, but not one that I would have wished anyone else to undertake.

I spoke of the sorrow and pain that Madeleine's 'unexpected' death had brought, most especially to her mother, sister and brothers, and said that Christian faith does not require us to deny our grief or mask our pain. The Crucifixion assures us that God shares our suffering, and at every Mass we re-enact the passion and death of Jesus. At the same time, we rejoice and give thanks for God's mighty acts – creating, redeeming, sanctifying. So, as we mourn Madeleine's death, we give thanks for her life and for all that she meant to so many people.

I then spoke about her faith and her work, mentioning the joy she felt on learning that her Augustinian sisters had recently accepted the new constitution which she herself had played a decisive part in creating. And I said that while she was a very special person in whose being the life and love of God seemed to pulsate with great power, to transform and inspire, she was also a very vulnerable person and rarely free from interior struggle and pain. 'Her coming to test her vocation in this Carmelite community, to whose Prioress and Sisters those who love Madeleine most will always be grateful, was, I suspect, the final attempt to deal with this particular, personal agony.'

The most painful moment for me was when the point of Communion was reached and, because I am an Anglican, I could not share in the sacrament with those with whom I was united in grief. The sin of Christian division could hardly have been more clearly demonstrated.

I had a long talk with the Prioress afterwards – she desperately needs reassurance from those who were closest to Madeleine – and when on the way home my travelling companions asked me to suggest a quotation to go with the press announcement they were preparing I could think only of St Augustine's words, 'Our hearts are restless, until they find their rest in Thee.' These will do.

Friday 13 July 1984

The Dalai Lama has visited the Abbey again, and unfortunately his coming, or at least his appearance at a public event in the Abbey, has created quite a furore in the Chapter.

This began when the Sub-Dean and I chanced to read in *The Sunday Times* that the Dalai Lama would be in Westminster Abbey on the evening of Saturday 7 July and be 'giving Buddhist teaching in depth'. This was the first anyone on the Chapter, apart from the Dean, knew of his coming, and some of us wondered if it was appropriate for 'Buddhist teaching in depth' to be given in a great Christian shrine.

The Sub-Dean raised the matter at the Chapter Meeting on Tuesday and I also expressed my concern. The Dean, who had invited the great man, apologized for failing to inform us about the occasion – it had been an oversight – and went on to explain that *The Sunday Times* report was incorrect inasmuch as no Buddhist teaching had been given.

Evidently the Abbey was quite full and the Dean simply put to the Dalai Lama a few questions as to how kindness and human feeling could be translated into corporate action. There were also questions about the contribution the East might make to the West and *vice versa*, and the significance of the office of Dalai Lama. After these questions had been answered there was two minutes of silence and the Dean ended the occasion with a quotation from a Shakespeare sonnet.

The problem was no more than a failure in communication – regrettable, but not really a disaster. The event had been greatly appreciated by those who were present. Quite so. It had, however, raised in my mind a much broader question about the jurisdiction of the Dean. Unlike the deans of cathedrals, who can do little without the consent of their chapters, the Dean of Westminster has the freedom to do more or less what he likes in Westminster Abbey. In practice, the present Dean is meticulous in consulting the Chapter before reaching a decision.

But is the Dean of Westminster subject to any constraints, or is he absolutely free to introduce into the Abbey Buddhist, or even atheist, teaching? In these changing times this seems to be a question worth exploring, so that we all know where we stand. The Dean is, however, rather hurt that the question has been asked and I don't think that I have much support in wanting to pursue it.

The whole incident is, I dare say, no more than a July thunderstorm – the kind of thing that tends to crop up at this time of the year when we are all feeling rather tired and tetchy, and when minor incidents are liable to be seen out of proportion and their significance much exaggerated. On one thing we are agreed, however: we are glad the the Dalai Lama came and was given an opportunity to speak in the Abbey.

Saturday 14 July 1984

Today being Miners' Gala Day in Durham, I went there to preach at the annual Miners' Service in the cathedral. It is several years since I was in the North East, and I was amazed how the improved rail service makes it possible to get from London to Durham in time for lunch with the Dean, then preach a sermon and be back in the Little Cloister before 9.00 p.m.

The event was a sombre one. Although the cathedral was full and three bands played, the Gala is a shadow of its former glory, as only a handful of Durham pits are still open. Those that are have produced nothing for the last eighteen weeks, as the miners are locked in a major dispute with the National Coal Board over colliery closures. While I was preaching in the cathedral, Arthur Scargill, the militant miners' leader, was holding forth to a large gathering of miners on the race-course.

What could a preacher say in so desperate a situation? I spoke of my own memories of the Durham mining community – of the last great disaster at Easington in 1951 when eighty-three were killed; of a young miner named Bobby Parker who ran the mission church in Leadgate parish, where I was a curate, and whose back was broken at the coal face, so that he never walked again.

I said that they would not expect me to produce a ready-made solution to the conflict, but nonetheless the Christian faith offered certain important insights necessary to the proper discussion and settlement of industrial, social and economic problems.

It asserts that people are more important than economics and that healthy community life is crucial to human well-being. Involvement in creative work is also necessary for most people, thus unemployment is a great evil. On the other hand, the faith has important things to say about openness to change and about the central place of reconciliation in relationships between individual and groups.

I went on to say that particular situations call for particular applications of these Christian insights and that the balancing of rival claims and the acceptance of compromise could only be done by those whose hands were dirty through personal involvement. Since this disqualified me from making any helpful comment on the strike, I spoke, instead, about friendship and how the excesses and furies of power must be curbed and tempered by the qualities that make for friendship between individuals and groups.

I spent the rest of the sermon teasing this out in terms of the North/South divide in Britain, the race issue and the need for justice, security and peace in the international order. I don't know if any of this was of the slightest help to that congregation of miners – something rather more folksy might have been better – but I said what I felt moved to say and I hope that at least a little of my deep concern got through.

Monday 23 July 1984

Patrick Cormack, my Churchwarden MP, has given me a copy of Hansard containing last week's House of Commons debate in which a General Synod Measure formulating changes in the procedure for electing bishops was firmly rejected. Some weird and not so wonderful things were said in the course of this debate because the subject provided an excuse for the voicing of a good deal of conservative (note the small c) unease about change in the Church of England.

The Measure sought to abolish the procedure under which a new Diocesan Bishop, nominated by the Prime Minister and appointed by the Crown, is elected by the Dean and Greater Chapter of the cathedral in which he will be enthroned. There is nothing faintly democratic about this, since there is only one name on the voting list and until fairly recently failure to elect could, in theory anyway, incur severe penalties under *praemunire*.

So the whole thing is a fair bit of nonsense and the General Synod decided it would best be abolished and a ceremony involving confirmation of appointment by the Archbishop of the Province concerned substituted. All very sensible and up-to-date. But the House of Commons would have none of this, and the MPs who took part in the debate – mainly churchmen – saw no reason why so harmless a piece of tradition should be cast aside at the whim of a recently constituted body like the General Synod.

What is more, the same General Synod (it was alleged) had alienated many actual and potential churchgoers by sidelining the Book of Common Prayer, merging rural parishes, dabbling in politics, undermining traditional doctrine and permitting other undesirable changes. Abolishing the election of bishops was one step too far.

So there we are: the House of Commons has asserted its authority. What next? The General Synod could return the Measure to Parliament and doubtless persuade the Government to force it though the Commons. But this would be unwise, and I have written to the Archbishop of Canterbury to tell him so. It really isn't worth having a church/state bust-up over something so unimportant.

Here is one of the big problems about the General Synod. It seems entirely devoid of any strategic sense. At a time of fundamental change involving forms of worship, patterns of ministry and the parochial system, it is not sensible to provoke further anxiety and irritation by proposing other changes in matters that are of no great consequence. This can only increase the sense of insecurity and instability and reinforce the opposition to any kind of change.

Wednesday 25 July 1984

The St Margaret's Appeal continues to absorb a good deal of my time, but apart from the frequent committee meetings, most of this work can be carried out in short daily spells – usually after I have conducted Prayers in the House of Commons.

There is a good deal of enthusiasm among the inner organizing circle, and the consultants are providing a top-class administration as well as numerous ideas. It is convenient to have it all located in my room in the Commons, and it is fortunate that I have such a room at my disposal, as the building cannot adequately accommodate all the Members. Finding spare space for an appeal office would have been quite impossible. For the time being, those wishing to see me on pastoral and non-appeal matters come across to my study in the Little Cloister.

The consultants keep emphasizing the importance of adequate preparation for the official launch in November, so names of potential donors continue to be listed, brochures are being designed, and I must draft a letter which can be sent, topped and tailed, to the Members of both Houses – about 1,400 in all, it seems.

The Chapter has agreed that the boxes in St Margaret's in which visitors leave donations can be used for the Appeal, and an exhibition is to be mounted in the church to demonstrate the need and to invite support. This should work, and become even more effective when the restoration work actually begins next year. Apparently it will be necessary to remove the entire roof for the first stage, and the Chapter is very properly insisting that no work be started until there is sufficient money available to cover the cost.

Monday 30 July 1984

I had a strong, indeed a rather rude, letter of protest this morning from the Provost of Lagos Cathedral, Samuel Johnson, about the sermon I preached in the Abbey yesterday on the Durham affair. Apparently he was in the congregation at Mattins and was enraged by a sermon which he believed to represent a denial of the Christian gospel.

I had not actually intended to preach again about the great controversy that has attended the appointment of David Jenkins to the bishopric of Durham. I devoted my sermon to it on the first Sunday of this month when I said that belief in the virgin birth of Jesus and in his physical resurrection (the two matters which have caused all the fuss) were not essential to Christian discipleship and membership of the church. I also said that I thought the new bishop had done well in his television programme to draw attention to the distinction between essentials and non-essentials in the realm of faith.

That seemed to be enough on the subject from the pulpit of Westminster Abbey. But the rights and wrongs of David Jenkins's appointment have occupied the media throughout this month and reached the ultimate in nonsense when, three days after his consecration as a bishop in York Minster, the roof of one of the transepts of that glorious building was destroyed by fire. A number of his conservative adversaries suggested that this was a sign of God's judgment on the consecration of a heretic.

The continuation of the controversy, combined with my recent visit to Durham, where I found no one concerned in the slightest by their new bishop's theological views, therefore led me to speak again on the subject. This time I suggested that the church's attempts, across the centuries, to express the Christian faith in terms of the secular philosophies of the day had led to the near-severance of its Hebraic roots which are essentially practical, not theoretical.

'It is the task therefore of some of our number, including bishops, to try to relate the truth of the gospel to other aspects of the truth – not forgetting the more recent developments in the social sciences, psychology, economics and politics. And where better for this to be done than in the North East of England, where unemployment ranges between fifteen and fifty per cent, where many of the young people have lost all hope of ever having a job, where the five-month-old miners' strike is now causing considerable hardship for large sections of the community? In such a place arguments about the virgin birth and the empty tomb seem, and are, absurdly irrelevant.'

I must send a polite reply to the Provost and suppose that the issue I was raising may look very different through Nigerian eyes.

Sunday 5 August 1984

I am struck by a paragraph in Hensley Henson's *Retrospect of an Unimportant Life* in which he said that during his time as Rector of St Margaret's (1900–1912) he never accepted an invitation to preach elsewhere on Sunday morning, because he believed it to be of the utmost importance that the Rector should always occupy the pulpit. During his terms as Canon-in-Residence in the Abbey he usually preached there at Evensong, though sometimes he preached at both places in the morning, taking advantage of the thirty minutes difference in the starting time of Mattins.

Sermons were more highly regarded in those days, but Henson's main point was that whereas the Abbey, by reason of its collegiate Constitution, had many different preachers, St Margaret's, being a parish church, had the opportunity to offer to its regular congregation consistency of preaching and sermons which over the course of time would provide 'a coherent view of faith and duty in the public mind'.

There is, I think, a lot of truth in this, even today, and all the Rectors since Henson seem to have made a point of being in the pulpit on Sunday morning – except of course when on holiday. This is my policy, too, though in these hectically busy times I am sometimes pleased to make way for the Dean or one of the other Canons of the Abbey. The assistant clergy also preach occasionally, but I do the greater part of it myself – sometimes to the astonishment of enthusiastic Americans who move from the Abbey to St Margaret's only to find the same preacher giving the same sermon.

Tuesday 25 September 1984

The problem of the Abbey's music during the second half of July and throughout August is again under discussion. The Choir goes on holiday in mid-July, the Lay Vicars return at the beginning of September, and the full Choir is in action again for the Battle of Britain service in mid-September. For about six weeks, therefore, the Sunday and daily services are sung by a sequence of visiting choirs.

Few of these are of a very high quality. Some come from parish churches where their contribution is doubtless much appreciated, but the Abbey often tests them beyond their capacity. Choirs from American cathedrals – we have had two of these this summer – are usually dreadful. Their inability to sing is aggravated by the desire of their directors that they shall give a première in Westminster Abbey of their own latest compositions. The best music is provided by relatively small choirs of trained singers – products of Oxbridge colleges or the London music colleges.

Simon Preston believes that we should employ professional choirs to sing the Sunday services during the holiday period and have 'said' services on all the weekdays. But this won't do, because July and August are the months when we receive the largest number of visitors, many of whom come from the ends of the earth and hope to hear choral music in the Abbey.

The Precentor and I believe the answer to the problem is to establish a second Abbey choir of a high standard that would lead the worship not only during the summer holiday, but also on other occasions when the main choir cannot be present. This is the only way in which the Abbey's music can be maintained at an acceptable standard all the year round.

The Chapter is not ready, however, for so radical a step, which would have significant financial implications, and there remains a strong feeling that it is good for parish church choirs to have an opportunity to sing in Westminster Abbey. No doubt it is, but it is much less good for those who have to worship in their company.

Wednesday 3 October 1984

More than two years have passed since we attempted to enter into a new deal with the Lay Vicars, but the only beneficiaries so far seem to be the lawyers representing the two sides. The object of the exercise, which is sometimes forgotten in the heat of battle, is to raise the musical standard of the choir of Westminster Abbey to a level which the Organist regards as acceptable.

And not only the Organist. The DGG Archiv recording company wrote to the Receiver General recently complaining about the standard of some of the men's voices in recent recordings and pointing out that the forthcoming recordings of unaccompanied music by Allegri and Stravinsky require a very high standard of excellence. They urged us to ensure that this standard be met.

According to Simon Preston, only six of the twelve Lay Vicars are capable of singing at this level, and he wonders if six competent deputies might be recruited to take the place of the others. But this would raise the question of whether the performing choir might honestly be described as that of Westminster Abbey, and in any case the displaced men would have to be paid the fee they would otherwise have earned. Postponement of these recordings is now being discussed.

Meanwhile, relations within the Choral Foundation are far from good. Leaving the present problems aside, some of this is, I believe, due to the fact that no one person is responsible for the welfare of the members of the Choir. The Dean, the Organist and the Precentor each have some responsibility, and this weakens the overall leadership.

Monday 22 October 1984

The Brass Rubbing Centre in the North Cloister has now added £250,000 to our income over the last eight years and been far more successful than anyone envisaged. I never fail to be astonished that so many people wish to rub facsimilies of brasses that are not even remotely connected with Westminster Abbey, and even when well done don't make what I would regard as beautiful house pictures. But a lot of our visitors of all ages find it great fun, and the opportunity to do something related to history in the Cloister and then carry it away as a souvenir is greatly valued.

The downside of all this is that a graceful cloister, which shelters many graves, is cluttered with the brass-rubbing equipment and resounds to the chink of money. And now it has become a place where pick-pockets flourish. Those pre-occupied with rubbing a brass are the easiest of targets, and security television cameras must now be added to the scene. It seems a long way from Galilee.

Tuesday 23 October 1984

Enoch Powell came this afternoon to discuss the arrangements for his funeral – still some way off, I guess, though his pallid skin and staring eyes give him a posthumous look. It was obvious that he had already given the matter a good deal of thought, even to the detail of asking to be buried in his wartime Brigadier's uniform. He also knew that an Intra-mural Burial Act, dating back to the early years of this century, precluded any consideration of his burial either in St Margaret's or in the Abbey. So he is going to approach the Royal Warwickshire Regiment to see if room for him can be found in the Regimental cemetery.

His chief concern today seemed to be to ascertain whether or not his funeral might take place in the Abbey. I told him that this was a decision for the Dean, but doubtless the subject would be discussed in Chapter if and when a formal request was made. There were, however, likely to be difficulties over precedent since it was the tradition to have funerals in the Abbey only for great state figures, such as Earl Mountbatten, and for members of the Abbey's own inner community. He saw the problem, but I undertook to discuss the matter with the Dean, which I must do, though I know that he will be horrified at the suggestion.

We then talked about St Margaret's, where he is a member of the Church Council, and where, as a member of the House of Commons, he has a clear right to a funeral. His only concern here is that the service should be in the traditional, i.e. 1662, form and, although I could not bind my successors, I was able to reassure him on this point. When I raised the possibility of a memorial service he replied, with a wintry smile, 'At that stage I shall need only a Mass for the repose of my soul.'

Tuesday 6 November 1984

The State Opening of Parliament is always a spectacular occasion, and today's ceremony was no exception. After Prayers I took up a position with the Speaker's Secretary just outside the Chamber, the doors of which were slammed shut. Soon afterwards, Black Rod, as elegant as ever in court dress, came across from the House of Lords and hammered on the door. The doorkeeper, having ascertained through a glass panel who the importunate visitor might be, threw open the doors. Advancing towards the Speaker, to the accompaniment of ribald remarks about the shape of his legs from Dennis Skinner, the Member for Bolsover, Black Rod summoned the House to attend Her Majesty the Queen in the House of Lords.

There followed what can only be described as a scramble. The Speaker, preceded by the Mace, led the way, the Secretary and I fell in behind as he passed through the doorway, the Prime Minister and the Leader of the Opposition followed us, and the rest of the Members formed an untidy and noisy crocodile behind them. As we passed through the Members' Lobby and the Central Lobby it was possible to see the Queen, a tiny figure in the distance, seated on a throne, splendidly attired and crowned.

The House of Lords itself presented a remarkable sight – peers in ermine, bishops in their robes, peeresses wearing tiaras, High Commissioners and Ambassadors in a variety of colourful garb. But there was space for only about six of us to witness this. Those behind the Prime Minister and the Leader of the Opposition were obliged to remain in a corridor, where they could neither see nor hear anything of the proceedings.

Not surprisingly, I suppose, the Members talked to one another, and the noise of their conversation made it difficult for the rest of us to hear the Queen's speech. 'Tell them to keep quiet' ordered Margaret Thatcher in her best schoolmistressly voice, but it made not a scrap of difference. They talked on until the speech ended, when they stood aside to allow the Speaker and his entourage to lead the way back to the Commons. Before long the champagne corks were popping at a reception in Speaker's House and a new session of Parliament was under way.

Thursday 8 November 1984

The Queen Mother came this morning on her annual pilgrimage to the Field of Remembrance in St Margaret's Churchyard and, as always, charmed the ex-service veterans by staying quite a long time and talking to the different regimental groups standing by their patches of lawn adorned with small wooden crosses each bearing a British Legion poppy. First, however, the Dean said a prayer for peace and I dedicated the Field, after which the Queen Mother was invited to plant her own cross of remembrance. This she did with greater agility than I could have displayed.

Accompanying her on the tour of inspection I found the decorations and campaign medals worn by the veterans of great interest. Those relating to the 1939–45 war I could easily identify, but the more recent medals defeated me. Their holders seemed pleased to explain their significance – Korea, Cyprus, Aden and the more recent Falkland Islands. A Gurkha officer whom I also noticed last year was wearing the VC.

Afterwards the Queen Mother came into St Margaret's to sign our services register and to rest for a while. She said that St Margaret's is one of her favourite churches and we talked about the various memorable occasions when she had visited the church and when she came to the Abbey for her wedding in 1923 and her crowning in 1937.

Wednesday 15 November 1984

Last evening I gave a paper on Christian Ethics in Personal and Public Life to a group of about fifty MPs meeting in Speaker's House. It was a fairly lengthy offering and drew heavily, as I am wont to do, on the thinking of Reinhold Niebuhr and William Temple.

My aim was to challenge, through rather careful biblical and theological analysis, two misunderstandings which are widespread in a House of Commons, where Conservative politics and Evangelical Christianity are frequently intertwined. It is often argued, or more frequently simply stated, that the Christian faith is primarily a personal matter and that the ethical teaching of Jesus has no social or political implications.

I tackled this by demonstrating that the ethical teaching of Jesus cannot be applied directly to the lives of either individuals or communities. The Sermon on the Mount offers examples of love in action at its highest level, but this is rarely possible to individuals living within the complexities of the modern world and exercising multiple responsibilities. Accepting the imperative of love, taught by Jesus, Christians are required to work out how this applies to the varied situations in which they find themselves – drawing on the wisdom of the past but not bound by its examples.

Since individuals cannot be separated entirely from their surroundings and are much influenced by the society to which they belong, the Christian faith has a social dimension. And since the way of love taught by Jesus cannot be turned directly into a political programme, it must be translated into ethical principles related to human dignity, liberty, justice, peace, responsibility and service.

But even these principles cannot easily be applied to political decision-making. This is partly because it is often possible to reach the same end by different means and partly because it is rarely possible in a sinful world for a political policy to do full justice to the ethical principle on which it is based.

The Christian politician is therefore required to operate in the realm of compromise – rarely permitted to make a straight choice between good and evil and all too often required to choose between the greater and the lesser evil. The Falklands War is a classic example of this. In the application of Christian ethical principles we may have to accept second-best, or least worst. But if second-best is the most moral course open to us, it ceases in that particular situation to be second-best, and becomes the best and most creative thing we can do.

The Kingdom of God is, I believe, generally advanced not by high-minded statements of Christian principle and the pursuit of morally perfect policies but by our courage and skill in distinguishing between Christian and un-Christian compromise. And the ethical teaching of Jesus, with its extravagant demands in the name of love, points us in the direction of our ultimate goal. This goal will not be reached in this life but – who knows? – the apparent craziness of the teaching of Jesus may take hold of us from time to time and surprise us, and those around us, by enabling us to achieve what had previously seemed impossible. When this happens it is always the work of divine grace.

My paper provoked a lively discussion, but there was too much in it for immediate assimilation and I have undertaken to provide copies for distribution among those who came to the meeting.

Thursday 22 November 1984

The St Margaret's Appeal was officially launched and got off to a good start this evening at a reception in Speaker's House. It has the support of the Lord Chancellor, the Prime Minister, five former Prime Ministers, and the Leaders of the main Opposition parties. Just over 100 other supporters and potential donors came to the reception. The Speaker spoke, and so did I, and we were followed by the fund-raising consultant, who explained the benefits of covenants.

A generous gift from the Queen Mother was announced, and by the end of the evening we had gifts and promises in excess of £60,000. The Bernard Sunley Foundation has promised £1 for every £10 given by others, up to a maximum gift of £100,000 by the Foundation, and as we near our £900,000 target we shall be claiming most of this.

The restoration will be the largest undertaken since the tower was rebuilt and the exterior of the building heavily restored in 1735. Indeed, all being well, we shall complete the mediaeval structure. The whole of the North wall facing Parliament Square is exceedingly unsightly, for the simple reason that it is not built of stone, but is only a cement rendering on rubble. It seems that the entire building was of this construction until the eighteenth century, when the South, East and West walls were replaced by Portland stone. Just why the North wall was left in this unsatisfactory form is unknown – perhaps the money ran out, or maybe houses abutted it – but we must now seize the opportunity to put this right. If not now, it may have to wait another two centuries.

Wednesday 5 December 1984

The memorial service for Sir Anthony Berry, the MP for Enfield Southgate who was killed in the Brighton IRA bombing, was, as anticipated, an exceedingly moving occasion. St Margaret's was absolutely packed – mainly with MPs, of course – and virtually the whole of the Cabinet was present, many of its members doubtless deeply thankful to have escaped injury, and possibly death.

The Princess of Wales was among the family mourners, the Prime Minister read the Beatitudes from the Sermon on the Mount, and the Speaker gave an address which was absolutely right in its sensitive combination of the personal and national dimensions of this tragedy. It is hard to believe that it could have been done better.

Sarah, the widow, chose most of the material for the service and insisted that the emphasis should be on reconciliation and peace. Thus, after my opening Bidding which mentioned the family's desire to avoid bitterness, George – a young Etonian son – bravely read the prayer normally (and mistakenly) attributed to St Francis of Assisi which begins 'Lord, make me an instrument of thy peace'. Another, older, son read from Kahil Gibran's *The Prophet*.

We sang 'Guide me O thou great Redeemer', reflecting Tony's Welsh connection – he was once editor of the *Western Mail* – and 'Hark, the herald angels sing', which was his favourite Christmas carol. A string quartet played before and after the service.

It felt right and Sarah told me that she was very grateful – though the service was really hers.

Tuesday 18 December 1984

The Speaker's official dinners are always pleasant and sometimes very interesting affairs, but the one held last evening seemed rather special. The Speaker was entertaining a delegation from the Soviet Union led by Mikhail Gorbachev, who is No.2 to President Chernenko and widely tipped to succeed him.

He is an impressive man and quite different from the dour personalities who normally occupy high positions in the Soviet Union. During the evening there was much joking and laughing, and his response to the Speaker's welcome was particularly warm. There was something of a

Western feel to him and one could imagine our own, and American, politicians doing business with him at a conference table.

His wife, Raisa, was also a great hit. She is a very attractive woman, with a vibrant personality, and seemed to be enjoying the occasion hugely. Apparently she is a lecturer at Moscow University and also has a high position in the Communist Party.

I was unfortunate enough to be seated with a Russian General who is one of the top people in the KGB and whose solemnity contrasted sharply with the bonhomie of the chief guests. He exuded the air of Siberia.

Monday 24 December 1984

St Margaret's is decorated and ready for the Midnight Eucharist, which is sure to be crowded, if only because the huge number of people seeking admission to the Abbey will be more than can be safely accommodated there, and some hundreds will be diverted to 'the church next door'. No doubt this will cause a measure of disappointment, but in fact these overflow people will do rather well, with a Mozart Mass magnificently sung, whereas the multitudes in the Abbey will have only a said service with carols.

There is a tradition at St Margaret's – I don't know if it is unbroken – which requires the pew ends to be decorated with rosemary, and bay trees to be placed near the altar. The Churchwardens' accounts indicate that in 1647 they paid eight pence for 'Rosmarie and Baies that was stuck about the church at Christmas'. But this was when the Puritans were trying to forbid the celebration of Christmas, and the Serjeant-at-Arms sent two messengers to arrest the Churchwardens and arraign them before the House of Commons where they were fined £5 (which must have been a great deal of money in those days) for 'permitting Ministers to preach upon Christmas Day and for adorning the church'. What action would have been taken, I wonder, against today's gaily decorated Christmas tree and the beautiful crib sculpted by a Wantage nun?

In 1575 the Churchwardens spent 2s 1d on holly and ivy, and holly wands. It is not, I think, commonly recognized that the decoration of churches with flowers dates back no more than 100 years.

Although St Margaret's is no longer the fashionable church it is generally thought to be, its congregation is still drawn mainly from the political and professional classes. This seems inevitable, given its location and history, and it is therefore all the more pleasing that our corporate life is relaxed enough to provide space for a number of unusual people who are quite a long way removed from the norm.

One such, Enoch Hall, we laid to rest today. Why he was always called Enoch I don't know: his real Christian name was Sidney. He was essentially a simple man. Maybe the accidents of his birth or something about his early upbringing left him without the normal powers of reasoning and drive. He lived in a small house in South London and a housekeeper was employed to look after his domestic arrangements.

But St Margaret's was his real home. He came to the church most days, and although ready to perform any simple tasks that needed doing, his main purpose was simply to be here. He asked nothing of us, except acceptance, and his response to a greeting or a few words of conversation was lovingly childlike.

No one enjoyed the worship more than Enoch, especially the music, and Saturday afternoon always found him at Evensong in the Abbey. One of the greatest moments of his life occurred when Simon Preston invited him into the organ loft to see the Organist in action. Music affected him profoundly.

He also enjoyed liturgical mishaps. If in the course of a service someone landed in the wrong place at the wrong time, whereas the rest of us would become uptight and cross at a failure of organization, Enoch would be greatly amused and fall about laughing. The failure was unimportant to him and I shall always be grateful for this insight into the mind of God which he shared with us.

So we have had a rather special person among us. This was recognized by members of the congregation who visited and cared for him during the final months of his life when pain and disability were exacting their cruel toll. He taught us to see more clearly what Jesus meant by 'Unless ye be converted and become as little children, ye shall not enter the kingdom of heaven.'

1985

Although the publicity for the Abbey's Christmas services was woefully inadequate, we had the largest congregation for many years at the Midnight Eucharist on Christmas Eve. Indeed, for safety's sake, the doors had to be closed long before midnight, and when a further 1,000 people had been crowded into St Margaret's, its doors also had to be closed.

No one can offer a convincing explanation for the increase, and I dare say that it is the result of a combination of several factors. What never changes is the proportion of our congregations that, on this occasion, actually receives Holy Communion. It remains consistently at fifty per cent. In 1982 I went into the pulpit at St Margaret's at the beginning of the service and exhorted everyone in the congregation to come to the altar to receive either communion or a blessing, but it made not a scrap of difference – just fifty per cent responded.

There is evidently still a great deal of vestigial Christianity around which surfaces at festivals such as Christmas, and on family or personal occasions, but which will not enter into the kind of commitment implied in the reception of the sacrament. I am sure that the Church of England, especially in places such as Westminster Abbey and St Margaret's, must continue to welcome people of this sort and to respect whatever faith they may possess.

Wednesday 23 January 1985

There has been much fuss over a proposal that a new Requiem, composed by Andrew Lloyd Webber, should be performed in the Abbey, its first performance having been given in New York by the choirs of Winchester Cathedral and St Thomas's Church, Fifth Avenue. It now seems that this will take place on 21 April, without the involvement of the Abbey Choir but with the Winchester Choir, the original soloists – Placido Domingo, Sarah Brightman, and Paul Miles-Kingston, a Winchester chorister – and the English Chamber Orchestra.

When the proposal was put to us earlier this month, Simon Preston was in South Africa and, having been contacted by telephone, indicated that he did not have a high regard for Lloyd Webber's music, that he would himself be away on tour in April, and that the Choristers would be on holiday. He was therefore against the idea and wished to have nothing to do with it.

Nonetheless we have decided to go ahead with the performance, partly because we think the Requiem will arouse a lot of interest, but also because it is intended to be a fund-raising effort for the Emergency Services and hospitals in Brighton which did such sterling work with the victims of last year's Brighton IRA bombing.

A Sunday evening event that disrupts the normal services earlier in the day isn't something we generally welcome, but an exception can be made for something special, and doubtless this will be a sell-out.

Wednesday 30 January 1985

Another very satisfactory financial year, with a surplus on the income and expenditure account of £360,437, and even St Margaret's achieving a £706 surplus. Apart from dividends and interest, every item of income shows an increase – over £230,000 in the case of visitors, and over £50,000 from the Bookshop and Brass Rubbing Centre. These two commercial operations now bring in over £250,000 annually, and we could not manage without them.

Income from the Church Commissioners' Property Pool has risen slightly to £64,000. Behind this lies the story of how, during the great ecclesiastical reforms of the nineteenth century, the Abbey yielded to the newly formed Ecclesiastical Commissioners its entire estates in return for a commuted sum of £25,000 per annum. These estates included the whole of Victoria Street in Westminster, Covent Garden (formerly the convent garden), the Hyde Park estate in West London, and large tracts of land in the City of London. This now seems, from our point of view, to have been a crazy transaction, since the commuted sum has risen only a little, but it must have seemed right at the time, since the then Dean announced, 'Never again will the Abbey want for money.'

The Abbey's estates, along with those of the ancient bishoprics and cathedrals, enabled the Ecclesiastical Commissioners to finance the building of new churches and the payment of their clergy in the growing industrial towns, and the income has helped to pay the Church of England's clergy ever since. So it has done some good, and it may be that had the estates been retained, the vast amount of money now yielded by them would have made indolence and corruption unavoidable. Churches are more likely to be destroyed by wealth than by poverty.

The total cost of running the Abbey and St Margaret's last year was £1.3 million, of which just over £1 million went in salaries. It is also the case that, besides the Abbey building itself (the restoration of which is being financed by the Trust), we have many other historic buildings to maintain, and only a small amount of the cost of this is shown in the income and expenditure account. Nearly all of this year's surplus will be used for maintenance purposes.

Thursday 31 January 1985

We have turned down a request from Chichester Museum for the loan of the Duchess of Richmond's parrot. They have an exhibition from June to September of items relating to the Richmond family, whose seat is at nearby Goodwood House, but the parrot is altogether too delicate and too precious for us to allow him to make the journey. In any case, many visitors to our own museum would be disappointed were he to be away from his usual haunts during the height of the tourist season.

The wax effigy of Frances, Duchess of Richmond and Lennox, was made immediately after her death in 1702 and is really very fine. She was apparently a great beauty and was the model for the original figure of Britannia on the copper coinage. Her effigy is clothed with the robes she wore at the Coronation of Queen Anne a few months before her death.

Earlier she was a maid of honour to Queen Catherine of Braganza and a mistress of Charles II and several other members of the Court, finally eloping with the third Duke of Richmond in 1667.

The West African grey parrot – her favourite parrot – died a few days after the Duchess and, having been stuffed, joined the company of her effigy. It is believed to be the oldest surviving stuffed bird in England and cannot be spared.

Friday 1 February 1985

The future of the Abbey's Wednesday lunchtime services in under discussion again. These were instituted many years ago and last from 12.30 to 1.00 p.m., consisting normally of a twenty-five-minute talk and a prayer given by one of the clergy. Recently a Service of Healing was introduced on the first Wednesday of every month.

Since I became Rector of St Margaret's I have been relieved of any responsibility for these services, but before then I did many four- to five-week stints, giving courses of addresses on subjects such as 'The Religious Significance of Some Recent Novels', 'Christian Belief Today', 'Signs of Hope in the World and in the Church', 'The Bible for Beginners'. Other members of the Chapter have given similar courses, and the standard has always been reasonably high.

Yet, in spite of good advertising in and around the Abbey, and on office noticeboards in Whitehall and Victoria Street, the attendance has never been large – twenty to twenty-five people maybe; perhaps a few more if a group of tourists arrive by mistake. Although one can never tell how individuals may be influenced by the talks, they represent quite a lot of work for such a small response.

My own view is that the content of the service is wrong for the place and time of day. People who have been working hard in their offices all morning and are faced with further labour during the afternoon are not disposed to spend most of their lunchtime listening to lectures on theological topics. They need something less intellectual if they are to be refreshed. Evidence for this is provided every May when the Wednesday slot is allocated to 'Come and Sing', and hymn-writers and church musicians, aided by choirs, give illustrated talks on hymns new and old. The Nave is then often full to capacity.

What is needed is one person with flair to compile a programme for the whole year consisting of music, drama, dancing, dialogue and other forms of communication which point to Christian truth without being intellectually heavy. The Chapter has agreed that we shall try to find such a person and not be confined to our own community in the search.

Thursday 28 February 1985

Something of a crisis has blown up over the question of the Organist's absences from the Abbey – a matter which has been causing concern for some time. When the Chapter agenda was circulated on Tuesday, both the Sub-Dean and I spotted under Matters to be Noted – To be Taken as Read the following item:

'To note that Mr Simon Preston has notified the Dean of his absence in America between 11 April and 30 May "in accordance with the agreement that I have with Chapter whereby I can add up my days off".'

The period includes about three weeks when the Choir is on Easter holiday and the first four weeks of the summer term, which includes among other events the major service to commemorate the fortieth anniversary of VE-Day.

Edward Knapp-Fisher and I both intimated to the Dean that we would welcome clarification of the situation, and this was provided at today's Chapter Meeting. I was not reassured.

The background to this problem is that Douglas Guest, Simon's predecessor, was away regularly on Mondays, Tuesdays and Wednesdays and often did not take up his duties until Thursday. In addition to his annual leave entitlement he was also absent for the Chorister holidays – a month after Christmas and Easter. Obviously this was unsatisfactory, and when Simon Preston was appointed, the Organist's service agreement was deliberately tightened so that he would be entitled to thirty days annual leave, i.e. six weeks, and no more.

Subsequently, Simon wrote to ask if he might sometimes be permitted to forego days off and accumulate these so that they might be used to enable him to undertake overseas tours. Apparently he had some such arrangement at Christ Church, Oxford.

Smelling a rat, we wrote a carefully-worded reply which said that he might accumulate days off in this way, but that absences for overseas tours would always require the Dean's permission and that long periods of absence would not be granted. Now, however, Simon simply informed the Dean of his forthcoming seven-week absence, without as much as a 'by your leave', and it emerged at this morning's meeting that when he was away in South Africa and America for four weeks in January he did not seek the Dean's permission then. In other words, the Dean is being taken for a ride and his charitable view of human nature is, I believe, being exploited – as I was at pains to point out.

It is important for us to recognize, of course, that Simon Preston is arguably the best organist in the world. Naturally he receives invitations from all over the world, and it is to be expected that a top organist of his sort will wish to perform on a world stage and employ an agent to arrange tours. We must also expect that someone of his artistic temperament will not always appreciate the niceties of sound administration.

Yet it is equally true that he is employed as the organist of a world-famous church, that visitors to the Abbey may reasonably expect to find him in action here, rather than in Chicago or Cape Town, and that his presence here undoubtedly makes a difference to the performance of the Choir – with which he has worked wonders since he came to us four years ago.

So some measure of give and take is needed, but this is not possible if Simon does not discuss his desired absences with the Dean and if he encourages his agent to arrange tours that require long absences from Westminster. It seems simple enough, but of course human nature is never simple, and someone at the top of his profession is never likely to submit happily to control by an institution.

Nonetheless, he is to be told that permission for a seven-week absence in April and May cannot be granted, that if he is away for as long as this he will be in breach of his contract, and that whatever happens he will be required to direct the music at the VE-Day service on 8 May.

I cannot believe, however, that this will be the end of the story.

Friday 1 March 1985

We have decided to restore the portrait and the desk of William Buckland, who was Dean here from 1845 to 1856 and is one of the present Dean's heroes. He was one of the nineteenth century's pioneer geologists, and although his work in this field lacked the scientific basis of those who followed him, he helped to open the door for the great discoveries of our own century. He was also a notable eccentric as well as a fine Dean, which is probably why Edward Carpenter is so fond of him.

Buckland became Professor of Mineralogy at Oxford in 1813 and the first Reader in Geology six years later. Like all the dons of those days, he was ordained, and in 1825 was made a Canon of Christ Church. He was a Fellow of the Royal Society and President of the Geological Society, undertaking numerous tours of exploration and producing many papers on his findings. He believed that the apparent design of the natural order proved the existence of God, and that the discovery of a vestigal sheet of ice from the Ice Age was proof of the Genesis story of the Flood.

Ever curious, he decided to eat his way through the world of living organisms and lost no opportunity to taste the exotic and the unusual, declaring a handful of blue-bottle flies to be the most unpleasant. He combined the Deanery with the Rectory of Islip, in Oxfordshire, where Edward the Confessor was born, and on one occasion was dining at the Manor House there when his host, a descendant of a former British Ambassador, produced for inspection the heart of Louis XIV of France. The relic, enshrined in a silk handkerchief, was passed round the table and when it reached Buckland he put it in his mouth, ate it and declared, 'See, I am eating the heart of *le roi soleil,* before whom all Europe trembled.'

On another occasion, when he was riding from Islip to Westminster with a friend, fog descended upon them and the friend feared they were lost. But Buckland dismounted from his horse, knelt down, sniffed the ground and announced, reassuringly, 'Uxbridge'.

At Westminster he used his scientific knowledge to instal pipe drainage – the first in London; he and his wife kept open house at the Deanery and engaged in much social work among the large number of poor people in the neighbourhood.

The memory of such a Dean ought to be decently preserved, and Edward is keen that the restored portrait and desk should return to the Deanery.

Tuesday 12 March 1985

There is some wavering among the Chapter over our handling of Simon Preston's absences. We had a special meeting about this last Saturday, at which two of the Canons expressed their misgivings about the proposal that permission for a seven-week absence in April and May should be refused. They believe that the repercussions of this would be very serious both for the Abbey and for Simon himself. Which is just the kind of situation in which we so often find ourselves whenever we try to impose some sort of managerial discipline on our staff.

We decided today, however, – by three votes to two – to send a letter to Simon pointing out that he is mistaken in believing that he can take his accumulated days off as leave whenever he chooses; that in arranging a long tour without permission he is in breach of an obligation to us and that this must not be repeated; that he is free to be away during the Choristers' holiday, 11 April – 3 May; and that whatever happens he must be here for the VE-Day service on 8 May.

This is a tough letter, but I think we have actually conceded that his tour will go ahead. Our chief effort now must be to ensure that this never happens again. The Dean is to have another discussion with Simon to see if some sort of understanding can be reached, but I am not optimistic about the outcome of this.

Wednesday 13 March 1985

The Queen's Almsmen, who are appointed by Royal Warrant, are members of the Foundation; their history goes back to Elizabeth I's Charter, when eight war veterans were given homes in the Abbey's precincts and a small pension. Today their ranks still include a number of elderly ex-servicemen, and in their scarlet gowns they make an impressive sight when walking behind the Dean and Chapter at Mattins on Sundays and at important special services. Indeed, members of the congregation often believe them to be the Dean and Chapter.

Recently, however, Bishop Edward Knapp-Fisher, who was on the way to a confirmation in South London, noticed the Almsmen talking in the Cloisters five minutes after Mattins had started. Other observers have noted their presence in Grandma Lee's, the café opposite Big Ben, during Mattins time, and it seems that they are in the habit of escorting the Dean and Chapter as far as the Sacrarium, then peeling off into Poets' Corner and leaving the building through its convenient door. They return after the sermon in time to help with the taking of the collection and to join the procession at the end of the service.

Since members of the Foundation are required to give priority to the offering of worship in the Abbey, this won't do, so we have decided that a row of seats near the Sacrarium be allocated to the Almsmen and that they be required to occupy these during Mattins. The Dean's Verger has objected to this on the grounds that he sometimes needs them to help with the distribution of service papers and the taking of the collection in the Nave, but they can hardly carry out these functions if they are talking in the Cloisters or drinking coffee in Grandma Lee's.

The Almsmen are in fact very decent chaps who recognize that they should be in the Abbey throughout Mattins, and are now rather pleased to have been given seats in a prominent place.

Monday 15 April 1985

A session this afternoon with my GP, who likes to keep an eye on my blood pressure, back problem, weight and so on. He is aware that I work under considerable pressure and wonders why something cannot be done about this. It isn't easy to explain to others how inflexible institutions such as Westminster Abbey normally are and how difficult it is for responsibilities to be fully shared.

That said, it remains entirely within my power to reduce my workload in any or all of the three spheres in which I operate. But my commitment to the special opportunities at Westminster makes it impossible for me to do this. Monica Furlong, who knows me pretty well and has a lot of insight, points out that the pattern of my ministry has always involved the piling up of commitments to people and projects until the only way of coping with the accumulated stress has been for me to leave the job and start afresh elsewhere. I hope this isn't going to be repeated here, but I can see that it may.

Saturday 20 April 1985

An unusual occasion today when London's Armenian community, led by Bishop Yeghishe Gizirian, came to St Margaret's to remember the seventieth anniversary of what has become known as the Armenian genocide. Until I was approached by the Bishop about the possibility of this service being held here I really knew nothing about the event it proposed to commemorate, so a little research was called for. I was astonished and appalled by what I discovered.

The onslaught on the Armenians began in 1894, and by mid-1896 some 300,000 of them had been massacred by the Turks or had died in the subsequent famine. Hurling them over high cliffs was, apparently, the most favoured method of murder. Another 30,000 were killed in 1909; then came the greatest tragedy of all, in 1915, when systematic genocide, carried out by the rulers of the Ottoman Empire in the ancient country now divided between the Soviet Union and Turkey, caused the deaths of 1.5 million Armenians. Some of the survivors of that massacre, now very old of course, were in the large congregation this morning.

The service was the liturgy of the Armenian Church – a new experience for me – and lasted about two hours. It combined, in a very good way I thought, elements of the Orthodox liturgy and the Catholic mass, and the singing, deeply-toned, was specially moving. The officiating priests had small bells attached to their vestments, which was rather jolly, and at the eucharistic prayer the Bishop removed his shoes.

At the planning stage the Bishop asked me to give an address at the end of the liturgy. I said that I would be most happy to say a few words of welcome at the beginning but did not feel that I had anything more to contribute to their important commemoration. At this he seemed hurt, so I relented. I am glad that I did.

Monday 22 April 1985

As anticipated, last evening's performance in the Abbey of the new Lloyd Webber Requiem attracted a full house and a lot of interest. The Prime Minister was there, in company with many other politicians who were in the Grand Hotel, Brighton, on the night of the IRA bomb

264

attack; provided the expenses are not too heavy, the Brighton Emergency Services and hospitals should receive useful donations.

I am not well enough educated musically to pass judgment on the quality of the Requiem. It certainly sounded well enough and, like all Andrew Lloyd Webber's music, was immediately accessible, but the Abbey's music establishment is being very sniffy about it, describing it as 'light-weight' and 'not up to standard for an Abbey performance'. What is far from clear, even to me, is what future use will be made of it, for it is far too difficult for parish church use and I cannot see it entering the repertoire of the cathedral choirs. I dare say that it will be performed occasionally for a special event and eventually fade into oblivion.

What came as quite a revelation to me, and to some others at Westminster, was the quality of the Winchester Cathedral Choir. We had come to take it for granted that the Abbey Choir was in a league of its own and of a much higher quality than a provincial cathedral choir. Winchester demonstrated otherwise. Because the Requiem is a fairly short work, the first half of last evening's performance was devoted to some classical choral items – Elgar, Stanford, Wood and so on – and these, together with the Requiem, were sung at a very high level indeed. Martin Neary, who was Organist of St Margaret's before moving to Winchester in 1972, has both ability and style.

Michael Stancliffe, the Dean of Winchester, came into the house for a drink before the performance and I asked him if he would like to return some time to the Abbey to preach (he was a Canon here and Rector of St Margaret's from 1957–69, and a notable preacher). But he politely declined on the grounds that he was at the moment too heavily committed to other work, and when I suggested that he might like to come next year he said, 'I expect you will have moved from the Abbey by then.'

Wednesday 1 May 1985

General Sir Anthony Farrar-Hockley, a scholar-soldier, who won a DSO and bar in the Korean War and was until 1982 Commander-in-Chief, Allied Forces Northern Europe, is anxious for a memorial plaque to go in the Abbey commemorating the 1,000 British servicemen who were killed or died as prisoners in the Korean conflict. Evidently he has always regretted the lack of any Korean War memorial, and now that it has been announced that the Queen is to unveil a Falklands War memorial in St Paul's he is renewing his efforts.

Certainly he has a point, and the Dean is quite keen to respond favourably, chiefly because the British forces were part of a United Nations force. Edward is a great supporter of the UN, believing, rather unrealistically I fear, that it holds the key to world peace. But the rest of us on the Chapter are much less sure about this proposal.

That those who lost their lives in the fearful Korean campaign should have a national memorial is fair enough. But does it have to be in Westminster Abbey? Apart from the Unknown Warrior, there is a strong tradition that military people are memorialized in St Paul's; hence the decision to place the Falklands memorial there. And there is no point in our complaining about a surfeit of memorials, of all kinds, in the Abbey if we persist in adding to their number.

The Dean is to consult the Ministry of Defence; if they decide to take the General's suggestion further, I hope they will move in the direction of St Paul's or some other appropriate site.

Wednesday 8 May 1985

The service in the Abbey this morning to mark the fortieth anniversary of the end of the 1939–45 war turned out to be a very moving and inspiring event, which is just as well, since it was seen by millions the world over on television. When the service was first mooted we had some misgivings, as a fortieth anniversary did not immediately strike us as being particularly appropriate. But the point was made that if we waited until the fiftieth anniversary, many of the war veterans would be either dead or too infirm to take part in it. In the event the Government was determined to have a service in the Abbey, and before we knew where we were the Prime Minister had announced in the House of Commons that it was to take place.

It was then decreed that the form of service would be devised by an inter-church committee meeting under the chairmanship of the Dean. Liturgy by committee is not normally a recipe for success, but this time it went well as a forum for ideas and our own Precentor, Alan Luff, worked wonders in converting these into a coherent act of worship.

This had four phases: Thanksgiving, Penitence, Reconciliation and Healing, and Hope and Dedication. I thought that the lighting of candles at the grave of the Unknown Warrior was specially effective. The candles were then carried in a procession consisting of church leaders from Japan, the two Germanys, Poland, Russia, Holland, France and the USA and placed around the Easter Candle – a symbol of the resurrection. When the church leaders reached the Sacrarium they were greeted and escorted to their seats by the leaders of the British churches.

The Archbishop of Canterbury preached an admirable sermon about the pity and cost of war, but declared himself convinced that this particular war was necessary, and that the victory which closed down Belsen, Buchenwald and Auschwitz was in itself sufficient cause for thanksgiving.

This was followed by as imaginative a piece of ritual as I have ever seen in the Abbey, when a group of children from the Royal Ballet School danced their way from the Great West Door to the Sacrarium, bearing flowers, which were placed on the floor to form a large white cross before the High Altar. While this was going on an RAF band played the Air from Handel's *Water Music,* and a schoolgirl read some powerful biblical texts on love and reconciliation.

The Queen and virtually the whole of the Royal Family were present, together with a host of political leaders and a large contingent of ex-service men and women. The inclusion of a war widow, a member of the Land Army, a merchant seaman, an ambulanceman and a fireman in one of the special processions was another imaginative touch.

Jo and I have much enjoyed entertaining Superintendent Eggo Hafermann, of the Lutheran Church in the German Federal Republic, who has spent a couple of days with us.

Tuesday 14 May 1985

Sir Robert Mayer, whose Memorial Service was held in St Margaret's today, died in January aged 105. His first wife died in 1974 and six years later, after he had passed the age of 100, he remarried – which caused some family complications over the organization of the memorial service. Fortunately the arrangements were in the hands of Robert Armstrong, the Secretary of the Cabinet, who is used to handling conflict.

It betrays great ignorance on my part that I had never heard of Sir Robert Mayer until the request for a service came to me. But obviously he was someone of very considerable influence. As Ted Heath pointed out in his address, when Mayer started his children's concerts in the 1920s, London was a musical desert. Today, however, London is the centre of the world of music and extraordinarily rich in talented young singers and instrumentalists.

Mayer played a key role in bringing about this transformation. Working in partnership with his daughter Dorothy, a notable soprano, he used his great wealth to sponsor all manner of music enterprises, but mainly among children and young people. And they knew how to

267

choose conductors, for the first series of concerts for children in 1924 was conducted by Adrian Boult, who continued until the outbreak of war in 1939; when the concerts resumed after the war, Malcolm Sargent was put in charge. In 1932 Mayer was co-founder with Sir Thomas Beecham of the London Philharmonic Orchestra. He also supported the development of music in the provinces and provided money for gifted students to be trained and for groups of musicians to undertake tours abroad.

Besides all this, he supported other youth projects, especially those concerned with delinquents, and his wide international interests led him to become a strong advocate of Britain's membership of the European Community. He was himself born in Germany, and Ted Heath told how at the age of four he won a piano-playing competition, the prize for which was the privilege of playing before Johannes Brahms, who encouraged him to continue his musical studies. What might have been the fate of British music had these words of encouragement not been given?

A large congregation, drawn from the world of music, came to the service; it is fortunate that the St Margaret's Choir is able to stand up to such scrutiny and to provide fine music for such an occasion.

Friday 17 May 1985

Although the St Margaret's Appeal reached £200,000 a month ago, we seemed at that time to have entered the doldrums over the locating of substantial new donations, and Clifford Boulton, the perceptive Clerk Assistant of the House of Commons and a member of the Appeal Committee, confided to me his belief that we might well have to settle for something less than our £900,000 target. In the May Newsletter, therefore, I expressed delight with the progress so far (it is essential to maintain a buoyant spirit) and looked forward to our soon reaching the £250,000 mark.

We have in fact now reached £440,000 and the aim is to reach £500,000 as quickly as possible. The explanation of this dramatic leap forward is that the Sainsbury family trusts have given us £65,000, a former Cabinet Minister has contributed £10,000, and our American committee has sent a first instalment of £100,000. These gifts have been augmented by £17,500 from the Bernard Sunley Foundation, who give us £1 for every £10 raised.

All of this is enormously encouraging and has restored confidence in our ability to reach the target. It also means that we can now begin the restoration of the roof, at an estimated cost of £350,000. The church will soon be covered in scaffolding, both outside and inside; although this will reduce its elegance, it should assist fund-raising considerably. The appeal can have no better advertisement.

Monday 20 May 1985

From time to time people complain about the behaviour of MPs during Parliamentary debates and the new Bishop of Portsmouth, Timothy Bavin, writes in his latest diocesan newsletter:

'I for one am fed up with public slanging matches in and out of Parliament, and find it hard not to be contemptuous of the noise, nonsense and childishness which apparently mark many of the debates broadcast on the wireless. Surely, I say to myself, people have something better to do with their time than to be part of what sounds like a bear garden.'

The broadcasting of Parliament, especially Prime Minister's Question Time on Tuesdays and Thursdays, has undoubtedly increased public awareness of some aspects of the work of the House of Commons, including its boisterous element. Not long ago the vicar of a Surrey parish wrote to the Speaker in terms similar to those used by the bishop. He wondered how he could be expected to inculcate good behaviour in the young people of his parish when, as he put it, MPs set such a bad example.

On receipt of this letter the Speaker immediately telephoned the vicar, invited him to lunch and provided him with a seat in the gallery. The vicar subsequently wrote to thank the Speaker for his hospitality and kindness and went on to say that he had found the debate that afternoon exceedingly tedious and boring. Which is of course just how it is for much of the time, as indeed it is in other democratic assemblies concerned with detailed legislation.

The Speaker often ventures to suggest at official dinners in his house that the behaviour of MPs today is much better than it was during the early years of this century. Hansard records that on one occasion the House broke up in 'indescribable chaos' and sittings often had to be suspended after the 'naming' of a dozen or more Members.

It is often forgotten that Parliament is the scene of a constant struggle for power about matters of the greatest importance, and about which Members may have very strong feelings. This is an essential part of our democratic system. So it is totally unrealistic to expect the House of

Commons, with its vast responsibilities and its fingers on the levers of power, to behave with the decorum of a village debating society.

Tuesday 21 May 1985

The Chilean Ambassador and his entourage came again this morning to lay a wreath on the memorial to Admiral Lord Cochrane – this being Chilean Navy Day. It is all very difficult, given the deplorable human rights situation, and we gladly gave permission to the Chile Committee for Human Rights to lay its own wreath on the memorial this afternoon as a protest against the Chilean government's policies.

We thought that they had better not distribute anti-Chilean government pamphlets in the precincts, but we were happy for them to bring a photographer in the hope of publicity in tomorrow's papers.

Wednesday 12 June 1985

The opening of the St Margaret's North vault this morning provided the Surveyor of the Fabric and me with a surprise. It had to be opened in order that engineers may determine whether or not its floor will bear the weight of the large network of scaffolding required for the building's restoration. We know that the body of Sir Walter Raleigh was placed in the central vault beneath the altar following his execution just outside the church in 1618, and that many other bodies were buried in the vaults during the seventeenth and eighteenth centuries.

It was to be expected, therefore, that the opening of the North vault would reveal many decayed coffins. But what we found was a huge deposit of soil reaching almost to the roof. Among this soil was debris of various kinds and human bones – a remarkable sight but not specially interesting.

The explanation of this seems to be that when the churchyard was cleared in 1880–81 and turned into the present lawns, all the surface soil and the results of the levelling, which included the remains of memorials and bones, were poured into the vault, which was then sealed. It must have been a mammoth task, but convenient for the disposal of unwanted material and appropriate for the burial of human remains.

Monday 17 June 1985

We had a long and not very satisfactory meeting with Simon Preston today over the issue of his absences. As anticipated, he went on his seven-week tour of the United States and flew back for the VE-Day service. Meanwhile our Legal Secretary, Clifford Hodgetts, has been drawn into the discussion, and the purpose of today's meeting was to present Simon with what seems to us a reasonable compromise for the future.

This provides for him to accumulate up to thirty-five days off in any one year, but these must always be taken during choir holidays, and the permission of the Dean must be obtained before the arrangements for any tours are settled. None of this would, of course, affect any engagements which he might accept in this country and which can easily be undertaken without affecting his Abbey responsibilities.

But Simon seems unwilling to accept this. He argued that he is free to take the days off to which he is entitled whenever he wishes and that any restriction of this is contrary to his contract. He acknowledged that the contract requires him to obtain the Dean's permission before going on overseas tours, but said that he would expect any reasonable Dean to agree to such tours unless there was a very strong reason for not doing so. He could not understand why we lacked confidence in his ability to decide what might or might not be harmful to the Abbey's music.

We tried to assure him of how greatly we appreciate the enormous improvement he has made to the Choir and explained that it was because of his great contribution to our life that we want him to be on duty at the Abbey as much of the year as possible.

But none of this got us much nearer to agreement. I think that it is the case that specially talented people, such as Simon, are often loners and don't really understand what is involved in belonging to a community. A revised version of the letter we drafted in March is to go to him for what we hope will be careful consideration.

Tuesday 18 June 1985

Last evening's reception at 10 Downing Street for the St Margaret's Appeal turned out to be a very pleasant occasion and we hope that some, at least, of those who felt honoured to be invited will feel equally honoured to contribute to the Appeal.

The Prime Minister was very affable and made a good and useful speech in support of St Margaret's. She said it was of the greatest importance that the Christian values which St Margaret's symbolized and existed to promote should remain at the centre of our national life, and went on to express the hope that the Church of England would always remain an Established Church, thereby reminding all in authority in the nation that they are subject to an even higher authority.

The size of the interior of No.10 is always surprising; we were encouraged to go into all the public rooms, including the Cabinet Room, with its huge table. The pictures of the former Prime Ministers which adorn the staircase are very numerous and of uneven quality, but there are some fine paintings and splendid porcelain in other parts of the house.

I spent quite a lot of time with Lady Charlotte Bonham Carter, who had come up from Hampshire for the occasion, though she is well into her nineties. Disability confined her to a chair, which can be isolating at parties, so we had a long talk, which revealed a very sharp mind. Apparently she was one of the first women to qualify as an air pilot and has had an adventurous life. I don't know if this included the acquisition of much money.

The champagne and canapés were paid for by Jeffrey Archer, the novelist and former MP, as a contribution to the Appeal. Although he is immensely wealthy, he has so far resisted all suggestions that he should make a donation to the Appeal, but he made a great thing of refreshments for the reception and presented the Prime Minister with a magnum of champagne as a thank-you for hosting the occasion.

Thursday 27 June 1985

Yesterday's Memorial Service in St Margaret's for Lord George-Brown aroused a lot of interest and some comment. *The Times* says, 'Like the man himself, the service was very unstuffy, populist, almost kitsch'. Sandwiched between 'Jerusalem' and 'The Battle Hymn of the Republic', the entertainer Tony Monopoly delivered a rendition of the Frank Sinatra song 'My Way', which George had adopted for the title of his autobiography.

George's brother, Ronald, who was himself an MP for a time, had a big hand in the arranging of the service and declared himself well pleased with the result: 'It represented virtually everything he stood for.' The presence of his long-suffering widow and the lady he deserted her for in the later stages of his life added a touch of drama, and no one disagreed with the description of George as 'a dynamic, compassionate and mercurial politician'.

The task of compiling a memorial service that does justice to such a man as George Brown is always a welcome challenge. Many of those present at the service were surprised to learn that his deep commitment to justice, truth, freedom and peace owed everything to the influence of Father Sankey, one of the old-style Anglo-Catholic socialist priests in whose church he was a choirboy. This left its mark, not only politically but also devotionally, and throughout his life George remained firmly attached to the high church sacramental tradition. Shortly before his final illness he became a Roman Catholic.

He was of course a flawed character, as most of us are to a greater or a lesser degree, and his colourful style called public attention to his chief failings, not least those associated with the bottle. This, together with the unfortunate rejection of him by the Belper constituency which he served so long and so well, has tended to obscure his stature and achievements. After all, he did hold at different times the offices of Deputy Prime Minister, Foreign and Commonwealth Secretary, and Secretary of State for Economic Affairs, and he might well have become Prime Minister had not Harold Wilson defeated him, by 144 votes to 103, in the final ballot for the leadership of the Labour Party following the death of Hugh Gaitskell in 1963.

All this acknowledged, however, it does no service to a man's memory to gloss over his weaknesses, and the general view seems to be that we got the balance right yesterday. George himself would not have wished to be remembered dishonestly as a plaster saint, and he would, I think, have greatly enjoyed the service.

Tuesday 9 July 1985

The Dean formally told us in Chapter this morning of his intention to retire at the end of November – three days after his seventy-fifth birthday. It was a moving moment, because we were all aware that Edward has spent thirty-four years in the service of the Abbey, first as a Canon, then as Dean, and we were equally aware that the decision to retire was a painful one, because the Abbey is his life and he is bound to be bereft without it.

Undoubtedly he has been a great Dean. It is hard to believe that any of his successors will ever match his record of such long and distinguished service to the Abbey. It has been sad, however, to witness the inevitable decline of these last few years – inevitable because the responsibilities of the Westminster Deanery are now so heavy that they simply cannot be carried out effectively by a man who has passed his three score years and ten.

The next few months will pass quickly, and we must do all we can to make Edward's remaining time with us as happy as may be. We all owe him a very great deal and I cannot forget that he was responsible for my coming to the Abbey.

Sunday 21 July 1985

St Margaret's is a remarkable church for its link with English history and the continuity of its life. Last Tuesday I baptized nine-week-old Arthur Harry David Soames, the son of Nicholas Soames and a great-grandson of Winston Churchill, who was himself married here in 1908 and, famously, led the Members of the House of Commons to the church in 1945 for an act of thanksgiving for the ending of the war in Europe. I recently discovered a form signed by him when he joined the Electoral Roll in 1924.

Then today I baptized a descendant of Speaker Arthur Onslow, who presided over the House of Commons from 1728 to 1761 and is reckoned to have been one of the greatest Speakers. It was during his time that the tower of St Margaret's was rebuilt with the aid of a grant of £3,500 from Parliament. His name, together with that of Prime Minister Robert Walpole, is inscribed on the North side of the tower. The inscription is now very faded, so I hope that when the present restoration is completed it may be re-cut and the name of the present Speaker added.

Tuesday 30 July 1985

Today we marked with a party and a presentation the retirement of Joe Bloomfield, who for many years has been responsible for monitoring the cleanliness of the interior of the Abbey and has held the office of Superintendent of the Attendant Cleaners – a title that only Westminster Abbey could produce for one of its more menial, albeit very important, posts.

Joe, a man of massive frame, outspoken tongue and the utmost loyalty, has ruled his kingdom with the firmest of hands. Thus the dust and debris inevitably created in an ancient building visited by multitudes has been kept at bay with remarkable success. Although Joe has been strict with his seven-man team, he has always fought tenaciously for their rights and not least for their proper pay.

The Dean and Chapter he has regarded with a mixture of respect, exasperation and wry amusement. We have never been left in doubt as to his views on this or that aspect of the Abbey's life, and his long hours on the 'floor' meant that little escaped him. A conversation with him could be guaranteed to yield valuable information and a gem of Cockney humour, though his vocabulary could lead to inaccuracy, as when he informed me that he was about to go into hospital to be circumscribed.

So Joe, a much-loved figure in our community, will be greatly missed. Today's farewell would have made a superb stage comedy. He could easily stand in for Ronnie Barker in the TV 'Porridge' series.

Monday 2 September 1985

Later today we shall go to our holiday cottage at Sandwich, and James Mansel will be left in charge of St Margaret's. I sometimes boast that I am the only Rector who has a knighted curate, for James is a retired priest who spent over a quarter of a century on the teaching staff of Winchester College and then exercised a remarkable pastoral ministry as Sub-Dean of the Chapels Royal, for which the Queen rewarded him with a KCVO. He is now seventy-eight, and loves St Margaret's, where he helps me with the Sunday services and undertakes most of the pastoral work among the non-Parliamentary members of the congregation.

He and I make an unusual partnership, and often tease each other about this, for he is an archetypal establishment figure, and the combination of Winchester College and Buckingham Palace takes some beating for privilege. But as with many others associated with William of Wykeham's foundation, there is an open, reformist side to him, and he has steadfastly supported the changes I have initiated at St Margaret's. One could not have a more loyal colleague.

When I moved across to St Margaret's he had already been serving as an honorary curate for several years and immediately did what he believed to be the gentlemanly thing by placing his resignation in my hands. There was, of course, no question of my accepting it, and he would have been devastated if I had. Yet every year he takes me aside and says, 'I am an old buffer now, who just witters away, and you may feel that the time has come for me to hang up my surplice. Please be frank with me about this.' Every year I assure him that he is still making an important contribution to the church's life, and I know that he is relieved to hear this. He potters off to the Athenaeum reassured and happy.

From time to time he also tells me that he is what was known in the eighteenth century as 'a painful preacher' – one who finds it painful to prepare a sermon and one whose congregation finds it equally painful to listen. I hardly need to be informed on this point, since he really is very disappointing in the pulpit. This doesn't much matter, because I require him to preach only infrequently, and he is so greatly loved by the regular congregation that his presence, rather than his words, communicate Christian faith.

My colleagues at the Abbey will preach while I am away, and James will ensure that everything else is maintained in good order.

Tuesday 24 September 1985

Now that everyone is back from holiday, we have been able to consider Simon Preston's response to the Dean and Chapter's letter about his future absences. In the end we were driven, by disagreement within the Chapter, to remove the reference to a maximum of thirty-five accumulated days off, and it was left that such days off, however many, must always be taken in Choir holidays and subject to the Dean's approval.

Simon still cannot accept this, and in his reply also said that he is under no contractual obligation to attend special services. The Legal Secretary has confirmed that he has an obligation, so we shall correct him on this point, as well as reaffirm our decision about extended periods of absence.

But we are not going to get this matter finally resolved until a new Dean has arrived and settled in. Already it has extended over seven months and damaged the relationship between the Chapter and the Organist. Which is a great pity, because Simon is an attractive character and hugely talented. The fundamental question for us, I suppose, is what price are we prepared to pay in order to have such a musician in our community.

Thursday 8 October 1985

The problem of recruiting Choristers becomes ever more serious. In spite of massive publicity, only nineteen candidates came to last Wednesday's Voice Trial, and Simon Preston decided that none of these was of sufficient calibre to be accepted. It was hoped to recruit five boys to replace those who will leave during the course of the next twelve months. At the previous trial last summer none of the candidates was accepted.

Various explanations are offered. It is, I think, undoubtedly the case that fewer parents are willing for their eight-year-old sons to enter boarding schools – even when, as at our Choir School, the fees are little more than nominal. With fathers working longer and longer hours to earn good salaries, mothers are now making more of the domestic decisions, and they want to keep their little boys at home.

The decline of parish-church choirs and the sidelining of singing in many schools has also reduced the supply of potential choristers, and I expect that the secularizing tendencies of our time are working against the attraction of a boy spending five of his early years in the cloistered life of an abbey or a cathedral.

I just wonder, however, and I voiced this in Chapter on Tuesday, whether Simon Preston might not be demanding too high a standard for entry to our choir. Of course he wants the very best, and we back him to the hilt in this, but there is a good deal of evidence to suggest that most boys, if they are keen on music and not actually tone-deaf, can, with adequate training, reach a high standard of performance. Many of the cathedrals have been driven to recognize this, and I find it significant that when a boy of considerable promise from my former parish in Ware came to us for a trial a few years ago he was turned down. But he was accepted for Ely Cathedral choir, where he is now the Head Chorister.

Because our failure to recruit at the last two Trials will leave too many vacant places in the Choir School, the Organist and the Headmaster have in fact now decided to accept two of last week's 'sub-standard' candidates, in order, as they put it, 'to maintain some notion that the Choir is at full strength and also that it is not impossible to get into Westminster Abbey Choir'.

My guess is that these boys will become good Choristers – provided, of course, that one or other of our organists is prepared to give time to their training.

Saturday 19 October 1985

There is much speculation about the appointment of Edward Carpenter's successor as Dean and various names are being bandied about – none of them altogether convincing. The truth seems to be that the cupboard is pretty bare, and I have no clear idea in my own mind as to the best man for this job. The need is for someone who will be sympathetic to the Abbey's vocation as a church for everyone and who is sufficiently visionary to discern how this vocation may be developed during the remaining years of the century. It would be useful also if he were a good administrator, and there is a lot to be said for Deans of Westminster having some intellectual gifts. Altogether, this combination is a tall order and probably cannot be met, in which case the first requirement is the most important.

Whenever senior appointments are discussed these days Edward Norman's name is always mentioned – usually with foreboding. He is an able church historian, has been Dean of Peterhouse, Cambridge, since 1971, and it is believed that his right-wing political views have won him high marks at 10 Downing Street. But he is said to be a very difficult man to work with, and that is the last thing we need here.

Patrick Mitchell, the elegant Dean of Wells, is highly thought of and might fit the bill. It is not normal for deans to be moved sideways, but Westminster is special and it might be tolerated. I am not sure how much of a visionary Patrick is.

Another name mentioned is that of Peter Pilkington, the Headmaster of King's School, Canterbury. He is certainly a substantial figure and should have administrative competence, but his outlook is conservative, and again I am not sure if he would develop the openness of ministry that has been such a marked feature of Edward Carpenter's reign.

There is a lot of pressure being applied from within the House of Commons for me to be appointed – chiefly, I suspect, because quite a number of people over there would like me to remain in Westminster. But this wouldn't do, and won't happen, though I would love to have the opportunity. There is always a predisposition against making internal appointments, and since such an appointment was made at the last vacancy, the odds against it happening again are overwhelming. Internal appointments can, I am sure, only be made successfully when there is a unanimous desire within a community that a particular person become its leader. Neither I nor anyone else on the present Chapter could command the unanimous support of colleagues, so we must have someone from outside and, provided the right man can be found, a fresh mind applied to our life can only be beneficial.

Tuesday 22 October 1985

This is a very strange place, or, rather, there are some strange people running it. Back in 1980 I proposed that the Norman Undercroft should cease to house our interesting, yet modest, museum and instead be converted into a coffee shop. This would bring in an annual income of £25,000, as well as provide a useful service to visitors. The museum exhibits would be housed elsewhere. But although that proposal was initially supported by a majority of the Chapter, the decision was eventually reversed. In 1980 the museum had to be closed for a time because it was losing money and is now financially viable only because it is manned by volunteers.

Notwithstanding all this, Anthony Harvey, our Steward, has produced a scheme for the refurbishing of the museum and for the setting up of a treasury in the Pyx Chamber that will cost us a huge amount of money – £210,600 for the first phase. Initially the total cost was put at £250,000, and Anthony was hopeful of raising this by means of grants from Trusts, but although the Goldsmiths Company and other bodies have given about £44,000, and it is hoped that the English Tourist Board will give a further £70,000, this leaves the Dean and Chapter to find almost £100,000 for the first phase alone.

Sebastian Charles, the Treasurer, is rightly protesting that much of the scheme is going ahead without his knowledge and without the opportunity for him to bring financial matters to the Chapter for authorization. The expenditure of £1,600 on a fund-raising brochure was quite unauthorized. At his suggestion, therefore, we have agreed to contribute £100,000 to the project – £50,000 of this coming from a £100,000 donation given to us by our good friend John Smith, of the Manifold Trust, and £50,000 from a hoped-for surplus on our current year's accounts. But this must be the limit of our financial commitment because, as the Treasurer points out, the running of a museum is not one of our primary objectives.

Monday 11 November 1985

The unveiling of the memorial to the leading poets of the 1914–18 war was a somewhat lower-key event than originally envisaged, but it was noteworthy all the same, not least because the memorial itself has some artistic merit. Instead of the usual black marble slab, incised with white lettering, we have the names of the poets – Rupert Brooke, Wilfred Owen, Siegfried Sassoon, Robert Graves, Edmund Blunden and others – intertwined in green to form a wreath.

We had hoped that the unveiling might be accompanied by a performance of Elgar's 'For the Fallen', but this had to be abandoned when we learned that the orchestra would cost about £4,000, that a female soprano would add another £500, and that our own choir and organists would have to be paid at Equity rates. Raising the money to pay for the memorial itself was a difficult enough task after Faber, the publisher of most of the war poets, declined to meet the cost.

So Ted Hughes, the new Poet Laureate, and various other people read from their works, there was a five-minute organ piece followed by appropriate prayers, and a reception afterwards for the thirty or so donors to the cost of the memorial. I wonder if there will ever be a memorial to the poets of the 1939–45 war? One doesn't hear much about them and I cannot name any, so I dare say there will be no demand.

Tuesday 12 November 1985

We have now been given the cost of phase 2 of the museum project, which has been put at £201,600 – making a total cost of £412,000. This is a ludicrous amount of money to spend on so small, and so relatively unimportant, a project. But Anthony Harvey's enthusiasm for it knows no bounds, and he is proposing to include a fund-raising expedition in a forthcoming lecture tour of the United States.

The chances of this raising very much are remote and, as I have emphasized at today's Chapter Meeting, there is a very real danger that the project will move forward so quickly that we shall be left with no alternative but to find another £200,000 to meet the cost of phase 2. Here is a dangerous trap, and it was agreed that, if necessary, the scheme will not be allowed to advance beyond phase 1.

This would leave us with a new Treasury, mainly for the St Margaret's Communion plate, in the Pyx Chamber and a new floor and better ventilation in the Norman Undercroft, but no refurbished museum. Not at all satisfactory, but this will be the position if the required money is not forthcoming from external sources.

Friday 15 November 1985

It is by no means easy to get first-class speakers to give our annual 'One People' oration, even though we can guarantee an audience of about a thousand. The number of people who can talk sensibly for three-quarters of an hour is, I suppose, limited.

Next year being the time for the reappearance of Halley's Comet, the Dean thought it would be a good idea to invite Patrick Moore, the astronomer, to give the oration, and the rest of us readily agreed. We had not, however, reckoned with the element of madness in his character that comes through so clearly in his television broadcasts.

He has declined the invitation on the grounds that 'it would be hypocritical for me to take part in church activities while the World Council of Churches continues to be involved indirectly in terrorism in South Africa'. We have, I am sure, had a lucky escape, and the search is resumed for an astronomer who is both articulate and sensible, and has some understanding of what is involved in living together in this world.

Tuesday 19 November 1985

The newly-elected General Synod came this morning for a Sung Eucharist, as part of its official opening ceremonies. As usual, the Queen attended, along with the Lord Chancellor, the Speaker and other notables from public life.

The impressiveness of the occasion was not marred by a heart-stopping moment in the sermon. Alistair Haggart, the able and attractive Primus of the Scottish Episcopal Church, was about two-thirds of the way through a powerful utterance when he suddenly paused. During what seemed like an eternity, he turned some pages of his script, ad libbed for a while, then resumed his flow and brought the sermon to a rousing conclusion.

The explanation turned out to be that, while putting on his robes before the service started, he had placed the sermon on the Deanery dining-room table and inadvertently left two pages behind. The ultimate nightmare of any preacher on a great occasion such as this, but Alistair – normally the best organized of men – did not seem unduly perturbed by his experience.

At a party in the Deanery Drawing Room afterwards, I found myself in the Queen's company for a time and, for want of anything better to talk about, mentioned the problem of preaching from an incomplete script. She sympathized with the plight of the Primus and added that before reading her official speech at the State Opening of Parliament she always double-checked the page numbers.

There is an interesting little question as to what is the appropriate action for the person standing next to the Queen at a modern liturgy, such as we had today, when the Peace is shared. Hugging is certainly out of the question, and a warm handshake is not the normal way of greeting the Queen. Faced with this problem five years ago, the then Speaker, George Thomas, improvised and simply bowed to the Queen, who bowed back, and this is now established as the correct procedure.

Friday 22 November 1985

Today is the first anniversary of the Speaker's Appeal, and the total raised is now just over £700,000. Although the Appeal was launched with much enthusiasm and there was talk of reaching the £900,000 in twelve months, I don't think that any of us really believed we would raise so much so quickly.

The fact that the Speaker is so deeply involved is undoubtedly a great help, because he commands wide respect and his own enthusiasm is infectious. We also have a strong committee which has secured some large gifts, and there have been many smaller donations – over 1,000 in all – which is a clear indication of the affection in which St Margaret's is held by people all over the world. The contributions of visitors to the collection boxes in church have brought in over £20,000.

But it has been, and continues to be, mighty hard work for all of us who are involved in the day-to-day running of the Appeal. I devote two or three hours to it most days, apart from weekends, and, besides topping and tailing some thousands of letters to potential donors, write a brief personal letter of thanks to all those who have responded.

There are, however, benefits extending beyond the financial, as there seems to be new interest in the church's work, and attendances at services have increased noticeably during the last year.

Now we need to raise the remaining £200,000, and although this should not be too difficult, it is important that complacency be avoided. The current high interest rates are bringing in a considerable income, and a number of special events have been planned, so it looks as if we are going to need another £100,000 in direct gifts. Meanwhile, we need to press on with the restoration work as quickly as possible before rises in building costs undermine the basis on which the Appeal was launched.

Sunday 24 November 1985

The death of Nicholas MacMichael, the Keeper of the Muniments, was not unexpected, but is not less tragic because of this. He was only fifty-two. There can only be great sadness that a life which embraced great talent in one particular area of knowledge also experienced great loneliness and much ill-health, exacerbated by an alcohol problem.

Naturally, we all now wonder if we, as a community, might have done more to save him from such an end, and there are guilty feelings around, related to what might be regarded as a serious failure on our part. I am not so sure about this. It is virtually impossible to combine disciplinary and pastoral functions, and, although everything possible was done to provide Nicholas with expert professional help, he – like many of his kind – was unable to accept this.

In the end the individual has to be responsible for himself, and perhaps the best thing we were able to do for him during his final years was to provide the security of a home in the Little Cloister and a place in the Library he loved. His contribution to the life of the Abbey over the last thirty years has been considerable, but it represented only a small part of the potential.

Thursday 28 November 1985

We said our Goodbyes to Edward and Lilian Carpenter at a great gathering in 'Up School' after Evensong. No one can doubt that we have seen the passing of an era, for Edward came here as a Canon as long ago as 1951, when the Abbey, like the rest of the nation, was still recovering from its wartime tribulations and was soon to be immersed in preparations for a Coronation. The changes that have taken place since then have been enormous – perhaps greater than at any time since the sixteenth century, when the Abbey ceased to be a Benedictine monastery – and Edward has been involved in and influenced them all, holding all the main offices: Steward, Archdeacon, rather improbably Treasurer, and, for the last eleven years, Dean.

His appointment to the Abbey when he was only forty-one owed everything to the then Prime Minister, Clement Attlee, who had personal knowledge of his work as Rector of Stanmore and approved of his ethical and social interpretation of the Christian faith. Apparently the Chapter strongly disapproved of the appointment, and during his early years here he had a difficult time – often left with nothing much to do.

Eventually, changes in the Chapter altered this, but not before he had built up a wide network of personal contacts with individuals and organizations that were engaged in humanitarian enterprises of one sort and another. These were eventually linked to the Abbey and helped to change the character of its ministry.

Although by training and inclination a historian, Edward will be remembered more as a 'modern churchman' – the last, in fact, in a line of scholars who led a liberal movement in the Church of England which had some influence in the 1920s and 1930s. Unlike the Christian radicalism of the 1960s, epitomized by John Robinson's *Honest to God*, the liberalism espoused by Edward and the rest had few, if any, biblical roots, and its openness to the truth, from whatever quarter it might be perceived to come, made its adherents suspicious of anything that seemed overly churchy or sacramental.

From almost every point of view this was an ideal background for a Canon, and later the Dean, of Westminster Abbey – a national church whose doors must be open to everyone and where a narrow ecclesiasticism should never erect fences to protest sectional interests – be they never so holy.

Under Edward's leadership, the Abbey has become a much more warm and friendly place. The last vestiges of stuffiness and privilege have been removed, and many of those who come to share in our life express surprise and pleasure at the warmth of the welcome they receive.

Clearly linked with this has been the opening of the Abbey to a large number of organizations and groups who have wished to mark some occasion or plead some cause in the context of worship in a great national church. Edward's wide contacts have encouraged this; so also his deep conviction that, under God, the human race is 'One People' (a phrase frequently on his lips) and that a Christian church can never be exclusive if it is to be true to its calling.

Another of his special concerns has been the cultivation of links between the Abbey and the Commonwealth – inspired again by his vision of a multi-racial world community living in peace. The annual multi-faith Commonwealth observance has always been one of the high points in his year, and his friendship with the Dalai Lama and deep involvement in the Council for Christians and Jews is all part of his vision of an ideal world in which sin has been crowded out by love.

Administration has never been one of his fortes, as he would be the first to admit, but with the ever-efficient Reg Pullen at his side there have been surprisingly few disasters. His working hours have been extraordinary: 7.30 a.m. Mattins in the Abbey interrupting work already started, then a long day of correspondence, meetings and interviews, Evensong at 5.30 p.m., followed by a formal dinner somewhere (often with a speech of unusual brilliance), back at the Deanery by midnight, in time for a couple of hours of writing the official biography of Archbishop Geoffrey Fisher – a project which has already occupied thirteen years.

Such a man is going to be greatly missed, and his successor is bound to be different. Although he preached at Evensong, he made no reference to his own imminent departure, and at the party afterwards, when many nice things were said about him and he was presented with a fine desk and a cheque, his response was of great embarrassment, as if he couldn't understand what all the fuss was about.

My abiding memory of him will, I think, be the sight of him arriving on his old bicycle at Buckingham Palace or some other important establishment. An old overcoat and scarf covered an even more elderly suit, while a brightly-coloured pullover provided extra warmth for a journey made exceedingly hazardous by the combination of near-blindness and London traffic. Having arrived safe and sound, he invariably neglected to remove his trouser clips during the royal or ambassadorial reception. Small wonder that he is so greatly and widely loved. As is customary, the Queen is sure to appoint him KCVO, though he is the last man on earth to be concerned about such an honour.

Monday 2 December 1985

The problem of securing an adequate choir for the Abbey's Midnight Eucharist on Christmas Eve is still not solved, and once again we shall have to call on the services of Miss Petronella Dittmer's Kensington Singers, who are more of a chamber choir and can offer no more than some beautifully sung carols during the administration of the Communion.

The Organist is not prepared to turn out, as he says it is not part of his contract that he should do so. The Lay Vicars take the same line, though they have indicated that they might be prepared to sing at midnight if they were to be let off Evensong on Christmas Day. The Legal Secretary has been consulted, yet again, and says that if the Midnight Eucharist is designated a special service the Dean has the right, under their contracts, to order the Lay Vicars to sing. But this would almost certainly be contested by them, and it is hardly in the spirit of Christmas to be driven to order anyone to church – and then have to pay them a hefty fee for doing so. As far as the Organist is concerned, it seems that if either he or the Sub-Organist plays at a Midnight Eucharist which has been designated a special service, the terms of his contract will have been met.

It is a sorry story. There is, I suppose, no cathedral or other great church in the country where the choir cannot be mobilized for the best-attended act of worship on one of the church's major festivals. Those coming to the Abbey from outside who regard it as Britain's main religious shrine would, I am sure, be utterly astonished if they knew the extent to which the Abbey's music is controlled by legal contracts and cash. One day, no doubt, there will have to be a showdown, but it will need to be a tough Dean and Chapter to cope with the immediate ramifications of such a showdown, because it may well involve a new start for the Choral Foundation.

1986/87

Thursday 16 January 1986

The surplus on last year's income and expenditure account was a record-breaking £675,803. It was one of those years when almost every item of income increased – some substantially, as in the case of visitors' entry fees and purchases from the Bookshop and the Brass Rubbing Centre, which brought in an additional £288,000. Rents, dividends and interest also increased by £30,000, and to crown our good fortune we received a donation of £100,000.

Tight control of expenditure kept costs below the £1.5 million level, so, all in all, we could not hope ever to do better. The surplus was some £279,000 above the amount budgetted. Such are the uncertainties under which we work. The introduction of budgets and quarterly financial statements in 1978 was just in time, for we can at least monitor the position and, if necessary, take some remedial action.

Most of last year's surplus will be spent on capital projects – mainly maintenance and renewal of buildings.

Saturday 18 January 1986

We have come to dread the final paragraph of Simon Preston's annual reports to the Audit Chapter and this year's warning was true to form:

> 'Finally, I would like to say that this has not been a good year for me personally in my relationship with Westminster Abbey. Chapter must be aware that the campaign they have waged against me, lasting from March until well into October, has taken its toll in the matter of my commitment to the musical life of Westminster Abbey. I can only say that whatever the Chapter may have hoped to achieve has been counter-productive, and the continuing uncertainty over my future here can only lead to a stagnation in the musical standards at the Abbey.'

The so-called 'campaign' was of course our effort to make Simon comply with the contractual requirement that he shall not absent himself from the Abbey for long periods and never without the Dean's permission.

It is, I think, fair to assume that no secular organization would be as tolerant as we try to be in these matters. Nor would any Board of Directors accept accusations such as this in an employee's annual report. But as a church which benefits enormously from the gifts of a Simon Preston, we have to do as much as we can to accept him as he is, and often enough tolerate the intolerable. Which doesn't mean that no limits are ever imposed: simply (and it is not simple) that we struggle to find compromises that are creative, rather than destructive. Sometimes I wonder if the struggle is worth it, but I have only to attend Evensong to be convinced that it is.

Monday 27 January 1986

So Michael Mayne is to be our new Dean. The announcement came from Downing Street this morning, and Michael and his wife came up from Cambridge to have lunch with the Chapter and to survey the Deanery.

This could be a good appointment. I have known Michael for almost twenty years, going back to the 1960s, when he was Mervyn Stockwood's chaplain at Southwark. Then we were both in parishes in St Albans Diocese at the same time, and I had some dealing with him when he was Head of the radio side of religious broadcasting at the BBC. Since he has been at Great St Mary's, Cambridge, he has twice preached in the Abbey at consecrations of bishops, and on both occasions gave a first-class sermon.

It would be difficult to think of a personality more different from that of Edward Carpenter. Although Michael undoubtedly shares many of Edward's liberal views, he is very much a Catholic churchman who lays strong emphasis on the importance of prayer and the sacraments. In this he is much closer to Eric Abbott and will, I suspect, be less at home with the secular element in the Abbey's life.

The biggest question mark, however, lies over his health. For the greater part of last year, apparently, he was out of action with a mysterious illness known as post-viral syndrome, or ME. The symptoms of this are a general lethargy and inability to cope with any work, and the medical profession, which has no treatment to offer, is divided over whether the cause is physical or psychological.

At one time it seemed likely that Michael would become Bishop of

Norwich, then ill-health intervened and now, although he seems a very long way from recovered, he has been given one of the most demanding jobs in the Church of England. The doctors say that recovery is certain, and we must hope that they are right, because the burden of running Westminster Abbey is taxing to the fittest. Someone – probably Bob Runcie – must have been utterly convinced of the rightness of Michael's appointment for such a risk to have been taken.

The suggestion now is that he shall spend more time completing his recovery, go abroad for a good holiday and, hopefully, be Installed as Dean during the early part of the summer.

Tuesday 4 February 1986

Not even the presence of the Prince and Princess of Wales could bring excitement to last evening's service commemorating the centenary of the setting-up of the General Synod's House of Laity. The bringing of lay people into church government was a very important move, but the fruits of this development have been meagre, and there really wasn't much to celebrate.

Nor were things improved by the failure of the new central heating which has been installed at enormous cost and, on a cold February night, left us all shivering. The Prince of Wales referred to this in his speech in the Whitehall Banqueting House at the reception afterwards, and although his remarks were jocular, the element of complaint was not hidden.

The appearance, behaviour and language of some Westminster School boys who were standing around in the Dean's Yard when the Prince and Princess departed shocked the police and Abbey staff who were present, and a letter of complaint is to go to the Headmaster.

Edward Knapp-Fisher, as Acting Dean, escorted the Prince out of the Abbey and I escorted the Princess who, as always, attracted a great deal of attention from a large band of Press photographers whose cameras were flashing constantly. But when I asked her if she was finding this troublesome, she replied, 'I would be much more concerned if they were not interested in me.'

A perceptive comment, I thought.

Wednesday 5 February 1986

Chapter discussed yesterday the point I raised at the Audit Chapter concerning the amount of money given away to charitable causes beyond the Abbey. Whenever I have raised this before we have always been quickly overtaken by a financial crisis of our own and the matter has been dropped.

Last year, however, we had a surplus in excess of £500,000, and the amount of money given away, derived from a number of designated collections taken at Abbey services and the special One People Fund, was no more than £15,000. This is not right for any Christian institution and compares ill with many parish churches, where up to ten per cent of income is given to overseas missionary societies and Christian Aid, besides the ever-increasing amount of money claimed by dioceses for central church funds.

If last year we had given away all the collections taken at services, the total would have amounted to just over £50,000, which would certainly have been an improvement and still left us with a large surplus. But, as I was quickly reminded by other members of the Chapter and powerfully by the Receiver General, the finances of the Abbey are complicated. For one thing, there can be, and often are, violent oscillations in our main source of income, which comes from the fees paid by visitors for entry to the Royal Chapels.

Since we have more than 170 people on our payroll, we need to safeguard their future and cannot responsibly run the place on a shoe-string. Over the last few years the staff have been constantly urged to help maximize the Abbey's income and to reduce expenditure. A decision to give away the benefits thus secured would not, it was suggested, be well received by most of our employees.

There is also the constant demand for money for capital projects of one sort and another. Hopefully, the Trust's fund-raising efforts will deal with the restoration of the fabric of the Abbey, but we have much historic property in the precincts, the Choir School is in urgent need of modernization, and almost anything we touch requires expenditure in excess of £100,000.

So the Chapter was unwilling to agree to a fixed percentage of income or surplus being given away every year and we shall, instead, consider at every Budget Chapter whether or not there is a real surplus and, if there is, how much of it is to be given away. This will be an improvement on the past, but it will be surprising if at these reviews there is deemed to be much of a surplus, and in due course the procedure will be quietly forgotten.

The good news from the music front is that Edward Knapp-Fisher, the Acting Dean, and Simon Preston, the Organist, seem to be getting on rather well, or at any rate have established a good working relationship. Thus Simon has sought permission to have three weeks' leave in April and to be away for a ten-day recital tour in Canada in July. Both requests have been readily granted.

Simon has also suggested that once a fortnight we should have a 'boys only' Evensong in addition to the existing Evensongs on six days of the week. This would give us a daily Evensong every other week and represent a welcome move forward, but it will require the collaboration of the Lay Vicars for a necessary change in their singing days, and this may or may not be forthcoming.

I don't know the reason for the change of attitude and atmosphere. Edward Knapp-Fisher is a formidable character, but by no means devoid of humanity, and there is never any doubting where one stands with him. Simon may be finding this easier to cope with than he did Edward Carpenter's benign tolerance, or maybe he has come to recognize that he can get most, if not quite everything, he wants from the Dean and Chapter through collaboration rather than confrontation.

Whatever the explanation, the change is an enormous relief to me. I hope that it may be the beginning of a new era, though the problem of the Lay Vicars remains intractable.

Wednesday 12 February 1986

Anthony Harvey, our Canon Steward and successor of the monastic Guestmaster, is an austere fellow. Essentially an intellectual, and indeed a distinguished theologian, from time to time he gets a bee in his bonnet about our outlay on entertainment. Thus there has been a scaling down of what we offer at farewell parties for members of the staff – now only wine and bits. Working lunches are no more than sandwiches and coffee. A recommendation that only a single cup of coffee be served at Chapter Meetings was rejected.

His latest assault is on the annual Audit Dinner. This is an occasion when we celebrate the end of the accounting year and thank the various professional people who have helped us during the year – lawyers, stockbrokers, property advisers, large donors and so on, and of course the auditor himself. Anthony is advocating greater vigilance on the serving of drinks before, during and after the meal because, he alleges, at last month's dinner some guests and staff had a drop too much.

I must confess that I saw no sign of this, and it is the case that our guests are often people who have saved or raised for us large sums of money – sometimes running into millions of pounds. In future, however, pre-dinner drinks will be confined to wine cup and sherry, there will be just one glass of white wine with the fish course, unless any of the guests wish to remain on white throughout the meal, and great caution will be exercised over the serving of brandy afterwards.

All very proper and responsible, no doubt, but not quite in the spirit of the occasion.

Wednesday 26 February 1986

There was a disturbing and macabre sequence of events at the eight o'clock High Communion in St George's Chapel this morning. Soon after the service started it was apparent that Sebastian Charles, the celebrant, was distinctly unwell. He had difficulty in standing, and was obliged to lean on the altar for support. Later his speech became slower, so Edward Knapp-Fisher, who was in the congregation, stepped forward and took over.

The duty Verger and I got Sebastian into the Vestry, sat him down, gave him a glass of water and summoned an ambulance. When this arrived, however, he refused to go, and just as the vehicle was about to return to its base a man collapsed and died at the Great West Door. So he was put into the ambulance instead and driven to Westminster Hospital.

Edward Knapp-Fisher, in his capacity as Acting Dean and pastor of the community, has been to enquire about Sebastian's health, but got no further than a front-door assurance that he is now quite well again.

Wednesday 5 March 1986

The splendid crown only recently fixed on Queen Elizabeth I's tomb to replace a long-lost earlier adornment has been stolen and the great Queen is once again bare-headed. It was not difficult for the thief to seize it and carry it away unobserved, as it is virtually impossible to protect so small a part of the monument with a security device.

The crown – a superb piece of craftsmanship in wood – was made by Arthur Ayres, who over the years did a great deal of work in the Abbey, but will do no more, as he died shortly after completing this piece. Peter

Foster, the Surveyor, is having a new crown made of metal which he thinks will be less easy to steal. Our insurers will meet the cost – £1,435. I wonder where the stolen crown will finish up? No doubt it will be described as dating from 1606, when King James I had the tomb installed.

Friday 14 March 1986

The interior of St Margaret's is now a scene of utter chaos. After a couple of minor hiccups, the contractors who are undertaking the restoration of the building moved in at the beginning of this month and within a matter of days had moved many of the pews, piled others high, lifted floor boards and brought in a great deal of concrete. This is now being used to create 'collars' around the bases of the eight main pillars at the Western end of the Nave.

These will provide a base for an elaborate network of scaffolding which will reach the clerestory windows and provide support for a temporary roof and for a working area for the stonemasons. The main roof is to be stripped of all its lead, so that defective timber can be renewed, and work will then start on the restoration of the seriously decayed stonework of the clerestory.

It is exciting to see this great restoration project getting under way, but it is inevitably creating some inconvenience, since the church has to be closed on weekdays for three weeks and the interior will be scaffolded for at least two years. Brides are not going to like this. The sight of the work going on should, however, be a great help to fund-raising as we look for the final £100,000 of the Appeal.

Monday 7 April 1986

The Sub-Dean announced at the Chapter Meeting this morning that the wedding of Prince Andrew and Miss Sarah Ferguson, whose engagement was announced on the 19th of last month, will take place in the Abbey on Wednesday 23 July at 11.30 a.m. So it seems that we are back to normal with the venue of royal weddings, and that the decision of the Prince of Wales to be married in St Paul's in 1981 was a one-off departure from tradition based on personal preference.

The July wedding will not be on such a grand scale as that of the heir to the Throne, and the Queen wishes it to be a family occasion, but it sounds as if it will not fall far short of that major national event, and much preparatory work will be needed. It remains to be seen whether or not the new Dean will be here to take part in the service, but the Sub-Dean will have to be involved in the planning. Most of the nuts-and-bolts preparation will be master-minded by Reg Pullen, the Receiver General, who was here for the Queen's wedding, the Coronation and the weddings of Princess Margaret and Princess Anne, so he will take this one in his stride.

The Archbishop of Canterbury will officiate at the actual marriage, and doubtless I and my fellow Canons will have some modest walk-on part.

Thursday 10 April 1986

Thanks to Clifford Dann, its immediate Past-President, the Royal Institution of Chartered Surveyors has played a notable part in the St Margaret's Appeal and now seems certain to have raised £100,000 towards the £900,000 target.

Its final effort this evening was a dinner for sixty specially chosen guests at its headquarters across the road in Great George Street, with the Prime Minister as the speaker. I am by no means one of Margaret Thatcher's greatest fans, but I must say that she has been very encouraging and helpful over this Appeal.

At the dinner she spoke passionately of the vital importance of religious faith and values in the life of the nation:

'Freedom and democracy depend ultimately on the Judaeo-Christian faith. Too many of our precious religious treasures have been put to one side, like items in a left-luggage office, and I believe it is time we brought them out again and put them to use. Here, we politicians require the help of the church – not to lecture us on social and economic matters, but to remind us of the fundamentals of faith and hope. And St Margaret's, with its historic link with the House of Commons, has a special role in this – a role that will be less easy to discharge if its building seems to be dilapidated and uncared-for.'

She went on to say that we ought to aim to raise more than £900,000 in order that a fund might be established to deal with the future mainte-nance of the building. It was a remarkable speech, not least for the burn-ing conviction with which it was delivered.

The involvement of Clifford with the Appeals Administrator, Patricia Jennings-Bramley, is now causing a certain amount of gossip, but I am doing what I can to play this down and it is rather important that it should not get into the papers. The Appeal now stands at £823,469, which is, of course, marvellous.

Wednesday 23 April 1986

This afternoon's visit to the Abbey by the King and Queen of Spain was, by common consent, one of the happiest state visits we have ever experienced. I was on parade this morning for their visit to the Palace of Westminster, which involved a good deal of pomp and ceremony, and where the King made a very good speech.

This afternoon was also intended to be a formal occasion when they came to lay a wreath on the grave of the Unknown Warrior. Usually the wreath-laying is followed by a brief and somewhat hurried tour of the Abbey before the visitor moves on to his next engagement. No sooner had we started the tour, however, with Edward Knapp-Fisher accompanying the King and me the Queen, than they asked if they could stay rather longer than planned, as they would value a quiet interlude before again facing the crowd outside.

The Queen was altogether delightful, displaying an unusual combination of dignity and informality. She was interested in the Abbey but also ready to ask questions and talk about all manner of other things – personal as well as national and international. We were sad when eventually they decided to leave, and I couldn't help feeling how remarkable it is that such a monarchy has developed from the long, repressive rule of General Franco. This was the first visit to Britain by a Spanish monarch for eighty-one years.

Sunday 11 May 1986

The death during the night of Eric Callaghan, the People's Warden of St Margaret's, will bring sadness to a large number of people in the congregation and among the many who over the last twenty years have come to the church for weddings and memorial services. Although dogged by ill-health for a long time, it seemed likely that he would go on for a few more years. Indeed, he attended a wedding in the church yesterday afternoon, and James Mansel, his friend and pastor, spoke to him on the telephone late last evening.

When he failed to appear this morning we knew that something serious had happened, for he was a lonely man and St Margaret's was his life. Not a day passed without his coming to the church and finding something to do either in the vestry or in the arranging of flowers – at which he was something of an expert. In 1984 when Fred Glee, the Verger, had to be away for six weeks undergoing heart surgery, Eric, though seventy-three and himself in poor health, took over his duties and would not allow me even to unlock the church door early in the morning.

There was a strange side to him, however, inasmuch as he led us to believe that his father was a priest, in fact an Honorary Canon of Birmingham Cathedral, and that he had himself been to Oxford and spent most of his life as a prep-school master. In fact, his father was a layman who owned and ran a prep school which he bequeathed to his two sons. The elder son bought Eric's share from him, and unfortunately the money was invested in a Birmingham motor-cycle company that went bankrupt. Thus he was driven to earn a living as a gardener, and won prizes for his achievements in the difficult soils of Central London.

The fantasizing about the past which protected him from its painful aspects was harmless enough, and he rendered great service to St Margaret's. He was specially good at welcoming visitors and at the seating of the congregation at services. At the annual church meeting, held just twelve days ago, there was nonetheless a feeling that the time had come for him to be replaced as People's Warden by a younger man.

Mercifully, the younger candidate just failed to be elected; otherwise it would for ever have been alleged that Eric Callaghan was killed by a ruthless congregation that deprived him of the post that provided the central focus of his life. Occasionally, when exasperated by something I had said or done, he would threaten to cut St Margaret's out of his will. But I shall be very surprised if he had anything to leave.

Wednesday 21 May 1986

Prince Andrew and Sarah Ferguson came for lunch with the Chapter and wives in the Jerusalem Chamber today. This was at the suggestion of Edward Knapp-Fisher, the Acting Dean, who is handling the wedding arrangements and seems to be getting on rather well with the couple.

Certainly the lunch was a pleasant occasion. Sarah is a bubbly sort of girl, easy to talk to, full of enthusiasm and, I should say, likely to bring a breath (if not a gale) of fresh air into royal circles. She is obviously very proud of her splendid engagement ring – ten diamonds and a large ruby – and told me that she thought she was one of the luckiest people in the world to have met Prince Andrew and now to be approaching such an exciting wedding and future married life. When I asked her if she might not find it difficult having the Prince away for long periods because of his naval duties, she said that, on the contrary, this would be an advantage, as she thought married people needed personal space in their lives. Jo sat next to the Prince and found him rather boorish.

After lunch the couple went into the Abbey to discuss the floral arrangements and other matters, and they also discussed the music with Simon Preston, who is displeased because they want to import some 'star' singers and not make much use of the Abbey Choir.

Tuesday 10 June 1986

One of the saddest things I have experienced since I came to the Abbey is the attitude of the Lay Vicars to the Installation of the new Dean in the course of Festal Evensong on 7 July. Since this is a Monday, only six of them are contracted to attend, but it will of course be a great occasion requiring the presence of the full Choir. The Lay Vicars are therefore demanding that the Installation be regarded as a special service and that they be paid a fee for their attendance.

The fact that we shall be welcoming the new head of our community – someone with whom they will be worshipping most days for many years to come – makes not the slightest difference to their attitude. Money is the priority. We have decided not to contest this, as it would be unfortunate if such a special moment in our corporate life were to be marred by a dispute of this sort.

A similar attitude by the Lay Vicars came to our attention last month over the proposal that at Evensong on Saturday 20 September there should be a sermon commemorating the 800th anniversary of the consecration as a bishop, in our St Catherine's Chapel, of St Hugh of Lincoln. Recognizing that this would involve the Lay Clerks staying on for an additional fifteen to twenty minutes, we offered them half a special service by way of compensation. But they won't accept this, arguing that a sermon turns a weekday Evensong into a special service, for which they must receive a full fee. We are not, however, ready to wear this and have decided that at the end of Evensong and before the St Hugh sermon, which is to be given by Gordon Wheeler, the former Roman Catholic Bishop of Leeds, the Choir will withdraw and thereby qualify for no fee.

All of which is very regrettable, but unless the whole attitude of the Lay Vicars to the life of the Abbey can be changed, we must resist many of their demands and get on as well as we can without them.

Plans for next month's royal wedding are now well advanced. Although the Queen said originally that it was to be simply a family occasion, it will be spectacular enough, and is expected to be seen by over 300 million television viewers world-wide.

A few matters with financial implications have had to be sorted out in Chapter, but these have presented no great difficulties. At first there were to be no instrumentalists involved in the music, but Lindy Runcie, the Archbishop's wife, suggested some items to the bride that require instrumental accompaniment, so eighteen musicians have been engaged at a cost of £130 each – this being the rate prescribed by the Musicians' Union.

Simon Preston appointed an American soloist, Arleen Auger, to sing during the signing of the registers, and although she is not charging a fee for her services, we must find about £1,000 for her travelling and accommodation expenses. Meanwhile Buckingham Palace signalled that they thought a British soloist should be used and, since it was then too late to withdraw the invitation to the American, Felicity Lott has been invited to lend a hand, too. This will be a popular choice.

The Vergers are worried about their loss of income from conducted tours during the days when the Abbey is closed for preparations for the wedding – about £25 each – but while we cannot reimburse them for this without running into precedent problems, we intend to bear their loss in mind when allocating gratuities.

Bearing in mind my experience as Treasurer at the time of Earl Mountbatten's funeral, I raised the issue of loss of income to the Abbey during the three-day closure for preparations, but was assured that the reduction in visitors' fees will be more than compensated for by fees for broadcasting facilities. It is also hoped to make about £40,000 profit on silver goblets minted to commemorate the occasion and sold to subscribers.

The main question in the Little Cloister is, will there be any tickets for the service for the families of the Canons and other resident members of the staff? About 1,800 guests have been invited, and fervent prayers are being offered in the hope that some will have to decline.

Monday 23 June 1986

It has been a dramatic weekend. The wedding in St Margaret's of the Speaker's god-daughter, Susan White, to a US Navy flying officer, stationed in Honolulu, was a happy enough occasion. Members of the congregation flew in from the ends of the earth and the reception in Speaker's House was appropriately grand.

But immediately after the bell-ringers had rung the bride into church, one of their number collapsed and died. The police and ambulance service were summoned, and while the service was going on below, his body was removed from the tower. Naturally, the rest of the ringers were deeply shocked, but they collected themselves sufficiently to be able to ring the bells at the end of the service and so avoided disappointing the bridegroom and bride. It was a noble effort and much appreciated by all involved in the wedding.

Then came the news this morning that another of the ringers, said to be one of the finest in the country, had been found dead in his home yesterday in suspicious circumstances. There is even a suggestion that he may have been murdered, but this has not been confirmed.

Our large team of ringers consists mainly of old-age pensioners, which is why they are generally available for the many mid-week events at St Margaret's, but fortunately their deaths are rarely attended by such drama.

Sunday 29 June 1986

Today being St Peter's Day there was Festal Evensong at three o'clock to mark the Abbey's Patronal Festival. But for some of us it was a gravely disturbing, rather than a celebratory, occasion.

As Canon-in-Residence, Sebastian Charles was the preacher, but when he arrived in the Abbey a few moments before the service was due to start he seemed distinctly under the weather. When we reached our stalls near the High Altar, it was apparent that he was unable to stand, and for the greater part of the first half of the service he lay across three seats.

I was in my usual stall beside him, and as the time for the sermon came ever nearer I implored him to allow me to take his place in the pulpit. I have preached on St Peter on a number of occasions, and although unprepared sermons are by no means my line, least of all in Westminster Abbey, there appeared to be no alternative to my taking over.

Sebastian refused to allow this, and during the hymn before the sermon pulled himself together to the extent that he was able to follow the Canons' Verger to the pulpit. Then came about ten minutes of incoherent nonsense, starting with the question 'What would Jesus be if he were alive today?' Answer, 'A general in the army'. At no point was there any reference to St Peter and the Patronal Festival, and the whole thing was an embarrassing disaster.

Immediately the service was ended, Edward Knapp-Fisher and I took Sebastian on one side and said that he was obviously unwell and he ought to seek medical advice immediately. But he refused to accept that there was any problem and after tea telephoned me to complain, still incoherently, of what he called our aggressive attitude to him at Evensong.

None of us has the authority to take in hand a problem that Edward Carpenter was unwilling to tackle, and I think we can only await the Installation of the new Dean and see what can be done then.

Monday 7 July 1986

Michael Mayne was Installed as our new Dean this afternoon, with appropriate pomp and ceremony, and just in time for him to take a leading part in the royal wedding a fortnight on Wednesday. He coped well with the Latin parts of the service and preached an excellent sermon – not too long and expressing a good understanding of the Abbey's distinctive life and witness. It will be good to have a new mind applied to this.

I must confess, however, to one or two worries. Michael still looks very unwell. I remind myself that his gaunt features and pallid hue have never given him a robust appearance. But this seems different, and the prospect of an unwell Dean assuming the dauntingly heavy responsibilities of the Abbey is quite frightening.

This is certainly not the moment in its history for weak leadership, since there are several nettles in our life that need urgently to be grasped. The final period of Edward Carpenter's reign saw a number of serious problems put to one side, and a strong hand must deal with these.

It would make an interesting study if someone were to investigate how often serious difficulties in the life of the nation and its major institutions have been caused by the physical frailty of those in positions of leadership. However, I am an inveterate worrier and my anxieties now may be quite unnecessary. I hope so.

Wednesday 16 July 1986

It could be said that the Speaker's Appeal for St Margaret's reached its £900,000 target today, not so much with a flourish as with a splash. We were looking for £20,000 to get there and it now looks as if the Summer Regatta, held on the Thames this afternoon, will raise about £50,000.

It ws the brainchild of Colin Moynihan, the diminutive Member for Lewisham East and a former Oxford and British Olympics cox. He obtained the promise of boats from Eton College and invited Members and staff of the two Houses to enter crews to row a 300-yard course on the Thames beside the Parliament terrace. Companies and other groups were invited to sponsor a boat for £1,000. A souvenir programme, T-shirts and straw hats were on sale. Colin put in a tremendous amount of work.

The whole thing caught on in a remarkable way and created so much interest that July – usually the most fractious of months in the House of Commons – is said to have been the most amicable in living memory. In the end over fifty crews entered, and this afternoon saw scenes of great festivity on and around the terrace.

I was to have been cox for the Speaker's crew recruited from his own office, but this morning a strong wind sprang up, making the river very choppy, and it was decreed that, for safety's sake, only experienced coxes would be allowed. Along with many others, I was therefore obliged to stand down.

The wind in fact made it very difficult for most of the crews to complete the course in anything like reasonable time, but in the end the judges declared one to be the winner. While the calculations were being made, Jim Callaghan, a former Prime Minister, managed to fall overboard from a Labour Party boat and had to be rescued – very cold but unharmed. Naturally the press and television, who were present in full force, loved this and there have been pictures on all this evening's news broadcasts.

Jim complained that shortly before entering the boat he had received the Archbishop of Canterbury's blessing and this made him wonder if there was any benefit in it; to which I replied that if he had confined himself to the ministrations of the Speaker's Chaplain he might have kept dry.

So the target has been reached and will be exceeded, as there are still some promised gifts and money-raising events outstanding. It has involved a very great deal of work, but the benefits have been more than financial. St Margaret's is very much on the map.

The wedding is over, the captains and the kings have departed, and the Abbey now stands silent, wonderfully decorated with roses in delicate cream and pink shades, and with the memory of one more royal event to add to the many others accumulated since King Edward the Confessor was buried here during the early days of 1066 and William the Conqueror was crowned here on Christmas Day of the same year.

Everything went as planned, and was a gloriously happy occasion. The service itself was as simple as that of many a country church wedding – the traditional Prayer Book rite, including the bride's promise to 'obey', the usual hymns ('Praise to the Lord, the Almighty, the King of creation', 'Lead us, heavenly Father, lead us'. and 'Come down, O Love, divine'), and a short Bible reading (Ephesians 3.14–21) instead of an address.

There were some familiar human touches, too. The eight children who attended the bride became somewhat unruly while awaiting the start of the service, the bride's father gave her away with the wrong hand, and the bride stumbled slightly over the bridegroom's Christian names. Amidst such panoply and perfection these were welcome lapses. It wasn't a stage show, the re-enactment of a fairy tale, after all.

The building took three full days to prepare and we had a long rehearsal yesterday afternoon. The Dean and Chapter were on parade at the Great West Door at 10.45, as there were many members of the Royal Family to be greeted, and the Queen's procession moved to the High Altar sacrarium at 11.15.

The Dean read the introduction, the Archbishop of Canterbury conducted the marriage, the Prince of Wales read the lesson, the Precentor led the versicles and responses, and prayers (one each) were said by Cardinal Hume, the Moderator of the General Assembly of the Church of Scotland, the Moderator of the Free Church Federal Council, the Chaplain of the Fleet, and the Archbishop of York, who also pronounced a blessing. This last element made me wonder, once again, whether in this ecumenical age it is necessary to have so many verbal participants. Certainly it is not very conducive to prayer, and it would be good to think that just one non-Anglican might represent the rest.

The music, by deliberate design, was a major part of the service, though Simon Preston was somewhat miffed that our Choir was permitted to make only a small contribution, with two plainsong verses of Psalm 48 and William Walton's 'Set me a seal upon thine heart'. The big stuff was Mozart's 'Laudate Dominum' and 'Exsultate, jubilate', with orchestra and splendid soloists, and for the final processions we had, from the organ, Elgar's 'Triumphal March' from *Caractacus* and Walton's 'Crown Imperial'. Nothing very demanding, but all contributing to a joyful and memorable day.

Most of the Abbey community who wished to be there managed to get seats, while the rest saw and heard everything on a large television screen in St Margaret's and rushed out to see the bridegroom and bride go by in their carriage afterwards. By 1.15 those of us who had had walk-on parts and had been standing for over two-and-a-half hours in full robes were feeling distinctly weak at the knees, and were as relieved that it was over as we were pleased that it had gone so well.

Thursday 24 July 1986

The effect of standing so long in a heavy cope at yesterday's Royal Wedding was painfully apparent today in my troublesome back. So I managed to get some treatment this afternoon at the School of Osteopathy near Trafalgar Square. At about five o'clock I answered my door bell and was handed a long white envelope marked Personal and stamped First Lord of the Treasury. Inside were two other smaller envelopes of the sort I had received when I was offered a Canonry of Westminster in 1976. One was marked Prime Minister and contained a letter topped and tailed by the Iron Lady herself:

10 Downing Street, SW1

My Dear Canon Beeson,

As you will be aware, the Very Reverend Michael Stancliffe is resigning from the Deanery of Winchester on 1 October 1986, and it is my duty to nominate a successor to Her Majesty The Queen.

After taking the appropriate advice and having considered the needs of Winchester with great care, it would give me great pleasure to put forward your name for this appointment if you are agreeable that I should do so. My Appointments Secretary will be in touch with you on procedural matters.

I very much hope that you will accept my proposal which I would ask you to regard as being in the strictest confidence.

Yours sincerely,

Margaret Thatcher

The other letter was from the Appointments Secretary, Robin Catford, who said that if he could be of any help to me in considering the Prime Minister's suggestion I was to let him know.

I showed the letters to Jo, who seemed somewhat shocked by their contents, and I said it was going to be a difficult decision, partly because of my heavy commitments at St Margaret's and in the House of Commons but also because Michael Mayne had only just arrived at the Abbey as Dean and Edward Knapp-Fisher, who had been holding the fort as Acting Dean, was due to retire early next year.

This is not a good time to leave Westminster.

Friday 25 July 1986

Inevitably, I suppose, I slept badly last night. The offer of a major deanery, such as Winchester undoubtedly is, is not to be taken lightly or wantonly. Had it been Westminster I would have had no difficulty in accepting, since my heart is very much here, but leaving at this juncture will be seen by some, perhaps many, in the Abbey community as something of a betrayal. I have been Rector of St Margaret's for only four and a half years, and my new approach to the Speaker's Chaplaincy requires consolidation if it is to make a lasting impact. Michael Mayne, who is still a long way from fit and lacking in experience, is certainly going to need a hand.

Yet I am aware that trying to do justice to three demanding jobs is putting me under considerable strain, and I am not sure for how long I can continue at this pace – certainly not until retirement – and some people are sad that I have had to give up writing and broadcasting.

There is also the difficult question of how easy I am going to find it to work under Michael Mayne's leadership, or for that matter how easy he will find it to have me as his senior Canon. It isn't simply the contrast between my decade of experience of the Abbey's life and his ignorance of the ways of these places: our temperaments are very different, and I have the impression that he has his own clear ideas about the direction in which the Abbey should be moving and isn't particularly keen to learn about our traditions from old hands such as myself.

These are the issues I must resolve – and fairly quickly.

Wednesday 30 July 1986

The appointment of a new Vicar of St Matthew's, Westminster – the responsibility of the Dean and Chapter – has encouraged the Bishop of

London to indulge in skulduggery. This parish, on the Abbey's doorstep, has a long Anglo-Catholic tradition and is therefore of special interest to the Bishop, whose outlook is much closer to that of a Vatican monsignor than to that of a prince of the Church of England.

St Matthew's is no longer one of the great centres of London Anglo-Catholicism, and indeed the church was burned down as a result of an arson attack in 1977. Gerard Irvine, who has just retired after exercising a faithful ministry for the last seventeen years, sensibly replaced it with a much smaller building – of chapel size.

Nonetheless, it is an appointment that calls for care, since the church provides the opportunity for a priest to minister in central London and to exploit the special opportunities this constantly offers. We have therefore conducted an extensive trawl and found the Team Rector of Newbury, who has impressed us all. He would be at home in the St Matthew's tradition, but his outlook is wider than the 'Yes, Father', 'No, Father' culture of former times. He even wears a grey, rather than a black, suit.

The prospect of such a man being appointed to St Matthew's is displeasing to the Bishop, but he realizes that he has no valid grounds for refusing our nomination. Instead, he has had a private meeting with the Churchwardens, who have informed us that our proposed nominee is unacceptable. At one time this would not have much mattered, and as Patrons, we could have enforced our choice. But in these more democratic times it is virtually impossible for Patrons to defy Churchwardens, and in any case, no priest would be prepared to go to a parish in the teeth of such opposition. Our man from Newbury has already withdrawn.

Needless to say, the Bishop has his own man waiting in the wings – the Rector of Porthleven in Cornwall, a priest of impeccable Anglo-Catholic orthodoxy who served under the Bishop when he was at Truro. It is no surprise to learn that the Churchwardens have welcomed the Bishop's suggestion, and although we must obviously interview him, it will now be very difficult for us to to say No.

Perhaps he will turn out to be a first-class priest, but there is nothing in his record to indicate that he will match our erstwhile candidate.

Thursday 31 July 1986

I have written to the Prime Minister agreeing to her suggestion that I should go to Winchester. On Tuesday I went down to Winchester incognito to talk things over with Colin James, the Bishop. I know him fairly well, having served under his chairmanship of the Church Information Committee a few years ago, and we have bumped into each other from time to time.

With a little time to spare before a kitchen-table lunch in the Bishop's Palace – Wolvesey – I decided to look in the cathedral. I once preached there (at a civic service, I think), but I had no memory of the building. Having made my £1 donation at the door, as suggested, I found myself at the West end of a magnificent nave. But before I could explore further I became aware that the Visitors' Chaplain on duty was none other than Charles Taylor, my son-in-law, who is now vicar of a parish on the edge of the city. So in the interests of confidentiality I fled.

My conversation with the Bishop was useful. He asked me if I was surprised to be offered the Deanery, to which I replied, 'Were you surprised that I was offered it?' A faint smile crossed his face; obviously he has had a fair say in the choice. He made it clear that he hopes I will accept, because a new and rather more vigorous approach is apparently needed.

Yesterday I went to 10 Downing Street to see the Secretary for Appointments. I was ushered into a spacious office on the first floor, where Robin Catford more or less confirmed what the Bishop had said about the need for the Cathedral doors to be opened wider and for the Dean to be more visible. When I asked to see a copy of the latest accounts, he went to a filing cabinet but then announced that they appeared to have been misplaced, adding reassuringly, perhaps hopefully, that Winchester's finances were in a break-even situation.

I then raised the problem of my leaving my present work, to which he responded, 'The Prime Minister has considered that and thinks it might be best for you to be under less pressure and have a chance to write again.' He added, pointedly I thought, 'I should tell you that if you decline this offer it will be difficult at your age to suggest anything more.'

On my way home a newspaper seller at the end of Whitehall exhorted me to 'Cheer up', so I must have been looking pretty grim, but now I have taken the plunge and decided to go to Winchester. A few close friends, including the Speaker and Nadir Dinshaw, whom I consulted in strict confidence, are against it, but I am not sure they are aware how exhausted and trapped I feel and just how difficult it is for me to contemplate continuing at Westminster for very much longer.

My difficulty in discussing the choice is that I have no clear idea of what Winchester really needs, and it may be that I am simply being put out to grass.

Returning to my house from the Abbey this afternoon I found a man carrying the television out of the back door. Challenged, he sought to explain that he was taking it to be repaired, but then put it down and made off. I followed and, having seized him by the collar, marched him into the Little Cloister and to the front door of my neighbour, Edward Knapp-Fisher.

This good bishop has a thing about tourists trying out his doorbell and disturbing his peace, so my violent pressing of the brass button brought him to his door in some fury. 'There is no need to ring like that,' he barked. But annoyance immediately gave way to astonishment as the burglar was bundled into his hallway accompanied by my admonition 'Call the police'.

I continued to hang on to the man's collar until the police arrived, and they took him away to Cannon Row Police Station. This is the third time during the last ten months that burglars have visited us – the previous ten years being quite incident-free in this regard.

The first, a young man, I observed climbing through the downstairs loo window one Sunday lunchtime. He seemed surprised to be greeted by me on the other side and the police told me later that he was after money for drugs. The second came one evening while I was out and Jo was watching television in the first-floor drawing room. Having helped himself to a few items of no great value from a china cabinet downstairs, he was evidently on his way to the first floor when he discovered that someone was at home. Mercifully, he fled without entering the drawing room and in his haste left his cloth cap on the stairs.

This one got away, but, as I pointed out to the Cannon Row sergeant this evening, my capture of two out of three burglars represented a much better clear-up rate than that achieved by the Metropolitan Police.

Saturday 6 September 1986

An avalanche of letters since the announcement last Monday. *The Times* and the *Telegraph* carried photographs and I went down to Winchester to meet local journalists and to be interviewed by TV and radio. Messages have come from all quarters and all are kind and encouraging, as is usual on these occasions.

Michael Stancliffe apparently hoped I would succeed him, so he is well pleased. Likewise Colin James: 'I could not be more delighted that you are willing to come here . . . in my bones I feel it to be right and meant. Yet I know how hard it will be for you to leave Westminster.'

The Westminster problem has been mentioned in many of the letters. Bob Runcie: 'I am delighted for Winchester, applaud the appointment, pray for your happiness with Jo in such a future but can't help feeling you are irreplaceable at Westminster. So when I was asked for my opinion (it actually happens even with the present occupant of No.10) I said they wouldn't do better for one W but should think of the effect on the other – "Let him decide".'

Edward Carpenter said he began with mixed feelings but, 'No! Mrs Thatcher has gone up in my estimation as a result of this nomination; but as I am desperately concerned that there should be a change of government I am hoping this will prove to be a death-bed repentance.'

George Thomas was characteristically enthusiastic – 'Halleluyah!!!! I am absolutely thrilled by the news . . . You are going to one of the greatest cathedrals in the world. When I was a student in Southampton, I used to go and sit in that cathedral. It is easy to worship there. In my student days I did not dream that one day I could claim friendship with the Dean!'

Another dean, Robert Holtby of Chichester, tempered his pleasure and, he said, his relief, with a warning, 'You will realize that (except at the Abbey) a Dean is a dogsbody. Enjoyable, nevertheless.'

Replying to all the letters is going to take some time, but if people are kind enough to send a personal message they had better have something personal back, even if it is long delayed.

Wednesday 1 October 1986

One thing has become absolutely clear during the last few years: it is impossible to combine effectively the posts of Canon of Westminster Abbey, Rector of St Margaret's and Speaker's Chaplain. My predecessors dealt with this problem by strictly rationing the amount of time they devoted to each responsibility. This was a valid, indeed a sensible, choice but it meant that the potentiality for mission and ministry in the three spheres was not fully exploited.

I have attempted to remedy this and have failed, to the extent that I have been driven into the ground by the demands of an impossible diary and still have not been able to use to the full the many opportunities open to me. Many clergy of the Church of England now find themselves in a similar position but, strategically, Westminster presents special problems, since there are responsibilities here which a national church simply dare not neglect.

My departure in January, coinciding with the retirement of Edward Knapp-Fisher, provides a rare opportunity to solve this problem. With two canonries falling vacant at the same time it will be possible to allocate the three tasks to two priests. One should combine his Canonry with the post of Speaker's Chaplain, the other with that of Rector of St Margaret's. The Parliamentary connection will, of course, require the Chaplain to function frequently in St Margaret's, but this should not be a problem, provided there is a modest degree of collaboration between himself and the Rector. Getting such collaboration between senior clerics is notoriously difficult, but in this instance there is ample space for each to minister without the creation of conflict.

All this I have outlined in a paper submitted to the Chapter and sent to the Speaker and the Churchwardens. The co-operation of the Speaker is essential, as he is entirely free to choose his Chaplain from either within or without the Westminster Chapter. The co-operation of Downing Street is equally important, since the Crown is responsible for the appointment of the new Canons and in these days the choice is influenced by the tasks that need to be performed.

The Chapter recognizes the problem and might be prepared to move in the direction I have recommended. But there is some reluctance to accept so high an investment of Canonical responsibility outside the Abbey itself and also an anxiety about the collaboration factor. Further assistance for the Rector in the form of priest-vicars is still seen as the best answer. This coincides with the view of Patrick Cormack, the Rector's Warden, and some other MPs, who say that they want the Speaker's Chaplain to be also 'our Rector' and believe it would be a mistake for the posts to be separated – even though they were always separated until 1890 and in the present century have not invariably been combined.

I think therefore that the chances of my proposal winning acceptance are quite slim, but I am sure that a radical solution is the only way of securing an effective ministry in all three of these unique spheres.

Tuesday 28 October 1986

A sad problem has arisen over the Night Watchman, who was recently discovered sitting in Samaria (one of the vestries) outside the Abbey, rather than on duty inside the main building. It seems that he finds the atmosphere of the Abbey at night so frightening that he dare not spend any time within its walls, and he does not believe he will ever be able to overcome this fear.

Which is of course no use in someone employed for security purposes. But the poor fellow has serious domestic and financial problems and is pleading with us to find him alternative employment on our staff. Unfortunately, there is no vacancy for any job he might conceivably do.

This particular problem has not arisen before, but I wonder how many people would find a night alone in the Abbey unnerving?

Friday 31 October 1986

The early retirement of Bill Beaumont from the office of Speaker's Secretary is a sad affair, not least because it has been occasioned by the serious illness of his wife, Kythé. He became Speaker's Secretary just a few weeks after I had started as Chaplain and we have been firm friends ever since.

Like me, he was in the RAF during the war, then, after Oxford, a short spell in teaching, and involvement in his family's wool business in the West Riding of Yorkshire, he became a senior civil servant in the Welsh Office. It was from there that George Thomas recruited him as his Secretary – a personal assistant role – and for the last four years or so we have daily walked side by side in the Speaker's Procession. And we have also met, at least weekly, to discuss matters of mutual concern in the House of Commons.

Bill had a very difficult time under George Thomas, who almost drove him to despair. The job of Speaker's Secretary must always be a difficult one for anyone coming to it new from outside the House of Commons. The arcane procedures of the House and the multitude of Members, most of whose names and faces are totally unknown, requiring some favour of the Speaker or making a complaint to him, is bound to be bewildering for a time. But George Thomas, who in public exuded an art of geniality and benign tolerance, could be a tyrant over his staff and Bill, who had resigned from the civil service in order to become Secretary, felt the full force of his unreasonableness. During his final months as Speaker, George once again turned on Bill and also on poor Ernest Armstrong, one of the Deputy Speakers, to vent his interior anger at the prospect of leaving the job which had made him world-famous.

When Jack Weatherill became Speaker the situation for Bill changed overnight and a good partnership between them was quickly established. Bill – a strong churchman – was always extremely helpful to me and to anything relating to St Margaret's, and he and Kythé, in their flat perched high alongside Big Ben, dispensed the most generous hospitality to all sorts of people associated with the House.

Now it is evident that the chemotherapy treatment which Kythé has been undergoing for the last year is not going to save her life, so they are returning to Wales for her final months and Bill has retired in order to care for her. Had he been able to remain in office for another three years until retirement age he would, like all his predecessors, have been given a knighthood. Instead he has a CB.

Monday 3 November 1986

We have appointed a new Receiver General who will succeed Reg Pullen when he retires early next year. This is a key post, effectively the head of the Abbey's administration, and one that gives its holder much influence and, in some circumstances, considerable power. Reg, who has been on the staff since 1947 and Receiver General since 1959, served under two Deans, Eric Abbott and Edward Carpenter, who had no great interest and skill in administration. Thus he took control of large areas of the life of the Abbey – to which he has been utterly devoted – and certainly during my time here it has been near impossible to get anything done without his approval.

There is agreement in the Chapter that things will have to be different under a new regime, but this will depend on whether or not the Dean and the Canons are ready to be more deeply involved in administrative matters. During the last few months there has been a tussle between the Chapter and Reg over the period of overlap necessary between the arrival of the new Receiver General and his own departure.

Reg, who has always carried a great deal of information in his head, rather than in files, originally suggested twelve months, but we, fearing a long period of indoctrination in existing practices, said that we thought about three months would suffice. For once Reg was in no position to resist. We then decided not to advertise the post but to carry out a trawl in the City and the Civil Service in the hope that a high-powered executive might welcome the opportunity to serve a unique national institution such as Westminster Abbey.

None seemed at all interested, so we fell back on a long-established recruitment agency for cathedrals, schools and charities – a Whitehall office for the placing of retiring senior officers in the armed forces. So today we interviewed two admirals and three brigadiers, any one of whom could have done the job. Our main task was to decide which of them would most readily fit into the Abbey's style and be easy to work with. To each of them we put the question we had ourselves been battling with: how long a period of overlap with your predecessor do you think would be desirable? The answers ranged from a few months to a few weeks, until Rear Admiral Kenneth Snow replied, 'Well, the Chief of the Defence Staff is given twenty minutes.'

It was not simply this response that encouraged us to offer him the job. He had impeccable references, interviewed impressively, and, having been Captain of the aircraft carrier HMS Hermes and Deputy Assistant Chief of Staff to the Supreme Allied Commander Europe, should be able to manage Westminster Abbey. We warned him, however, that he would be faced with problems no less tricky than some of those arising in East–West relations and that a much smaller staff would leave him with many menial tasks to perform. He was not deterred and will join us at the end of February, which will give an overlap of just one month.

Monday 1 December 1986

Donald Gray, the Rector of Liverpool, is to succeed me as Canon of the Abbey and, I trust, as Rector of St Margaret's and Speaker's Chaplain. His name was, I gather, suggested to Downing Street by the new Dean and, although I don't know him well, I think he will fill the bill very nicely.

For the last twelve years he has been responsible for a major parish church which has considerable civic responsibilities. Twenty years as a Territorial Army chaplain suggests a clubability that won't come amiss in the House of Commons. And as a scholar-member of the Liturgical Commission, he is known to the wider church and will bring a particular expertise to the life of the Abbey and St Margaret's.

This could cause problems at St Margaret's, however, since the congregation is firmly wedded to the Book of Common Prayer and the Churchwardens stated firmly in their submission about the kind of new Rector required that they wish the Prayer Book tradition to continue. Donald may be ready to accept this, but liturgists are notorious for their unwillingness to compromise and my predecessor at the Abbey, Ronald Jasper, who was chairman of the Liturgical Commission, became very frustrated when he was not allowed to practise what he preached about liturgical reform. This should now be less of a problem in the Abbey, as the Dean has let it be known that he wants to take the worship 'in hand' – which generally means make it more eucharistic.

Meanwhile Anthony Harvey is making things difficult by insisting that it must not be taken for granted that Donald Gray will be the next Rector of St Margaret's, since this appointment is no longer made by the Crown and is in the gift of the Dean and Chapter. In this he is absolutely correct, but Downing Street was specifically asked to appoint a Canon who could take on St Margaret's, and apparently no other member of the Chapter wishes to become Rector, so it seems unnecessarily legalistic to insist on rights which can only cause undesirable delay in continuity at St Margaret's and in the House of Commons.

I must recognize, however, that none of this is my responsibility and that I must let go of the tasks which have occupied me for the last ten years.

Tuesday 9 December 1986

I chanced to meet the Prime Minister in the Library corridor this morning and she stopped to ask about Winchester. 'We are all very sorry to be losing you,' she said, 'but you should have the chance to run your own cathedral.' She then asked about the Deanery: 'Is it a large house? Is it furnished?' When I told her it was huge and unfurnished she expressed astonishment. 'How are you going to manage? Won't the church do something for you? What does your wife make of it?' And so on.

This little incident was a good illustration of something about Margaret Thatcher which I have often noticed, but which is not generally known about. The bossy, combative woman at the despatch box becomes someone totally different when dealing with individuals about personal matters. Then a compassionate, caring person emerges. This is specially so when anyone is in trouble.

There was no reason at all why a Prime Minister with 101 other things on her mind should be interested in my removal to Winchester and concerned about my housing arrangements. But she took the trouble to enquire and to comment. It is a pity that more of this side of her cannot find its way into the Government's welfare legislation, but then – as I have discovered since becoming Chaplain to the House – politics cannot be separated from power.

Monday 15 December 1986

The new Treasury created in the Pyx Chamber was officially opened at noon. It has been beautifully designed by Stanton Williams, who are said to be the best people working in this field, and Roy Strong, the

Director of the V & A, and various other notables from the museum world graced the occasion.

The St Margaret's Communion plate, which I rescued from a bank vault, looks splendid, though I am not sure how many people are likely to pay to see it. Fortunately, Lord and Lady Eccles, whom I married in St Margaret's a couple of years ago, he then being eighty, have been persuaded by Anthony Harvey to meet most of the cost of phase 2 of the Museum project, so all should be well in the end. But the expenditure of over £400,000 on so modest an enterprise is not easily justified, and to add insult to injury, the £25,000 spent on archaeology yielded no finds. The archaeologists said that the discovery of nothing was just as significant as the unearthing of a hoard would have been.

Tuesday 16 December 1986

My final memorial service at St Margaret's turned out to be something of a disaster. Sir Gordon Richards – one of the most famous jockeys in racing history who rode a record 4,870 winners – deserved better.

I became a little anxious at the rehearsal yesterday. Peter O'Sullevan had agreed to read the lesson, and it turned out that although he is a most brilliant BBC commentator and uses a lip microphone with consummate skill to describe the drama of a horse-race, he is almost incapable of using an ordinary microphone to make himself heard in a large church. A certain amount of discreet coaching brought some improvement, but not much.

The problem with the giver of the address was no less serious. Scobie Breasley, a contemporary of Gordon Richards and also of great fame, had come from Australia for the occasion. In common with other jockeys, he is small of stature, and when we got him into the pulpit his head was barely visble to those seated in the pews below. This was remedied by the provision of a wooden box on which he was invited to stand – and, vitally, to stand still. This improved the visibility but not the audibility, because he was obviously without experience in public speaking and had not the faintest idea of how to use his voice effectively.

It was with some foreboding, therefore, that I joined the large company of the racing fraternity who had assembled, with Gordon Richards' family, in the church this morning. I was unprepared, however, for the disaster that struck some twenty minutes before starter's orders when the electricity supply failed totally and we learned that, because of a major fault in Parliament Square, the supply would not be restored for some hours.

This not only made the microphones ineffective and their users completely inaudible; it also put the organ out of action. A piano was hastily brought from its corner to the front of the church and the organist played with great verve, but it lacked the volume for the accompanying of so large a gathering in such a building, and the hymn singing was abysmal.

All in all an embarrassingly sad send-off for someone whose previous finishing posts were attended by excitement and glory.

Wednesday 17 December 1986

Since the American bombing of Libya in April and the consequent terrorist threat to American citizens, the number of visitors to London has declined sharply throughout the summer, and in spite of the Royal Wedding, there have been noticeably fewer visitors to the Abbey. Thus this year's surplus is about £298,000, some £62,000 less than that achieved last year. In the circumstances, indeed in any circumstances, it is a very satisfactory result.

Surpluses are, however, quickly spent. £55,000 has been allocated to the Museum project to secure its completion; likewise £40,000 to the Organ restoration, £49,000 to a computer and word processors for the Chapter office, £14,000 for improvement of the sound reinforcement system in the Abbey, £16,000 for the repair and re-siting of stained glass, £25,000 for new lavatories in the Choir School and Cellarium. The lists of needs is endless, and several other important items have had to be deferred.

When I came to the Abbey in 1976 the annual running costs totalled about £520,000. The budgeted expenditure for the next twelve months is just over £1,850,000. Both figures exclude any expenditure on the restoration of the fabric of the Abbey and St Margaret's. Such has been the effect of inflation and also, it must be said, some development of our life and witness.

Staff costs will always account for about 70% of outgoings, for the simple reason that Westminster Abbey can be run only by people, not machines. The Choir is always going to be expensive – £284,000 last year – if the present superb quality of music to be be maintained.

Our financial advisers constantly remind us that we are seriously under-capitalized, and this must be true, since we are absolutely at the mercy of the number of visitors coming to London, and with a salaried staff of over 170 and a life and witness of international repute to maintain, it is simply not possible to make rapid adjustments without courting disaster.

These great churches have affinities with medium-sized companies, with the result that they are now in danger of becoming finance- rather than Spirit-driven. I expect that Winchester will be much the same, though the financial scale will be lower. And forty-two years ago I left the services of a bank in order that I should not have to devote my working life to money matters.

Saturday 3 January 1987

The Taizé pilgrimage to Westminster has just ended and, in spite of the appalling wet weather, has been an impressive success. Over 20,000 young people from all over Europe have spent the last five days here and 10,000 of them have been fed in tents erected on St Margaret's churchyard. It has been a most remarkable experience.

The Abbey was one of the main churches for their distinctive forms of worship and the evening services, held in candlelight, with long periods of silence interspersed with Taizé psalms and songs, have shown how a national shrine such as ours can become a place where young people feel at home and create an atmosphere of devotion that often eludes us.

The organization of the event, which included study and entertainment, has been a triumph for the Taizé administration and our own staff, and I wonder if such a powerful expression of Christian witness has ever before taken place in the capital. Significantly, the media have virtually ignored it.

Sunday 4 January 1987

At the Sung Eucharist this morning my ministry at St Margaret's ended, and after the service the official Goodbyes were said. Princess Margaret was present at the service, not because of my departing but simply because she chanced to be in London this weekend and wanted to attend a Book of Common Prayer Holy Communion. Nonetheless, on the way out she said a few kind things about my work at the Abbey and at St Margaret's and hoped that I would be equally happy at Winchester.

I preached on the text 'Jesus Christ is the same yesterday, and today and forever', which seemed appropriate for the first Sunday in the New Year as well as for the point of transition at St Margaret's. I spoke of the church's vocation to proclaim and live the gospel in the context of a special ministry to those involved in government.

'It is our task here to uphold those Christian values which enable a proper balance between justice, compassion and prosperity to be achieved, or at least attempted. Rarely are we in a position to tell politicians what they ought to be doing. Our task is to stand along-side them and to share in the struggle to discern what the gospel of love requires of us in our personal and corporate lives.'

In my 'Thank you' speech afterwards, following words and presentations from the Speaker and Patrick Cormack MP, the Rector's Warden, I reflected further on the significance of St Margaret's and caused some amusement by quoting from my book *The Church of England in Crisis* (1974) in which I suggested that St Margaret's was a classic example of the extravagant use of resources and ought to be demolished.

Five years of service as its Rector has certainly taught me differently. The historic relationship between St Margaret's and the House of Commons is still very much alive and is capable of further dynamic development. The importance of this in our increasingly secularized age cannot, I believe, be exaggerated.

The church also exercises an important function complementary to that of the Abbey. Because it is smaller than the Abbey and has a regular congregation, with a priest charged with pastoral responsi-bilties, it can exercise a more personal ministry. The international, the national – and the local – are all needed at this central point in the nation's life.

During the last five years I went into the church several times every day, and hardly ever did I find it without a number of people engaged in prayer. It is a place that inspires devotion, and no priest could ever have received stronger support from a congregation than I have been given here.

It had better not be demolished.

Winchester   **Thursday 15 January 1987**

The removal firm completed the loading of two furniture vans late this afternoon and will begin the delivery at Winchester tomorrow morning. It has been a mammoth task, since the vans could come no closer to the Little Cloister than the Poets' Corner entrance to the Abbey and every item from our three-storey house had to be carried across the garden and through two sets of iron gates. To make matters worse, since Tuesday there has been heavy snow, and with the onset of a hard frost today, it began to look as if our car journey to Winchester would have to be postponed. In the end, we decided to chance it and found the normally crowded M3 virtually deserted. Careful driving on icy roads got us to the Winchester home of our daughter, Catherine, and her husband Charles soon after nine o'clock.

I remain a Canon of Westminster until the end of this month and must return to London for some Chapter meetings and farewell parties in the House of Commons and the Jerusalem Chamber. But my days at the Abbey have effectively ended and I must quickly pick up the reins of Winchester Cathedral.

Westminster has been a marvellous experience and I do not know what I can have done to merit such a privilege of ministering there for nearly eleven years. Nothing, of course, and Jesus once solemnly warned his followers, 'To whom much is given, of him shall much be required.' So I am left wondering just how well I have used the remarkable opportunities that have come my way since I was Installed in the Abbey on May Day 1976. I find consolation in some words of St Teresa of Avila: 'God does not ask a perfect work, only infinite desire'.

Index